Israel's Declaration of Independence

Israel's Declaration of Independence brings to life the debates and decisions at the founding of the state of Israel. Through a presentation of the drafts of Israel's Declaration of Independence in English for the first time, Neil Rogachevsky and Dov Zigler shed new light on the dilemmas of politics, diplomacy, and values faced by Israel's leaders as they charted the path to independence and composed what became modern Israel's most important political text.

The stakes began with war, state-building, strategy, and great power politics, and ascended to matters of high principle: freedom, liberty, sovereignty, rights, and religion. Using fast-paced narration of the meetings of Israel's leadership in April and May 1948, this volume tells the astonishing story of the drafting of Israel's Declaration of Independence, enriching and reframing the understanding of Israel's founding and its ideas – and tracing its legacy.

Neil Rogachevsky is Clinical Assistant Professor and Associate Director at the Straus Center of Yeshiva University, where he teaches Israel studies and political thought. His writing has appeared in the *Wall Street Journal, Tablet, Mosaic, Jewish Review of Books, American Affairs, Ha'aretz* and other publications.

Dov Zigler is an investor and Chief International Economist at Element Capital in New York.

Israel's Declaration of Independence

The History and Political Theory of the Nation's Founding Moment

NEIL ROGACHEVSKY

Yeshiva University

DOV ZIGLER

Independent Scholar

Shaftesbury Road, Cambridge CB2 8EA, United Kingdom

One Liberty Plaza, 20th Floor, New York, NY 10006, USA

477 Williamstown Road, Port Melbourne, VIC 3207, Australia

314–321, 3rd Floor, Plot 3, Splendor Forum, Jasola District Centre, New Delhi – 110025, India

103 Penang Road, #05–06/07, Visioncrest Commercial, Singapore 238467

Cambridge University Press is part of Cambridge University Press & Assessment, a department of the University of Cambridge.

We share the University's mission to contribute to society through the pursuit of education, learning and research at the highest international levels of excellence.

www.cambridge.org
Information on this title: www.cambridge.org/9781316514771

DOI: 10.1017/9781009090841

First published 2023

Printed in the United Kingdom by TJ Books Limited, Padstow Cornwall

A catalogue record for this publication is available from the British Library.

ISBN 978-1-316-51477-1 Hardback

Contents

Notes on the Text   *page* vii

Introduction: Israel's Declaration of Independence: History
and Political Theory   1

    PART I THE SETTING

1 Government: The Origins of Israel's Declaration
   of Independence   19

    PART II POLITICAL THEORY

2 Natural Rights   43

3 From Natural Rights to Labor Zionism: Tzvi Berenson
   and the Legal Department's Draft   79

4 International Law: Herschel Lauterpacht's Draft   113

    PART III HISTORY

5 Diplomacy: Moshe Shertok's Draft   139

6 Politics and Law: Debating the Declaration   167

7 Natural and Historical Right: David Ben-Gurion and
   Israel's Declaration   195

PART IV LEGACY

8   The Laws of Israel and the Declaration of Independence   235

Conclusion: Sovereignty, the Jewish State, and Principles of
Political Right   261

Afterword and Acknowledgments   286

*Appendix: Address by Zalman Rubashov (Shazar) to the
Zionist Actions Committee, April 12, 1948*   292
Bibliography   295
Index   311

Notes on the Text

Zionism in the nineteenth and twentieth centuries often constituted a personal transformation: many who arrived in the land of Israel, including key Zionist figures, took on entirely new Hebrew names or Hebraicized existing ones at some point in their lives.

Our practice is to refer to individuals as they were known (officially) in the days leading up to Israel's Declaration of Independence in 1948. Thus, the future prime minister Golda Meir is Golda Meyerson, the future prime minister Moshe Sharett is Moshe Shertok, etc. Figures who had already Hebraicized their names formally, such as David Gruen, who had been known as David Ben-Gurion for years, are referred to accordingly.

Despite some accompanying stylistic infelicities, we have chosen to transliterate certain Hebrew proper names, particularly those of organizations, military groups, political parties, and other institutions of the Jewish settlement in Palestine (which we always call the *Yishuv*). Thus, we refer throughout to the new governing bodies set up in April 1948 as *Moetzet ha'Am* and *Minhelet ha'Am* rather than as the National Council and National Administration. This leads to some grammatical problems – any Hebrew speaker will chuckle at occasional references to the *Moetzet ha'Am* – but we thought that the benefits of using Hebrew names while keeping the English language straight for a non-Hebrew speaker outweighed the costs.

Of some additional importance: this book studies the early drafts of Israel's Declaration of Independence. In examining the early drafts, it was at times necessary to focus our study on a single text which was one amongst a sequence of similar drafts. The differences between these drafts are generally relatively minor, however, occasionally, they take on added significance. We explain our choices throughout the text. These deserve some attention.

An important primary source for this book has been the official minutes of the meetings of Zionist and *Yishuv* executive and deliberative bodies in the weeks leading up to independence, particularly those of *Minhelet ha'Am*, *Moetzet ha'Am*, and *Va'ad ha'Poel ha'Tzioni* (which we generally refer to using a dated but revealing translation, the Zionist Actions Committee, itself an English form of the original "Actionscomité.") We treated the content of these minutes, and the discussion and speeches they contain, as accurate renditions of what was said at these meetings (as we have done for the records contained in *Foreign Relations of the United States* and elsewhere). Though the quality of these minutes is high, no such historical texts are free of possible elisions, oversights, abridgements, misquotations, and even additions. The reader should keep this in mind when encountering a direct quote from any of these meetings.

Unless otherwise noted, all translations are our own.

Introduction

Israel's Declaration of Independence: History and Political Theory

At four o'clock in the afternoon, we declared independence. The nation was jubilant – and again I mourn amidst the rejoicing.

—David Ben-Gurion's diary, May 14, 1948

On Friday, May 14, 1948, David Ben-Gurion presided over the declaration of an independent Jewish state. The proceedings were held at the inconspicuous Tel Aviv Museum on leafy Rothschild Boulevard, a two-story building believed to be less susceptible to Egyptian aerial bombardment than the larger and better outfitted Habimah Theatre down the street.

When at 4 pm Ben-Gurion rapped his gavel from a hastily erected stage in the museum's main hall, the attendees rose unprompted and sang *Hatikvah*, the anthem of the Zionist movement and its settlement in Palestine, the *Yishuv*. The exuberance was so great that the communal recitation began before the Jewish Philharmonic Orchestra, placed on the second story balcony in order to conserve floor space for dignitaries, was able to commence the musical accompaniment.[1] Its words – "To be a free people in our homeland, the land of Zion, Jerusalem" – must have never sounded more poignant to the generation that had turned the Jewish people's national hope into a state.

Amidst the rapture, Ben-Gurion declaimed soberly: "I will read to you the founding declaration."[2] Standing in front of a portrait of Theodor Herzl hung between two floor-to-ceiling flags bearing the Star of David, Ben-Gurion

---

[1] Ze'ev Sharef, *Three Days*, trans. Julian Meltzer (London: W. H. Allen, 1962), p. 282.
[2] Protocols of the National Council, Afternoon meeting, May 14, 1948, p. 24. The minutes are available by request from the Israel State Archives.

I

declared the coming into being of a new state, a Jewish state, a state which some of those assembled were surprised to learn was called Israel.

The reading was followed by the recitation of *Shehecheyanu*, the Jewish blessing used to mark holidays and lifecycle events. It is a prayer of gratitude. The crowd responded resoundingly: "Amen."

Ben-Gurion then moved to consolidate the new government's political control: "By the power of the Declaration of Independence, published today, *Hey b'Iyar*, May 14, 1948, and according to which the provisional State Council and provisional government of Israel have been established, we hereby declare: the provisional National Council shall hold legislative authority." The government's first act: lifting the hated British restrictions on Jewish immigration.[3]

Members of the new government were next requested, in alphabetical order, to sign what appeared to onlookers to be the Declaration of Independence, but was in fact a blank piece of parchment. There had not been time in advance of the ceremony to write the "Declaration of the Establishment of the State of Israel," Israel's Declaration of Independence, onto a formal scroll. The text had been settled upon and approved by the leadership of the *Yishuv* only hours before.

Hatikvah was then performed again, this time with the orchestral arrangement. In the words of one onlooker, "it seemed as if the heavens had opened and were pouring out a song of joy on the rebirth of the nation ... . The audience stood motionless, transfixed, listening to the melody coming from above."[4] When the last notes of the melancholy anthem faded away, the meeting's Chairman, Ben-Gurion, concluded on a procedural note: "The State of Israel has arisen. The meeting is ended."[5]

The gravity of the events in the museum yielded to the ebullience of a street party on the boulevard outside. When the politicians, bureaucrats, journalists, writers, and rabbis left the museum, they were met by a throng of people celebrating the proclamation of the new state. The meeting was supposed to have been kept secret for reasons of safety. It was the worst kept secret in Tel Aviv. Revelers from outside flooded the hall and folk music blared from loudspeakers. On Rothschild Boulevard, dwellers of Tel Aviv, now for the first time Israelis, celebrated the achievement of statehood well into the night.[6]

---

[3] Ibid., p. 26.   [4] Ze'ev Sharef, *Three Days*, p. 287.
[5] Protocols of the National Council, Afternoon meeting, May 14, 1948, p. 26.
[6] See Moshe Gurari, "Havlei leidata shel megilat ha'atzmaut," ("The Birth Pangs of the Declaration of Independence,") *Davar*, May 11, 1973.

David Ben-Gurion, for his part, had just become the leader of a state. He joined neither in the reveling nor in the prayers at a Sabbath service that would take place at Tel Aviv's Great Synagogue. He was preoccupied with other matters. While Israel's Jews celebrated their political independence, Ben-Gurion mustered only four terse points on the subject in his diary entries for May 14, 1948.

- One P.M. at the National Council. We approved the text of the Declaration of Independence. At four o'clock in the afternoon, we declared independence.
- The nation was jubilant – and again I mourn amidst the rejoicing as I did on the 29th of November.
- At four o'clock in the afternoon, Jewish independence was announced and the state officially came into being. Our fate is in the hands of the defense forces.
- Immediately after the declaration ceremony, I returned to Headquarters and reviewed the worsening situation.

The next entry in his diary reads: "We decided to requisition rifles from agricultural settlements for the new brigade." His notes for May 14, 1948 end with an ominous question: "Will Tel-Aviv be bombed tonight?"[7]

ISRAEL'S DECLARATION OF INDEPENDENCE

"The Declaration of the Establishment of the State of Israel," the formal name of the text of Israel's Declaration of Independence, changed everything for the Jewish people. The act of a declaration of political independence represented a shift from statelessness to a state. From private life to public life. From being ruled to ruling. From a society and culture without a state to a state developing its society and culture. From a life fleeing politics to a life of politics.

David Ben-Gurion decisively broke with nearly two millenia of Jewish history when he read this sentence: "By virtue of our natural and historic right and on the strength of the resolution of the United Nations General Assembly, [We] hereby declare the establishment of a Jewish state in *Eretz-Israel*, to be known as the State of Israel."

---

[7] Quoted in Tuvia Friling and S. Ilan Troen, "Proclaiming Independence: Five Days in May from Ben-Gurion's Diary," *Israel Studies*, Spring, 1998, 3, 1, pp. 170–194.

The relevance of Israel's Declaration of Independence was first and foremost political. It represented a rupture with the past and the opening of a new volume in Jewish history. But Israel's Declaration of Independence is also a text. The Declaration of the Establishment of the State of Israel that Ben-Gurion recited on May 14, 1948, not only asserted the fact of Israel's independence, but also elaborated the reasons why there ought to be an independent Jewish state in the land of Israel.

This book is a history of the composition of Israel's Declaration of Independence – and thus a political history of how Israel came to declare independence. For David Ben-Gurion's public reading of Israel's Declaration of Independence was itself a supreme political act, a political declaration of the independence of a new political entity. The history of the composition of the text of the Declaration therefore provides a unique window into Israel's path to independence.

Political history is generally thought of as the history of wars and decisions – with justification. No differently from most political history, the period of Israel's independence is largely studied through the prism of Israel's War of Independence, the 1948 War. This is likely because of the visible drama of the war: the question of whether or not Israel could survive its declaration of independence took precedence both at the time of independence and indeed since. The history and historiography of the war remains alive even to this day because the war itself cast such a grave and severe shadow over the events of 1948.

Texts and speeches are also acts and decisions. What the *Yishuv* would say to the world upon the end of the British Mandate constituted the weightiest decision that stood before its leadership as the moment of British departure from Palestine on May 15 approached. This book presents the history of the debates and choices that culminated in David Ben-Gurion reading Israel's Declaration of Independence on May 14, 1948.

The choices were momentous. When and how to create a government? How to navigate international politics? Would the *Yishuv* rely on the UN and international law to support independence? Or would it act on its own and thus risk that independence would run afoul of the very process of international diplomacy that had brought the *Yishuv* to the verge statehood? Its leaders had to balance the needs of diplomacy with domestic considerations. Decisions that might help the state in the short term might hinder its long run development. What the leaders of the *Yishuv* would say and how they would say it would, they all knew, shape their nation's founding and carry consequences that could not be predicted. This book tells a part of this story.

It does so not only by narrating these decisions, but also through the history of a text. Israel's Declaration of Independence was written over the course of roughly three weeks beginning in late April 1948. There are five major drafts that were produced along with a sixth political text delivered on April 12 delegating political authority to a leadership council headed by David Ben-Gurion. There are additional extant working drafts that show how these texts took shape. Further fragments and edits shed more light still. These texts, when properly pieced together, raise the pivotal political questions that confronted the leadership of the *Yishuv* as they hurtled toward the end of the British Mandate and the creation of the first Jewish state in more than 1,800 years.

Understanding the contents of Israel's Declaration and its drafts requires a journey beyond the texts themselves. The texts address long-forgotten political, legal, and diplomatic matters that were in fact at the center of controversy and the substance of decision at the time.

These are raised in the minutes of the meetings of the leadership of the *Yishuv* who debated three of the drafts of Israel's Declaration of Independence. These debates are interspersed amidst discussion of the other decisive political events of May 1948 – war, diplomacy, and much else – from which the draft texts of Israel's Declaration of Independence cannot be separated. There is a further mix of memos and letters from 1948 and oral histories compiled afterwards that illuminate the events of the spring of 1948.

When the drafts of Israel's Declaration and indeed its final text are read in light of these documents and this history, they come to life and present a view of the issues on the minds of the leaders of the *Yishuv* at the moment of independence. In this way, a study of the composition of the Declaration of Independence becomes a study of decision-making and statesmanship at the moment of the founding of Israel.

The Declaration of Independence is also a political text containing political ideas. This book is a study of those ideas. The first draft of Israel's Declaration of Independence drew on the American Declaration of Independence and the Hebrew Bible for its arguments and even its language. The intermediate drafts relied on completely different sources, arguments, and considerations: Labor Zionist ideology, the *Yishuv*'s obligations under UN Resolution 181, and the diplomatic pressures its leaders felt. The final text said of the Jewish people: "Here they wrote the Book of Books." It declared the independence of the Jewish state on the basis of the Jewish people's "natural and historic right."

This book traces this intellectual journey and unpacks its meaning. It explains the origins of Israel's Declaration of Independence, the ideas and circumstances that gave birth to it and which animate it, the choices which were made in compiling it, and the meaning and merits of those choices – as well as their alternatives. If the creation of a sovereign Jewish state changed everything for the Jewish people, then the text which announced, explained, and justified that change offers a view not only of the past, but also of the trajectory onto which it cast the Jewish people.

Through these texts and debates, studied in this book in-depth, we see the first leaders of Israel grappling with both practical and abstract questions of politics. The history of the drafting of Israel's Declaration of Independence is thus the story of the heart of Israel's founding. It is the story of the ideas at the root of the founding of the state.

THE FACT OF THE FOUNDING VERSUS THE REASONS FOR FOUNDING: STUDYING ISRAEL'S DECLARATION OF INDEPENDENCE

The goal of independence was fundamentally met by The Declaration of the Establishment of the State of Israel. Sovereignty presented an immediate and obvious rupture in *deed* from the Jewish past. It formed a culmination of the *Yishuv*'s practical project, Zionism's ideological aim, and Judaism's national striving.

Independence had an immediate impact on material developments. Britain relinquished sovereignty over its protectorate Palestine and a new sovereignty, the sovereignty of Israel, was established. The official language of the land switched from English to Hebrew and Arabic, its laws from those of Britain to those of the new state of Israel. Even its currency changed from the old British-administered currency to a new national currency in 1952. Its armed forces were no longer those of the British military but rather its own. Hundreds of thousands of Jews immigrated to the new state in under a year, many from displaced persons camps in Europe or as exiles from the Arab countries now at war with the new state.

These changes were contested. There was a war which lasted ten months following Israel's independence. The state of Israel stands today with a population of nearly nine million people living in a country called Israel where before there were two million people living under British rule. A new territory was etched into the world map, its contours still changing to this day. This element of rupture and break with the past was not enacted by the precise substance of the words of Israel's Declaration of Independence but by its simple fact – by Israel's declaration of independence. This rupture was plain for all to see on May 14, 1948.

The mere fact of the creation of a state, however, omits the substance of the question of the founding of a new state. Yes, a state was born. But what would be its nature: its aimed for conduct, its government, the principles of its government, its laws? How would the state conceive of its citizens' rights? To what aims would the state aspire?

This book presents a study of the drafting and composition of Israel's Declaration of Independence. It does so not only to recount the composition of Israel's Declaration of Independence but also with an aim to excavating and illuminating the ideas that lie at its heart.

The Declaration of the Establishment of the State of Israel is structured with a straightforward internal logic. It begins with history: *Eretz-Israel* was "the birthplace of the Jewish people." Zionism transformed their hope for "restoration" into a political agenda of migration "in masses." And diplomatic statements starting with the Balfour Declaration of 1917 conferred international legitimacy on the Jewish "national home," culminating in UN Resolution 181 in November 1947.[8]

The Declaration also explains the need for Jewish independence – *why* the state is being declared. There are material justifications: to "make the deserts bloom" with "cities and towns" thus bringing "the blessings of progress to all the country's inhabitants." The tragedy of Jewish history is raised, including the Holocaust and the Jews' self-evident need "to be masters of their own fate." And the text raises a spiritual rationale: in the land of Israel the Jews "created cultural values" of "universal" meaning by giving "to the world the Eternal Book of Books."

Indeed, the state is declared in light of these arguments: "By virtue of our natural and historic right and on the strength of the resolution of the United Nations General assembly, [We] hereby declare the establishment of a Jewish State in *Eretz-Israel*, to be known as the State of Israel."

And finally, the Declaration describes the new state's characteristics and aspirations.[9] "The ingathering of the exiles" gets pride of place. Pluralism is emphasized: Israel will "foster the development of the country for the benefit of all its inhabitants." The "basis" of the state is defined in liberal-democratic terms: "freedom, justice, and peace as envisaged by the prophets of Israel." The state will "ensure complete equality" of

---

[8] The official English translation of Israel's Declaration of Independence is available at www .mfa.gov.il/MFA/Peace+Process/Guide+to+the+Peace+Process/Declaration+of +Establishment+of+State+of+Israel.htm. We will consider lacunae in the translation later in the book.

[9] See Chapter 8 for a detailed analysis of the formal account of the parts of the Declaration as developed in Israeli jurisprudence and legal scholarship.

"social and political rights" to "all its inhabitants irrespective of religion, race or sex"; it will "guarantee freedom of religion, conscience, language, education and culture"; it "will safeguard the Holy Places of all religions"; and "it will be faithful to the principles of the Charter of the United Nations."

The Declaration concludes with an oath. The signatories place their trust in "*Tzur Yisrael*," a term from Jewish liturgy translated as "Rock of Israel" and always used to refer to God, but which, not being one of the Bible's explicit names for God, could be viewed by a nonbeliever as an earnest invocation of the state or the Jewish people as well.

What does the text mean by "Jewish state"? What is "complete equality"? What are political rights? What are social rights? How far do these extend? How will the state balance the obligations of religion with the demands of civic life? How will it ensure complete equality while being a Jewish state? Such questions, raised by the Declaration of Independence of Israel, have been at the heart of defining controversies in Israel since its founding in 1948. They are first-order questions that demand first-order reflection if they are to be addressed.

The Declaration of Independence of Israel is important because it is the only document in Israel's entire founding period that attempts to address foundationally these foundational questions. It is the purpose of this book to consider and evaluate how the Declaration addresses these questions by unearthing and evaluating the ideas that made their way into its text – and those that were excluded. It analyzes the drafts and the final text. It is a map. It shows the path that was taken – and those which were not.

A study of the Declaration of Independence of Israel is a study of the spirit of the laws of Israel, a journey to the heart of the principles of the state of Israel as they were considered at the founding of Israel. It is a tour of the principles.

The Declaration of Independence is amongst the vital texts of Israeli life today and a case can even be made for it as *the* vital text. It is the basis for many of Israel's most recent Basic Laws – Israel's constitutional laws. "Basic Law: Human Dignity and Liberty" (1992), "Basic Law: Freedom of Occupation" (1994), and the recently passed "Jewish State Law" (2018) all draw on The Declaration.

This is for good reason. The Declaration is cited in Israeli jurisprudence as a source of "principled guidance" in interpreting other laws and rights. Moshe Smoira, the first president of Israel's Supreme Court, wrote in the case of *Ziv* v. *The Tel Aviv Administrator (Gubernik)* in 1948 that the Declaration expresses "the nation's vision and its basic credo." In 1958, in the case of *Kol Ha'am Ltd. v. The Interior Minister*, Supreme Court Justice Agranat added to Smoira's claim, writing that "if the Declaration reflects the vision and basic credo of the nation, then, it is incumbent upon us to carefully examine its contents when we come to interpret and lend meaning to the state's laws."[10]

Justice Aharon Barak, in an essay published in 1998 while he was President of the Supreme Court, argued that the Declaration is an essential source for Israel's "fundamentals" accompanying Israel's piecemeal constitution of Basic Laws:

There is currently a full realization of the existence of a formal constitution in Israel. These are the eleven "basic laws" of Israel .... . The judge learns about fundamental values from the basic documents, such as the constitution itself. From our constitution, we learn that values of the State of Israel are those of a Jewish and democratic state; that the constitution's fundamental rights are founded upon the recognition of human value, and of the sanctity of human life and liberty. From the Declaration of Independence, we learn that Israel was to be founded on fundamentals of liberty, peace, and justice, and was to grant full equality of social and political rights to all of its citizens.[11]

This assessment makes the vital point: Israel's Declaration is a source of the country's principles.

Despite its manifest importance, the Declaration, and moreover its prior drafts, have surprisingly not received the attention they deserve. There is the scholarly unearthing of the documents in the 1990s and 2000s by Yoram Shachar and the valuable essays he composed to situate it. There is copious legal writing, jurisprudence, and some scholarship, concerning the doctrines of the use of the Declaration in the courts. And there have been the beginnings of textual interpretation, mainly in recent years.[12] However the Declaration has not been studied against the

---

[10] Quoted in Elyakim Rubinstein, "The Declaration of Independence as a Basic Document of the State of Israel," *Israel Studies*, 3, 1 1998, pp. 195–210.

[11] Aharon Barak, "The Role of The Supreme Court in a Democracy," *Israel Studies*, 3, 2 10, 2, 2009 1998, pp. 6–29.

[12] Essential sources include: Bejamin Aksin, "Ha'khraza al ka'mat ha'medina," (Declaration of the Founding of the State) in *Sefer ha'yovel l'Pinchas Rosen*, ed. Haim Cohen, 1962; Aharon Barak, "Megilat ha'Atzmaut ve'haKnesset k'reshut mechonenet," ("The Declaration of Independence and the Knesset as a Constituent Authority,"), *Hukim*, 11, 2018; Martin Kramer, "The May 1948 Vote That Made the State of Israel," *Mosaic*, April 2, 2018; and Elyakim Rubinstein, "The Declaration of Independence as a Basic Document of the State of Israel," 195–210. Yoram Shachar's writings are of particular importance, particularly: "Jefferson Goes East: The American Origins of the Israeli Declaration of Independence," *Theoretical Inquiries in Law*, 10, 2, 2009; "Ha'teyotot ha'mukdamot shel hakhrazat ha'atzmaut," ("The Early Drafts of the

backdrop of political science or political philosophy – the necessary context for understanding its thought.

This book is organized in accordance with the history of the drafting of Israel's Declaration of Independence. It tells the story of Israel's political independence through the window opened by the drafts of the text that ultimately announced its independence.

But it also examines the Declaration and its drafts in light of political thought. The significant drafts of Israel's Declaration produced in the weeks leading up to Israeli independence are of course historically important insofar as they shed light on the moments of decision at the founding of the state. Yet they also do much more. These early drafts represent an attempt to justify the state in theoretical terms – to articulate the purpose of the state. Each of them, in often strikingly different ways, attempts to address first-order questions about the meaning of the state. Within the drafts and the debates surrounding them, we find ideas about rights, duties, liberty, equality, theology, labor, international law, nationhood, religion, realpolitik and idealism, war and peace.

To be fully grasped, these texts need to be studied in light not only of the context of Tel Aviv in the spring of 1948, or even within the context of Zionist writing and thought, but especially in light of the essentials of political thought. They are works of political ideas that must be examined for their political ideas. When seen through the prism of political thought, Israel's Declaration and its drafts present a uniquely revealing portrait of the Israeli mind at the founding of the state of Israel. They offer the starkest portrait of the kind of state the founders of Israel thought they were founding.

The study of the political theory of Israel's Declaration, its drafts, the debates surrounding them, and its final text is thus vital for two reasons. First: the debates over the text of the Declaration of Independence lie at the root of the most important political matters contested today in the here and now. The definition of a "Jewish and democratic state," the balance between the natural inherent civil rights of the citizen and the political and security needs of the collective, the interaction between Israel's Jewish and secular character, the question of Israel's borders –

Declaration of Independence," *Iyunei Mishpat* (November, 2002); Eliav Lieblich and Yoram Shachar, "Cosmopolitanism at a Crossroads: Hersch Lauterpacht and the Israeli Declaration of Independence, *British Yearbook of International Law*, 84, 1, 2014; and Israel Dov Alboim, ed., *The Declaration of Independence with an Israeli Talmudic Commentary* (Rishon Lezion: Yedioth Aharanoth, 2019).

these are the core political debates at work in Israel and the wider Jewish world today. And yet, they can only be intelligently answered by asking deeper questions about the nature of politics and the state – deeper questions that are pointed to, and often explicitly raised, in Israel's founding documents and debates.

The second and more vital reason why we must strive to answer these questions of political first principles is linked to the first, but greater than it because its object is higher. Inquiry into the first order questions of politics helps us understand our own basic condition: the human condition. The study of politics is important because it is the only way to think about the mysteries of life. Man is the political animal and so to better understand the mysteries of life, life must be studied as it is lived: in political communities.[13] And it must be studied at its high points such as at the moment of the founding of a state.

The study of politics, political science and political philosophy, is an endeavor to understand the deepest questions, the overarching questions, the questions that the Mishnah claims that Abraham asked as he departed from Ur Kasdim and the questions that Socrates is said to have asked as the beginning of inquiry.[14]

CHAPTER HEADINGS

The first section of the book sets the stage for Israel's declaration of independence. The journey begins in the smoke-filled rooms of the Zionist Actions Committee, the executive body of the World Zionist Organization, at a meeting held in Tel Aviv during the second week of April 1948. The British Mandate over Palestine, which would end on May 15, was already receding, leaving chaos, political void, and war in its wake. David Ben-Gurion, the de-facto leader of the *Yishuv*, pulled together Zionist leaders from around the world in order to win authorization and legitimacy to create a Jewish government, with him at its head, that would be capable of directing a state and bringing it to independence.

---

[13] Aristotle, *Politics*, Book I, trans. Jowett: http://classics.mit.edu/Aristotle/politics.1.one.html

[14] For Abraham and Ur-Kasdim, see Maimonides, *Mishneh Torah* 1:3 and *Guide of the Perplexed*, 3:29. For Socrates' beginning of inquiry, see "Philosophy of Plato" in Al-Farabi, *Philosophy of Plato and Aristotle* (Philosophy of Plato), trans. Mushin Mahdi (Ithaca, NY: Cornell University Press, 2001).

After six days of colorful debate and dispute amongst Labor Zionists, Revisionists, Communists, and a mix of Zionist dignitaries from abroad, the Zionist Actions Committee meeting culminated in the adoption of a "Declaration of the Establishment of the Government" written by Labor Zionist politician and newspaper editor Zalman Rubashov (Shazar). This was not a declaration of independence for a Jewish state but a beginning toward one. This book's first chapter tells the story of the political steps that were needed to make a declaration of independence possible. It tells the story of what one central participant would call "the first foundation of our political independence."

The next section of the book presents an intellectual tour of the political theories that vied for dominance in Israel's Declaration of Independence. It begins with Chapter 2, discussing the first significant draft of Israel's Declaration of Independence, and through it, a path not travelled by the state of Israel: the path of the natural rights discourse of the Declaration of Independence of the United States.

The first draft of Israel's Declaration of Independence was based directly on America's, even including the phrase "life, liberty, and the pursuit of happiness." It was composed by a young lawyer moonlighting in a government office named Mordechai Beham who used the resources of Rabbi Harry Davidowitz, an older rabbi who came to Tel Aviv by way of America, to write the first draft of Israel's Declaration of Independence on an afternoon during the Passover holiday.

The text that Beham produced is not just interesting for its reliance on the American Declaration of Independence as source material but also for the ideas that it drew from it. Beham, possibly with the help of Davidowitz, attempted to meld the natural rights doctrines and realpolitik of American political thought with an explicitly Hebraic idea of the legitimacy of a Jewish state.

With the exception of a few notable aspects, Beham's first draft was revised and redacted out of existence as the text encountered Beham's fellow legal bureaucrats. Israel's founding document would take a different tack. The story of Beham's text is thus a tale of a road not taken by Israel, one which, if it cannot exactly be retraced, leads to reflections germane to Israel today.

Chapter 3 turns to the Labor Zionist vision of national independence expressed in the draft of Israel's Declaration composed by lawyer and future Supreme Court Justice Tzvi Berenson. In justifying independence on the basis of the ethics of labor, Berenson built on and elaborated the arguments laid out in Rubashov's "Declaration of the Establishment of the Government" – one of the main documents Berenson worked with. The chapter considers the meaning of the doctrines of Labor Zionism by studying Berenson's text which justified the state on their basis.

Chapter 4 considers the relationship of national independence to the law of nations such as it is examined through the fulcrum of international legal theorist Herschel Lauterpacht's draft of Israel's Declaration of Independence. While visiting New York where he was involved in creating the nascent UN's legal infrastructure, Lauterpacht met with the Jewish Agency's delegation to the UN. It included a young diplomat and relative of Lauterpacht's by marriage named Aubrey Eban, later to be known Abba Eban – one of Israel's most prominent and successful diplomats. The result was a document that drew both on then-in-vogue arguments for international peace through global federalism and advocated for an independent Jewish state. This chapter evaluates the dream of international law and cosmopolitan peace by way of a close reading not just of Lauterpacht's text but also of its underlying ideas.

The third section of the book relates the political history of Israel's Declaration of Independence: the debates surrounding its composition, the political calculations of its authors, the dilemmas that they confronted, and the choices that Israel's leaders ultimately made – both concrete political choices and abstract philosophical ones. It begins with Chapter 5, which returns to the world of international diplomacy and politics. This is the necessary lens through which to understand the penultimate draft of Israel's Declaration, written by the *Yishuv*'s de-facto foreign minister and Israel's second prime minister Moshe Shertok (later Sharett) just a few days before Israel's independence.

The chapter addresses the possibilities of politics: the limits and strictures as well as the possibility of departures and novelties. Shertok's eyes were expressly fixed on the *Yishuv*'s diplomatic situation in May 1948. He was a pivotal actor in events then still unfolding at the UN and in Washington. This caused him to limit his draft of the Declaration to the task of fitting a new state within an already existing political and legal pattern. The chapter walks the reader through the drama of Shertok's political maneuverings in Washington and looks at the radical form of departure that the creation of a new state in fact requires.

Chapter 6 continues to reflect on this theme – namely, the extent to which a new state must be *new*, or *entirely new* – how it must in some elemental sense depart from the modes and orders of the past. It considers this through an unfolding of the *Yishuv* leadership's May 13 debate on the text of Shertok's Declaration.

In this chapter, David Ben-Gurion emerges as the first man of the *Yishuv*, the indispensable politician for the creation of Israel. The pull-no-punches debate on the fundamental issues at play in Israel's Declaration of Independence sees Ben-Gurion, Shertok, Golda Meyerson (later Meir), and the other colorful leaders of the *Yishuv* arguing about the essentials of statecraft and politics.

Ben-Gurion understood what was essential in the creation of a new state. It had to create a new reality and legislate new laws to meet that new reality. In criticizing Shertok's draft, and stressing what the Declaration had to include, Ben-Gurion in these debates provides a timeless lesson on the hierarchy between politics and law at the moment of a political founding.

Having mastered the debate over Shertok's draft of the Declaration, Ben-Gurion took upon himself the task, as he put it modestly, with the help of "a committee," of "editing" Shertok's draft on May 13. Chapter 7, the final chapter of the book surveying the drafting process, interprets Ben-Gurion's Declaration – that is, The Declaration of the Establishment of the State of Israel as it is known to us.

Before setting to work, Ben-Gurion told his colleagues that he was a "practical" man, that the Declaration's first purpose was simply to declare a Jewish state which would be, by its very nature, independent and sovereign. If the Declaration did this, said Ben-Gurion, it would be enough. The text "did not have to be recited by schoolchildren in one hundred years."[15]

And yet, in spite of himself, or somewhere deep in his being, Ben-Gurion instinctively knew that a Declaration of Independence worthy of its name would have to be recited by schoolchildren in 100 years – as Israel's Declaration of Independence is today. And thus, Ben-Gurion too attempted to articulate the nature of the state.

The core of his effort was the attempt to explain the "natural and historic right" of the Jews to a state. There are glimpses at his view regarding the essence of the inherent rights that citizens naturally possess. His success and his failure, the clarity of his document on some fundamental issues and its ambiguity on others, has left deep questions with which Israel must continue to reckon.

The fourth section of the book discusses the legacy of the Declaration of Independence. Chapter 8 explains how the Declaration of

---

[15] Protocols of the National Administration, May 13, 1948, p. 126.

Independence became, in the words of one jurist, the "basic credo" of the state of Israel: a source of normative principles, moral argument, and pivotal to legal interpretation, rising not to the level of constitution, but in some ways at once less and more. For the Declaration holds the status of an elevated text, one of the sources of arch-constitutional first principles for Israel.

The Declaration of Independence had something clear to say about political sovereignty. Its lesson on this front is most visible in the remarkable story of Israel's recognition by the US government as the clock struck midnight to bring in May 15, 1948 – at the first possible minute. This legacy of Israel's Declaration of Independence is related in the conclusion.

There are ambiguities and paths left open by Israel's Declaration which map to the ambiguities of the state of Israel itself. The final chapter explores how the paths not taken in the Declaration's composition themselves point to a way forward.

PART I

THE SETTING

I

Government

The Origins of Israel's Declaration of Independence

"Declaration of Jewish Independence" read the April 12, 1948 headline on the front page of the Tel Aviv daily *Davar*. *Ha'aretz* said something similar: "The Zionist Actions Committee declares Jewish Independence." Beneath the *Davar* article ran the full text of a document announcing the creation of "the highest authority of our political independence."[1]

Of course, Israel did not declare independence on April 12. The title "Declaration of Independence" is reserved for the text read by David Ben-Gurion on May 14, 1948, hours before the British Mandate over Palestine ended at midnight. Why did the *Yishuv*'s leading newspapers think that Jewish independence was being declared one month before the anticipated British departure?

The previous night, the Zionist Actions Committee or ZAC (in Hebrew: the *Va'ad Ha'Poel Ha'Tzioni*), the highest body of international Zionism, had produced a document culminating in a ringing assertion: "We say, at last, on behalf of the World Zionist Movement, and with the agreement of all the House of Israel: with the end of the disappointing rule of the Mandatory government, the rule of foreigners in the land will end. The nation will claim its inheritance and establish its political independence."[2]

The ZAC's text was not in fact what *Davar* and *Ha'aretz* had called it. Its contents did not announce the creation of a Jewish state. Rather, the ZAC produced and ratified a motion on "The Declaration of the Founding

---

[1] *Davar*, *Ha'aretz*, April 12, 1948. Note: *Davar* was the official organ of David Ben-Gurion's *Mapai* Labor Party.

[2] For a full translation of the text adopted by the ZAC, see the Appendix. The ZAC has sometimes been referred to in English as the "Zionist General Council."

of the Government." This was no small matter. It represents a turning point in the political history of the *Yishuv* – one that has not been adequately acknowledged or understood by historians or the wider public.[3]

The April 1948 ZAC meeting was the moment when the multitude of Jewish political and communal leadership bodies, both in Palestine and throughout the world, agreed to create a unified *political* body – one that could and indeed would declare political independence roughly one month later. The text which was composed announcing the creation of such a political body ultimately exerted a profound influence on the text of the Declaration of Independence. The April 1948 ZAC meeting is thus where the story of Israel's journey to declaring political independence and the tale of the drafting of Israel's Declaration of Independence both begin.

The significance of the ZAC's declaration was recognized by acute observers at the time. *The New York Times* took notice: "Ben-Gurion Urges Zionist Set-Up Now," it explained.[4] The Chief Secretary of the British Mandate Administration in Jerusalem, Sir Henry Gurney, thought that the ZAC declaration was a clear sign that the Jews were bent on statehood after the British departure from Palestine – irrespective of how other local or international actors might react: "The General Zionist Council has come out with a formidable concoction of religion and polit-ics," he wrote in his personal journal. The document that appeared in the Tel Aviv daily newspapers seemed to him to be "designed to assert their intention of establishing a Jewish State on the 16th of May, at all costs."[5]

David Ben-Gurion was the principal actor in the drama, both leading the ZAC to unify the Zionist world's political authority in April and then using that political authority to declare independence and political sover-eignty in May. To his mind, the creation of a unified political body was in many ways as important as the actual declaration of independence.

As Ben-Gurion put it in his memoirs: "With respect to foreign affairs, the decision of the Zionist Actions Committee did not have force, since there

---

[3] Yoram Shachar discusses the ZAC text in his vital "*Ha'teyotot ha'mukdamot shel hakhrazat ha'atzmaut*," *Iyunei Mishpat*, 2002. David Ben-Gurion speaks of the significance of the ZAC meeting in *Medinat Yisrael ha'Methadeshet* (*The Renewed State of Israel*), vol. 1 (Tel Aviv: Am Oved, 1969), p. 81. Also see Samuel Sagar, "Israel's Provisional State Council and Government," *Middle Eastern Studies*, 14, 1, 1978, pp. 91–101, and Walter Laqueur, *A History of Zionism* (New York: Shocken, 2003), p. 585.

[4] Dana Adams Schmidt, "Ben-Gurion Urges Zionist Set-Up Now," *The New York Times*, April 6, 1948.

[5] Motti Golani, ed., *The End of the British Mandate for Palestine, 1948: The Diary of Sir Henry Gurney* (New York: Palgrave MacMillan, 2009), April 13, 1948, pp. 117–118.

was more than a month to go of British rule. But with respect to domestic affairs, there was in the Zionist Actions Committee's decision the opening to the Declaration of Independence that was accepted on May 14."[6]

Yosef Sprinzak, a *Mapai* member and future first speaker of the Knesset who chaired the meeting, summed up the ZAC's work at its closing session: "We have secured the first foundations of our existence and independent politics in our land." It was a first foundation, but not the ultimate one.

What kind of institutions did the ZAC create? How did it lead to the "Declaration on the Founding of the Government?" And how in turn did this lead to "The Declaration of the Establishment of the State of Israel," Israel's declaration of independence, one month later? What did the ZAC say, and why did it say it?

Though the state of Israel was born on May 14, 1948, Israel's government was born on April 12, just after midnight, in a school classroom after a weeklong conference of the ZAC in Tel Aviv. It was not a given that such a body would be created, nor did the full political leadership of the *Yishuv* agree to this path at the time. This is the story of how it happened anyways.

CHANGES AND THE VOID

The April 1948 meeting of the ZAC brought together 77 representatives of Zionism's major political, cultural, and social organizations both in the Diaspora and the *Yishuv*. They were an eccentric crew, ranging from scholars and polemicists to Jewish communal officials, bureaucrats, trade union activists, rabbis, and military officers. They gathered as members of the permanent "actions committee" ("*actioncomité*" originally) of the Zionist Organization, an institution Theodor Herzl himself created following the First Zionist Congress in Basel in 1897.

Some arrived from as far afield as France, South Africa, Britain, and the United States. A number of them had to break the Arab blockade then separating the Jews of Jerusalem from the coast – already in force for months. Others only had to walk a few short blocks in Tel Aviv to arrive at the high school where the conference was held.

Judith Epstein, the 52-year-old American president of the Zionist women's organization Hadassah, had traveled by air from the United

---

[6] *Medinat Yisrael ha'Methadeshet*, vol. 1, p. 81.

States to Palestine. There were no direct flights in 1948. She likely stopped numerous times on a journey whose length was measured in days.

The changes she experienced as she traversed half the globe were less amazing to her than those she witnessed in Palestine itself. She said in an address to the ZAC, delivered in English:

> My first experiences in the land convinced me that the state was a fact. We left the Lydda airport under British protection. But twenty minutes later, we actually entered the Jewish state. Our passports were checked by Jews. One had the sense of crossing a Jewish frontier.[7]

Palestine's political reality was in flux. The British Mandate that had governed Palestine since 1920 was withering away. Epstein felt as if she had crossed the first Jewish border to exist in roughly 1,800 years.

Epstein also raised the other unavoidable fact which any visitor to Palestine in April 1948 would immediately observe: Palestine was at war. "Yesterday I was taken to a training camp for the new army," she explained. "I saw the youth training for the ugly but necessary task of war .... The next day a large-scale attack on Mishmar ha-Emek was launched."

Here Epstein is referring to heavy fighting that took place in the Western part of the Jezreel Valley in early April 1948. Epstein was not exaggerating. War had followed Britain's creeping withdrawal from Palestine. What had begun as an Arab general strike on December 1, 1947, with ambushes of Jewish busses and civil violence morphed into a war over the winter of 1948.[8] By February, Jerusalem had been blockaded by local cleric Haj Amin al-Husayni's militiamen.[9]

In the spring, the *Yishuv* began to undertake its own offensive campaigns. During March and April, the *Yishuv*'s *Haganah* fighters began to mass into company- and even battalion-sized formations. And similarly, an Arab Liberation Army composed of both local and Lebanese, Syrian, and other foreign volunteers had formed in the north. *Haganah* attacks grew into efforts to secure *Yishuv* lines of communication and supply. Within 10 days of the ZAC meeting's conclusion, *Yishuv* military action would see battles in Haifa and then the Jaffa area.[10]

---

[7] Protocols of the Zionist Actions Committee, Central Zionist Archives, S/5/322, April 7, 1948.

[8] Martin Gilbert, *Israel* (New York: William Morrow, 1998), p. 155.

[9] On the relative paucity of scholarship on al-Husayni, see Avraham Sela and Alon Kadish, eds., *The War of 1948: Representations of Israeli and Palestinian Memories and Narratives* (Bloomington: Indiana University Press, 2016), pp. 1–24.

[10] Tom Segev, *One Palestine, Complete* (New York: Henry Holt Press, 2000), p. 509.

The experience of political upheaval and violence that Epstein described was a function of what was called in the *Yishuv* – quoting the language of Genesis 1:1 – "the void," *Tohu va'Vohu*, the nothingness that exists before creation in the Bible's telling of the beginning of existence, almost in defiance of logic and thought itself. The ZAC was convened during a period of indeterminacy and political retreat caused by Britain's withdrawal and the UN's abdication of the responsibility that Britain had passed on to it.[11] The void was being filled with war.

UN RESOLUTION 181

The formal process of British withdrawal from Palestine had started on February 14, 1947, when the British government, under military and economic strain and with India and Pakistan independence fast approaching in September, referred what was called the "Palestine problem" to the United Nations.[12] Nearly 10 months later, the Resolution on the Report of the Ad Hoc Committee on the Palestinian Question (Resolution 181), now known simply as Resolution 181, was adopted by the UN on November 29, 1947. It was meant to settle the Palestine issue once and for all by decreeing the creation of two states – one Arab and one Jewish – in Palestine.[13] Indeed, that is what Resolution 181 is known for today. Needless to say, Resolution 181 was front and center at the ZAC.

That is because Resolution 181 was not as cut and dry as it may seem. A key element in the story of Israel's independence lies in the details of Resolution 181. This will be a subject of some focus in this book. For Resolution 181 did more than just declare eventual partition of Palestine: It set out a complex path whereby what it called "Jewish" and "Arab" states were to be created. The navigation of this process, even as the process had come undone under the realities of war, was a key

---

[11] The term was already in use before the passing of UN Resolution 181. See *Ha'aretz*, November 18, 1947. Also see David Ben-Gurion's speech to *Minhelet ha'Am*, Protocols of the National Administration, April 18, 1948.

[12] Ellen Jenny Ravndal, "Exit Britain: British Withdrawal from the Palestine Mandate in the Early Cold War, 1947–1948," *Diplomacy & Statecraft*, Fall: 2010, p. 417.

[13] *Official Records of the Second Session of the General Assembly, Ad Hoc Committee on the Palestine Question*, 32nd, 33rd, and 34th meetings. www.un.org/unispal/document-source/general-assembly-ad-hoc-committee-on-the-palestinian-question/. Also see, H. Eugene Bovis, *The Jerusalem Question, 1917–1968* (Palo Alto, CA: Hoover Press, 1971), pp. 41–50.

consideration at the *Yishuv*'s highest echelons of diplomacy and politics in 1948 and a vital matter on the minds of the delegates to the ZAC.

The Jewish and Arab states envisioned by Resolution 181 were to come into being in phases as various political criteria for statehood were met. This path to independence was to be administered by a UN "Commission ... [with] authority to issue necessary regulations and take other measures as required."

This Commission was to preside over the establishment of "provisional councils of government" by April 1 and the election of constitutional assemblies by October 1. It was also tasked with certifying that the Jews and Arabs were following the UN plan. They were to compose and ratify constitutions, adhere to the ethics of the UN Charter, and participate in an economic union with one another (and with what was to be a UN-administered Jerusalem).

Most important of all, peace was to prevail between them. Quoting Resolution 181, the plan was for "Independent Arab and Jewish States and the Special International Regime for the City of Jerusalem ... [to] come into existence in Palestine two months after the evacuation of the armed forces of the mandatory Power has been completed but in any case not later than 1 October 1948."[14]

While this all sounded good on paper, the reality was that Resolution 181 had been an immediate failure. By the time the ZAC convened in April 1948, the process set out by Resolution 181 was in tatters. In late January 1948, only two months after the passage of Resolution 181, the UN Palestine Commission issued the first report of its proceedings. It was gloomy and concluded that the UN's scheme was unlikely to work. John Fletcher-Cooke of Britain's delegation to the UN Palestine Commission reported as follows:

> The Arabs have made it quite clear and have told the Palestine government that they do not propose to co-operate or to assist the Commission, and that, far from it, they propose to attack and impede its work in every possible way. We have no reason to suppose that they do not mean what they say.[15]

The failure of Resolution 181 had led US diplomats to propose a program of UN Trusteeship of Palestine that would have forestalled

---

[14] The text of Resolution 181 is available at https://documents-dds-ny.un.org/doc/RESOLUTION/GEN/NR0/038/88/PDF/NR003888.pdf. Also see Martin Gilbert, *Israel*, p. 153.

[15] United Nations Palestine Commission Report, January 29, 1948, available at https://unispal.un.org/DPA/DPR/unispal.nsf/fd807e46661e3689852570d00069e918/feca435dae3b3deb85256c6000615518.

partition into states and thus Jewish independence. Epstein explained the matter starkly: "It is not easy to be a citizen of a country in whose ideals you have believed deeply and to witness the reversal on partition, which was a betrayal of the Jewish people and American honor." Trusteeship was not to come about, a subject discussed in Chapter 6. And there is good reason to believe that *Yishuv* leadership did not believe it to be a serious possibility. But it was on the minds of the delegates as the ZAC assembled.

The void created by the British withdrawal invited intensifying violence. By springtime, it was a war. "An afternoon of battle and bullets," wrote the laconic and anti-Jewish Chief Secretary Henry Gurney in his diary on March 21. "And the [British] army playing football among them. Another lovely day."[16]

This was the Palestine into which Epstein and the other delegates to the ZAC arrived: riven by war and in political flux. But like the rest of the Zionist leadership, Epstein understood that the *Yishuv* had to embrace these challenges if it was to achieve statehood. Epstein saw the historical path on which the *Yishuv* was now set: "There are dynamics in a movement that lead you from one step to another," she said. The step that the *Yishuv* was next compelled to take was toward continuing in its war and establishment of the state: "I found here a very deep realism ... and a complete understanding of our needs and the relationship of our forces to meet the enemy we are facing," Epstein continued. But there was a missing ingredient needed to confront these challenges, and it was with this that she concluded her remarks to the ZAC: "We must be assured of Jewish unity of purpose. Perhaps unity is not the right term, for it has so often been misused ... . The common danger must draw all of us together ... ."[17]

THE CREATION OF A GOVERNMENT

It was this very common danger and a search for unity of purpose and action that caused David Ben-Gurion to convene the ZAC's weeklong gathering in April 1948. This wasn't a mere rhetorical point: the *Yishuv* faced a crisis. Ben-Gurion's *Mapai* party colleagues put the issue on the

[16] March 21, 1948, *The End of the British Mandate for Palestine, 1948: The Diary of Sir Henry Gurney*, p. 45.

[17] Protocols of the Zionist Actions Committee, April 7, 1948.

table at a March 6, 1948, internal party leadership meeting that set the table for the ZAC meeting in April.

Eliyahu Dobkin, a senior *Mapai* politician, summarized the dilemma: "Our first goal is the creation of a political body recognized by the family of nations that can implement the decision of the United Nations on the founding of a Jewish state," he explained. The Jews were supposed to have established a "provisional council of government" according to Resolution 181. They hadn't. And so, even as the Resolution 181 process was crumbling, they had to get moving on it already.

"But this isn't enough – there's another goal," Dobkin continued. "To right away found an effective authority for the material direction of all the affairs of state ... in place of the crumbling [British] rule."[18] The military and other vital agencies reported up a jumble of bureaucratic chains of command, some under the aegis of the Jewish Agency, others to Mandate agencies in Palestine, and still others to the World Zionist Organization leadership.

Ben-Gurion stood at the head of all of the major pan-Zionist organizations. But each had separate rules and procedures, and were composed of different governing councils. They couldn't simply be commanded through a unified organization – even though that was necessary. The red tape had to be cut.

There was a third imperative for creating a unified authority to govern the *Yishuv:* declaring political independence in May. *Mapai* politican Avraham Katznelson spelled it out: "The foundation of a [authoritative body] is important for May 15," he explained. Sure, it is also helpful "to prevent *Tohu va'Vohu* in many areas if we have tools to act and the necessary authority." But there was a more important rationale for centralizing power: "There has to be a single table for the *Yishuv* and the Zionist movement to prepare for May 15."[19] The end of the British Mandate on May 15 would require a single authority convening around a single table to make the decisions that would have to be made regarding independence.

It was with these imperatives in mind that Ben-Gurion had convened the ZAC in Tel Aviv in April 1948. Rising to address the Committee on the first day of the meeting, Ben-Gurion gave a Churchillian speech complete with echoes of the 1940 "Never Surrender" address:

---

[18] Protocols of *Mapai*, March 6, 1948, Labor Party Archives, 2-023-1948-49.   [19] Ibid.

We have no choice but to defend ourselves. I refer to all Jews, both in the land of Israel and in the Diaspora, who are able to live just one sort of life: an independent Jewish life in their homeland .... To those Jews, I say, there is no choice except: we cannot surrender. Not to the Mufti, not to the leaders of the Arab league, not to the government of [British Foreign Secretary Ernest] Bevin, not to other nations that will assist Bevin with his intrigues.[20]

Ben-Gurion was playing to the crowd. It was time for the Jews to stand their ground. No one was going to disagree in a *Yishuv* that had been bloodied and with Jerusalem under siege.

But Ben-Gurion's rhetoric was in the service of his political agenda. If the *Yishuv* was to defend itself, if it in fact was to avoid surrender, it would need to procure weapons, he explained. And to buy weapons, the *Yishuv* needed a government – "for only governments can do this."[21]

To meet the challenge, Ben-Gurion called in his address for the creation of a "central high authority" that would be solely responsible for the politics and self-defense of the *Yishuv*. He put his cards on the table. The aim of the ZAC meeting would be to wrest that authority from the ZAC's various constituent parts and place it in an actual governing body located in the *Yishuv*. The ZAC was to vote itself out of relevance, if not existence.

The new central authority that Ben-Gurion envisioned would possess powers beyond war, he explained. It would be responsible for "manpower, army, market, industry, agriculture, finance, and political services in the *Yishuv* and the land of Israel." This authority would have the legitimate monopoly on politics, violence, social affairs, and even the entire economy.

Ben-Gurion spoke candidly to the assembled delegates. This would represent a transfer of power, the final transfer of power, from the institutions of world Zionism to local leaders of the *Yishuv* – to the leaders of what would soon become known as Israel. War requires a break with formality, bureaucracy, and the way that things in the Zionist world had conventionally been done. Now was not a time to protect organizational turf: "The job of the Zionist Actions Committee is to arrange things for the *Yishuv* and the Zionist movement not according to the Zionist [Organization] constitution, or according to our rules, not how it has been habitual with us for the pasty fifty years. It must act completely according to the needs of self-defense."[22]

This wouldn't be the end of Zionist institutions abroad, Ben-Gurion half-reassuringly explained. The new authority would "depend on support

[20] Protocols of the Zionist Actions Committee, April 6, 1948.   [21] Ibid.   [22] Ibid.

from the Zionist movement and the Jewish people around the world."[23] But Zionism had to change to meet the needs of the moment: "There is a necessity that in place of all such institutions, however important and dear to us, there now emerges, in this hour of emergency, without any connection to what was decided at the UN . . . a central authority," he said.[24] The Jews faced a choice, Ben-Gurion put it, without understatement, that they hadn't faced "in 1,800 years."

IDEOLOGICAL DISTRACTIONS

Ben-Gurion had set an absolute position: He needed to concentrate political authority. The assembled delegates would either have to agree or make their disagreement explicit. It was a dynamite opening to the conference. But of course, Ben-Gurion's agenda wasn't the only one represented at the ZAC. There would be plenty of ideological hair splitting and argument.

For starters, far-left members of the ZAC, belonging to the *Mapam* political party, supported the consensus *Yishuv* position about the need to fight the war. But they were not focused on this urgent issue. Instead, they wanted to argue for, of all things, communist anti-imperialism. They urged the ZAC to array the *Yishuv* squarely in political opposition to America and Britain. As *Mapam* member Yaakov Riftin put it: "The central question isn't a 'single higher authority'. . . . The most pressing question is one of money." And, he continued, ludicrously in hindsight, it was the "socialist countries" who were truly in a position to help.[25]

The Communist Moshe Sneh, who had led the general staff of the *Haganah* during World War II, similarly denounced "Anglo-Saxon imperialism" and warned that America and Britain might intervene aggressively against the *Yishuv*.[26] Neither of them mentioned the name Stalin or the Communist International openly, but the two were effectually calling on the *Yishuv* to ally with Moscow.[27] In later years, evidence would mount that Riftin was likely a Soviet agent.[28]

And so, in a second speech on April 7, Ben-Gurion protected his left flank. He demolished Moshe Sneh's assertion that the Jews should only commit to the fight against "Anglo-Saxon" imperialism and align with

---

[23] Ibid.   [24] Ibid.   [25] Ibid., April 7, 1948.   [26] Ibid.   [27] Ibid.
[28] See Ronen Bergman, "The KGB's Middle East Files," *Ynet*, October 28, 2016, www
.ynetnews.com/articles/0,7340,L-4870004,00.html

the socialist countries. "Seven million Jews live in the Anglo-Saxon world," stated Ben-Gurion, "I don't understand why when this word 'Anglo-Saxon' is uttered by us [in Hebrew], we use such a racist tone."[29]

The Soviet Union was hardly paradise. "Even before Stalin," Ben-Gurion said, "Kautsky [the Communist theorist] decreed that the Jewish people were not a people and had no right to a future." Ben-Gurion may have tipped his preference for the "Anglo-Saxon" world over the Soviet one in this speech, but his decisive rationale was geopolitical. Both the Soviet Union *and* the United States had approved the partition plan, he reminded the ZAC. And Britain, though clearly hostile, already had more than one foot out the door from Palestine. For the time being, Ben-Gurion argued, the *Yishuv* should not align one way or another. The priority was to build up independent strength.

The stormiest sessions at the meeting concerned whether, and on what terms, *Etzel*, the militia of the Revisionist Party, could be integrated within a single chain of command. Attempting to bring order to a late-night session on the subject that was repeatedly interrupted by shouting, insults, and vitriol, the meeting's chairman Sprinzak pleaded with the delegates: "If this is how the leaders behave, what will happen on the street?"[30] Though the integration of *Etzel* was approved at the meeting, the matter would not be settled definitively. Only after Israel's independence on May 14, 1948, could a national army be said to exist. And even after independence, tensions persisted. The traumatic Altalena incident, discussed later in the book, would take place that summer.

While Ben-Gurion and his Labor Party allies had much to say about these issues, they endeavored to bring the assembled group back to the real task at hand: the creation of a government. In a speech on April 7, Ben-Gurion's ally Golda Meyerson (later Meir) cut to the essence of things: "We're here to do one thing: decide how to organize our powers." Meyerson criticized colleagues on the Left and on the Right for losing sight of this central goal amidst petty ideological quarrels: "Our different worldviews will be irrelevant if we are all dead."[31]

Levi Shkolnik (later Eshkol), Israel's third Prime Minister who led the country to victory in the Six-Day War, was also an important point man for Ben-Gurion in keeping the ZAC focused on the creation of a single high authority or government: "In this Committee we have not only

---

[29] Protocols of the Zionist Actions Committee, April 7, 1948.
[30] Quoted in *Ma'ariv*, April 12, 1948.
[31] Protocols of the Zionist Actions Committee, April 7, 1948.

people from the land of Israel. This is our right. This is our good fortune, that we have a global movement, and not just the *Yishuv*," he explained. But leadership of the *Yishuv* on both domestic and foreign affairs, he continued, now had to be "localized." This was necessary, he claimed, to "direct the war and achieve our independence."[32]

Ben-Gurion also had support from the broad Zionist center – Zionism's silent majority. Members of the General Zionists party spoke fervently about the need for unity thus lending support to Ben-Gurion's program. Dr. Haim Bograshov, the General Zionist who had been the founder and principal of the Herzliya Hebrew high school, called for cohesion and respect amongst all parties: "The Talmud presents Beit Shamai as well as Beit Hillel. *This and this* is the way of the living God," the *Yeshiva*-trained educator said, quoting one of the Talmud's great dictums.

Unity at that moment, Bograshov continued, meant generally following the course of David Ben-Gurion: "One person says: 'I want a dictatorship of the proletariat. Ben-Gurion is not proletarian enough.' Another side says: 'Ben-Gurion is the symbol of the proletariat' .... If we start this way, we'll never succeed in steering our ship of state."[33]

Emanuel Neumann, an American Zionist leader who helped write the meeting's concluding text, deferred to the *Yishuv* leadership:

It is not for us [American Jews] to indicate to the *Yishuv* the degree of risk and peril which the *Yishuv* should assume and bear .... All that we can do or say to you here is that in our judgment, in my judgment certainly, there was never a moment with [sic] the Jews of the United States were prepared more so than now to stand fully behind the *Yishuv* in whatever decisions it adopts, and to give it their fullest backing, financial, moral, and otherwise.[34]

Another American speaker, Beba Idelson, urged the ZAC to follow the example of the Allied nations in World War II who were able to put aside partisan divisions in wartime: "We haven't yet put aside our party arguments. We have to remember that the most important thing is the defense of Jewish lives and of the land of Israel."[35]

A STATE OR A GOVERNMENT?

Even as the focus of the ZAC meeting was the concentration of power in the hands of a new governing council, Ben-Gurion and his allies did not hesitate to say openly that the new institutions would ultimately form the

---

[32] Ibid., April 6, 1948.   [33] Ibid., April 7, 1948.   [34] Ibid.   [35] Ibid.

government of an independent *state*. "Our agenda is a Jewish state," said David Ben-Gurion. "We weren't afraid previously when we were told that it's not possible to demand a Jewish state because the progressive nations wouldn't like it."[36]

The right-wing Revisionists, however, thought that the Zionist executive leadership was too cautious. The time to declare a state is now, they argued. Meir Grossman, the writer and one-time associate of the founder of Revisionism Vladimir Jabotinsky, made the case in a fiery speech: "We think that this meeting of the Committee must immediately declare a Jewish state and authorize the creation of a Jewish government that can immediately begin to operate," he argued. "And when I say 'Jewish government' I refer to an actual government and not to some murky body of international authority about which one no one is clear and everyone interprets differently."[37]

Grossman here drew an important distinction. He and his party were not interested in declaring a "provisional council of government" as the Resolution 181 text had stipulated. They did not see logic in following a dead political process. They held little hope that the UN would itself respect it and one day recognize a Jewish state. Rather they wanted a Jewish government and state right then and on Jewish terms.

Aryeh Altman, another American Revisionist academic, accused Ben-Gurion's party of dangerous evasions and half-measures that would wreck the possibility of an independent state: "Ben-Gurion and Shkolnik [Eshkol] spoke of creating an 'office' .... That's not a government. To wait until May 16 is legalism. There's no place for that. Declare an independent state today before the UN subjects us to something new."[38]

Mapai and its allies disagreed on one of these points and didn't address the second – probably because they weren't yet decided on it themselves. They argued ardently that declaring political independence before the British Mandate actually expired in May would be a fool's errand. And at this early stage, they were yet to settle the issue of whether to declare a "provisional government" or a state upon the departure of the British.

Mapai politician Zalman Aharonovich (later Aranne) launched a caustic attack against the Revisionist demand for an immediate declaration of independence: "The Revisionists are not only saying 'everything or nothing' today, when we have 700,000 Jews here. They said the same thing when there were 120,000." Aharonovich had heard it all before from the

---

[36] Ibid.   [37] Ibid., April 7, 1948.   [38] Ibid.

Revisionists: "If we had listened to them, if we followed their logic of 'everything or nothing,' we would never have strengthened our numbers, our capabilities, and power in the *Yishuv*."[39]

Aharonovich argued that the ZAC should steer a middle way between the extremist ideas of Sneh the Communist and Altman the Revisionist: "The Zionist leadership hasn't faltered," he argued, "And we're on the cusp of a Hebrew state."[40] The mathematician and future president of the Hebrew University Selig Brodetsky added that an immediate declaration of independence would equate to an actual declaration of war on Britain, a rash move that would likely cancel the path to independence: "If we can wait five weeks until the end of the Mandate ... it's better to do that."[41]

And then there was information that may not have been known to the Revisionists, but was known to the *Mapai* leaders: British authorities had explicitly warned the *Yishuv* leadership against any declaration of independence while the British Mandate was in force.[42] There is a reason that ideological fervor tends to mellow amongst those in positions of political authority.

THE VOTE

On April 11, the debate was finally brought to a head. There would be a vote on the ZAC's ultimate position. The left-wing *Mapam* party, center-leaning *Mapai*, and the right-wing Revisionists each drafted separate resolutions. The *Mapam* resolution called for the *Yishuv* to pursue statehood by fulfilling its side of the bargain as envisioned by UN Resolution 181. It called on the UN to fully implement both the principle and the details of Resolution 181. It rejected the plan of Trusteeship that had been floated, whereby Jewish and Arab independence would have been put on hold indefinitely. And, in homage to *Mapam*'s firm belief in the principle of dividing Palestine among Arabs and Jews, it called for independence for "both nations."[43]

The Revisionist resolution, in contrast, explicitly renounced the details of the UN plan for Palestine. According to the Revisionist text, read out loud by Revisionist leader Joseph Schectman, Resolution 181 was important insofar as it was a "final and irrevocable recognition of the natural right

[39] Ibid.   [40] Ibid.   [41] Ibid.

[42] Ze'ev Sharef, *Three Days*, trans. Julian Meltzer (London: W. H. Allen, 1962), p. 45.

[43] Protocols of the Zionist Actions Committee, April 11, 1948.

of the Hebrew nation to renew its independence on its national soil."[44] However, the Revisionists asserted, things had gone awry from there:

The Jewish Agency's consent to the curtailment of the territory of the Jewish State was given as part as [sic] an attempt to reach an agreed solution of the Palestine Problem ... . The Arabs unconditionally combat the partition scheme in all its implications and the United Nations are obviously not ready to enforce it. The Actions Committee therefore declares that the consent by the Jewish Agency to the territorial provisions of the United Nations decision of November 29 is therefore revoked.[45]

The Revisionists, whose party had always opposed partition, remained obsessed over the issue of borders.

The Revisionists also called for the *immediate* establishment of a "temporary government."[46] But it would only be temporary insofar as elections needed to be held to legitimate it in the future – not because it was a waystation on the path to a sovereignty that would require the approval of the UN. "The Jewish state exists," said Shechtman. "We should announce it and create the Hebrew government." This logical deduction exactly presages what David Ben-Gurion would tell the leadership of the *Yishuv* one month later as they debated Israel's independence. Indeed, Ben-Gurion would even invoke a "natural right" to political independence, albeit in a different formulation than the Revisionist text presented. But Ben-Gurion saw that the time was not ripe to declare this publicly, for all the world to hear, one month prior to the British departure from Palestine.

Ben-Gurion's *Mapai* resolution ultimately had the most votes: it was supported by his party, the General Zionists and *Mizrahi*, the religious Zionists. Their collective "majority resolution" was issued in bullet point form highlighting its main operational features. And attached to these bullet points came a "pronouncement."

The essence of their resolution was distilled in two statements: (1) "The Jewish people and the *Yishuv* in the land of Israel will oppose any measure designed to delay or cancel the creation of the Jewish state"; and (2) "immediately upon the end of the British Mandate, and no later than May 16, a provisional Jewish government will begin to act, and will cooperate with representatives of the United Nations that will be in the country then."[47]

The ZAC meeting had crystalized the political intentions of the *Yishuv*: a government and a state at the end of the British Mandate. But the

[44] Ibid.   [45] Ibid.   [46] Ibid.   [47] Ibid.

adopted resolution also paid some attention to the general tenor of United Nations Resolution 181. Unlike the Revisionists, the majority did not declare a government of a state immediately. The majority resolution created "a provisional Jewish government" that would only begin to take authority from the British Mandate following Britain's withdrawal. Also, unlike the Revisionist revolution, the majority resolution said that the Jewish government would "cooperate with representatives of the United Nations."

On the other hand, unlike the *Mapam* resolution, the majority declaration did not explicitly call for the fulfillment of the details of Resolution 181. "Cooperation with the United Nations" does not imply either fulfillment of Resolution 181 or opposition to it. Essentially, the majority left the question of the place of Resolution 181 ambiguous and vague. The matter of the United Nations, unaddressed at this stage, would emerge again and again in the weeks ahead.

RUBASHOV'S PROCLAMATION

The ZAC also issued a formal "declaration." This is the text that would be highlighted in the press the next day. The union organizer and *Davar* editor Zalman Rubashov wrote it with some assistance, on both format and substance, from other members of the ZAC including the Americans Israel Goldstein, Emanuel Neumann, and Samuel Margoshes as well as the Mizrahi leader Yeshayahu Wolfsberg (later Aviad).[48]

Rubashov read "The Declaration on the Founding of the Government," as the address is titled in the minutes of the meeting, to the assembled body of the ZAC after midnight on April 12.[49] Rubashov's speech cannot be called a declaration of independence since the document scrupulously avoided declaring an independent or sovereign state. To do so would have been in contravention of the aims of Ben-Gurion and the *Mapai* leadership. The state would have to wait until the Union Jack came down.

But Rubashov's speech is clear in its aim. Its first sentence asserted the founding of a Jewish "provisional government" with studied effort to try to make it sound like something more: "The Zionist Action Committee, the highest office of the world Zionist movement, declares today our

---

[48] Yoram Shachar, ""Ha'teyotot ha'mukdamot shel hakhrazat ha'atzmaut," p. 32.
[49] For the full text of Rubashov's address, see the Appendix.

decision to found in this country the highest authority of our political independence."

Rubashov's text continued on to discuss many of the themes that would appear in the eventual drafts of the Declaration of Independence proper. It organized itself following the simple logic of the American Declaration of Independence: a list of grievances regarding the British Mandate culminating in the declaration ... not of independence but of a future hope for it.

And hence we say, at last, on behalf of the World Zionist Movement, and with the agreement of all the House of Israel: with the end of the disappointing rule of the Mandatory government, the rule of foreigners in the land will end. The nation will claim its inheritance and establish its political independence.[50]

The state to be known as Israel would not come into being until May 14. It was hard to imagine any turning back on April 12. The text paid heed to this reality and promised future action both in the name of Zionism and the "House of Israel." And yet, it studiously avoided overcommitting to any distinct political-diplomatic path.

Rubashov's text was also ambitious. He began the work of articulating a vision of the future state. Rubashov wrote:

The Jewish state that the Jewish nation will found in the land of our inheritance will be a state of justice and of freedom, of equality for all its residents, without respect to religion, race, sex, and land of origin, a state of the ingathering the exiles and the blossoming of the wilderness, a state of uprightness and understanding, and the vision of the prophets of Israel will illuminate the way for us.

This paragraph, discussed at greater length in Chapter 3, offers a formulation that would have great resonance both in the *Yishuv* in the spring of 1948 and later in the state of Israel. It distills an outlook regarding fundamental human rights that deeply spoke to many in the *Yishuv*. A version of it would find its way into Israel's Declaration of Independence.

Rubashov likewise called "to the Arabs of the Hebrew state ... in brotherhood, peace, and cooperation. We are the nation of peace we have come to build peace." This found its way, in modified form, into the May 14 Declaration. Rubashov's text presented many a noble sentiment that would prove worthy of emulation later in the drafting of Israel's Declaration of Independence.

[50] Protocols of the Zionist Actions Committee, April 11/12, 1948.

Rubashov's text also represented an at-best partially thought-through approach to the character of the state and government. The wording of his text's operative section – declaring the creation of the "provisional council of government" as a "highest political authority" – had been carefully considered by the *Mapai* leadership. This formulation deliberately said what needed to be said and left the rest ambiguous. There would be a "provisional council of government." That was the concrete meaning that mattered.

Other self-evidently important questions had not been as carefully considered or vetted and seem to have been left to Rubashov. His declaration that a Jewish state would respect vital human rights, in particular justice, freedom, and equality, was noble but inadequate. It ignored many obvious other human rights. Moreover, Rubashov did not root those rights in any basis that could be used to defend them: he simply stated them. There was no clear thinking about the basis for the state, whose emergence he justified on the grounds of the "judicial authority" and "moral authority" of Resolution 181. The state would and indeed did rest on other firmer foundations than those Rubashov considered.

While it would be incorrect to call Rubashov's text the first draft of Israel's Declaration of Independence, many of its fundamental aspects were grafted onto the roots that were subsequently planted in the drafting process. And although his text was careful precisely *not* to be a declaration of independence, it contained a literary aspiration to be more than the proclamation of a provisional government – which is what it in fact was.

"THE 13" AND "THE 37": THE CREATION OF *MINHELET HA'AM* AND *MOETZET HA'AM*

Rubashov's speech also avoided saying who would be in the Jewish provisional government. Of course that mattered – especially to Ben-Gurion and his associates. As in all things, the details were of the highest interest to the practitioners. The resolutions giving life to the provisional government were hammered through the ZAC on the morning of April 12.

After the ZAC had voted on its intention to create a provisional government, Ben-Gurion's key lieutenants rushed through the authorization of a "Council of 13" and a "Council of 37." These bodies would serve as the new central authority that the *Mapai* leadership had been insisting upon all week.

This had long been planned. At the same March 6 meeting at which the *Mapai* leadership had addressed the issue of centralizing political authority, there had also been debate regarding that most important of questions: Who would rule? How would the governing council be organized? And who would sit on it?

At the March 6 Labor Party meeting, Ben-Gurion himself had made the case that "it is necessary that there will emerge a single authority which has to be split in two: a larger constituent council and a smaller body, the executive." And while denying that he even wanted to play a role in the government, he ensured that his key lieutenants, who inevitably would conscript him, would be council members.[51]

Ben-Gurion and his allies left nothing to chance at the ZAC meeting. The ZAC was not given leave to debate the membership of the Council of 13. During the prior week of ZAC meetings, narrow ideological issues had been debated at length. On the ZAC's final day, the creation of a small council with power over war, diplomacy, and market was concluded in a few short hours. It was clear to all that it would be controlled by Ben-Gurion.

The creation of these bodies – what became *Minhelet ha'Am* and *Moetzet ha'Am* – had to be submitted to a vote. There was the expected quarreling along party lines. The Revisionist Meir Grossman argued that the Council of 13 should be expanded to 14 and be conducted on the basis of "unity" – that is, by including a Revisionist member.[52] Ben-Gurion's ally Pinhas Lubianker (later Lavon) swatted away the suggestion, noting that "whoever wants to be part of the government ... can be in it only if he holds a loyal relationship to the Resolution of the United Nations" – which the Revisionists opposed.[53] This statement was a way to throw down the ideological gauntlet.

An expert hatchet man, Lubianker brought the matter to a vote rapidly. The ZAC, by a vote of 38 to 24, approved the Lubianker-*Mapai* motion to create a Council of 13 that would exclude the Revisionists as well as the most stalwart Communists.[54] This council would be the executive. All powers of war and peace were transferred to it.

On the other hand, the larger Council of 37 would act as a kind of overarching legislative body – a council to audit the executive council. It would include all parties, of course encompassing Revisionists and Communists. A proto-executive and proto-parliament for the Jewish state

---

[51] Protocols of *Mapai*, March 6, 1948.
[52] Protocols of the Zionist Actions Committee, April 12, 1948.   [53] Ibid.   [54] Ibid.

had been created. Ben-Gurion had been adamant that this was necessary too at the March 6 *Mapai* meeting, arguing that representation in the council must be according to "maximum unity of the *Yishuv*."[55]

In a certain sense, this vote marked a culmination, at least in terms of political authority, for the old institutions of international Zionism that traced their origin to Theodor Herzl. World Zionism had played a fundamental role in building and legitimating the *Yishuv*. The *Yishuv* now needed self-government, as all states do. The ZAC voted to leave certain important authorities in the hands of the Jewish Agency and World Zionism. *Aliyah*, education, the development of Jerusalem – these were to remain under the purview of the old bodies, perhaps in the case that independence failed.

All matters of war, peace, and government were to be in the hands of the new political authorities. To recall Sprinzak's concluding sentence at the end of the ZAC: "We have secured the first foundations of our existence and independent politics in our land."[56]

To Ben-Gurion, the creation of this entirely new order of government with authority to direct the affairs of the *Yishuv* was a vital and seminal moment. It was the necessary if not sufficient condition for independence. For if the Jews could not organize the powers to carry forth their independence, the words of a future declaration of independence, however strident, would be empty.

Ben-Gurion said as much at the first meeting of the "Council of 13" (named at that very meeting *Minhelet ha'Am*) on April 18: "The Zionist Actions Committee had decided ... that, in the areas that it treats, this body has sole authority. This [body] is a new tool, and if it succeeds, a new chapter may open in the history of our people and the [Zionist] movement."[57]

Much of the heavy lifting on the political-bureaucratic front toward the creation of a Jewish government was accomplished at the ZAC, one month before the end of the Mandate. This in turn means that some of the essential conditions for the *Yishuv*'s declaration of independence in the middle of May had been met one month earlier as well. The sufficient criterion for the creation of a new state may be political: a declaration of political indendence, a rupture with the past and a move into a new political future. But the necessary criteria are institutional and premised

---

[55] Protocols of *Mapai*, March 6, 1948.
[56] Protocols of the Zionist Actions Committee, April 12, 1948.
[57] Protocols of the National Administration, April 18, 1948, p. 6.

and indeed built upon the past: creating state capacity and institutions, forming a political basis conferring legitimacy on the the state, and then consolidating institutions and legitimated political bodies into an operating government. The *Yishuv* had accomplished these goals in the 1930s and 1940s. This accomplishment was brought to the fore at the April 1948 ZAC meeting.

But as the debate at the ZAC shows, crucial issues had been left open. There had been consensus to create a "provisional council of government" and to create the "first foundations of our political independence." But it had not been the right time to declare political independence. And there was legitimate dispute regarding whether it would be wise or prudent to deviate from the UN's path and declare a "government" or "independence" as opposed to provisional versions of both upon the departure of the British one month later.

There was also the issue of the text that Rubashov had read. Was it a proper basis for a declaration of independence? Ben-Gurion and his associates paid the most attention to the creation of a provisional council of government. The words that were used to justify the decision had been delegated lower down the chain. That would remain the case for some subsequent weeks before the text of the Declaration of Independence emerged as a vital matter in the days prior to independence, thus becoming a subject of keen interest for Ben-Gurion and the other leaders of the *Yishuv*.

Ben-Gurion had moved the *Yishuv* a step closer to independence at the ZAC. However, the most important political questions that the *Yishuv* would face had been deliberately left open. What kind of government would the *Yishuv* announce? What extent of independence would the *Yishuv* declare? Ultimately, what kind of state would the *Yishuv* form? Would there be a new state in the full sense of the term or just a "provisional council of government"?

These were the vital questions that Ben-Gurion deliberately left unanswered at the ZAC. This exemplified his bureaucratic tact. For he had won the ability to address these matters and have the final say on them in the newly formed council of government – a council that Ben-Gurion would lead. The greatest questions at the foundation of Israel would be addressed in the weeks to come by the Council of 13 that Ben-Gurion had created.

PART II

POLITICAL THEORY

2

Natural Rights

In 1948, the year in which the State of Israel came into being, Saturday, April 24, was the first day of Passover, the Jewish holiday commemorating the exodus from Egypt – the Jewish political beginning. Like millions of other Jews, a 33-year-old Tel Aviv lawyer named Mordechai Beham gathered with his family 1948 to recite the Passover *Hagadah*, the classical Jewish text which narrates Israel's flight from Egypt and deliverance to the land of Israel.

Many that year must have fixed their minds on the possibility that the dream of renewed political independence with which the *Hagadah* culminates – the singing of the phrase "next year in Jerusalem" – was on the verge of becoming a reality. And this especially must have been the case for Beham. For he had just been assigned the job of writing Israel's Declaration of Independence.[1]

A state's declaration of independence can be either a procedural or a monumental work: it can be a simple legal document that declares independence for a state, following in the tradition of international law, or it can, in addition, be a foundational, bedrock document that sets an overarching ethical and even philosophical framework for a country. The prime example of a declaration of independence that is a bedrock

[1] Yoram Shachar is owed enormous gratitude for his work uncovering Beham's draft. See "Ha'teyotot ha'mukdamot shel hakhrazat ha'atzmaut," ("The Early Drafts of the Declaration of Independence"), *Iyunei Mishpat* (November, 2002), and "Jefferson Goes East: The American Origins of the Israeli Declaration of Independence," *Theoretical Inquires in Law*, 10, 2, 2009, "Yomano shel Uri Yadin," ("Uri Yadin's Diary,") *Iyunei Mishpat*, 3, 1991; "Israel as a Two-Parent State," *Zmanim*, 2007. The original texts are available through the Israel State Archive, 2/8227-א.

national document is the American Declaration of Independence. It is a proclamation of self-evident truths: humans are created equal; they are endowed with the rights to life, liberty, and the pursuit of happiness by the simple act of their being; and a state must be established in the service of those rights. A declaration of independence can declare mere independence, or it can declare why a state must have independence.[2]

The text that Beham produced belongs in the second of those two categories: it aimed high. It represented an attempt to define the nature of the Jewish state, not merely declaring its independence, but declaring why it would be independent; not merely laying down a law, but providing a reason for the laws. It did this by combining the source texts of the Jewish tradition with the political thought embedded in the American Declaration of Independence of 1776. It is a document that attempts more than just the legal declaration of an independent Jewish state. It presents an overarching set of ideas, one which could serve to shape future law-making and the spirit of the country coming into being.

Its aim can thus be seen as nothing less than shaping the political discourse of the state of the Jewish people. Its unique contribution would be an attempt to shape it in the direction of the discourse of natural rights – in the direction of the political concepts drawn together in the American Declaration of Independence, the document from which he drew a great deal of his first draft verbatim.

Beham did not succeed. His text was largely lost to history until it was publicized in the 1990s. Its major arguments were redacted as the text was edited by *Moetzet ha'Am*'s Legal Department, which included, it must be said, Beham himself. The text's form, some stylistic elements of its content, and some of its literary innovations, such as the use of the term *Tzur Yisrael* – "rock of Israel" – to describe God, would make it into Israel's Declaration of Independence. Its essential points regarding natural rights would not. But what these essential points were, what the text attempted, and why it did not succeed – therein lies a tale.

---

[2] On the view of a declaration of independence as a national ethical or even philosophical framework, see Harry V. Jaffa, *A New Birth of Freedom* (Lanham: Rowman & Littlefield, 2000), p. 121. For a review of the influence of the American Declaration of Independence, see David Armitage, *The Declaration of Independence: A Global History* (Cambridge, MA: Harvard University Press, 2007), p. 104; Jure Vidmar, "Conceptualizing Declarations of Independence in International Law," *Oxford Journal of Legal Studies* 32, 1, 2012, pp. 153–177.

THE BACKGROUND AND THE ASSIGNMENT

The job had come to Mordechai Beham by way of Felix Rosenblüth (later Pinchas Rosen), the Berlin-born Zionist politician who was at the time assembling the future state's Justice Ministry, and who would indeed lead the Justice Ministry for most of the first decade-and-a-half of Israel's existence.[3] On Thursday, April 22, Rosenblüth had asked Beham, a junior member of his team, to prepare a draft of a "proclamation" that would be published upon the termination of the British Mandate, set for three weeks later on May 15. Rosenblüth instructed Beham by memo:

The Legal Department is of the opinion that on the day of our political independence ... we should publish a first proclamation that notes in its introduction the unfolding of events that brought about the founding of independent rule, and which sets out that the provisional governing council has taken in its hands the authority and responsibility to govern the state.[4]

There is no extant record of discussions between Rosenblüth and Beham about the project. Perhaps in conversation Rosenblüth spoke to Beham more expansively of what he had in mind. But his terse memo – the only outstanding document detailing Beham's assignment – left the task unclear.

The memo does, however, offer a window into the agenda of the *Yishuv* a little more than three weeks before the state of Israel would come into being. Most strikingly, it takes for granted that there will be "a date of our political independence" on May 16. It also states that the "provisional governing council" should become the government at that moment.[5] And thus, finally, it is concerned with legitimating the authority of the bodies of the so-called temporary or provisional governing council, the National Council (*Moetzet ha'Am*) and the National Administration (*Minhelet ha'Am*), both of which counted Rosenblüth as a member.

The establishment of a provisional governing council had been mandated by the governing bodies of the *Yishuv* and of the international Zionist movement at the Zionist Actions Committee meeting: the "provisional council of government" envisioned in the UN Resolution 181 path to statehood would be declared. The bodies required to do so had already

---

[3] Fania Oz-Salzberger and Eli Salzberger, "Die Geheimen Deutschen Quellen Am Israelischen Obersten Gerichtshof," ("The Secret German Sources of the Israeli Supreme Court,)" *Kritische Justiz*, 31, 3, 1998, p. 291.

[4] Quoted in Yoram Shachar, "Ha'teyotot ha'mukdamot shel hakhrazat ha'atzmaut," p. 532.

[5] The Hebrew translation used for provisional has a strong connotation of being temporary. This issue is discussed in later chapters.

been created by the ZAC, and indeed, *Minhelet ha'Am* had already convened. Now Rosenblüth and the Legal Department would put those decisions into formal legal effect in a "proclamation."

But this account does not do the issue justice. There remained the deeper question of whether or not the provisional council of government would be an actual government of an actual state – or a provisional council that could assume control of a future state.

To offer a sense of the ambiguity, on April 22, the same day that Rosenblüth gave Beham his assignment, the Jerusalem Legal Department of the *Yishuv*'s old governing bodies, which reported to the Canadian-born *Mapai* politician Dov Yosef, also serving as governor of Jerusalem, had issued a similar memo. Attached to it was a "Proclamation" establishing the "Provisional Council of Government of a Jewish State." That document, even as it proclaimed the authority of the Provisional Council of Government, did not proclaim the independence of a Jewish state: it rather proclaimed that the establishment of the provisional council's authority was "a necessary prerequisite in founding such a state."[6] Rosenblüth's memo to Beham went further: it called for establishing a provisional government "on the date of our political independence."

These were the foremost considerations of high politics at the time. But there were internal political reasons for requiring a declaration as well. Though three members of the Labor Zionist Party's political antagonists, Menachem Begin's Revisionist Party, were included in the new *Moetzet ha'Am*, and would sign the Declaration of Independence, the Revisionists had also threatened to declare independence themselves.

Rosenblüth and Ben-Gurion had just heard the Revisionist leadership demanding as much during April's Zionist Actions Committee conference, a position that had been of a piece with maximalist demands by Revisionist leaders over the prior two years.[7] Indeed, the Revisionists had

---

[6] See Yoram Shachar, "Ha'teyotot ha'mukdamot shel hakhrazat ha'atzmaut," pp. 523–534. Also see Israel State Archive, 111/3/ ג. The Legal Department's Uri Heinsheimer claimed to have brought a copy of this document to Tel Aviv, though it is unlikely to have been consulted by others and Rosenblüth did not mention it.

[7] Ofira Gruweis-Kovalsky, "Between Ideology and Reality: The Right Wing Organizations, the Jerusalem Question, and the Role of Menachem Begin 1948–1949," *Israel Studies*, 21, 3, 2016, pp. 99–101. Also see Protocols of the Zionist Actions Committee, Central Zionist Archives, S/5/322, April 6–7, 1948.

boycotted *Yishuv* elections in 1944 roughly on those grounds, only giving up their boycott of *Yishuv* institutions in 1946.[8]

Menachem Begin, who could count on the support of his own relatively small but loyal military forces, had not ruled out the possibility of declaring independence himself if the so-called Organized *Yishuv* failed to act.[9] In January, Begin had announced that he sought immediate national independence through armed struggle: "No more cease-fire in the land of Israel between the people and the Hebrew youth and the British administration . . . . The leadership will be placed immediately in the hands of a temporary Jewish government."[10] Begin had not changed his mind as the spring came. He would explain in a public notice in early May:

The Hebrew government will be established. There is no maybe–it will rise. If the official leadership establishes a government, we will back it. But if the government gives in to threats, our forces and the majority of the land's youth will back the free government that will grow from the underground.[11]

This was an obvious shot at *Minhelet ha'Am* and pointed to the issue at hand: asserting the power of the newly formed government.

For Rosenblüth, then, declaring independence had great diplomatic, legal, and political import. From a diplomatic and legal perspective, the new institutions had to be framed as the culmination of the UN Resolution 181 process. From a practical perspective, the highest governing bodies of the *Yishuv* and international Zionism had set the ball rolling in this direction, and the new orientation had to be clarified and stated plainly. From a political perspective, the leadership of the *Yishuv* had to avoid being undercut by a potential rival declaration of independence. The less organized, smaller, and poorly-armed Revisionist movement could not be allowed to call the legitimacy of the *Yishuv*'s actual governing bodies into question.

---

[8] See Lilly Weissbrod, "Economic Factors and Political Strategies: The Defeat of the Revisionists in Mandatory Palestine," *Middle Eastern Studies*, 19, 3, 1983, p. 344 and Mark Tessler, *A History of the Israeli-Palestinian Conflict* (Bloomington: Indiana University Press, 2009), p. 205.

[9] Dan Horowitz and Moshe Lissak, "Authority without Sovereignty: The Case of the National Centre of the Jewish Community in Palestine," *Government and Opposition*, 8, 1, 1973, p. 60.

[10] Quoted in Avi Shilon, *Menachem Begin*, trans. Danielle Zilberberg and Yoram Sharett (New Haven, CT: Yale University Press, 2012), p. 51.

[11] Quoted in Martin Kramer, "The May 1948 Vote that Made the State of Israel," *Mosaic*, April 2, 2018.

Those imperatives explain part of Rosenblüth's agenda. But what about his demands regarding the substantive content of the document? What "unfolding of events," to use Rosenblüth's phrase, would Israel's Declaration narrate? Did Rosenblüth want Beham to focus only on recent developments, such as the passage ofResolution 181?[12] Did he envision a description of the circumstances surrounding the end of the British Mandate, the causes of which were hotly disputed between the *Mapai* and Revisionist leaderships? Did he hope the text would stretch further back in time and capture a broader sweep, covering the Balfour Declaration of 1917, the diplomacy of Theodor Herzl, or the history of the Zionist movement and the *Yishuv*?

Or did Rosenblüth have in mind the true sweep of history? Was he considering the story of Jews in the land of Israel and the Jewish diaspora? How would any such proclamation relate to abstract questions about sovereignty and national independence? And what of Jewish ideas? Independence for what kind of state? Indeed, we do not know whether Rosenblüth sought a technical statement, a political statement, or a deeper text that would articulate the purposes of Jewish independence.[13]

Whatever Rosenblüth's own thoughts about the content of the proclamation he commissioned, his attentions during this time were largely directed elsewhere. He was busy setting up a Justice Ministry and a system of laws.[14] The leading lawyers of the *Yishuv* were split between Tel Aviv and Jerusalem, which were cut off from one another. The *Hagannah* was having little luck breaking the siege.[15] Preparing a proclamation of independence was simply not Rosenblüth's only priority. He thus sought to delegate the responsibility, at least in the first place, to Mordechai Beham.

---

[12] Jonathan Fine, "Establishing a New Governmental System: The Israeli Emergency Committee, October 1947–April 1948," *Middle Eastern Studies* 44, 6, 2008, p. 982.

[13] According to Ze'ev Sharef, Rosenblüth initially wanted two separate proclamations. The first would explain the "unfolding of events" while a second proclamation would detail the powers and responsibilities of the new state. This, however, does not clarify Rosenblüth's view of what kind of a document the Israeli declaration should be. *Three Days* (Doubleday: New York, 1963), p. 124.

[14] See the description of the work by one of the main staff lawyers on this work, Shabtai Rosenne, "Revisiting Some Legal Aspects of the Transition from Mandate to Independence: December 1947–15 May 1948," *Israel among the Nations*, ed. Alfred Kellerman, Kurt Siehr, and Talia Einhorn (The Hague: Kluwer Law International, 1998), p. 319.

[15] Benny Morris, *1948* (New Haven, CT: Yale University Press, 2008), p. 130.

THE TURNING

So it came to pass that Mordechai Beham, likely with the help of an American-trained Rabbi named Harry Davidowitz, would write what would become the preliminary draft of Israel's Declaration of Independence over the first days of Passover in 1948. What we call "Beham's draft" would ultimately set the structure of what became Israel's Declaration of Independence, building the plan of the document and introducing many of the rhetorical flourishes and literary devices which would filter through its various edits and editions.[16] This draft ensured that Israel's Declaration would be a true political text, a declaration of independence properly understood, rather than simply a technical or legalistic document. For this reason alone, it deserves attention.

Yet there is more to the story. Beham's draft of Israel's Declaration is perhaps the most theoretically ambitious attempt in Israel's founding period to express the meaning of the re-established state in terms of both Jewish ideas and political philosophy. This is the case precisely for the reason that makes the text at first pass seem almost dilettantish. The text is based on the American Declaration of Independence, which Beham transcribed verbatim and subsequently translated into Hebrew, subsequently transposing its form and key elements into a new Declaration of Independence for a Jewish state while blending in numerous quotations from the Hebrew Bible.

This could lead to the mistaken view that Beham's work is flawed for being unoriginal. But in its relationship to the American Declaration, which itself draws heavily on prior texts in the Anglo-American tradition of political thought, Beham's draft implicitly incorporated the philosophical ideas that lie at the American Declaration's source. And in its citation of the Hebrew Bible it ventured to the roots of Jewish ideas to justify the creation of a Jewish state. It combines an elaboration of natural rights justification of modern political sovereignty grounded in the inherent rights of the individual with arguments drawn from the deepest wells of Jewish tradition.

In 1948, this was unique. Until the final hours before Israel's independence was declared, no one else even attempted this. And it's easy to understand why. With a few exceptions, the founders of the state of

---

[16] Beham's drafts can be found in Israel State Archives, 8227/א7 and other drafts can be found in 5664/20/ג.

Israel were not readers of political philosophy.[17] While they were doubtless a learned group, and some had formal religious instruction growing up, or had even learned in *yeshivas* in their pasts, many saw themselves as explicitly breaking away from Jewish religious study, Talmudic disputation, and other versions of classical learning.

When Zionist politicians looked beyond the politics of their time, their frame of reference was far likelier to be more recent Russian or Western European literature.[18] When it came to Jewish antiquity, the intellectual sources holding the highest social repute were the Hebrew Bible and ancient archaeology.[19] The most influential politicians and writers of the *Yishuv* were far more likely to draw on Marx and other socialist thinkers than the American *Federalist*, to say nothing of Plato, Aristotle, and renaissance political theory.[20]

And even at that, the Marxism of the Labor-Zionist socialists was antidoctrinaire, "practical," and almost anti-intellectual. Berl Katznelson, David Ben-Gurion's ideological partner and a founder of the Labor-Zionist movement, who had died in 1944, saw over-reliance on "theory" as weakness.[21] The influential political economist Ber Borochov (1881–1917) in his most important work, *Nationalism and the Class*

---

[17] David Ben-Gurion was a voracious reader of both Jewish texts and the non-Jewish classics. He especially admired Plato, Thucydides, and Spinoza, traveling often with the Greek text of Plato's *Laws*. But he was unique in this among the leaders of the *Yishuv*. Revisionist political leader Vladimir Jabotinsky, who died in 1940, was another notable exception. Dante, whose works he translated into Hebrew, and other classics of particularly a continental bent, were integral to his intellectual formation. Abba Eban had benefitted from a first-rate Cambridge education in classics and languages. On Jabotinsky, see Hillel Halkin, *Jabotinsky* (New Haven, CT: Yale University Press, 2014), p. 130.

[18] See *Zionism and Religion,* ed. Shmuel Almog, Jehuda Reinharz, and Anita Shapira (Hanover, NH: University Press of New England, 1998). Cf. Leo Strauss, "Why We Remain Jews," in *Jewish Philosophy and the Crisis of Modernity,* ed. Kenneth Hart Green (Albany: State University of New York Press, 1997), p. 319. "I was struck by the fact that the substance of the intellectual life of some of these estimable young men [leading Zionist German youth] ... consisted of their concern with people like Balzac."

[19] Tali Tadmor Shimony, "Teaching the Bible as a Common Culture," *Jewish History,* 21, 2, 2007, p. 159.

[20] David Ben-Gurion's interest in Greek writers, and indeed philosophers more generally, was rather "pantheistic." He elided key differences between different thinkers and different traditions. Isaiah Berlin recalls meeting an incognito Ben-Gurion in Oxford in the 1950s. Ben-Gurion greeted him with these words: "Socrates, gurus, rebbes[sic]–same thing, no difference, deep wisdom." *Personal Impressions: Updated Edition,* ed. Hardy Henry, Isaiah Berlin, Annan Noel, and Lee Hermione (Princeton, NJ: Princeton University Press, 2014), pp. 238, 235–242.

[21] See Amos Perlmutter, "Berl Katznelson and the Theory and Practice of Revolutionary Constructivism," *Middle Eastern Studies,* 13, 1, 1977, p. 72, and Anita Shapira, *Berl:*

Struggle, counseled his readers away from the study of Marxist ortho-
doxies and steered them to action instead.[22] The next chapter will delve
further into the dialectics of the Labor Zionist movement.

Such was the zeitgeist in which Mordechai Beham's text was to appear.
And that is why it is so surprising that the text orients Israel's founding
moment in the direction of the political theory of the United States and
England – a break with the Marxist nationalism of Labor Zionism that
was at the heart of the *Yishuv*'s political origins. Its introduction of
principles of political justice drawn from the classics of the Anglo-
American tradition, and ultimately the classics of political theory, into a
Hebrew and indeed Jewish vernacular was thus an effort, whether deliberate or otherwise, to refound the basis of the *Yishuv*.

THE RABBI'S STUDY

Who was Mordechai Beham? Born in Ukraine in 1915, following World
War I he moved with his family first to Germany and then Palestine in
1924. In Tel Aviv, Beham's father Yehuda quickly established a successful
law practice. Mordechai's mother died young. Mordechai is said to have
been taciturn and competent in his studies. Like other well-to-do young
men in Mandatory Palestine and indeed throughout the British Empire,
Beham had the opportunity to attend university in Britain, studying first
at the London School of Economics and then training in law at the Inns of
Court. In his final year law exams in 1939, he ranked eighth out of
eleven.[23] He stayed on as a barrister at the Middle Temple for a number
of years before returning to Palestine. Through his studies and work in
London, he likely imbibed something of the Anglo political and legal
traditions which he would employ in 1948.[24]

A *Socialist Zionist*, trans. Haya Galai (Cambridge: Cambridge University Press, 1984),
   p. 345.
[22] *Nationalism and the Class Struggle* (New York: Poale Zion Alliance of America, 1937).
[23] Inns of Court Archives, MT/13/BER/2/1.
[24] Less than a handful of leading figures in the *Yishuv* had Anglo or American origins. No
   signer of Israel's Declaration of Independence several weeks later was born in Western
   Europe or an English-speaking country. The British citizen Chaim Weizmann and the
   South African-born, London-raised Abba Eban were principally engaged in diplomacy
   abroad, and especially during the months leading up to independence. For biographies of
   the signers of the Declaration of Independence, see Mordechai Naor, *Yom ha'shishi
   ha'gadol* (*The Great Friday*) (Tel Aviv: Dekel, 2014).

Back in Palestine, Beham first found work in Jerusalem for the British Mandate Administration. After World War II he joined his family law firm in Tel Aviv. His father Yehuda was by then one of Tel Aviv's most prominent lawyers. In 1948, Yehuda Beham was appointed to the legal advisory council of the *Yishuv* where he advised Rosenblüth.[25] When in the spring of 1948 Rosenblüth was scrambling to assemble the Justice Ministry out of the *Yishuv*'s Legal Department, Yehuda suggested his son Mordechai as an assistant who could help with various legal and administrative projects. Among these was the draft of the "proclamation" of independence.

Given the ambiguity of Rosenblüth's instructions regarding the drafting of a proclamation, it is no wonder that Mordechai Beham was perplexed by his assigned task. The story of Beham's authorship of the text is largely based on family lore. The story goes as follows: over lunch on Saturday, April 24, with his family, Beham spoke of his secret assignment and confessed he was not sure not where to begin.[26] Someone reminded Mordechai that a learned Rabbi lived down the street. Perhaps the Rabbi could help? After lunch, Mordechai Beham paid an impromptu visit to the home of Rabbi Harry Davidowitz.[27]

If Mordechai Beham had a British education, Harry Solomon Davidowitz had experienced a most American *paidea*. Davidowitz was born in Lithuania in 1887 and had emigrated to the United States with his family in the first years of the new century. The Davidowtizes settled in New York. There, Harry pursued both religious and secular studies.

In religion as well as philosophy, Davidowitz latched on to the then-ascendant Progressivism. Religiously, this led him to join the Conservative Movement.[28] For a while, it seemed like Davidowitz would pursue a conventional rabbinic career in the United States, serving as a rabbi in various cities.[29]

---

[25] Yoram Shachar, "Ha'teyotot ha'mukdamot shel hakhrazat ha'atzmaut," p. 532.

[26] Yoram Shachar, "Jefferson Goes East: The American Origins of the Israeli Declaration of Independence," p. 602. Cf., Judgment in Jerusalem District Court Case, *Beham v. State of Israel*, 08/22/2017, www.psakdin.co.il/Court/%D7%AA-%D7%90-58927-11-15-%D7%9E%D7%93%D7%99%D7%A0%D7%AA-%D7%99%D7%A9%D7%A8%D7%90%D7%9C-%D7%95%D7%90%D7%97-%D7%A0-%D7%91%D7%A2%D7%94%D7%9D-%D7%95%D7%90%D7%97#.YOMry-lKj_S

[27] Davidowitz lived at 5 Arnon Street, near the Tel Aviv Marina. Ibid.   [28] Ibid.

[29] Arlene Fine, "Cantor's Jewish Journey Set to Music," *Cleveland Jewish News*, October 9, 2011.   www.clevelandjewishnews.com/archives/cantor-s-jewish-journey-set-to-music/article_366a28fa-fa91-11e0-bd9f-001cc4c002e0.html

Yet his restlessness and unconventionality shine through all of his decisions. In World War I, for instance, Davidowitz returned to Europe as a chaplain for the US Army in France. Similarly, Davidowitz's *aliyah* to Palestine in 1934 cannot be explained by anything other than Zionist reasons.[30] Having married well, Davidowitz was financially comfortable in the United States. There was no necessity to leave, and certainly no social pressure. Though 1934 through 1935 was the peak of interwar Jewish immigration to Palestine, only a very small number of immigrants came from the United States.[31] And, to be sure, the market for the services of a Conservative rabbi in interwar Palestine was not robust.[32]

It seems that this suited Davidowitz just fine. After settling in Tel Aviv, Davidowitz devoted himself to literary pursuits. The learned, polyglot, possibly under-employed "man of culture" was well-known in the *Yishuv* in the 1930s. Many of these were of German origin. Thanks in part to Amos Oz's recollections, this type is more easily associated with the already comfortable garden neighborhood of Rehavia in Jerusalem than with the teeming streets of Tel Aviv.[33]

Precisely because of their European origins, and as well due to the *Yishuv*'s struggle with Britain, most of the *Yishuv*'s intellectuals held at best a dismissive attitude toward British and American ideas much as was the case in the political sphere.[34] Though he had left America behind,

---

[30] In a review on a book on Zionism in 1922, the young Davidowitz wrote: "It is borne in upon [the reader] with the force of truth that eventually the one successful mode of righting the most ancient wrong, of offering to Eastern Europe a solution of a vexing problem, and to persecuted Israel salvation, is the one presented by the author–political Zionism." See Harry S. Davidowitz, "Recent Books on Palestine and Zionism," *The Jewish Quarterly Review*, New Series, 13, 2, 1922, p. 227.

[31] Jacob Metzer, "Jewish Immigration to Palestine in the Long 1920s: An Exploratory Examination," *Journal of Israeli History*, 27, 2, 2008, pp. 221–251.

[32] To this day the Conservative Movement has had great difficulty establishing a foothold in the Jewish state, and that was even more true of its station in the proto-state in 1948. Harvey E. Goldberg, "The Ethnographic Challenge of *Masorti* Religiosity among Israeli Jews," *Ethnologie Française*, 43, 4, 2013, pp. 583–590.

[33] Rehavia as capital of the intellectual life of the *Yishuv* is well described by Amos Oz, who recalls his father pointing out scholars with a "worldwide reputation" on the streets of the neighborhood. *A Tale of Love and Darkness*, trans. Nicholas de Lange (New York: Harcourt, 2004), p. 3. On German roots in the *Yishuv*, see Jennifer Hansen-Glucklich, "Father, Goethe, Kant, and Rilke: The Ideal of *Bildung*, the Fifth Aliyah, and German-Jewish Integration into the *Yishuv*," *Shofar*, 35, 2, 2017, pp. 21–53.

[34] Interest in America, if not its founding political texts, grew after independence. See Ilan S. Troen, "The Discovery of America in the Israeli University: Historical, Cultural, and Methodological Perspectives," *The Journal of American History*, 81, 1, 1994, pp. 164–182.

Davidowitz was different. He kept up his love of the classics of English and American literature. He translated a number of Shakespeare's works into Hebrew, and his editions were standard in Israel for many decades.[35] Davidowitz also edited and translated a little-known Arabic text, "The Treatise on Ultimate Happiness," about which he had written a thesis. This text has often been attributed, probably mistakenly, to Maimonides.[36] His wife Ida had similar literary inclinations. She became the first theater critic of the *Jerusalem Post*.[37]

Davidowitz allowed his Jewish ritual practice to slacken when he moved to Palestine. Yet he remained committed to Zionism and the Jewish cause.[38] Davidowitz was perhaps not a strict proponent of the Cultural Zionism movement that had often denigrated political action and saw Jewish culture as a substitute both for *halakhic* Judaism and the moral compromises inherent to power politics.[39] Yet, as a translator of literary and philosophic works, he certainly aspired to advance education, general culture, and perhaps philosophic understanding in the *Yishuv*.

How well did Mordechai Beham know Harry Davidowitz? This is unknown. They could have been regular friends, or they could have been fairly removed from one another. Davidowitz may have been someone members of the Beham family knew well, or he could have been someone they simply saw around the neighborhood. Perhaps the Rabbi had a reputation for learning – and his private collection of texts. At the time, Tel Aviv had no university. The municipal library, Sha'ar Zion, was

---

[35] "Danny Maseng," *A Dream of Zion: American Jews Reflect on Why Israel Matters to Them*, ed. Jeffrey Salkin (Nashville, TN: Jewish Lights, 2009), p. 87. For instance, his Macbeth: http://collections.shakespeare.org.uk/search/library/81054017-macdbeth-a-tragedy-translated-into-hebrew-by-h-s-davidowitz/view_as/grid/page/1326

[36] See "Dropsie College Theses," *The Jewish Quarterly Review*, New Series, 24, 1, 1933, p. 101 and Yoram Shachar, "Ha'teyotot ha'mukdamot shel hakhrazat ha'atzmaut," p. 529. For the text in English, see W. Bacher, "The Treatise on Eternal Bliss Attributed to Moses Maimuni," *The Jewish Quarterly Review*, 9, 2, 1897, pp. 270–289. For a discussion on why the text's notion of happiness is more pietistic and thus unlikely Maimonidean, see Avi Elqayam, "The Metaphysical, Epistemological, and Mystical Aspects of Happiness in the Treatise on Ultimate Happiness Attributed to Moses Maimonides," *Journal of Jewish Thought & Philosophy*, 26, 2018, p. 174. We are grateful to Kenneth Hart Green for this note.

[37] "Danny Maseng," *A Dream of Zion: American Jews Reflect on Why Israel Matters to Them*, p. 87.

[38] Yoram Shachar, "Jefferson Goes East," p. 603.

[39] Allan Arkush, "Cultural Zionism Today," *Israel Studies*, 19, 2, 2014, p. 2.

cramped and underfunded.[40] Rabbi Davidowitz had an extensive private library that Beham could consult.

Like so many of the events surrounding the first draft of Israel's Declaration of Independence, there is no record of the conversation between Beham and Davidowitz. What can we reasonably imagine? They probably shared a common vocabulary and a common way to conceive the challenge due to their shared education in the Anglo-American political tradition. It is similarly likely that the learned and older Davidowitz would have offered Beham some thoughts on how to proceed. Like all Americans of his generation, he would have had a keen appreciation for 1776 and its founding documents which were taught to all Americans in grade school.[41] It is likely that Davidowitz had a sense that a declaration of independence offers a unique opportunity to shape the political and ethical direction of a country for the years to come. And Beham, the former Middle Temple barrister, would have been receptive to the invocation of the ideas of the Anglo-American political tradition.[42]

As the story goes, Beham spent a few hours that Saturday afternoon in the Rabbi's private library. By the end of the day, he had copied out, in English, segments from the American Declaration of Independence, the English Bill of Rights of 1689, the King James Bible's rendition of Deuteronomy 1:8, and some notes on the United Nations Resolution 181 of November 1947.[43] It as well is possible that, in Davidowitz's company, he had used these texts as the basis for an English draft of Israel's Declaration of Independence modeled upon them.

That text is the subject of this chapter. Its exact provenance remains unknown and unlikely ever to be established with certainty – whether it was written by Beham alone after conversing with Davidowitz, by Beham

---

[40] On Tel Aviv's libraries see Shmuel Sever, "Some Social Aspects of Public Library Development in Israel," *The Library Quarterly*, 38, 4, 1968, p. 395.

[41] The progressive critics of the American founding largely targeted the US Constitution rather than the Declaration of Independence. See, for instance, Theodore Roosevelt's paean to the American Declaration of Independence in his "New Nationalism" speech of 1910. https://teachingamericanhistory.org/library/document/new-nationalism-speech/ See R. J. Pestritto, *American Progressivism: A Reader* (Lexington, VA: Lexington Books, 2008). On American textbooks, see Julie A. Reuben, "Beyond Politics: Community Civics and the Redefinition of Citizenship in the Progressive Era," *History of Education Quarterly*, 37, 4, 1997, p. 51.

[42] For a treatment of how the idea of a "founding" developed in early America, see James Ceaser, "The First American Founder," *National Affairs*, Summer: 2018. Cf. Max Beloff, "Is There an Anglo-American Political Tradition?" *History*, 36, 126/127, 1951, pp. 73–91.

[43] Yoram Shachar, "Ha'teyotot ha'mukdamot shel hakhrazat ha'atzmaut," pp. 537–538.

with Davidowitz, or by Beham alone without input from Davidowitz. The documentary record, as it exists, consists of a number of pages of text written in Beham's hand. These include, in English, selections from the aforementioned sources. Beham kept those sheets in his safe for decades, storing them along with his first English draft of the Declaration, a Hebrew translation of that draft which he subsequently edited, almost certainly with the help of a colleague in the Legal Department named Uri Heinsheimer (Yadin), and a final clean version of the heavily edited text which he and Heinsheimer had produced. These documents were the subject of an extended legal dispute between the Beham family and the State of Israel. They are now held in the Israel State Archives.[44]

Before analyzing what Beham copied out in Davidowitz's library, it is important to note the documents to which Beham did *not* turn. If Davidowitz had a copy of the French Declaration of the Rights of Man and of the Citizen in his library, or other texts of continental history, Beham did not copy them. Nor did he use any modern Zionist statements or writings, whether by the poets or political writers then active in the *Yishuv* or founders of the Zionist movement such as Theodor Herzl, Ahad Ha'am, or Leon Pinsker.

With respect to Herzl, Beham elected at least at this moment to omit him (though Beham would later have a change of heart). When Beham, along with other colleagues in the Legal Department, was later asked to review the draft of the Declaration written by Tzvi Berenson (discussed in the next chapter), he suggested that the name of Herzl be included. As the Legal Department team laconically put it in a memo: "After the prophets of Israel, we've mentioned Theodor Herzl. In our opinion there's a need to mention his name, especially since [Arthur] Balfour's name was mentioned. For all Balfour's importance, he does not exactly rank among the righteous of the nations."[45]

[44] For the Jerusalem District case, see: www.psakdin.co.il/Court/%D7%AA-%D7%90-58927-11-15-%D7%9E%D7%93%D7%99%D7%A0%D7%AA-%D7%99%D7%A9%D7%A8%D7%90%D7%9C-%D7%95%D7%90%D7%97-%D7%A0-%D7%91%D7%A2%D7%94%D7%9D-%D7%95%D7%90%D7%97#.YOMry-lKj_S. For the Supreme Court Case, see: https://supremedecisions.court.gov.il/Home/Download?path=HebrewVerdicts\17\230\083\n14&fileName=17083230.N14&type=4. Also see Yaacov Lozowick, "Who Owns Israel's History?" *Tablet*, August 05, 2009, www.tabletmag.com/sections/arts-letters/articles/who-owns-israels-history. On whether Beham wrote the text himself or with Davidowitz, see speculation in Yoram Shachar, "Ha'teyotot ha'mukdamot shel hakhrazat ha'atzmaut."

[45] Memo to Felix Rosenblüth, May 9, 1948, 5664/20/22/124 ?

Herzl's name would of course appear in the Declaration of Independence of Israel that David Ben-Gurion read under a portrait of Herzl.[46] Yet this was more a recognition of the importance of Herzl's actions rather than an invocation of anything Herzl wrote or said.

None of Beham, Ben-Gurion, or any other drafters of the Declaration of Independence referred to any of Herzl's written works, such as *The Jewish State* (1896), which had galvanized an important swath of world Jewry half a century before.[47] This is less difficult to explain than one might think. The key theme in the writing of Herzl, like many other early Zionist thinkers, was the persecution of Jews.[48] This was not Herzl's only theme. His writing also expressed a vision of the ennobling effects that political sovereignty could have on the Jewish people: Herzl believed that national independence would produce for the Jewish people a "great radiance."[49]

However, as Benzion Netanyahu has argued, emphasizing Herzl's texts obscures the significance of Herzl: Herzl cast the Jewish quest for autonomy into the political sphere – he insisted that the Zionist movement enter the realm of international politics and achieved it. His organizing galvanized a movement that led to the creation of a state. And thus, with a Jewish state about to be proclaimed, his importance as a founder of a movement exceeded his draw as a provider of ideas regarding the nature or content of the state that his movement was so instrumental in creating.[50]

The persecution of Jews could not be ignored. It was the proximate cause, the most necessary and implacable problem, that Jewish sovereignty aimed to address. However, Beham's text intuited that a justification for the Jewish state as simply a plausible antidote to the problem of Jew hatred was not enough. While this may make intuitive sense seventy five years later, in Beham's context and time, this was radical. The

---

[46] The official English translation of the Declaration of Independence was not finalized until the early 1960s. It is found at https://mfa.gov.il/mfa/foreignpolicy/peace/guide/pages/declaration%20of%20establishment%20of%20state%20of%20israel.aspx

[47] Daniel Gordis, *Israel* (New York: Harper Collins, 2016), p. 22.

[48] Alan Dowty, *The Jewish State: A Century Later* (Berkeley: University of California Press, 1998), p. 5.

[49] Quoted in Yoram Hazony, "Did Herzl Want a Jewish State?" *Azure*, 9, 2000, http://azure.org.il/include/print.php?id=288.

[50] Benzion Netanyahu, *The Founding Fathers of Zionism* (Geffen: Jerusalem, 2012), pp. 67–105, See Shlomo Avineri, *Herzl's Vision* (Katonah, NY: Bluebridge, 2014), and Cf., Yoram Hazony, "The Jewish State at 100," *Azure*, 2, 1997, www.yoramhazony.org/wp-content/uploads/2013/11/the_jewish_state_at_100_azz_hazony_yoram.pdf

principal sources that Beham's text would draw upon for the articulation of the essence of the new Jewish state were to come from outside the main texts and wellsprings of inspiration for Zionists of his time: beyond Labor Zionism and Herzl.

THE SOURCE TEXTS

To meet the tall task of articulating the nature of the first Jewish state to rise in Israel in nearly 2,000 years, Mordechai Beham relied on no less than the bedrock texts of the English-speaking democracies and of the Jewish people – the American Declaration of Independence, the English Bill of Rights, and the Bible.

The significance of an effort to root the founding of the State of Israel in the political ideas contained in these texts can hardly be understated. But before considering the weight of the ideas implicit in the text Beham produced, let us first turn our attention to Beham's source materials. From the American Declaration of Independence, Beham copied the first two paragraphs in his preparatory notes:

When in the course of human events, it becomes necessary for one people to dissolve the political bonds which have connected them with one another, and to assume among the Powers of the earth, the separate and equal station to which the Laws of Nature and of Nature's God entitle them, a decent respect to the opinions of mankind requires that they should declare the causes which impel them to the separation. We hold these truths to be self-evident, that all men are created equal, that they are endowed by their Creator with certain inalienable Rights, that among these are Life, Liberty, and the pursuit of Happiness. That to secure these rights, Governments are instituted among Men, deriving their just powers from the consent of the governed .... [51]

Beham then skipped the paragraphs elaborating the "long train of abuses" of King George III against the American colonists, returning to quote the final paragraph of the document:

We, therefore, the Representatives of the United States of America, in General Congress, Assembled, appealing to the Supreme Judge of the world for the rectitude of our intentions, do, in the Name, and by Authority of the good People of these Colonies, solemnly publish and declare, That these United

---

[51] Beham's handwritten draft is available through the Israel State Archives at 8227/א and has recently been digitized, available online at ooɪɪdyn. Before Beham's texts were publicly available, Yoram Shachar had access to them, identified their significance, and transcribed them. See "Ha'teyotot ha'mukdamot shel hakhrazat ha'atzmaut," p. 585.

Colonies are, and of Right ought to be Free and Independent States, that they are Absolved from all Allegiance to the British Crown, and that all political connection between them and the State of Great Britain, is and ought to be totally dissolved; and that as Free and Independent States, they have full Power to levy War, conclude Peace, contract Alliances, establish Commerce, and to do all other Acts and Things which Independent States may of right do. And for the support of this Declaration, with a firm reliance on the Protection of Divine Providence, we mutually pledge to each other our Lives, our Fortunes, and our sacred Honor.[52]

Beham extracted both of the most salient facets of the American Declaration: the passages that reflect the concepts of political right that animated the American founding, as well as the reflections on practical politics that made the effort to realize those concepts plausible.[53] These are, first, the "propositions" at the American Declaration's beginning, the source of what has been called America's propositional character, the self-evident truth of man's freedom.[54] The end of the American Declaration focuses on what states must do in order to cement security and good order so as to safeguard a society that respects its citizens inherent rights. It reminds its readers that acts of state must be brought in full force if communities of human justice are not "to perish from the earth."[55]

It is worth thinking about the principles that Beham drew upon to better understand the text that he would write based upon them. When Thomas Jefferson wrote in the American Declaration that the equality of human beings is self-evident, he meant that this equality is intelligible to the human mind.[56] In order for the proposition "all men are created equal" to be self-evident, there must be a plane of human equality that is theoretically recognizable to every human. This is the equality of our status as human beings irrespective of our differences. The most self-evident truth regarding humankind is that each of us belongs to the human species. It is *not* self-evident that any one human – each being as

---

[52] Ibid.

[53] The interpretation of the US Declaration of Independence remains a subject of ongoing debate and interest in America. See Danielle Allen, *Our Declaration* (Liveright: Norton, 2014).

[54] According to G. K. Chesterton, Americans were bound by a "creed" that was "set forth with dogmatic and even theological lucidity in the Declaration of Independence." *What I Saw in America* (London: Hodder & Stoughton, 1922), p. 7.

[55] See Ralph Lerner, *Naïve Readings* (Chicago: University of Chicago Press, 2016). For the text of the American Declaration of Independence, www.archives.gov/founding-docs/declaration-transcript

[56] For a related though somewhat different take on self-evidence, see Michael P. Zuckert, "Self-Evident Truth and the Declaration of Independence," *The Review of Politics*, 49, 3, 1987, p. 323.

human as any other – has any implicit right to dominion over the others. No newborn child is self-evidently different than any other, regardless of the claims of genetics, which at their most extensive only speak to human potential as opposed to what humans will actually be.[57] This natural sameness of condition precludes any one human from having a basis to declare ownership or mastery over any other; it precludes the possibility of ethical rule without consent.

From this limited equality, the formulation's original author, John Locke, derived the political right to limited or negative freedom – freedom to enjoy our own lives, liberties, and property. He derived the idea of political equality from the equality of our most fundamental condition.[58]

Even if there may be politically-relevant differences among humans, no single human has adequate or definitive recourse to the wisdom that would be needed to definitively discern these differences. No human is capable by dint of reason of sorting anonymous groups of people into political classes, discerning among strangers the good humans from the bad, the better humans from the worse, or of delineating one group of humans the master by implicit right over the other.

One does not require access to any circumstantial or historical evidence to understand that no one human being could on the basis of a separate *nature* rule groups of human beings without consent, the way that God is said to rule over the universe and the way that human beings rule over horses or dogs without their consent by the very nature of things.[59] The idea of a human being, and a single human species to which every individual belongs, supplies this politically-relevant evidence without recourse to external knowledge. Such is the argument of the American Declaration for natural rights that Beham had identified and copied out.

But Beham didn't stop there. He copied out more. While natural rights may exist on an intellectual plane, they must be safeguarded politically in the world as it exists.[60] Some political entity must guard those rights for

---

[57] Anne Chapman, "Genetic Engineering: The Unnatural Argument," *Techné: Research in Philosophy and Technology*, 9, 2, 2005, https://scholar.lib.vt.edu/ejournals/SPT/v9n2/chapman.html#2.

[58] The *locus classicus* of the argument for the equality of human beings as compared to the natural rule of human beings over the lower beasts remains John Locke, *First Treatise*, ed. Peter Laslett (Cambridge: Cambridge University Press, 1988), p. 160. Locke, of course, draws on Biblical texts for this side of his argument, particularly Genesis 8.

[59] Jaffa, *A New Birth of Freedom*, p. 121.

[60] Ralph Lerner, "Jefferson's Summary View Reviewed, Yet Again," in *Principle and Prudence in Western Political Thought*, ed. Christopher Lynch and Jonathan Marks (Binghamton: State University of New York Press, 2016), p. 259.

each distinct community, laying down the laws to secure those rights as well as marshaling military force to protect them. This is the purpose of the conclusion of the American Declaration that Beham copied out. That text explains that it is in the name of the natural rights elaborated in the text's beginning that the American state will "have full Power to levy War, conclude Peace, contract Alliances, establish Commerce, and to do all other Acts and Things which Independent States may of right do."

The equal natural rights of individuals are abstract and universal. In practice, however, they must be put into force and protected.[61] The abstract nature of these rights justifies the state's use of its power to secure freedom on behalf of a single group of people. In the American Declaration, the political independence of the United States is meant to serve those rights. The United States comes into being as a grand experiment to prove that a government whose purpose is the protection of the inherent rights for its citizens is feasible and plausible.[62] It aims to make universal or God-given rights concrete for a single people.[63] Beham had identified the importance of this aspect of the American Declaration too.

The other major Anglo-American document to which Beham turned was the English Bill of Rights of 1689, signed by William and Mary after the Glorious Revolution. The English Bill of Rights had been a significant source for Thomas Jefferson's efforts in writing the American Declaration of Independence a century later.[64] From this text, Beham however copied just a few short words: "the true, ancient, and indubitable rights and liberties of the people."[65]

What did the English Bill of Rights offer Beham that could not be found in the American Declaration? "Indubitable" and "inherent" rights

---

[61] See Abraham Lincoln, Letter to Henry L. Pierce and others, April 6, 1859, www .abrahamlincolnonline.org/lincoln/speeches/pierce.htm. "All honor to Jefferson – to the man who, in the concrete pressure of a struggle for national independence by a single people, had the coolness, forecast, and capacity to introduce into a merely revolutionary document, an abstract truth, applicable to all men and all times, and so to embalm it there, that to-day, and in all coming days, it shall be a rebuke and a stumbling-block to the very harbingers of re-appearing tyranny and oppression."

[62] *Federalist*, no. 1, ed. Charles Kesler (New York: Signet, 1993).

[63] Cf. Jefferson's draft of the Declaration of Independence, from: *The Papers of Thomas Jefferson*, vol. 1, 1760–1776, ed. Julian P. Boyd (Princeton, NJ: Princeton University Press, 1950), pp. 243–224, www.loc.gov/exhibits/declara/ruffdrft.html

[64] David S. Lovejoy, "Two American Revolutions, 1689 and 1776," *Three British Revolutions*, ed. John Pocock (Princeton, NJ: Princeton University Press, 1980), p. 257. See also: Stephen E. Lucas, "The Rhetorical Ancestry of the Declaration of Independence," *Rhetoric and Public Affairs*, 1, 2, 1998, p. 151.

[65] Yoram Shachar, "Jefferson Goes East," p. 602.

are extremely close to natural rights and perhaps synonymous.[66] It is significant enough to note here that Beham had settled on the concept of inherent or natural rights as the lynchpin of both the British and the American political traditions.

But the important word which the Bill of Rights adds in contradistinction to the American Declaration is "ancient." Jefferson's Declaration of Independence severs the connection between rights and their antiquity; it ignores tradition. The text of the English Bill of Rights, on the other hand, plainly states that the rights of the English are not only inherent but firmly grounded in historical practice.[67] It argues that King James II's purported slide toward tyranny was particularly outrageous because he had not denied newly established rights but rather stamped out rights long established.

Edmund Burke famously argued that the English had possessed these rights throughout their history, dating from no particular moment.[68] There is no 'Sinai moment' in British history, no single moment when independence or freedom had first been gained.[69] English liberties are indubitable for their being ancient. The long-established fact of a practice has ethical weight in defending that practice not simply due to its antiquity. Rather, the antiquity of the practice can be thought of as the

---

[66] On the frequent use of all such terms in the American context at the time of the Revolution, see Chester James Antieau, "Natural Rights and the American Founders: The Virginians," *Washington and Lee Law Review*, 3, 1, 1960, p. 71.

[67] Cf. Joyce Lee Malcolm, "The Creation of a 'True Antient and Indubitable' Right: The English Bill of Rights and the Right to Be Armed," *Journal of British Studies*, 32, 3, 1993, pp. 226–227.

[68] Edmund Burke, *Reflections on the Revolution in France* (London: Everyman's Library: 2015), p. 451 "Their *whole care* was to secure the religion, laws, and liberties that had been long possessed, and had been lately endangered" (emphasis added). On the problem of tradition without founding, see Neil Rogachevsky, "Nathan the Wise: An Ambiguous Plea for Religious Toleration," *Mosaic*, June 29, 2016.

[69] See, for instance, the conclusion to Blackstone's *Commentaries*, "The protection of THE LIBERTY OF BRITAIN is a duty which they owe to themselves, who enjoy it; to their ancestors, who transmitted it down; and to their posterity, who will claim at their hands this, the best birthright, and the noblest inheritance in the world." https://avalon.law.yale .edu/18th_century/blackstone_bk4ch33.asp. English liberty, he elsewhere says, had prevailed from the Saxons, from "the earliest times." See George Anastaplo, "William Blackstone, Patrick Henry, and Edmund Burke on Liberty (1765-1790)," in *Reflections on Freedom of Speech and the First Amendment* (Lexington: University Press of Kentucky, 2007) pp. 26–35.

school which nurtured and cultivated the good and expunged the bad from whatever practice existed at the origin.[70]

Evolutionism of this kind is best thought of as Maimonidean. Did not Maimonides stress Abraham's evolution and his learning as the truest foundation of Israel? Jewish tradition and its history can and must be seen as the proving ground of that tradition's ethical logic. This is a central argument of Maimonides's masterwork *The Guide of the Perplexed*.[71] It is only fitting then for Beham to have sought to explain the legitimacy of Jewish sovereignty in light of the Jewish cultivation of the ethical tradition that still animates the Western world at its best moments today.

For the Jewish state, Beham's text intuits that turning only to sources in the Anglo-American tradition would not be sufficient. It is not a declaration of independence of a state of English-speaking people, but of a Jewish state declaring independence from the British empire. Jewish tradition weighed upon Beham's shoulders too – perhaps it should have even weighed more heavily. For in taking its cues from the American Declaration, Beham's text would have to articulate a Jewish perspective that would stand in harmony with nature and history.

Beham's notes thus next turn to the Hebrew Bible, albeit in the King James rendition. (It is notable that Davidowitz's grandson claimed that the Rabbi enjoyed declaiming from the King James rendition for the benefit and amusement of his family.[72]) Beham copied out Deuteronomy 1:8:

Behold, I have set the land before you: go in and possess the land which the Lord sware unto your fathers, Abraham, Isaac, and Jacob, to give unto them and to their seed after them.[73]

There are any number of locations in the Bible which might stand as proof texts for justifying restored Jewish sovereignty. King David, Moses, Joshua, Abraham, Isaac, and Jacob are plausible points of departure for Jewish political sovereignty.[74] Beham's text settled on God's promise to Moses, Israel, and the patriarchs before them. They are promised that

---

[70] Cf. Steven J. Lenzner, "Strauss's Three Burkes: The Problem of Edmund Burke in Natural Right and History," *Political Theory*, 19, 3, 1991, pp. 364–390. Also see: Dan Edelstein, *The Terror of Natural Right* (Chicago: University of Chicago Press, 2009).

[71] See James Diamond, *Maimonides and the Hermeneutics of Concealment* (Binghamton: State University of New York Press, 2012), p. 144, and *Maimonides and the Shaping of the Jewish Canon* (Cambridge: Cambridge University Press, 2017), p. 111.

[72] Yoram Shachar, "Ha'teyotot ha'mukdamot shel hakhrazat ha'atzmaut," p. 539.

[73] Israel State Archives, online at 001idyn.

[74] On King David, see especially Michael Wyschogrod, "A King in Israel," *First Things*, 2010, www.firstthings.com/article/2010/05/a-king-in-israel

their descendants will make a great people and possess a great land. This passage expresses the covenantal notion embedded in the most traditional readings of Deuteronomy 1:8: God issues a promise of the land of Israel to the Children of Israel because of Israel's chosenness in this text; and it is this divine chosenness and promise that stands as almost a religious-legal right to the land in this passage. That is the interpretation of the biblical commentator ha'Netziv, for instance.[75]

Beham (or perhaps Rabbi Davidowitz) must have seen something in this passage that would resonate within the political culture of the *Yishuv*. Yet the same passage would also have been unsettling for many of the elite of the *Yishuv*, who saw labor as the chief means of redeeming Jewish sovereignty.[76] The passage implies that labor, however important, is not an end in itself. Possession of the land, it might seem on this reading, is meaningful precisely because it expresses God's promise to Israel. Beham's citation of this passage attempts to draw a link between the modern Zionist project of building with the most basic interpretations of the biblical covenant. This sentiment, if aired publicly, would have managed to unite secular Zionist leaders *and* non-Zionist religious authorities in opposition.[77]

In addition to the three historical sources, Beham also made his own notes related to UN Resolution 181. Resolution 181 was the key legal and political text upon which Jewish claims to independence rested. And in April 1948, it was also still the "milestone" toward independence that stuck the most clearly in the minds of residents of the *Yishuv*.[78] No discussion of the "chain of events" that led to the establishment of the state, as Rosenbluth had requested, could ignore the United Nations vote.

From Beham's source texts taken together, one gets a glimpse of the spirit with which he hoped to imbue his document. Beham wrestled with combining the events of 1947–1948, the claims of Jewish history, modern Zionism, the biblical promise of God to the children of Israel, and the modern doctrine of natural rights all in a single framework.

---

[75] ha'Netziv on Deuteronomy 1:8, www.sefaria.org/Haamek_Davar_on_Deuteronomy.1.8

[76] On the redemptive power of labor see, especially, A. D. Gordon, "The Dream of the Aliyah," *Selected Essays* (New York: Arno Press, 1973), p. 1. Cf. John Locke, *Second Treatise on Government*, p. 285.

[77] On historic and current Haredi attitudes toward Zionism, see Yoel Finkelman, "The Ambivalent Haredi Jew," *Israel Studies*, 19, 2, 2014, p. 267.

[78] Circular of American Zionist Emergency Council, quoted in Martin Gilbert, *Israel* (New York: William Morrow, 1998), p. 150.

THE DRAFT

Having assembled his sources, Beham then proceeded, possibly with Davidowitz, or possibly on the evening of April 24 without him, to write his own proclamation, in English. Here is Beham's longhand draft.[79]

Declaration of the Jewish State

WHEREAS this Holy Land has been promised by the Lord God to our fathers, Abraham, Isaac, and Jacob, and to their seed after them, and

WHEREAS our ancient Jewish People had for a millennium and a half its state in this Holy Land

AND WHEREAS the ancient Jewish State in this land ceased to exist after the destruction of our Holy Temple in Jerusalem by the Roman Legions, and the exile from Palestine of the greater part of our people and their dispersal amongst all the nations of the world AND WHEREAS throughout the centuries of their exile our people has suffered loss of life and property by the hands of their many oppressors such as no people has been called upon to endure since time began, culminating in the cruel extermination of one third of our people at the hands of the enemies of mankind since the outbreak of the Second World War

AND WHEREAS the opinions of mankind, as represented in the Balfour Declaration and in the Palestine Mandate of the Council of Nations has given recognition to the historical connection of the Jewish People with Palestine and to the grounds of reconstituting their national home in this country

AND WHEREAS by the Resolution of the General Assembly of the United Nations it has been resolved that an independent Jewish State should come into existence in Palestine

AND WHEREAS by virtue of the said Resolution a Provisional Council of government should have been established in the Jewish State by the Commission set up under the said Resolution

AND WHEREAS the said Commission has failed to establish a Provisional Council of Government in the Jewish State

AND WHEREAS his Britannic Majesty has laid down the Mandate in respect of Palestine conferred upon him by the League of Nations and has withdrawn his government from Palestine

AND WHEREAS it is the true, ancient, and indubitable right of the Jewish People to reconstitute their state in this Holy Land, and to

---

[79] The text is available through the Israel State Archives, 0011dyo.

assume among the Powers of the earth, the separate and equal station
to which the Laws of God and Nature entitle them, to secure and enjoy
the inalienable rights to Life, Liberty, and the pursuit of happiness

AND WHEREAS to secure these rights, governments are established
among men, deriving their just power from the consent of the
governed

NOW THEREFORE, WE, the Representatives of the Jewish People in
solemn gathering assembled, and appealing to the Supreme Judge of
the world for the rectitude of our intentions do, in the Name, and by
authority of the Jewish People, solemnly publish and declare the
Establishment in Palestine as of right of a Free and Independent
Jewish State, Absolved of all allegiance to or political connection
with any other State, and that as a Free and Independent State, it has
the full power to levy War, conclude Peace, contract Alliances,
establish Commerce, and to do all other Acts and Things which
Independent States may of right do.

AND for the support of this Declaration, with a firm reliance on the
Protection of Divine Providence, we do, in the name and on behalf
of our Jewish People, mutually pledge to each other our Lives, our
Fortunes and our sacred Honour.

One finds an enormity of ideas about the Jewish people and their state
in Beham's text. The ideas range from more superficial questions of the
legal right to the land of Israel (the "common opinions of mankind"
embodied in the Balfour Declaration, etc.) to questions of the purpose
of the Jewish people (the allusion to the *Brit,* the covenant, between the
Jewish people and the God of the Bible), to the question of the purpose of
government in general (the securing of the "natural rights" of the citizens), to the tension between the rights of citizens, and indeed universal
rights, and *raison d'état* (the powers of the state). These are foundational
questions since they address foundational issues.

Of course, these considerations were not original to Mordechai
Beham. The allusions to principles of political right are literally ripped
from the American Declaration of Independence, copied verbatim.
Thomas Jefferson had followed the Virginia Declaration of Rights and
John Locke, with slight amendment, and had proclaimed the right to
"Life, Liberty, and the Pursuit of Happiness."[80] Beham's text adds from

---

[80] Allen Jayne, *Jefferson's Declaration of Independence* (Lexington: University of Kentucky
Press, 2000), p. 41.

the English Bill of Rights that these are the true, ancient, and indubitable rights of the Jewish people. He had basically stolen from the texts that he had copied out just as Jefferson had stolen from the Virginia Declaration and Locke.

We have already discussed the meaning of the propositions of the American Declaration at some length, but it is worth further discussing the American Declaration in the context of Beham's reformulation of it. The American Declaration differed in some important ways from its predecessor document, the Virginia Declaration of Rights of 1776, authored principally by George Mason.[81] That document's first article declares:

> That all men are by nature equally free and independent and have certain inherent rights, of which, when they enter into a state of society, they cannot, by any compact, deprive or divest their posterity; namely, the enjoyment of life and liberty, with the means of acquiring and possessing property, and pursuing and obtaining happiness and safety.[82]

The important distinction between the American Declaration and the Virginia Declaration of Rights is that the latter sets out an object of the inalienable and "inherent" freedoms of humanity: pursuing and obtaining happiness and safety.[83] The political "happiness" of the Virginia Declaration is a vague objective, but it is also the objective that Plato's Socrates claims that men pursue in building states, the objective that Aristotle in his *Nicomachean Ethics* claims that human action strives toward, and the aim of all political organizing and theorizing according to Maimonides' "second teacher" Al-Farabi.[84] If the content and even meaning of political happiness is vague, it is because it is necessarily unknown. As Aristotle also says, it is adequate if we get close to achieving it.[85] Freedom in a modern free city or state, on the face of the American formulations, is for the attainment of a political happiness that is obscure.

---

[81] Matthew S. Holland, *Bonds of Affection: Civic Charity and the Making of America – Winthrop, Jefferson, and Lincoln* (Washington, DC: Georgetown University Press, 2007), p. 93.

[82] Text available at http://avalon.law.yale.edu/18th_century/virginia.asp.

[83] Herbert Lawrence Ganter, "Jefferson's 'Pursuit of Happiness' and Some Forgotten Men," *The William and Mary Quarterly*, 16, 4, 1936, p. 558.

[84] Limin Bao and Lin Zhang, "'Justice Is Happiness'? – An Analysis of Plato's Strategies in Response to Challenges from the Sophists," *Frontiers of Philosophy in China*, 6, 2, 2011, pp. 258–272. Al-Farabi, *The Philosophy of Plato and Aristotle*, trans. Muhsin Mahdi (Ithaca, NY: Cornell University Press, 2001).

[85] Robert C. Bartlett, "Aristotle's Introduction to the Problem of Happiness: On Book I of the 'Nicomachean Ethics,'" *American Journal of Political Science*, 52, 3, 2008, pp. 677–687.

Beham's text reveals the initial stirrings of the reconciliation of the securing of a free state for free citizens and a substantive goal to be pursued with that freedom: the effort to provide an *object* for the citizens of the Jewish state. It begins with a quintessential text of God's promise of the land of Israel to the Jewish people. It reminds readers of the promise "by the Lord God to our fathers, Abraham, Isaac, and Jacob, and to their seed after them."[86]

If this citation from the Bible has a limit, it is the limit of its context. Rather than trying to cite the promise that God makes to Israel of a land that will be made holy by Israel's works, Beham's text employs a passage that stands as a testimonial to God's promise of the land of Canaan to the Jewish people as a quasi-legal right. The preceding Biblical passages delineate the borders of the land, and the subsequent passages recapitulate the Biblical narrative of Israel's arrival to the cusp of entry to the land of Israel. The simple reading of Beham's text, which continues with an invocation of the suffering of the Jewish people in its exile and especially in the Holocaust, and of the promises made to the Jews of a state by the powers of Europe between 1917 and 1947, would make it seem as though its citation of the Bible is but another proof-text that the particular land of Israel has been bequeathed to the Jews. Indeed, as the extant documentary record shows, that seems to be how Beham understood it.

Though this is a fair reading – and likely the decisive reading – we should also look deeper into the text of Deuteronomy to further contextualize the quotation that Beham's text used. At Deuteronomy 4:5, three chapters after the quotation in Beham's text appears, Moses says that Israel's right to the land of Israel in fact derives from Israel's adherence to God's wise law. The land is being given to Israel so that Israel might live in accordance with the law-giving:

Behold, I have taught you statutes and ordinances, even as the LORD my God commanded me, that ye should do so in the midst of the land whither ye go in to possess it. Observe therefore and do them; for this is your wisdom and your understanding in the sight of the peoples, that, when they hear all these statutes, shall say: "Surely this great nation is a wise and understanding people." And what great nation is there, that hath statutes and ordinances so righteous as all this law, which I set before you this day?[87]

---

[86] This is not the only statement of covenant in the Bible. The central one, which Beham does not cite, is the *brit bein he'batrim*, the "Covenant of Parts," at Genesis: 15. On the various covenants in the Bible, see *The Jewish Political Tradition*, vol. 1, ed. Michael Walzer, Menachem Lorberbaum, and Noam J. Zohar (New Haven, CT: Yale University Press, 2000), p. 5.

[87] Deuteronomy 4:5.

The Jewish tradition interprets this to mean that the greatness of Jewish law is its accordance with human justice revealed to the mind; that the purpose of political Israel is the wisdom of the law.[88] The wisdom of the law should be plain to all: it is evinced not by its divine source but by human observation of the wisdom of its application. This is the missing bridge from the Beham draft's articulation of the principles of political right of the American Declaration of Independence to its efforts to incorporate the train of Jewish thought and history in the founding document of the first Jewish state to arise in Israel in 1,800 years.

It goes without saying that Jewish history did include centuries of exile and great suffering. As Beham's text elaborates, that suffering had culminated in the Holocaust. This was a form of persecution whose cruelty and evil had no historical parallel in its scope, a perverse turning of the full range of modern state power to the most evil ends.[89] The text implicitly holds that Jewish suffering over the generations – the Jewish insistence on cleaving to the Jewish law and the Jewish texts amidst persecutions of the vilest nature – was in the name of a higher principle. That is the only possible sense to these sufferings that the text can find, a sense which it lends by connecting the suffering described at the text's beginnings to the Jewish principle. This argument was a hard one to make to the survivors of the Holocaust, but is also the only one.

The text situated the Biblical promise of the land of Israel in the context of other promises of the land of Israel to the children of Israel: the promises of the British Empire, the League of Nations, and the United Nations. This, along with the assurance that the provisional government of Palestine is mandated by the "Council of Nations" to govern, forms the bulk of the content of Beham's Declaration.

LIBERTY, SOVEREIGNTY, AND THE JEWISH PEOPLE

Had Beham's text simply followed the format of the American Declaration, commencing with a narration of the historical roots of independence and culminating in a declaration of the state, it would have been historically interesting, but lacking relevance beyond its literary features.

---

[88] Ibn Ezra, "Commentary on Deuteronomy," 4:5, www.sefaria.org/Ibn_Ezra_on_Deuteronomy.4.5?lang=bi

[89] Adam Tooze, *The Wages of Destruction* (London: Penguin, 2006).

But Beham went beyond formalistic copying. His text included the core ideas in the American Declaration of Independence and the English Bill of Rights: human foundational political equality and the natural freedoms that derive from this inherent human condition. These ideas represent one of two differing concepts of political freedom: they represent the idea of "negative liberty," freedom *from* oppressions of implicit rights, as opposed to the idea of implicit "positive" liberty, freedoms to enjoy particular goods.[90]

The distinction between these two ideas of liberty was at the core of the major political theoretical disputes within the Western democracies of the twentieth century.[91] And these disputes remain with us even today.[92] For the distinction between forms of liberty ultimately governs one's views on the purpose of the state. Does the state exist to secure the citizens' natural and inherent rights? Or are rights the privileges bestowed on citizens by the beneficence of the state? Is the human right to liberty the same as the human right to the common goods that government can procure through collective action?

There is an implicit answer in the text's choice: if humans have natural rights, their securing must, by the nature of the proposition, be the very purpose of the state. Consequently, to write about securing natural rights as the purpose of a state is to take a firm view on the question of the nature of human rights. At the time that Beham was writing, a different view of human rights was being articulated. The United Nations Declaration of Human Rights, which would include rights to social security and other positive goods, was to be published at the end of 1948.[93] This document sought to bridge the concepts of political liberty and positive political obligations of the state as the bedrocks of human rights, following on the heels of Franklin Roosevelt's "Four Freedoms" as well as other twentieth-century notions of liberty.[94] We do not see the spirit of this compromise in Beham's declaration of the rights of citizens of

---

[90] Isaiah Berlin, "Two Concepts of Liberty," *Four Essays on Liberty* (Oxford: Oxford University Press, 1969), pp. 118–172.

[91] François Furet, "La Passion Révolutionnaire," in *Penser le Vingtième Siècle* (Paris: Robert Lafont, 1997), p. 519.

[92] See Niall Ferguson, *The Great Degeneration* (New York: Penguin, 2014).

[93] Jack Donnelly, *Universal Human Rights in Theory and Practice* (Ithaca, NY: Cornell University Press, 2013), p. 27.

[94] Daniel J. Whelan, *Indivisible Human Rights: A History* (Philadelphia: University of Pennsylvania Press, 2010), p. 18.

the state that would later be called Israel. The text shows itself to be allied to the cause of political liberty.

Rooting political rights in the tradition of political liberty as opposed to the tradition of political obligation implies concrete differences in the apparatus of the state. For in one case, the state's responsibility is to safeguard the natural liberty of the citizens; in the other the state is the creator and rationer in some ways of the freedoms that citizens should enjoy. In one case, the state's laws must be formulated to ensure that the citizens can pursue the state's agreed-upon essential object (or discover that object). In the other, the state must furnish agreed upon objects.[95] In this way the politics of political liberty differ entirely from the politics of political obligation. In the one case, politics govern the securing of freedom, hopefully a freedom from tyranny that is used to freely pursue good.[96] In the other, politics govern the securing of goods.

Of course the one need not preclude the other. As Beham's draft subsequently explains, following the text of the American Declaration, it would be impossible to secure the liberty of the citizens without building an apparatus of state to secure the rights of the citizens; it would be impossible to secure rights without securing bodies. "As a free and independent state," the new Jewish state would require the full power, in the unforgettable words Beham copied from America's Declaration, "to levy War, conclude Peace, contract Alliances, establish Commerce, and to do all other Acts and Things which Independent States may of right do."

Beham's text is not articulating the minimalist "night watchman state" of libertarian dreams.[97] It calls for an energetic state as described in Alexander Hamilton's meditations on the nature of state power in *The Federalist*. Hamilton saw the state as requiring "energy," as being divided in powers between executive, legislative, and judiciary not only to limit the scope of government, but also in order to assure the strength of government.[98] The American state's later constitution which Hamilton

---

[95] Isaiah Berlin, "Two Concepts of Liberty," pp. 145–148.

[96] Though we borrow from Isaiah Berlin here, our understanding of negative liberty differs from him. Berlin saw "negative liberty" as an end-in-itself since he thought that there was no firm basis for privileging one end or good over another. See Stanley Rosen, "Reviewed Work: Against the Current: Essays in the History of Ideas by Isaiah Berlin," *The Journal of Modern History*, 53, 2, 1981, pp. 309–311.

[97] Geoffrey Sampson, "Liberalism and Nozick's 'Minimal State,'" *Mind*, 87, 345, 1978, pp. 93–97.

[98] On the distinction between the scope and strength of a state, see Francis Fukuyama, *State-Building* (Ithaca, NY: Cornell University Press, 2004).

defended and explicated in *The Federalist*, in order to bring this principle to life, would endow an "energetic executive" with the scope to marshal all of the tools of modern state power in the defense of the state.[99] It would be an unlimited state in its defense of a limited government.

Beham's text is hitting on an important reality: a strong state is a prerequisite for limited government. For in the cruel world of states, the only world that in fact exists, a state that cannot survive cannot also secure the rights of its citizens.[100] There is not even a hierarchy of needs or aims of the state into which state strength falls: there is just the simple fact that states need to survive. And they cannot survive without a strong and capable apparatus of the modern state which both assures prosperity through protection of the commerce of the citizens, and then uses that prosperity to assure that the state's arms suffice in the never-ending clash of states against states.

The purpose of the state whose independence the text was proclaiming might be to secure limited government – government in which the natural rights of the citizens to life, liberty, and property are not threatened. It is a Jewish state, in which the freedom of the citizens is a freedom that strives to honor and abet the resuscitation in political form of the Jewish people and their mission.

The state's *raison d'être* would not simply be freedom: it is in the service of a higher calling than the political organization of its citizens. More classically understood, the state, as all states are, is the stage on which humanity instantiates its fullest callings, the stage which the political animal requires to play its role to its fullest and at its highest. And in the Jewish state, the direction is without confusion: it is for the Jewish people to write their next chapter.

In Beham's text, this is to happen in the context of a free state, a state in which all citizens' inherent liberty and equality is respected. This is a prerequisite to the fulfilment of the state's positive ends; for the positive ends point to the pursuit of the good, and the common good cannot be served without the protection of the inherent liberties of the individual. That vision must be accomplished, can only in the living world be accomplished, in a state. And states are what they are. States, to repeat the great words quoted by Beham, "levy War, conclude Peace, contract Alliances, establish Commerce, and to do all other Acts and Things which Independent States may of right do."

---

[99] *Federalist* no. 70.   [100] *Federalist* no. 2.

The text concludes by announcing its authorship. The authors of the Declaration are "representatives of the Jewish people," thus, answering, simply, a question that agonized both representatives of Jews around the world and leaders of the *Yishuv* in those days and since. The Declaration of Independence of the Jewish state is, in this text, a declaration in the name of the Jewish people as a whole, not simply those who happen to live in the *Yishuv* and owe allegiance to its laws.[101]

Directly copying the concluding sentences of the 1776 American Declaration, this draft of Israel's Declaration notes faithfully the proclaimers' firm reliance on divine providence and pledges the authors' "lives, fortunes, and sacred honor." The text's chosen Hebrew equivalent for divine providence – *Tzur Yisrael* – would make it through all future drafts and enter the final text of the Declaration, touching off a fascinating debate about religion and state which we discuss further in Chapters 6 and 7.

The phrase "lives, fortunes, and sacred honor" would have struck a discordant note in the *Yishuv*.[102] In translating the text into Hebrew, Beham struggled with the right Hebrew equivalent for "fortunes": no single Hebrew word connotes both fate and property. The Hebrew text includes a correction and revision: Beham crosses out the Hebrew word for "fate" and replaces it with the Hebrew for "property."

Though not all the elite of the Yishuv lived in *kibbutzim*, many did, and in any event, in keeping with the *Yishuv*'s ethos of equality, communal mission, and labor, very few had any substantial property to speak of. And some thought that the state should ultimately work toward the severe limitation or eradication of private fortune.[103] Yet Beham was trying to affirm the pious belief that the efforts in declaring independence were strengthened by faith in a God who cared about the outcome of human struggle. Even the secular leaders of the *Yishuv* would pledge their earthly goods – be they privately or communally held – upon the Rock of Israel.

CONCLUSION: "THE VIRTUES OF INDEPENDENCE FOR AN INDEPENDENT NATION"

The English draft seems to have been followed quickly by a quite literally translated Hebrew version. When the Hebrew text was written is also

---

[101] Yoram Shachar, "Jefferson Goes East," p. 616.   [102] Ibid., p. 610.

[103] See Johan Franzén, "Communism versus Zionism: The Comintern, Yishuvism, and the Palestine Communist Party," *Journal of Palestine Studies*, 36, 2, 2007, pp. 6–24.

uncertain. Was it written on the evening of April 24? Was the translator Davidowitz in any way involved? Or was it written at the office the next day? The first remaining draft of the Hebrew text is dated April 27, but the Hebrew text as it exists has copious revisions and amendments, and Beham would claim that the date was only added when the final revisions were made.

There are some small differences between the Hebrew and the English texts, but these tend only to cause Beham's draft to be *more* traditional, less of the twentieth century, more abstract, and more religious. For instance, the name "Palestine" does not appear in the Hebrew text even as it is used in English. In the Hebrew text, the ancient Jewish state is said to have existed for 1,500 years from the time of Joshua to the destruction of the Second Temple; in the original English, Joshua and the temple are omitted. The opening paragraph in the Hebrew removes a promise to Abraham, Isaac, and Jacob from "the Lord God" and replaces it with a promise to Abraham, Isaac, and Jacob from *"Tzur Yisrael"* – "rock of Israel" – the same formulation used to describe God in the Declaration's final paragraph. The omission of the name "God" is likely a religiously motivated change: it is considered profane to write the name of God in Hebrew. The Biblical promise in the first paragraph is extended. The English version only mentioned the promise of the land of Israel to the Jews; the Hebrew version adds that it was promised, further quoting Deuteronomy, to be their "eternal holding." And of course, Beham's Hebrew text introduces the term *"Tzur Yisrael"* to replace the American Declaration's oath upon "divine providence."

The Hebrew text is most notable for Beham's effort to render the English text and its source ideas, as literally as possible, into Hebrew. Beham goes out of his way to innovatively translate English words with no obvious Hebrew equivalent. He finds original and literal coinages for the words "indubitable," "inalienable," "oppressors," and other hallmark language characteristic of his Anglo-American source texts. He translates "levy war" literally. He translates "do all the other acts and things which independent states may do" using equivalently simple, plain, and thus striking prose – but in Hebrew. The Hebrew word choices throughout betray Beham's aim: they are commendable examples of the art of literal translation.

In 1968, Beham would write to Ze'ev Sharef, by then Minister of Trade of Industry, and in 1948 the Secretary of *Moetzet ha'Am* and *Minhelet ha'Am* and subsequently the first Cabinet Secretary of Israel, with some recollections of the heady days of 1948:

On the occasion of the 20th anniversary of Israel's Independence, I removed from my safe the files that I have kept from the period prior to the Declaration of Independence and among them – the first draft of the Declaration that I prepared at the time. In connection to this, I was reminded of our conversation a few years ago in which I promised you that I would produce for you a copy of the draft and I'm happy to herewith keep my promise. In relation to this, I am here attaching two copies: the first, a copy of a draft in my own hand that was prepared by me in the first half of April 1948, and which, after it was revised [alt. trans.: corrected] by way of a conversation between me and Uri Yadin (Heinsheimer), was typed up and printed on 27.4.1948. The words at the top, "secret, first draft, 27.4.1948" are in Yadin's handwriting. The second copied document is a version of the draft as it was typed up by Gabi Levy (the first clerk of the "Legal Department to-be") which she sent me during the second half of the month of April, when that "department" was in fact just a room in the office of the lawyer Dunkelbloom, of blessed memory, at 13 Ahad Ha'am Street, Tel Aviv. By the way, as I used the American Declaration of Independence as a precedent for the text, I wrote my draft first of all in English, and afterwards I prepared the Hebrew text. In the name of "the whole picture," I'm attaching also a copy of that English text.[104]

Beham's letter is notable for two reasons. First, it is the only available written document articulating Beham's intent in drafting the English text and its literal Hebrew translation. "I used the American Declaration of Independence as a precedent for the text," he writes, and so "I wrote my draft first of all in English." The English text was written in order to capture the spirit of the American Declaration of Independence so that it could be translated into Hebrew.[105]

The second notable aspect of the letter is that it clarifies the process of the editing of Beham's Hebrew text – its transformation as it came into

---

[104] The letter is reproduced from the judgment in the case: Jerusalem District Court, *State of Israel v. Beham, 58927-11-15, 13/08/2017*

[105] The letter also introduces some historical ambiguity: Is it possible that Beham had in fact drafted the text, as he claims, in the first part of April? That seems unlikely: The memo from Rosenbluth assigning the task of writing a Declaration of Independence to Beham is dated April 22. The Zionist Actions Committee had only concluded its meeting on April 12. While Beham may have started his work a day or two later in anticipation of the great events to come, that seems unlikely. It surely would contradict the Beham family story related by Yoram Shachar in "Ha'teyotot ha'mukdamot shel hakhrazat ha'atzmaut" which holds that the work began in Davidowitz's library on the 24th – and which seems more plausible given the chronology of the events surrounding Israel's independence. One possibility is that Beham means in the letter that he had begun his drafting in the first *part* of April, and the swirl of his memory twenty years later had divided the month into a period before and after his most intense work in the Legal Department. Another possibility is that an ambitious Beham had indeed used Davidowitz's library and even conferred with him, but that this had been drawn out over time, and not just done on the afternoon of the 24th. We will likely never know.

contact with the rest of the Legal Department. Beham's original Hebrew text as it exists has copious markings and changes above an original text.[106] The original Hebrew text is the literal translation of the English text. The Hebrew text as amended by the markup is quite different. The revisions strike out the most important language borrowed from the American Declaration of Independence. "Life, Liberty, and the Pursuit of Happiness" are eliminated. So too is the "ancient and indubitable right" of the Jewish people.

Clearly Beham was involved in the editing. It seems that most of the markings to the text are made in his own handwriting. The letter to Sharef clarifies that the editing was a collaborative effort with another one of the legal professionals working under Rosenblüth: Uri Heinsheimer. The next chapter will delve further into the reception of Beham's stark argument drawn from the classics of Anglo-American political thought. But suffice it to say, for now, that the document would not be received well. It would be pared down and edited further until its major similarities to the original English text were formal as opposed to intellectual.

When Beham presented his text to Rosenblüth after the initial consultation with Heinsheimer, he included a simple memo that laid out what he had attempted to accomplish. The memo said:

1: The Declaration was written from the belief that one has to rely not only on the UN and League of Nations decisions, but the historical rights of the Jewish people in light of the law of nations.
2: The three forefathers of the nation are mentioned explicitly, since they were the recipients of the promise regarding the land of Israel in its entirety in the Bible.
3: Regarding the Executive Committee, its other responsibilities were not included in the draft in order to avoid questions regarding the transfer of government and its roots.
4: The words "laid down the Mandate" are drawn from the law of the English Parliament regarding the end of the Mandate.
5: The last paragraph of the Declaration, like the whole body of the Declaration, is drawn essentially from the American Declaration, and gives legal expression to the virtues of independence for an independent nation.[107]

Beham had seen the essence of things. He thought that a government should be declared simply and unambiguously. His first drafts had assured the rights of the citizens and explained that the rights were

---

[106] See Israel State Archives, 8227/2-א.
[107] Beham memo in Israel State Archives, 5664/20/10 ב, and Yoram Shachar, "Ha'teyotot ha'mukdamot shel hakhrazat ha'atzmaut," p. 534.

inherent, derived from the nature of things and not from conventions. The text was to be issued in the name of the Jewish people, and the declaration of independence was to be made within that context, drawing on the texts and history of the Jewish people. It was to draw on the insights of the American Declaration of Independence. Human beings are free and devise governments to ensure and protect that freedom. It delineated a doctrine of sovereignty and state power, and explained the rationale for state power: to protect the rights of the citizens. And the text was to be an explicitly Jewish text for a Jewish state even without being a religious text. In Beham's memorable phrase, to repeat, he wanted to give "expression to the virtues of independence for an independent nation."

We have no record of Rosenblüth's reaction to the text and the memo that Beham presented. We don't know if he ever saw or even heard of the original. We do know that Rosenblüth didn't hate the work as presented to him enough to prevent further revisions to it by Beham as well as other bureaucrats. Beham and his colleagues would continue to pare down his text, shaping it with the other lawyers who worked for Rosenblüth.[108] The author of the next significant draft of the Declaration, the lawyer Tzvi Berenson, consulted the output of the Legal Department's drafting process in writing his own draft.

There is much to commend in Beham's first draft. The text earnestly attempts to rise to the occasion: it betrays a sense that a declaration of independence is not merely a technical procedure. It offers a unique opportunity to state the ethical and political principles of the state. The text, produced by Beham, repairing to the library of an unusually literary neighborhood Rabbi, takes it upon itself to try to articulate the purpose of the new state. Referencing the Bible and the texts of Anglo-American political independence and natural rights, it understands that the Jewish state, on an elemental level, could not but be rooted in the people of Israel's covenantal texts on the one hand and the inherent natural rights of each individual on the other.

Beham seems to have known to a good degree what he was doing. The memo he sent to Rosenblüth along with his draft as well as the letter to Sharef twenty years later say it all: it was important not to merely mention the recent United Nations recognition of the Jews right to a state, or even the Hebrew Bible and the historical rights of the Jewish people to the land

---

[108] Yoram Shachar, "Jefferson Goes East," p. 614.

of Israel. The text had to distill the virtues of independence for an independent nation. Beham knew that it was necessary to aim high.

Beham's first draft is the most direct attempt in the founding period of modern Israel to connect the founding of the state on the one hand to Jewish ideas and the Jewish mission, and on the other hand to the political and philosophical logic that lies at the heart of the great free states of the modern world. Traces of Beham's work would make their way into the final document. As mentioned above, the basic format would be retained. And most famously, the phrase for divine providence, *Tzur Yisrael,* would gain particular notice.

But the text's combination of the concept of political natural right and the concept of the Jewish mission would not be picked up and carried forward. Such an effort would only emerge again in the final text of the Declaration. And there it would spring from different soil: the mind of David Ben-Gurion. The other leaders of the *Yishuv* had different intellectual and practical priorities. For reasons examined in the coming chapters, Beham's text, with its effort to fuse the spirit of doctrines of inherent or natural rights with the spirit of Jewish ideas, would remain a matter for the historical record.

3

From Natural Rights to Labor Zionism

Tzvi Berenson and the Legal Department's Draft

The dominant political theory of the *Yishuv* was Labor Zionism. But it was more than a theory. It comprised the institutions of national economic life such as the *Histadrut* labor union and the rural *kibbutzim*. It dominated the apparatus of national security in the *Haganah* and its strike force the *Palmach* whose soldiers and commanders addressed one another as comrade. The cultural markers of daily life such as the *Hashomer Ha'tzair* youth group with its red bandanas and youth communes, the worker's bank cooperative itself owned by the *Histadrut* (along with the worker's health and life insurer), and the purchase of food and clothing from grocery and clothing cooperatives – these were all carriers of the spirit of Labor Zionism in its many forms and textures.[1]

The same was true of the *Yishuv*'s political institutions. By 1948, the main bodies of the *Yishuv* were almost entirely Labor Zionist-run enterprises. The Jewish National Council, the *Yishuv*'s official representative body under the British Mandate, was chaired by the head of the Labor Party and governed in the main by a coalition of like-minded Labor-Zionists.[2] *Moetzet ha'Am* and *Minhelet ha'Am* – the institutions that would bring the Jewish state into being – were dominated by the Labor Zionist *Mapai* party and its allies.

---

[1] For a thorough treatment of Labor Zionism at the founding of the state, see Ze'ev Sternhell, *The Founding Myths of Israel*, trans. David Maisel (Princeton, NJ: Princeton University Press, 1994).

[2] Cf. Aviad Rubin, "Political-Elite Formation and Transition to Democracy in Pre-State Conditions: Comparing Israel and the Palestinian Authority," *Government and Opposition*, 44, 3, 2009, pp. 262–284.

It should thus come as no surprise that the Legal Department did not know what to make of Mordechai Beham's draft of the Declaration of Independence. Beham's draft had no roots in the theories of Jewish revival through labor – the theories that had propelled thousands to the swamps, deserts, and hard living of Palestine. It had Thomas Jefferson and John Locke, but not A. D. Gordon, Ber Borochov, Karl Marx, or Leon Trotsky. Beham's text was in many ways a foreign implant. And thus, his colleagues in the Legal Department, with Beham along with them, took to radically revising it. In this vein, Mordechai Beham's first effort at Israel's Declaration of Independence would be nearly totally reoriented from a focus on natural rights to a focus on the underlying tenets of Labor Zionism.

This chapter describes the change and reorientation of Israel's Declaration of Independence from the political theory of natural rights toward the political theory of state authority, progress through material development, and positive egalitarianism that formed the basis of Labor Zionism. This pivot would ultimately come to characterize the later versions of Israel's Declaration of Independence, including to a large degree the final one. It is not just a turning point in the history of the writing of Israel's Declaration. It is also an important marker in the intellectual and political makeup of the state at its founding.

The drama takes place both within and between the lines of the draft of Israel's Declaration produced by Tzvi Berenson (1907–2001), then legal advisor to the *Histadrut* labor union, an advisor in Felix Rosenblüth's Legal Department, and subsequently, from 1950 onwards, an influential judge on the Supreme Court of Israel.[3] As detailed below, even before Berenson set to work, major edits and revisions to Beham's first draft had been made by other members of the Legal Department along with Beham. After these revisions and Berenson's redrafting, very little was to remain of the substance of Beham's first draft.[4]

The revisions to Beham's first draft upended its main ideas. The priority and sovereignty of the natural rights of the individual was replaced with the priority and sovereignty of the state. The state is legitimated in terms of the material progress it delivers to its population and not the

---

[3] Nir Kedar, "Democracy and Judicial Autonomy in Israel's Early Years," *Israel Studies*, 15, 1, 2010, p. 30.
[4] See Yoram Shachar, "Ha'teyotot ha'mukdamot shel hakhrazat ha'atzmaut," p. 545.

abstract rights that it protects. The state's Jewish moral, religious, and even historical tradition is replaced with the history of Labor Zionism and mid-century ideas of democratic rights that would soon be enshrined in the United Nations Universal Declaration of Human Rights.[5]

The first revisions to Beham's draft and the subsequent drafting of an almost entirely new version of Israel's Declaration by Tzvi Berenson marked a reorientation away from the effort to ground Israel's national political life in the ideas of natural political rights and duties on the one hand, and in a search for an appropriate articulation of the Jewish mission on the other. The political independence of the Jewish people articulated in Beham's draft was recast as the political independence of the twentieth-century Labor Zionist state.

TZVI BERENSON'S DECLARATION

In later years, Tzvi Berenson would always claim that, having been asked to write a draft of Israel's Declaration by Felix Rosenblüth, he wrote from a blank slate on May 5–6, 1948.[6] On the contrary, it is nearly certain that Berenson had seen, and worked with, texts derived from Beham's first draft. He also had available the proclamation that Rubashov wrote at the conclusion of the April ZAC meeting.[7] Finally, Berenson's work subsequently received input from other members of the Legal Department, including Beham.[8]

In a certain sense, the documentary record's refutation of the letter of Berenson's claim is immaterial to judging Berenson's work. To Berenson's mind, he was tasked with inventing a declaration of independence. While he did not literally do this, the figurative importance of his claim is that the main intellectual aims and for that matter legal calculations implicit in the initial efforts were of limited use to Berenson. Even if Berenson had no direct exposure to Beham's first draft where the issue of natural political

---

[5] On the universal human rights and the UN, see Jack Donnelly, *Universal Human Rights in Theory and Practice* (Ithaca, NY: Cornell University Press, 2013), pp. 24–39.

[6] Yoram Shachar, "Ha'teyotot ha'mukdamot shel hakhrazat ha'atzmaut," p. 560. For Berenson's account of his work see *Megilat Ha'atzmaut* (*Declaration of Independence*) (Israel Ministry of Culture: 1988), pp. 5–6.

[7] Yoram Shachar, Ibid.

[8] See below for a discussion of Beham's colleagues Uri Heinsheimer (Yadin) and Moshe Zilberg.

justice was put most starkly, Berenson's own work is notable as a departure from that basic framework.

Here is the text of Tzvi Berenson's draft:

Declaration on the Founding of a Jewish State

By right of the unbroken historical and traditional connection of the people of Israel to the land of Israel, and by right of the labor and sacrifice of the pioneers, builders, and protectors, who made the land's wilderness bloom, and established it anew as the national home of the Jewish people;

And in accordance with the will of the conscience of humanity as expressed in the Balfour Declaration, the mandate over the land of Israel as given by the League of Nations, and the decision of the General Assembly of the United Nations of 16 Kislev, 5708, (November 29, 1947) regarding the establishment of a Jewish state in the land of Israel;

And in order to remove the curse of the exile of the Jewish people and its dependence on strangers in almost every land, to ingather the dispersed and promise them a life of work and creativity, freedom and independence, in a state of their own;

We, the National Council, the representatives of the Zionist movement and the *Yishuv* in the land of Israel, gathered here in joyous assembly at the end of the British Mandate, hereby proclaim the establishment of a Jewish, free, independent, and democratic state in the land of Israel, within the borders delineated by the General Assembly of the United Nations, with all the rights and authorities that the laws of nature and international law grant to independent states.

We declare that from today until the establishment of permanent governing institutions through a constitution, which will be approved by a constituent assembly of the Jewish state, the National Council [*Moetzet ha'Am*] shall be the provisional government, which possesses full powers of lawmaking and rule in the state, the obligation to safeguard its security and to defend its territorial integrity and independence.

We declare that the British White Paper for the land of Israel from 1939 is illegal and inoperative, and every law, regulation, and directive issued on the basis of its authority are invalid and abolished.

The Jewish state will be a state of the ingathering of the exiles and free immigration for Jews, [a state] of freedom, justice, and peace in the spirit of the vision of the prophets of Israel and Jewish history and in accordance with the principles of the Charter of the United Nations, and one law will apply to all residents regardless of race, religion, language, or sex.

All residents of the country are required to obey the provisional government and authorities established by it, and are required to ensure quiet and peace and to cooperate for the good of the whole.

We call especially to the Arabs in the Jewish state to cooperate as citizens bearing equal rights and duties, extend our hands in peace and brotherhood to the peoples of the Arab countries and look forward to the assistance of all nations.

And with trust in the Rock of Israel we sign with our own signatures in witness of this declaration, here on the soil of the land of Israel, this day, *motzei Shabbat*, 7 *Iyyar*, May 15, 1948.[9]

There is a great deal to commend in Berenson's draft. To begin with, Berenson introduces the noble vision of "freedom, justice, and peace in the spirit of the vision of the prophets of Israel and Jewish history" into the text – a formulation that would ultimately appear in the final text of the Declaration. It calls, notably and uniquely, for a "democratic" state to be built. It calls for the drafting of a constitution (even as we will see that the impetus for this was external). And it makes explicit the call to Arab residents of the Jewish state, Muslim and Christian, to "cooperate as citizens bearing equal rights and duties," extending a hand in friendship to the state's Arab neighbors. The document has a clear aspiration: it intends for the new state to base itself on principles of justice and equality before a just law.

Berenson's draft further articulates the principle, common to Anglo-American liberalism as well as to Judaism, of both equal rights of citizens and rights for the "stranger that lives amongst you."[10] In the new state "one law will apply to all residents regardless of race, religion, language, or sex." The emphasis on the equality of the sexes added here, quoting from the United Nations Charter of 1945, should of course be noted.[11]

Most of all, Berenson's emphasis on "one law for all" is a useful, and perhaps a still fruitful, method of framing equality within the context of a Jewish state. A Jewish state can be Jewish in that it will be constituted largely by Jewish people, seek to embody their ideas and practices, and aspire to advance the Jewish people's aims. Yet this does not make it a state of so-called Jewish privilege in its daily operations. In affirming that a single law will be applicable to all, Berenson's text asserts that non-Jews and Jews shall be subject to the same rights and eligible, under the letter of the law, to the same privileges. The document in this way expresses a spirit of patriotism, justice, and civic friendship that might enrich the politics of the country.

---

[9] Copy in Israel State Archives, 5664/20/10 ‎ב. In his reflection on the Declaration of Independence published by the state of Israel in 1988 as *Declaration of Independence: Vision and Reality*, Berenson reprinted a copy of "his" Declaration that differs from the one existing in the archives. Berenson's later document reflects further edits/revisions to Berenson's initial effort undertaken by himself and others in the Legal Department.

[10] See, for instance, Leviticus, 19:33–34.   [11] www.un.org/en/charter-united-nations/

These statements are clear in their moral and ethical hope for a community of equality and justice, calling for the creation of a democratic state that lives up to the highest vision of egalitarian principles. This vision should be familiar to the reader: it is largely borrowed from Zalman Rubashov's "Declaration on the Founding of the Government."[12] The same "equal rights and duties" that Rubashov's text envisioned for the Arabs of the Jewish state are articulated in Berenson's draft. The same extension "of our hand in peace, friendship, and cooperation" that Rubashov's text proclaimed is offered by Berenson.

While the similarity between Berenson's text and Rubashov's might make it impossible to believe Berenson's claim that he wrote the text from a blank slate, it does make evident the degree to which Berenson's noble ideals were shared within the *Yishuv*. These ideas and this vision were not simply Berenson's own, but rather were the official ideas of the *Mapai* party and passed muster with a majority of the Zionist Actions Committee just one month earlier. It is thus no surprise that its principles found their way into Berenson's text as well.

The ideas of equality, freedom, and rights, and the extension of these rights to all, including the Arabs of the land of Israel, had a long and consistent provenance in Zionist thought in general and in the thought of the Labor Zionist *Mapai* party, from which both Rubashov and Berenson both came, in particular. The language regarding finding common purpose with and respecting the common citizenship of the Arab citizens of the future state was a long held aspiration of *Mapai* – an aspiration that would be challenged by the events of the war, as we explain further in this chapter's afterword. Rubashov's views were entirely consistent with the writing in *Davar*, the *Mapai* newspaper of which he was the editor-in-chief. He had honed these ideas for years. Berenson's text was a natural channel for them. And Berenson had added to them: His text declares "a Jewish, free, independent, and democratic state in the land of Israel." His text sets out a high ethical marker for the state-to-be.

---

[12] While it is certain that Rubashov was the central figure in the composition of this text, he likely had assistance from other members of the Zionist Actions Committee. He certainly received input about the language of the draft or its general tenor from the Americans Israel Goldstein, Emanuel Neumann and Samuel Margoshes as well as the *Mizrahi* leader Yeshayahu Wolfsberg (Aviad). See Yoram Shachar, "Ha'teyotot ha'mukdamot shel hakhrazat ha'atzmaut," p. 32.

FROM NATURAL RIGHTS TO LABOR

At the same time that one must salute Berenson's vision, it is important to lay out the political structure and assumptions that underlie Berenson's political aims – and to contrast them with the aims in Mordechai Beham's original draft. For not only the narrative structure of Berenson's document, but as well its very language, represent a conscious political-theoretical reorientation away from the vision and principles that characterized Beham's text.

The two texts might share certain structural similarities. They begin from a historical narration of the justice of the founding of a Jewish state, declare the state's coming into being, proceed to outline a vision of laws, and conclude with an oath upon *Tzur Yisrael*. But beyond those structural or formal similarities, in substance the two documents could not be more different.

Berenson's draft presents an entirely different justification for Israel's founding, changes the substantive purpose of the state being founded, and makes final political judgments about important questions of policy in the declaration of the state which Beham had deliberately left open: the borders of the state, the status of its Arab residents, then bearing arms against the state in many prominent instances, and even the extent of the state's reliance on the United Nations as the source of its principles and legitimacy.

Finally, Berenson's text locates sovereignty in the state and not in the people. Beham's and Berenson's documents might at first glance seem like a natural evolution, the one proceeding from the next. In fact, they are anything but. The change is, by in large, toward the ethos of Jewish Palestine in the 1940s and away from the political theories of natural rights that Beham had cited and relied upon.

To start with the beginning, Berenson's text opens by citing an "unbroken historical and traditional connection of the people of Israel to the land of Israel." The emphasis on the "traditional" and "historical" connection between the Jewish people and the land of Israel deliberately omits the vexed question of Judaism and religious claims to the land – an issue which Beham had addressed by trying to find a harmony between revelation and reason in the texts of revelation.

Berenson perhaps hoped to find some neutral common ground on controversial religious questions by encompassing them in the phrase "historical and traditional." Surely the religious honor the historical and traditional connection between the Jews and Israel. And surely the irreligious would not deny these either. Instead of writing, as Beham did, of the Bible's promise and thus implicitly its moral universe, Berenson subsumes this idea under the notion of "tradition."

This rhetorical turn solves one problem but raises new ones. The argument presented in Berenson's text is that an enduring connection of a people to its land is enough to explain that people's presence (or return) there. That might have been enough to justify the *Yishuv* – or even more than enough. The fighting of the *Haganah* would of course be the ultimate material test.

As a logical matter, however, this type of argument struggles to ground exclusive claims. From the Knights Templar to the followers of Saladin, to the ancient Canaanites and Hittites and Amalekites and Assyrians, to say nothing of the nineteenth century Arab populations, other individuals and groups had held a cherished connection to the land now claimed for the new state.[13] What is the reason for privileging any historical or traditional connection to the land? An invocation of history and tradition cannot offer an answer. History is not an explanation for itself.[14]

Berenson's text shows that he intuited this difficulty. He understood that a "historical and traditional" claim alone would not suffice to explain the Zionist enterprise. This prompted him to offer deeper justification for the state: "the right of labor" and the "sacrifice of the pioneers." In Berenson's text, the right of labor takes the place of the natural right of individuals as the source of legitimacy for the national enterprise. Indeed, the heroes of Berenson's Declaration are the pioneers. It was these men and women who by labor, blood, sweat, and tears turned a barren land into the national home of the Jewish people.[15] The opening paragraph says it all. The state is declared "by right of the labor and sacrifice of the pioneers, builders, and protectors, who made the land's wilderness bloom, and established it anew as the national home of the Jewish people."

Labor as a basis for possession, both individual and collective, has a distinguished lineage in political thought. As John Locke put it in the *Second Treatise*:

---

[13] For review of the question of connection to the "land" of Israel, see Ilan S. Troen, "Israeli Views of the Land of Israel/Palestine," *Israel Studies,* 18, 2, 2013, pp. 100–114.

[14] See Chapter 7 for a discussion of how David Ben-Gurion attempted to wrestle with this problem.

[15] Ben Halpern and Jehuda Reinharz, "The Cultural and Social Background of the Second Aliyah," *Middle Eastern Studies,* 27, 3, 1991, pp. 487–517.

God commanded, and his [man's] wants forced him to labour. That was his Property which could not be taken from him where-ever he had fixed it. And hence subduing or cultivating the Earth, and having Dominion, we see are joined together. The one gave title to the other.[16]

The subduing and cultivating of the earth begets political dominion: labor produces political right, with political right coming into being to protect the ability to enjoy the fruits of labor.[17] This is Locke's famous doctrine of possession.

The limits of Locke's argument are well known. For one, and as a matter of fact, labor alone is never responsible for the possession of land. Locke's discussion assumes the existence of a historical or imagined state of nature – primitive individuals arriving at uncultivated and uninhabited land as he imagined had been the case in the Americas. In geographic Palestine, the pioneers, for their part, were able to work the land because the land had been purchased and the pioneering effort supported in its infant form. The efforts of philanthropists as well as pooled contributions from Jews and others around the world had been vital.[18] So too was a mix of aid and labor from Palestine's Arab communities. A full acknowledgment of the resettlement of Palestine would therefore need to acknowledge capital as well as labor.[19]

Labor in the *Yishuv* also depended on arms – as Berenson acknowledged when he wrote of the pioneers as "builders and protectors." The Earl of Shaftesbury may have famously said of Palestine that it was a country without a people for a people without a country. It would be trite but at the same time necessary to point out the obvious lacunae in this view.[20] Survey work indicates that the largely Arab population of the coast and the Galilee had been growing along with the general population of Palestine in the nineteenth century. The numbers are hard to pin down.

---

[16] John Locke, *Two Treatises of Government* (Cambridge: Cambridge University Press, 1988), p. 292.

[17] Ibid.

[18] For a helpful review of philanthropic efforts, see Michael Berkowitz, "Toward an Understanding of Fundraising, Philanthropy and Charity in Western Zionism, 1897–1933," *Voluntas: International Journal of Voluntary and Nonprofit Organizations,* 7, 3, 1996, pp. 241–258.

[19] Jonathan Helfand, "Baron James de Rothschild and the Old *Yishuv*," *Proceedings of the World Congress of Jewish Studies,* 1985, pp. 55–58.

[20] Adam Garfinkle, "On the Origin, Meaning, Use and Abuse of a Phrase," *Middle Eastern Studies,* 27, 4, 1991, pp. 539–550.

The population of Nablus in 1850, for instance, is subject to wildly varying estimates that range from 9,000 to 20,000.[21]

Nationalism too had come to Acre and Jerusalem and Haifa and Jaffa, even if its currency and the commitments that it demanded may not have reached the levels of say Egypt in the nineteenth century.[22] As Jewish immigration picked up in intensity, so too did Arab national consciousness. And the economic growth of the joint Jewish and Arab enterprise attracted further regional migrants. The population grew.

Whatever truth may lie in Shaftesbury's statement relates to the lack of an organized rival national Arab polity in Palestine preceding the *Yishuv*, or at least not one of sufficient scope as to have been evident to Shaftesbury and other statesmen in England or for that matter to the land's nineteenth-century Ottoman overseers. There may have been people but there was no local state and only the decaying remnants of Ottoman rule. The land thus knew the ravages of what is now called the weak state. The local villages raided one another. The highways knew banditry. The *Yishuv*, as one of its slogans went, was built "under the tower and the stockade."[23]

Capital and arms may have played their part. And still, even after considering the obvious caveats to a labor-centric framework, one must grant the laborers their central role. They did indispensable work. Paper ownership of untended land in the Galilee, or on the coastal plane, or on a rocky hill on the outskirts of the Old City of Jerusalem, would have been of limited utility to the creation of a new dominion in Palestine had not the laborers actually engaged in the work of building *kibbutzim, moshavim*, neighborhoods, and, indeed, cities. Locke made this same argument too:

If we will rightly estimate things as they come to our use, and cast up the several Expenses about them, what in them is purely owning to Nature, and what to labour, we shall find, that in most of them 99/100 are wholly to be put on the account of labour.[24]

This comment has special resonance in the case of the Jewish settlements of the nineteenth and early twentieth centuries, which often had transformative

---

[21] Beshara B. Doumani, "The Political Economy of Population Counts in Ottoman Palestine: Nablus, circa 1850," *International Journal of Middle East Studies,* 26, 1, 1994, p. 2.

[22] See Zachary Foster, "The Invention of Palestine" (Unpublished PhD thesis), Princeton University, 2017, https://dataspace.princeton.edu/handle/88435/dsp01g732dc66g

[23] See Elhannan Orren, *Hetyashvut be'shnot ma'avak (Settlement Amid Struggles)* (Jerusalem: Yad Yitzhak Ben Tzvi, 1978).

[24] John Locke, *Two Treatises of Government*, p. 296.

and fruitful effects in an indifferent or actively hostile climate, in a land that at the time was counted amongst the most impoverished in a region that itself was amongst the poorest in the world.[25]

FROM LABOR TO CREATIVITY

There were of course clear differences between the views that prevailed among the pioneers of the *Aliyot* and the theorist of capitalism John Locke. In particular, Locke argued that both private property and unequal possession were built into the human condition itself. Along with the inevitable introduction of money as a medium of exchange, Locke argued that each individual has a right to the enlargement of possessions. The "condition of human life," in his famous formulation, requires private property; by putting a value to money "by consent," humanity acknowledges what Locke called natural inequality in property.[26]

This view would be contested most influentially by Karl Marx, who argued that private property was merely an interim stage in the managing of human labor, a waystation on the way to socialized ownership.[27] And the ideological vanguard among the Jewish pioneers were Marxists, motivated by the idea of collective ownership of lands in Palestine and the nullification of private property. The *kibbutzim*, to take the most obvious example, were an experiment in collective ownership and collective living.[28] Locke's doctrine is political in that it advocates for a state, that, among other things, must protect private property.[29] The *Yishuv* was anything but a quest to attract and expand the domain of private property.

In Berenson's text, labor's goal goes beyond ownership. Its aim is to offer Jews a "life of work and creativity." This phrase immediately calls to

---

[25] The major source remains the "Palestine Report on Immigration, Land Settlement, and Development" (London: 1930).

[26] John Locke, *Two Treatises of Government*, pp. 292–293. On Locke's justification of private property, see C. B. MacPherson, *The Political Theory of Possessive Individualism* (Oxford: Clarendon Press, 1962).

[27] As Marx and Friedrich Engels put it in "The Communist Manifesto," "The Theory of the Communists may be summed up in the single sentence: Abolition of private property." Karl Marx and Friedrich Engels, *Collected Works*, vol. 6 (New York: International Publishers, 1976), p. 498.

[28] Alison M. Bowes, "The Experiment That Did Not Fail: Image and Reality in the Israeli Kibbutz," *International Journal of Middle East Studies*, 22, 1, 1990, pp. 85–103.

[29] John Locke, *Two Treatises of Government*, p. 296.

mind Karl Marx's *Das Kapital*, and its promises of liberation under state socialism.[30] As Marx put it in "The German Ideology":

> In Communist society, where nobody has one exclusive sphere of activity but each can become accomplished in any branch he wishes, society regulates the general production and thus makes it possible for me to do one thing today and another tomorrow, to hunt in the morning, fish in the afternoon, rear cattle in the evening, criticise after dinner, just as I have a mind, without ever becoming hunter, fisherman, shepherd, or critic.[31]

This strand of thought found special resonance among certain thinkers of high repute in the *Yishuv*. In particular, "creative work" is a not inapt way of defining the central idea of the writer A. D. Gordon (1856–1922), a cofounder of the political party *Ha'poel Ha'tzair* (The Young Worker) and a spiritual father of the Labor Zionist movement.[32] In his essays, Gordon writes about the transformative and redemptive quality of labor, which he thinks can reconnect modern, alienated humanity to its natural essence and permit the restitution of full human power.[33]

Gordon described his aims almost mystically: "Our entire spirit living within us, all the powers of our body and spirit, must be repaired. They must find expression in our life, in the creation of our life from start to finish, in every labor, and every kind of work, and every deed."[34] When Berenson promises the Jews a life of "creative work" in the new state, it is this Gordonist tradition of Labor Zionist thought to which he unwittingly or not refers.

THE PRINCIPLES OF THE UN

In addition to labor and creativity, the other positive end that Berenson argues for the state to uphold is the set of principles enshrined in the

---

[30] G. A. Cohen, "Bourgeois and Proletarians," in *Lectures on the History of Moral and Political Philosophy*, ed. Jonathan Wolf (Princeton, NJ: Princeton University Press, 2014).

[31] *Karl Marx: A Reader*, ed. John Elster (Cambridge: Cambridge University Press, 1986), p. 180.

[32] Amos Perlmutter, "A. D. Gordon: A Transcendental Zionist," *Middle Eastern Studies*, 7, 1, 1971, pp. 81–87.

[33] See Hillel Halkin, "The Self-Actualizing Zionism of A. D. Gordon," *Mosaic*, February 15, 2018.

[34] Quoted in Avraham Shapira, *Hope for Our Time: Key Trends in the Thought of Martin Buber*, trans. Jeffrey Green (Albany: State University of New York Press, 1999), pp. 141–142.

United Nations Charter. Indeed, the state's principles are to be truth, peace, and justice, both in "the spirit of the prophets" and also "in accordance with the principles of the Charter of the United Nations." Surely Berenson must have imagined that this rhetorical nod to the UN would win the state some international support, to say nothing of legitimacy. And indeed, UN Resolution 181, along the lines of which the Jewish state was being brought into being per Berenson, explicitly demanded that the new state adhere to the UN Charter's principles.[35]

It is worth delving into those principles: to what was Berenson committing the state? It happened that just as the *Yishuv* was preparing its own independence, the newly-born United Nations was preparing its Declaration on Human Rights. The UN Declaration had been in the works since 1946, when French theologian Jacques Maritain assembled a so-called Philosopher's Committee to craft a charter of rights applicable everywhere.[36]

The UN Charter built on the expansive definition of rights best embodied by Franklin D. Roosevelt's Four Freedoms.[37] On its face, the UN Charter is the inheritor of the rights tradition of Anglo-American liberalism and of the Rousseauian Declaration of the Rights of Man of the French tradition.[38] The US Declaration of Independence defines natural rights as life, liberty, and the pursuit of happiness. The French Revolutionary works speak of a bond of fraternity and thus common obligation and sympathy among people in concert with liberty and equality.

The UN Charter, in its ninth chapter, extends further still to "higher standards of living," "full employment," and "conditions of economic and social progress," "solutions of international economic, social health, and related problems," and more. It also outlines "universal respect for, and observance of, human rights and fundamental freedoms for all without distinction as to race, sex, language, or religion," a passage that Resolution 181 and Berenson would draw from.[39] The open-ended definition of human rights in the UN Charter would find its form in the

---

[35] See Chapter 4.
[36] "The Long and Influential Life of the Universal Declaration of Human Rights," in *The Universal Declaration of Human Rights in the 21st Century: A Living Document in a Changing World*, ed. Gordon Brown (Cambridge: Open Book Publishers, 2016), pp. 29–38. The committee's work was ultimately approved by, among others, Eleanor Roosevelt.
[37] Glen M. Johnson, "The Contributions of Eleanor and Franklin Roosevelt to the Development of International Protection for Human Rights," *Human Rights Quarterly*, 9, 1, 1987, p. 20.
[38] See Paul Magnette, *Citizenship: The History of an Idea* (Essex: ECPR Press, 2005).
[39] www.un.org/en/charter-united-nations/

Universal Declaration of Human Rights of 1948, which would explicitly mention the freedom of "speech and belief" and freedom from "fear and want" as the "highest aspiration of the common people," implicitly citing FDR's Four Freedoms.[40]

The catalogue of rights mentioned in the UN Declaration is far-reaching. Some of these, such as the freedom to practice one's religion and the recognition of the natural dignity of human beings, clearly derive from the inherent natural rights doctrine of the American Declaration of Independence.[41]

But many others represent the more encompassing understanding of positive rights articulated in the Depression-era New Deal and in the World War II-era Four Freedoms, of which Amartya Sen would become the most articulate defender and exponent in the 1980s and 1990s.[42] On this view, the state must defend not only inherent liberties; it also has a noneconomic obligation to the provision of economic goods. The basic idea: governmental bodies are obligated to provide positive goods that human beings require by justice. This can refer to basics such as food, shelter, and health services, but can grow beyond these basic needs as well to encompass the realms of human dignity.

Both in developed and perhaps more so in developing states, the politics of growing state obligation have led to a lack of economic dynamism in the state and an entrenchment of economic interests in the maintenance of governing programs.[43] State politics can devolve into a fight over the allocation of scarce resources. A violent populism pitting classes and regions against one another in a contest for limited resources comes to typify the state.

Instead of the state as the guarantor and protector of encroachments upon the liberty and dignity of the individual, here we have the state taking on an added species of duties that can sit in tension with the protection of the individual's inherent liberties and dignity. It is to this then-novel sense of rights and obligations that Berenson's text orients the new state when it appeals to justice "in accordance with the principles of the Charter of the United Nations."

---

[40] David Kennedy, *Freedom from Fear* (Oxford: Oxford University Press, 2001).

[41] On the natural right to religious liberty, see, for instance, Vincent Phillip Muñoz, "George Washington on Religious Liberty," *The Review of Politics*, 65, 1, 2003, pp. 11–33.

[42] See, for instance, his "Human Rights and Capabilities," *Journal of Human Development*, 6, 2, 2005.

[43] Cf. Daron Acemoglu and James A. Robinson, "Persistence of Power, Elites, and Institutions," *The American Economic Review*, 98, 1, 2008, pp. 267–293.

DEMOCRACY

Perhaps the most noted accomplishment of Berenson's text is its addition of the word "democracy" in its description of Jewish independence. The operative clause of the text, the one which declares the establishment of the state, reads: "We, the National Council, the representatives of the Zionist movement and the Yishuv in the land of Israel ... hereby proclaim the establishment of a Jewish, free, independent, and democratic state in the land of Israel ...."

What did Berenson likely mean by this? The sense of rights and obligations embodied in the UN Charter had come during World War II to be associated with a single word: democracy. It was common at least in the US and the UK to refer to World War II as a battle between democracy and fascism or totalitarianism.[44] The free countries – the United States, the UK and its Commonwealth, and even the rebellious rump of invaded countries like France – were the democracies.[45]

Democracy was popularly defined as the antonym of the Third Reich and the Japanese Empire. In the wake of the war, even some of the newly formed states under Soviet control would thus call themselves democracies: for instance, the German Democratic Republic also known as East Germany. Democracy was becoming the only ethically acceptable form of legitimation, even for nondemocracies.

Thus, on the face of things, there is little to say about Berenson's decision to characterize the new state as a democracy.[46] What else would he have possibly said? Although democratic nomination of leaders was yet to sweep the entire world in 1948, by the advent of the Third Wave of democratization in the 1990s, the work would be complete, and democracy would become essentially the only manner in which political leaders could be legitimated.[47] States with political systems as diverse as the social democracy of Germany, the parliamentary democracy of Canada, the dysfunctional kleptocracy of the Democratic Republic of Congo, and the theocracy of Iran would all shift to democratic legitimation of rulers, abandoning either monarchic or other non-popular forms of legitimating political leaders and succession.

---

[44] Roland Quinault, "Churchill and Democracy," *Transactions of the Royal Historical Society*, 11, 2001, pp. 201–220.

[45] This rhetoric was used both by Churchill as well as by Roosevelt. Ibid., p. 213.

[46] Zalman Rubashov (Shazar) had also characterized the state as democratic. Berenson seems to have been following Rubashov's lead here.

[47] Samuel Huntington, "Democracy's Third Wave," *Journal of Democracy*, 2, 2, 1991, pp. 12–34.

This variety of states that employ democratic nomination and legitimation underscores the diversity of systems of government of states that in some form or another describe themselves as being democratic. The point of highlighting this difference and variety of self-described democracies is to underline the limitations of democracy as a political category when the word is simply taken on its face. A thick definition of democracy is required. A thin one is an invitation to abuse of the word so as to deprive it of meaning.

In substance, when one speaks of democracy, one generally means a system of overall government and political arrangements that represent political choices: fair courts, rule of law, the rights of the individual are protected, government by representatives, and so on. This is thick democracy.

Democracy, in its bare-bones and literal sense, in contrast, is a simple method of political choosing. It is not necessarily determinative of any particular political choice. On major questions of political constitution, such as the question of the rights of individuals, the scope of the state, and even the fundamentals of law and order, the democratic method of nominating rulers is silent. A state may have the outward semblance of democratic institutions, such as elections, without respecting the rights of the population, of individuals, and without orienting its purpose toward encouraging the happiness, justice, or flourishing of its people.

In this regard, a thin democracy's formal aim is merely upholding the integrity and legitimacy of the state and its governing institutions via episodic elections. A state in which the *demos*, the people, is *kratos*, or strongest merely and thus insufficiently implies a political constitution of majority rule.[48]

Majority rule would prove in the second half of the twentieth century not to suffice as an adequate criterion for determining whether a country was substantively democratic. There would be too many self-described democracies where basic rights of citizens were not taken into account. The word itself could not suffice as a code for the series of political goods that it represented to so many in the wake of the Second World War. Berenson had not fully thought these questions through. For Berenson in 1948, the word "democracy" was enough.

---

[48] See Aristotle, *Politics*, Book III.

INGATHERING

Berenson's Declaration pointed to an explicitly Jewish positive aim: drawing on the history of Zionist thought, Berenson emphasized the importance of remedying the "curse of exile" as another substantive aim of the state. The curse of exile had been a key theme of modern Zionism, starting particularly with Leon Pinsker, the founder of *Hovevei Zion* (the *Lovers of Zion*) and author of the seminal text, *Auto-Emancipation*.[49] For Pinsker, life in the Diaspora, life as wanderers, had taken a terrible toll on Jews – they were walking "ghosts" in his strident terminology; absent self-rule, even Jewish learning was empty formalism and legalism.[50] Only a restoration of national self-rule would in his view make the Jews a vibrant people again. The "ingathering of the exiles" would be the means of ending not just the recurring physical devastation and emotional heartbreak brought on by persecution in the Diaspora, but also what Pinsker saw as the political and sociological curse of diaspora. This was one face of the "ingathering of the exiles" to which Berenson's text refers.

But there was also a more trenchant and immediate reference. A state of ingathering of exiles would also be a means for bringing the masses of Jews then resident in refugee camps in Europe to the new Jewish national home. The Second World War had ravaged the society of European Jewry from which the Labor Zionist leadership largely hailed. Between one half to three quarters of European Jewry had been murdered.[51] The suffering had occurred on a scale of cruelty and grotesque exceeding anything seen before. Children and the elderly were killed in such numbers that it came to be possible to speak of humans being exterminated. Men and women were worked to emaciated and weakened form and then left to perish from their starvation and illness or killed when their economic utility waned, to be replaced with new slave labor in a senseless spiral of enslavement and slaughter. Others were simply murdered en masse by the Nazi army and its accomplices, which created special military units of death and later even industrial factories of death to more rapidly kill Jews.[52] This had been the fate of European Jewry who fell under the rule of the Third Reich.

---

[49] "Auto-Emancipation" (London: Association of Youth Zionist Societies, 1932).

[50] Marc Volovici, "Leon Pinsker's Autoemancipation! and the Emergence of German as a Language of Jewish Nationalism," *Central European History*, 50, 1, 2017, p. 51.

[51] https://encyclopedia.ushmm.org/content/en/article/remaining-jewish-population-of-europe-in-1945

[52] Adam Tooze, *The Wages of Destruction* (New York: Penguin, 2008).

After the Third Reich's fall, Europe still teemed with Jewish refugees, people who could not or more often and understandably would not return to the places of residence from which their neighbors had in many cases sent them to perish as slaves or worse. All of this bears on the question of the ingathering of the exiles. And yet astonishingly, unlike Beham's draft and the final drafts of the Declaration, Berenson's text does not mention the *Shoah*.

The context for eliding the Holocaust, and referring only instead to the ingathering of the exiles, would have touched deep chords in the *Yishuv*. For the earlier opening of Palestine to immigration could have averted this horror and genocide at least to some degree. Some ratio of the deaths may have been averted had there been somewhere for the targets of the Holocaust to flee. These wounds, which still feel fresh today, were open and gaping in 1948. The human toll could be seen via a quick tour of the Displaced Persons camps of Europe – from which the British administrators of Palestine were still preventing immigration to Palestine.[53] And, in this way, the ingathering of the exiles was more than Zionist dialectics. It was a family matter for nearly every household in Jewish Palestine.

Expressed here by Berenson, and again by David Ben-Gurion in the final draft of Israel's Declaration, the principle of ingathering exiles articulated the aim of the Jewish state to ingather the Jews within a single national community – an initiative whose necessity had been demonstrated by the terror experienced by Jews around the world over the prior decade. The Law of Return, the law of the state that grants immediate citizenship to any Jew who moves to Israel, became the most practical manifestation of this. David Ben-Gurion famously, and publicly, went further, denying the legitimacy of a Jewish Diaspora.[54] As far as the future of the Jewish people was concerned, it was Israel or nothing for him.

Practically speaking, ending the curse of exile meant the abolition of the White Paper of 1939. A casual reader might wonder why Berenson's text references the abolition of a policy white paper in what purports to be a document of national founding. The White Paper of 1939 was a policy paper issued by the British Government strictly limiting Jewish immigration to 75,000, plus another 25,000 "emergency cases" over the next five years. It made future immigration subject to approval by the Arab majority. The document was widely seen as a treacherous betrayal of the Jews

---

[53] See the National Film Board of Canada film *Memorandum*, Donald Brittain and John Spotton, 1965. www.nfb.ca/film/memorandum/

[54] Avraham Avihai, "Israelocentrism: A Guiding Doctrine of David Ben Gurion," *Proceedings of the World Congress of Jewish Studies*, 1973, pp. 355–366.

of Europe, who were already living in grave fear in 1939 following the persecution of the Jews of Germany and Austria over the prior three years. It was also a reversal of the Balfour Declaration of 1917, which had pledged British support for the establishment of a Jewish national home in Palestine.[55]

Limiting immigration during the Holocaust, the White Paper became a catalyst for the revolt against British rule in Palestine in the 1940s, undertaken principally by Revisionist Zionist groups at first, and joined to a certain degree by the Labor establishment after the war.[56] Revoking the White Paper, opening the gates of the state to Jewish immigration, was to be a defining feature of renewed Jewish sovereignty.

BORDERS

Berenson also addressed the borders of the state. His text proclaimed the establishment of "a Jewish, free, independent, and democratic state in the land of Israel, within the borders delineated by the General Assembly of the United Nations." This was an issue avoided by Beham and, perhaps not coincidentally, also absent from the Declaration of Independence of the United States. It would also prove to a be a subject that David Ben-Gurion would elect to elide in the final draft of Israel's Declaration. Why?

First there was a legal component. UN Resolution 181 promised to give the Jews control over the coastal plane, a corridor to the Sea of Galilee, as well as much of the Negev Desert.[57] To the lawyer Berenson, it was vital that the legal text establishing the state accord with the legal framework brining the state into being: Resolution 181.

There was an ideological component as well. The borders of a potential Jewish state in the Middle East had been a highly contested issue since the Balfour Declaration of 1917, not only as a matter of international politics and diplomacy, but among the Jews themselves. In its latest version, on November 29, 1947, the leaders of the *Yishuv* had publicly accepted UN Resolution 181 in all its dimensions. This became a rallying cry on the left and center left. In contrast, the Revisionist movement, led by Menachem Begin, held to the idea that only sovereignty over both sides of the Jordan River would create a viable state for the future.

[55] Martin Gilbert, *Israel* (London: Harper, 1998), p. 34, 97.
[56] Tom Segev, *A State at Any Cost: The Life of David Ben-Gurion*, trans. Haim Watzman, (New York: Farrar, Straus, & Giroux, 2019), p. 281.
[57] Ibid., p. 665.

On November 30, 1947, Begin declared in a radio address that partition of the land was illegal.[58] The conflict between Labor and Revisionists in its final phase before the founding of the state featured the politics of borders prominently.

As much as the politicians and ideologues might have squabbled, and as much as the diplomats might have sought ingenious compromises, the precise borders, as borders always are, would be determined by the force of arms.[59] Immediately after November 29, Arabs in Palestine began the so-called civil war stage of the War of Independence, more reasonably thought of simply as a war, recognizing no distinction between areas granted to a future Jewish state they rejected and a future Arab state they hoped would come into being. Violence was visited upon those bearing arms on behalf of the *Yishuv* and civilians alike.[60] Even as David Ben-Gurion had publicly accepted the UN Resolution, including its borders, he noted, in his capacity as de-facto commander-in-chief, that all Jewish settlements would have to be defended in the coming war. "We shall not restrict ourselves territorially," he told staff officers before the UN vote.[61]

SOVEREIGNTY OF THE PEOPLE VERSUS SOVEREIGNTY OF THE STATE

Berenson's text reoriented the source of sovereignty from the people to the state itself. Mordechai Beham's text had evoked the right to life, liberty, and pursuit of happiness for the Jewish people. His text, in its recasting of the American Declaration, had said that to secure the "separate and equal station" that the laws of nature and of nature's God afford to the Jewish people, governments are established, drawing their legitimacy from the consent of the governed.

Rights belong to the people, and the state is constrained or oriented in its purpose toward securing those rights through the "consent of the governed." The state in this view is thus oriented toward the rights of individuals and the rights of the citizens.

---

[58] Daniel Gordis, *Menachem Begin* (New York: Schocken, 2014), p. 69.

[59] Avi Shlaim, "Britain and the Arab-Israeli War of 1948," *Journal of Palestine Studies*, 16, 4, 1987, p. 55.

[60] Uri Milstein, *History of Israel's War of Independence*, vol. 1, trans. Alan Sacks, (Washington, DC: University Press of America, 1998). On the reasons not to refer to this as a "Civil War," see Segev, *One Palestine, Complete* (New York: Henry Holt, 2000), p. 501.

[61] Martin Gilbert, *Israel*, p. 149.

Berenson, in contrast, speaks of "the rights and privileges that the laws of nature and international law grant to independent states." This peculiar locution stresses exclusively the rights of states; the law of nature and international law grants *states* rights and privileges. This is the exact opposite of the original use of this locution in the American Declaration of Independence. Nothing is said about the natural rights of the citizens who are to make up that state.

One might say that the work that "consent of the governed" does for Beham, and, for that matter, for the American Declaration of Independence, is fulfilled by the word "democratic" which Berenson introduces to describe the state. This, alas, does not suffice: the term democracy must be characterized to give it meaning.

In fairness to Berenson, this statist shift was not entirely his doing. The echoes of Beham's draft in his own imply that Berenson's work must have been connected to that initial effort – whether seen by Berenson or not. What can be said with certainty is that Berenson's connection to Beham's work was mediated by the work of the *Yishuv*'s Legal Department in Tel Aviv. These lawyers too had a say. And it is to the changes that they made to Beham's document that we will now turn.

THE WORK OF THE LEGAL DEPARTMENT

Tzvi Berenson's innovations were not the first "re-drafting" of relevance after the work of Beham.[62] Between April 27 and May 4, a team of staffers in the Legal Department, which included Beham, reviewed, revised, and redrafted Beham's initial efforts. This group produced at least four further drafts, two of which were likely internal provisional drafts for office use only.[63] The team made extensive and fundamental edits to Beham's original rather than writing drafts from scratch.[64]

Until May 4, Beham himself was involved in the process. The archives contain copies of Beham's first draft heavily redacted and commented upon by Beham and Uri Heinsheimer a number of days following his completion of his work citing Jefferson.[65] In crafting his first draft over a Sabbath away from the office, as the story goes, Mordechai Beham had

---

[62] Indeed, we do not know whether Felix Rosenblüth ever saw the first draft of Israel's Declaration written by Mordechai Beham.

[63] Copies in 5664/20/ʌ

[64] Yoram Shachar, "Ha'teyotot ha'mukdamot shel hakhrazat ha'atzmaut," pp. 545–551.

[65] Ibid.

been influenced by or inspired by the American Rabbi Harry Davidowitz or at least his library.

When he was back in the Legal Department office, Beham was one member of a team of legal bureaucrats, the most important of whom were Uri Heinsheimer and Moshe Zilberg.[66] Over the next week, these three would edit, draft, and redraft Israel's Declaration. It is difficult, and perhaps impossible, to delineate the specific roles of each of these three in this process. Yet it is clear that, at this juncture, Heinsheimer and Zilberg took on a role as significant – and probably greater – than that of Mordechai Beham.

Beham's new collaborators had extremely German legal educations. Heinsheimer, born Rudolph in Baden-Baden, was from an upper middle-class German family which included doctors and lawyers. He studied law at Heidelberg and elsewhere. He would go on to have a distinguished career in Israel's legal bureaucracy and the Faculty of Law at the Hebrew University.[67]

Like Berenson, Moshe Zilberg would himself ascend to the Supreme Court, serving from 1950 until 1970.[68] Born a religious Jew and raised in the Litvak traditions of Jewish legalistic study, Zilberg's family moved to Germany in 1920 and he studied philosophy and law at Marburg.[69] Friends with the most prominent poet of the Jewish world in the first half of the twentieth century Haim Nachman Bialik, and author of a popular series of lectures on the Talmud, in 1964 Zilberg would win the Israel Prize for Jurisprudence.[70] Both Heinsheimer and Zilberg were on the cusp of careers at the pinnacle of the Israeli legal profession in 1948. Mordechai Beham would return to private practice.

On April 27, the first formal draft of the Declaration produced by the Legal Department based on Beham's original and incorporating revisions made with Heinsheimer was typed up in Hebrew with the title "First Proposal."[71] This first proposal retains strong similarity with Beham's draft. This proposal still begins with God's promise to Abraham, Isaac, and Jacob.

---

[66] Copies in 5664/20/ב.

[67] On Yadin's life and work, *Sefer Uri Yadin*, ed. Aharon Barak and Tana Spanitz (Jerusalem: Bursi), 1990.

[68] Nir Kedar, "Democracy and Judicial Autonomy in Israel's Early Years," *Israel Studies*, 15, 1, 2010, p. 30.

[69] For Zilberg's see, see the Touro College encyclopedia on the founders of Israel. Tidhar, D. (1947), *Entsiklopedyah le-halutse ha-yishuv u-vonav* (vol. 2, p. 1027).

[70] Ibid.

[71] The copy in the archive exists only with further redactions toward the second draft.

Yet it also cuts away at references to the Anglo-American political tradition. Beham had cited the English Bill of Rights to assert the "true, ancient, and indubitable right of the Jewish People to reconstitute their state in this Holy Land." In the April 27 "First Proposal" this is replaced by a somewhat bland statement to the effect that "the Jewish people never abandoned their right to establish anew their state in the land of Israel." The crucial phrase asserting the natural rights of *individuals* – "to secure these rights, governments are established among men, deriving their just power from the consent of the governed" – is likewise dropped.

This "First Proposal" also cuts the enumeration of what free and independent states may do: the responsibility of the state to pursue national wealth and military might. It retains "Life," "liberty," and "happiness" as goals of independence, but cuts out the *pursuit* of happiness. This ambiguous locution would not and could not last. For it leaves unclear whether the state must *guarantee* happiness or whether it must merely allow individuals to pursue it. The locus of happiness in this strange formulation seems to be found in the state itself, rather than, as in Beham's text and Jefferson's before it, for the individuals who had consented to form a state to protect their natural rights.

The "First Proposal" does still refer to "representatives of world Jewry" as the source of legitimate representation for the Declaration. Yet it distinguishes between world Jewry and the representatives of the "Jewish settlement in the land of Israel." Berenson would take the next step of removing the representation of world Jewry in the Declaration of the state all together.

On May 4, after a week of further debate, cuts, and edits, a "Second Proposal" was typed up by the Legal Department. If the "First Proposal" was a significant modification of Beham's first draft, this "Second Proposal" should be understood as a total transformation. Gone completely are any reference to the Bible or the Anglo-American texts. Foreshadowing Berenson's draft, the text simply cites a "historical connection" of the Jews to the land, beginning as follows: "Whereas the Jewish people has, from its very beginnings, been connected historically to the land of Israel . . . ."

The draft goes on to assert simply that Jews maintained a connection to the land through their exile and dispersion. It continues by stating that the Jews have begun to build their state anew over the past few generations. The Labor Zionist effort of rebuilding is thus given pride of place. Beham's reference to the Holocaust is dropped. The work that Berenson would build upon commences. It seems almost assured that Berenson looked at and worked from drafts in this lineage.

Both the "First Proposal" and "Second Proposal" rely heavily on bureaucratic language both new and borrowed. Much of the text of the "Second Proposal" is given over to a quotation of the UN Security Council resolution authorizing a Jewish state in Palestine. In this draft, the November 29, 1947, act of the UN seems to serve as the single most important justification for the establishment of a new state. The "Second Proposal" also fails to mention world Jewry. The authors of the text are said to be the "representatives of the Zionist movement in the Diaspora and the *Yishuv* in the land of Israel."

A few other drafts were produced by the Legal Department, but the changes were minor. By the time Tzvi Berenson set to work on May 4, the *Yishuv* was already a long way away from Mordechai Beham's afternoon in the library with Harry Davidowitz.

BERENSON AS SPOKESPERSON FOR LABOR

It is not at all surprising that drafters of Israel's Declaration of Independence would turn in the first instance to Labor Zionism in establishing the principles and intellectual roots of the state. The *Yishuv*'s dominant ideology was Labor Zionism, and so Labor Zionist ideas would permeate the founding document of the modern state of Israel. To be sure, labor ideology was not the only going ideological enterprise in the *Yishuv*. It faced division within its own ranks, spawning a multitude of contending Labor Zionist political parties. And there was competition from the Revisionist Zionist movement, religious Zionism, and, most implacably, the traditionalism of most new immigrants to Palestine and then Israel after the Second *Aliyah*.[72]

Leading Labor Zionist political figures compromised with traditional Jewish beliefs, economic practices, and other political sensibilities existing in the *Yishuv* and among the Jewish people more generally. Indeed, it might be said of Ben-Gurion that his labor ideology was by 1948 largely subsumed by and subordinate to his general Zionism. Yet in ways both large and subtle, the ideological patina of Labor Zionism suffused and would continue to suffuse many of the institutions and mores of the *Yishuv* and then the state of Israel in its early decades.[73]

---

[72] Cf. Lily Weissbrod on the ideological "routinization" of Labor ideology. "From Labour Zionism to New Zionism: Ideological Change in Israel," *Theory and Society*, 10, 6, 1981, p. 778.

[73] See Neil Rogachevsky, "The Not-So-Strange Death of Labor Zionism," *American Affairs*, 4, 3, 2020; and Ze'ev Sternhell, *The Founding Myths of Israel*.

Tzvi Berenson was very much a member in good standing of the Labor Zionist elite. As the legal advisor for the *Histadrut* national labor union in 1948, Tzvi Berenson was one of the *Yishuv*'s most significant lawyers in one of its most significant institutions. Many *Histadrut* leaders would go on to populate the upper echelons of every part of the political institutions and bureaucracy down to the 2000s at least.[74]

As a young man, Berenson had started out as an intern in Felix Rosenblüth's private law practice, stayed on as a lawyer, and had remained in touch with Rosenblüth through the years.[75] In these weeks of April and May, Berenson had been informally loaned by the *Histadrut* to the Legal Department in order to assist Rosenblüth with various legal tasks.[76] During the time that Mordechai Beham had been working on his draft of the Declaration, Berenson had been working on other legal matters of immediate political or economic concern, particularly setting up national insurance schemes for the new state.[77]

Berenson was one of the few Palestine-born individuals who participated in the process of creating Israel's Declaration of Independence. Born in Tsfat in 1907, he studied in yeshiva there as a young man but was increasingly drawn to secular and technical subjects, specifically physics and mathematics, which he studied at the Scots College in Tsfat.[78] In 1931, he matriculated as an affiliated student at Jesus College, Cambridge, where he enrolled in the famed 'mathematical tripos' course, receiving his BA in 1933.[79] Subsequently he took up law and was admitted to the bar as a barrister. When he returned to Palestine, he joined the law firm led by Rosenblüth.

Following the founding of the state, Berenson served on the Supreme Court starting in 1954 until reaching the mandatory retirement age of 70 in 1977.[80] Working on public sector arbitration in his later years, he was counted among the elder sages of Israeli law until his death in 2001.[81]

In 1948, Berenson had done the work that his history and community had asked of him. He reflected as much in his own account of his drafting

---

[74] Samy Cohen, "Politiques Et Généraux En Israël Aux 20 E Et 21 E Siècles," *Vingtième Siècle. Revue D'histoire*, 124, 2014, pp. 99–110.
[75] Yoram Shachar, "Ha'teyotot ha'mukdamot shel hakhrazat ha'atzmaut," pp. 560–561.
[76] Ibid.   [77] Ibid.
[78] University of Cambridge Archives, UA Graduati 12/20, Exam. L.47.   [79] Ibid.
[80] For Berenson's biography, see *Sefer Tzvi Berenson*, in particular Berenson's own "Perkei hayyim vezikhronot" ("Chapters of Life and Souvenirs"), in ed. Aharon Barak and Hayyim Berenson (Jerusalem: 1997), pp. 29–81.
[81] Aharon Barak, "Human Rights in Israel," *Israel Law Review*, 39, 2, 2006, pp. 12–34.

of the Declaration. In a monograph published in honor of the fortieth anniversary of the state, titled *Declaration of Independence: Vision and Reality*, Berenson reflected on his role in 1948:

In the limited time that I had, and under the difficult conditions of the time, I was unable to acquire and to make comparisons between other declarations of independence and constitutions of other countries. Even the UN declaration on the partition of the land of Israel into two states – Jewish and Arab – I did not have in front of me. I thought it was necessary to prepare a short, succinct statement that would ground the rights of the people of Israel to the land of Israel in light of its historical connection to the land and the recognition of the nations of this right; that would declare the foundational principles upon which the regime of the state and the life of its citizens would be based; and that would fix the first ruling institutions of the state.[82]

Berenson's recollection is of course overstated. Clearly he was working with the help of the Legal Department's prior drafts and with the text of Rubashov's pronouncement. But the larger point holds. He intended to put "the foundational principles upon which the regime of the state and the life of its citizens would be based" into the text. He reached for foundational principles that were familiar. He found them in the Labor Zionism of the *Yishuv* in 1948 and UN Resolution 181. And he wrote them into Israel's Declaration of Independence.

CONCLUSION: LABOR VERSUS NATURAL RIGHTS

The "foundational principles" upon which Berenson sought to ground "the regime of the state and the life of its citizens" were twofold: labor on the one hand, and the political consensus of the post-war West on the other.

It was altogether fitting that labor as seen through the prism of the achievements of the pioneers would be recognized at the founding of the state. With Israel approaching the status of a modern state in 1948, it was without question that the work of pioneers was a basis for political independence. They had built viable new settlements across the country, institutional structures of a proto-state including military forces, unions, and even organs of government. They had built or revitalized old and new cities. One thinks in particular of Tel Aviv, whose first stone was laid on an empty patch of sand north of Jaffa in 1907 and had by 1948 grown to be an

---

[82] Tzvi Berenson, *Declaration of Independence* (State of Israel Publications, 1988), p. 6.

urban center not so different at the time from San Diego, albeit somewhat less well off. Likewise, the building of the foundational neighborhoods of what would become West Jerusalem such as Rehavia.[83] Massive capital and charitable efforts driven by philanthropists were of course essential to these enterprises.[84] Yet the deed to the new lands would have ultimately proved unenforceable without the immigrants themselves there to work, possess, and protect the land as Berenson wrote.

Labor, too, was an ideology. It is hard to imagine a school of thought or set of ideas that could have animated as large a swath of Europe's Jewry to migrate to Palestine and undertake the hardships of breaking empty ground. On the face of things, Labor Zionism was a counterpart for the idealistic nationalisms of Europe that galvanized diffuse towns to form modern nations. The challenge of accomplishing this feat for a Jewish people spread across different lands and with no experience of the type of frontier-breaking labor and migration required to build Palestine into a modern state is today difficult to conceive. This ideological function was surely one of the accomplishments of the myth of labor.

But Labor Zionism's ideological utility was broader. It cut through the religious disputes and expectations that had hindered prior efforts to gather the Jewish people in Palestine. It replaced this dispute over religious points with an appeal to the socialism that promised, but would fail to deliver, liberation for oppressed minorities from the monarchs and emperors of Central and Eastern Europe and Russia. It took socialism, the ideological vogue of the early twentieth century in these lands, and oriented the spirits that it animated among Jews toward the building of a Jewish state in Palestine – even as many of the socialist Zionist groups themselves denied any connection to Judaism. It is among history's ironies that socialism and organization in unions and socialist ideal communities did in fact prove to be a source of liberation for the Jews of the Pale of Settlement and Russia. But this was only the case in geographic Palestine.

Here we find the core insight of Labor Zionism. Labor and the solidarity of labor could be a tool for the freeing of the Jews; but it would only be the case if their labor was organized toward the national goal of building a state in Palestine.

---

[83] Michael Seelig and Julie Seelig, "Architecture and Politics in Israel: 1920 to the Present," *Journal of Architectural and Planning Research*, 5, 1, 1988, pp. 35–48.

[84] Abigail Green, "Rethinking Sir Moses Montefiore: Religion, Nationhood, and International Philanthropy in the Nineteenth Century," *The American Historical Review*, 110, 3, 2005, pp. 631–658.

Hidden reversals seem to adhere to the politics of ideology. It would turn out that in this most socialist of milieus – the Declaration of Independence of the Labor Zionist state – the arguments of John Locke for the primacy of property would win out. Berenson's arguments, even if not explicitly in the text and perhaps even if the text aspired to its opposite, were torn from John Locke in his *Second Treatise*: Berenson in effect argued that cultivation of the land is 99 percent of ownership.[85]

Of course this must be distinguished from the argument that might makes right. Here, the use-case, the outcome, the flourishing of the polity, makes right. This accords with the actual work of cultivation and protection that was an essential ingredient in the Zionist enterprise – as it is in any state or political enterprise. Buying up land in Palestine would not have been enough to create a state, just as the vast colonial territorial claims of France and Spain in North America could not withstand the confrontation with the activity of the American settlers in what we now call the United States. If Jewish pioneers had not actually been willing to move to Palestine and build it up, no national home could have been declared, or rather, the declaration would have been meaningless.

These ideas were in profound tension with the core socialist *zeitgeist* which prevailed in the *Yishuv*. There were *kibbutzim* where portraits of Marx and Trotsky and even Stalin had pride of place in the communal dining hall; but none with portraits of John Locke and first editions of the *Treatises of Government*. Even the name John Locke was foreign in the *Yishuv*, and in an interesting twist, the *Two Treatises of Government* were not even available in Hebrew until 1948.[86]

The two intellectual edifices do not fit. Possession and cultivation as a title to ownership defended by the tower and the stockade – the argument in practice of Labor Zionism – is intellectually difficult to fit with a world of universal brotherhood and the abolition of ownership – the world of Marx and even of later European democratic socialism. And an intellectual edifice of this nature, constructed of classical arguments of liberalism combined with the rhetoric of early twentieth-century Marxism, a house divided on itself, could not and would not stand. Lockean and Marxian conceptions of property in one document make, to say the least, for strange and uncomfortable bedfellows. As the first principles for a state that would require legal and political recourse to first principles, as the intellectual bedrock of Israel, they are almost impossible to hold together.

---

[85] John Locke, *Two Treatises of Government*, p. 293.
[86] Translated by Yosef Or, Magnus Press, 1948.

And so, as we will see in a later chapter on the jurisprudence that has flowed from the Declaration of Independence, the doctrines and the realities would continue to raise questions.

There is also the matter of what Berenson emphasized unwittingly from the Lockean tradition – and what was omitted. By the time Berenson's document was sent up the bureaucratic chain, the Declaration had been stripped of any semblance of the discourse of the inherent rights of individuals. Between the lawyers at the Legal Department and the work of Berenson, the rights to "life, liberty, and the pursuit of happiness" that proved a durable guidepost in the United States, and the "indubitable and ancient rights" that had steered free townspeople in England since the end of feudalism – these had been cast aside.

One might charitably argue that this might have been because Berenson and the other lawyers were confident that a constitution would follow: the UN demanded it, and work toward it had begun within the *Yishuv*. But there are limits to this argument. Berenson inserted an entirely different and new "rights tradition" and argument for rights. He had inserted the conceptions of positive rights and duties taken from Roosevelt's Four Freedoms and from the Charter of the United Nations in their stead.

This would prove to be a most fateful change but one that in hindsight was if not inevitable at least probable. For where else in the world in 1948 was the discourse of natural rights and the effort to return to the fundamental principles of political right prevalent? Who were the philosophers who steered minds toward the perpetual enquiry into the uncovering of the fundamentals of human nature and the political lessons that could be derived from such an exercise? And where in the settlements of the *Yishuv* behind the stockade and the tower could such an initiative be found? It was hard enough to find this at Oxford or Cambridge or Harvard or the Hebrew University of Jerusalem or the University of Chicago in 1948. Somehow a connection to this tradition had made itself manifest in Beham's text.

Instead, Berenson went where the times had taken him: to the Four Freedoms, the UN, and the discourse of democracy. This led him as well to a statism that endowed sovereignty in the state and not the individual. He had diplomatic and political motivations. Above all, the declarers of Israeli independence were hoping to ground their legitimacy against international claimants who might deny it. The state had to be seen as legitimate in international ciricles.

Alas, in offering this view, Berenson presented no limiting principle to the state. The state is necessarily, though not sufficiently, a fruitful way of advancing the safety, happiness, and independence of individuals. Surely one cannot imagine these things without a state. Absolute libertarianism exists in the world in the lawless lands of the failed states – no one wishes that upon themselves. Liberty properly understood is freedom under laws that themselves have a limited scope and are enforced impartially – but are enforced by a state.

Berenson's draft does not seek to orient the state toward the purpose of securing natural rights. The state is an aim in itself. It can do what it wants. Its only limit is ultimately democracy, the will of the people to use the state. The frequent complaints in subsequent Israeli history of a bureaucratic government typified by a lack of accountability, poor decision making, and neglect for liberty and liberties – this species of complaint has a comfortable home in the type of framework that Berenson formulated.

Until the unearthing of Mordechai Beham's draft of the Declaration, it was thought that Tzvi Berenson's ideas were the only options on the table, the only realistic considerations being made for a declaration of independence at the beginning of the founding moment. Berenson's articulation of Labor Zionism's core was thought to be the ur-text and the prism through which the later work for the rooting of the state of Israel had to be viewed. In this way, the discovery of Beham's draft casts an even more exact and stark light on the positive choices that Berenson made. It shows us that the path that the Legal Department, Berenson, and later the leaders of the *Yishuv* would take was not the only path.

AFTERWARD: IDEALS AND REALITY ("TO THE ARABS OF THE STATE ...")

One hallmark of Berenson's text is its articulation of a vision of harmony between "the *Yishuv* in the land of Israel" and both "Arabs in the Jewish state" and "the peoples of the Arab countries" to whom it addresses distinct messages: it calls for civic comity among the state's citizens and aspires to peace and cooperation between Israel and its Arab neighbors. Berenson wrote:

We call especially to the Arabs in the Jewish state to cooperate as citizens bearing equal rights and duties, extend our hands in peace and brotherhood to the peoples of the Arab countries, and look forward to the assistance of all nations.

The commendable ideal of fraternity and common citizenship articulated in Berenson's text echoed language in the pronouncement by Zalman

Rubashov which Berenson had drawn upon – only Rubashov had been more florid. He had added:

To the Arabs of the state and to our neighbors around us ... We are the nation of peace and to build peace did we come here. We will rise and build our nation as equal citizens equal in rights and equal in duties .... Our freedom is the daughter of your freedom, and in the rightness of our partnership shall we bring its blessing to all of the land's inhabitants and neighbors.

These sentiments encapsulated the consensus stance of the leadership of the *Yishuv* on the eve of its independence. Bechor Sheetrit, a politician from the *Sepharadim v'Edot ha'Mizrakh* party, was a future minister of police and the lone Sephardic member of *Minhelet ha'Am*. On May 10, in his capacity as the member of *Minhelet ha'Am* responsible for Arab affairs, he would compose an official memorandum on "The Arab Problem." It covered the issue of wartime conduct with respect to the future state's Arabs. The memorandum seems to have been written at the suggestion of David Ben-Gurion in light of concern regarding army behavior towards Arab populations.[87]

The memo is notable for its civility amidst the violence of wartime. It sets out policy regarding Arabs living in territory that falls under control of *Yishuv* forces. Arabs in the new state will have "equal civil rights." Leaders must conduct themselves so as "to maintain fair and proper relations with those who had stayed or who will want to stay among us or return among us." If, in the course of the war, "criminal deeds" have already transpired, they must be addressed and future misdeeds stopped.[88] This is but one of countless examples of this sentiment expressed at the highest levels of government at the time. It shows the government's policies virtually mirroring Berenson's and Rubashov's ideals.

Policy, alas, is seldom the full extent of reality. Sheetrit's memo itself pointed to the significant numbers of Arab refugees fleeing the *Yishuv*'s territory through April 1948. This would continue as 1948 unfolded, culminating in the Palestinian refugee crisis. This subject remains among the most hotly litigated of historiographical disputes to this day. We do not address its history or causes here. To do so would involve either writing a new historiographical book summarizing the vast scholarship

[87] Bechor Sheetrit, "Memorandum of the Ministry for Minority Affairs," May 10, 1948, Quoted in Benny Morris, *The Birth of the Palestinian Refugee Problem Revisited* (Cambridge: Cambridge University Press, 2004), p. 170.

[88] Benny Morris, *The Birth of the Palestinian Refugee Crisis Revisited*, p. 170.

in the field or treating the subject partially and inadequately in a few paragraphs that would inevitably fail to do it justice.[89]

What is not disputed is that there was a meaningful refugee crisis by the end of the war. The Israeli government estimated that 520,000–530,000 Arab refugees were created by the war. The UN estimated 726,000, the British 711,000–766,000 (depending on classification of illegal residents under the British Mandate and other complex differences in definition). Estimates from Arab sources range all the way up to 1,000,000. The rough assessment: at war's end, two thirds of the refugees were resident in either the West Bank or Gaza after fleeing their homes before or during the war, with the remainder having mainly moved to Jordan, Syria, Lebanon, and Egypt.

The estimates of the total quantity of refugees, even as they vary quite widely, are notable for their rough consensus on the essence of the issue: a large refugee population in the context of the total Arab population resident in the territory that became Israel was created by the war. As compared to these numbers, between 102,000 and 120,000 Arabs remained in the territory of the State of Israel after the 1949 armistice, and roughly 35,000 refugees returned in the period that immediately followed.[90]

As the war drew on and took a grim toll on the new state of Israel, ultimately killing slightly less than 1 percent and wounding nearly 2 percent of the Jewish population, the mood of the new state's leadership hardened against the repatriation of the Arab refugees. The refugees were born of a war which their communital leadership had started upon the passage of UN Resolution 181 – a resolution calling for Arab and Jewish states to coexist in peace. The flight occurred sometimes well in advance of battles, sometimes amidst military action, sometimes in war's wake following *Yishuv* successes. Throughout the war, the *Yishuv*'s political leadership rejected a policy of expelling the Arab population and went to some lengths to speak out against such a course, even as, at an operational and tactical level, its military action, itself authorized by the *Yishuv*'s

---

[89] While the standard work is Benny Morris's *The Birth of the Palestinian Refugee Crisis Revisited*, since its publication in 2004, additional materials have come to light which add texture to the study, and a vivid literature of "micro histories" relating particular incidents in the war continues to add complexity and nuance to the account.

[90] Benny Morris, *The Birth of the Palestinian Refugee Crisis Revisited*, p. 603, cf. Efraim Karsh, "How Many Palestinian Arab Refugees Were There?" *Israel Affairs*, 17, 2, 2011, pp. 224–246.

political leadership, led to, sometimes encouraged, and even occasionally directly precipitated refugee flight.[91]

The bulk of the refugees were what most refugees are: refugees fleeing a warzone, in this case, a warzone created by the Arab attack against the *Yishuv* following the passage of UN Resolution 181, but increasingly typified by successful Jewish counterattack. In some regions, the vast majority of the Arab population became refugees; in others, very few, as Israel's large Arab community both after the war and until today attest. Like in any war, military documents offer a record of contrasts: cruelty and kindness, humanity and bureaucratic coldness, inspiration and despair. The extent of the refugee movement shocked the leadership of *Yishuv*. Ben-Gurion, perplexed by the emptiness of Arab Jaffa upon its fall to *Yishuv* forces, did not know what to make of it.[92]

As the war progressed, the overall return of the refugees to Israel became inconceivable to the country's leadership. Proposals to that effect seemed to them to be an impossibility mid-war. How could the hostile refugee population be reincorporated in the middle of hostilities? It risked introducing an opposing force mid-war. And there was opportunism. The war was turning in favor of the *Yishuv* and the borders of the state were expanding.[93] Of course, there were Jewish refugees and evacuees from the warzones too, though the numbers are comparatively small, if still surprisingly significant. Estimates are 60,000–70,000.[94]

---

[91] Ibid., pp. 588–601.

[92] Benny Morris has argued that this issue must be analyzed in the context of the global history of war, the violent and total nature of the wars of the 1940s, the stated war aims of the Arabs and Jews, the operational and tactical imperatives of the war, and the context of terrible violence against civilians that the Jews of the *Yishuv* had experienced during the 1920s, 1930s, and through 1947–1948. Seen in that light, the record of Jewish leadership regarding Arab civilians, prisoners of war, and wartime conduct, while not without failures, blemishes, and corruptions, bears no comparison to the war records of any of the major powers during the 1940s. But the war record also reflects a greater truth: war. See Benny Morris, *1948*, pp. 392–420.

[93] Benny Morris, *The Birth of the Palestinian Refugee Crisis Revisited*, pp. 309–340.

[94] There would be a much larger flow of Jewish refugees from Arab lands, though this did not begin in earnest until well after the end of the war. An estimated 260,000 Jews ultimately left Arab countries between 1948 and 1951. See Colin Shindler, *A History of Modern Israel* (Cambridge: Cambridge University Press, 2008), pp. 63–64. All told, by the end of the twentieth century, more than 600,000 Jews had migrated, often under great duress, from Arab countries to Israel. On the numbers, see Carole Basri, "The Jewish Refugees from Arab Countries: An Examination of Legal Rights – A Case Study of the Human Rights Violations of Iraqi Jews," *Fordham International Law Journal*, 26, 3, 2002, pp. 656–720. On Jewish evacuees and refugees in the 1948–1949 war, see Nurit Cohen-Levinovsky, *Plitim yehudim be'milhemet ha'atzmaut* (*Jewish Refugees in the War*

At the conclusion of the war, Israel put two offers related to the Arab refugees on the table in its efforts to arrive at peace. The first consisted in the absorption of the encircled Gaza Strip, with its population of approximately 250,000, including roughly 150,000 Arab refugees, as part of a peace arrangement. And when that proposal was rejected, Israel offered to resettle 100,000 refugees as part of a peace treaty. That too was rejected by Arab leaders who were generally uninterested in diplomacy and peace.[95]

Berenson's vision of egalitarian civil rights for Israel's entire population would indeed become reality: Arab legislators were elected in Israel's first parliamentary election in 1949 reflecting the equal citizenship of all Israelis, Jewish or otherwise, in the parts of the state not under military administration. And the military administration of the Galilee, which still preempted the civil rights of some, was abolished in 1966, extending complete civil rights to all – as the Declaration had envisioned.

By the end of the war, perhaps a hand remained extended by Israel to the neighboring Arab states in the spirit of peace, as the sentiments of Rubashov and Berenson had expressed the *Yishuv*'s position in April and May 1948. It was, however, a colder hand in the wake of the casualties and losses in war and the clear rejection of peace overtures.

The ideal of peace between the *Yishuv* and its Arab neighbors found clear expression throughout the founding moment. Language similar to Berenson's would find its way into the Declaration's final text. And Berenson's formulation captured the prevailing view – of worldwide Jewry as embodied in the Zionist Actions Committee, of the *Yishuv*'s ministers serving in *Minhelet ha'Am*, and ultimately of the Declaration itself. But the cruel realities of a war begun by the Arabs of Palestine and their allies against the *Yishuv*, in rejection of the principle of political partition, ensured that these ideals were tested by the most harsh of realities during 1948 – and compelled to make their compromises with it.

---

of Independence) (Am Oved: 2014). Her estimate is that approximately 10 percent of the *Yishuv* population became evacuees or refugees during the war.

[95] Benny Morris, *The Birth of the Palestinian Refugee Crisis Revisited*, pp. 549–587.

4

International Law

Herschel Lauterpacht's Draft

The hope that the nations of the world could be governed by an overarching system of law rose to the forefront in the wake of the horrors of the Second World War. The United Nations Charter promised to ensure that "justice and respect for the obligations arising from treaties and other sources of international law can be maintained."[1] This hope was echoed in the rhetoric of the leaders of its founding states. US President Truman had said upon the signing of the United Nations Charter that:

[t]he Charter of the United Nations which you have just signed is a solid structure upon which we can build a better world .... With this Charter the world can begin to look forward to the time when all worthy human beings may be permitted to live decently as free people.[2]

Truman's rhetoric underscored the broader public narrative: hopes for the peace of the world rested on the success of the endeavors of the United Nations. And among the first major matters brought before the UN was the issue of the British withdrawal from Palestine, ultimately leading on November 29, 1947, to the passage at the UN of Resolution 181 calling for the creation of two states – one Arab and one Jewish.[3]

This chapter relates why that process failed both on a practical and an intellectual level. And it tells the story of the most ambitious effort in the founding of Israel to take the promise and the hope represented by the UN

---

[1] www.un.org/en/charter-united-nations/

[2] Harry Truman, "Address in San Francisco at the Closing Session of the United Nations Conference in San Francisco," June 26, 1945, www.trumanlibrary.gov/library/public-papers/66/address-san-francisco-closing-session-united-nations-conference

[3] https://unispal.un.org/DPA/DPR/unispal.nsf/o/7F0AF2BD897689B785256C330061D253

at face value. It does so by analyzing a draft of Israel's Declaration of Independence written in New York, 9,000 kilometers away from Tel Aviv, by acclaimed international lawyer, human rights activist, and architect of the UN's system of international law Herschel Lauterpacht.

PROFESSOR LAUTERPACHT GOES TO NEW YORK

The arrival of the UN to its preliminary headquarters at Lake Success, NY, in 1946 had brought with it not only an entire diplomatic corps to represent its member countries, but also theorists and legal practitioners to assemble its rules and its various governing procedures. Over the next few years, the UN would rely on a host of internal and external advisors for the task. One of these was a 50-year-old University of Cambridge academic named Herschel Lauterpacht. He had arrived to offer expert counsel to United Nations bureaucrats who were building up the infrastructure of international law within the UN in April 1948.

Born to an Orthodox Jewish family near Lvov in 1897, Lauterpacht was by 1948 one of the world's most respected theorists and practitioners of international law. He had already spent much of 1948 on leave from Cambridge traveling the world as a legal adviser and practitioner. That winter, he had been at the newly-formed International Court of Justice at The Hague. There, as a member of the British Delegation, he participated in the Corfu Channel Case (*United Kingdom* v. *Albania*) which concerned the question of the responsibility of states for damages at sea.

This was the first matter argued in front of the ICJ, and Lauterpacht helped secure a favorable result for the British side.[4] In April, he came to New York as an adviser to the UN International Law Commission which had been established the previous year in order to promote, in line with the idea in the UN Charter, "the codification and progressive development" of international law.[5]

And yet, as so often in Jewish history, chance in the form of family relations intervened. The *Yishuv* had a diplomatic delegation at the United Nations in New York. They had fought for and indeed accomplished the diplomatic coup that was UN Resolution 181 in the fall of 1947, and they remained on hand to continue to advance the *Yishuv*'s cause in the spring

---

[4] Elihu Lauterpacht, *The Life of Hersch Lauterpacht* (Cambridge: Cambridge University Press, 2010), pp. 299–301.
[5] Ibid., p. 301.

of 1948. One member of the delegation was the 33-year-old Aubrey (Abba) Eban, later Israel's Ambassador to the United Nations, Ambassador to the United States, Foreign Minister of Israel, and an accomplished writer.[6] The South Africa-born, London-raised, and Cambridge-educated Eban was married to the niece of Rachel Lauterpacht, Herschel Lauterpacht's wife.[7]

Though separated by two decades, the two Cantabrigians must have shared a certain commonality in outlook even as their life paths had diverged and would continue to diverge. Lauterpacht had been involved in Zionist politics for most of his early life. By 1948, however, his renown was not as a Zionist figure but as an expert in the burgeoning field of international law. Eban certainly held the belief that international law rightly understood was not unfavorable to the national self-determination of the Jews.[8] And Eban knew much of the ways of Cambridge and the academic world of the United Kingdom. Indeed, he had rejected an available life as a Cambridge academic and devoted himself first to Zionist activism and later to a difficult attempt to ascend the greasy pole of Israeli politics.

Many details about the what, when, and where of Lauterpacht's involvement with the *Yishuv* diplomatic team in New York are unknown. Lauterpacht in later years would downplay any involvement he had in the diplomacy of the founding of Israel. Yet at a certain moment in March or April of 1948, a member of the diplomatic team, likely Eban, asked Lauterpacht to either state the legal basis for Israeli independence, write a declaration of independence, or both.

Lauterpacht composed a two-part document by early May 1948 which amounted to a declaration of independence. It is unclear who else may have influenced it, whether or not Eban contributed to it, or if anyone else was involved in its production. After it was completed, Lauterpacht's documents were sent for comments to Jacob Robinson, another New York-based Jewish international lawyer who was more closely affiliated with the Zionist establishment.[9] And when Moshe Shertok, Israel's first

---

[6] Though his writing was certainly in part ghost-written, his books remain a most valuable resource for understanding Zionism in the twentieth century and the history of the first decades of Israel. See Asaf Siniver, *Abba Eban: A Biography* (New York: Harry Abrams, 2015) and Neil Rogachevsky, "Who Was Abba Eban?" *Mosaic*, February 17, 2016, https://mosaicmagazine.com/observation/israel-zionism/2016/02/who-was-abba-eban/

[7] Elihu Lauterpacht, *The Life of Hersch Lauterpacht*, p. 305.

[8] See, for example, his *The Tide of Nationalism* (New York: Horizon Press, 1959).

[9] Eliav Lieblich and Yoram Shachar, "Cosmopolitanism at a Crossroads: Hersch Lauterpacht and the Israeli Declaration of Independence," *British Yearbook of International Law*, 84, 1, 2014, pp. 8–9.

foreign minister and the head of the Jewish delegation at the UN, left for Palestine on May 9 to prepare for the end of the Mandate, he brought a copy of Lauterpacht's work along with him.[10]

When *Minhelet ha'Am* assembled on May 12 for a pivotal meeting that discussed both the declaration of political independence for the Jewish state and the text which would announce it, Lauterpacht's work was in the briefing book and on the table. And when it commissioned yet another draft of the Declaration of Independence, a decision we will discuss in Chapter 5, Lauterpacht's work was melded into Berenson's to produce a new text. In this way, the ideas that animated Lauterpacht's work at the UN, and his concerns about what the UN had in store for Israel, made their way into the production of the ultimate draft of Israel's Declaration of Independence.

Let us now look at what he produced in more detail. Here is the text of Lauterpacht's two-part declaration.

HERSCHEL LAUTERPACHT'S ACT OF INDEPENDENCE AND DECLARATION OF THE ASSUMPTION OF POWER BY THE PROVISIONAL GOVERNMENT OF THE JEWISH REPUBLIC

The Act of Independence

WHEREAS justice requires that the Jewish people should be enabled, through an independent State in its ancient home, to preserve the life and the culture of the Jewish race, to carry on the torch of its contribution to the spiritual values and to the welfare of mankind, and to provide for the survival and the happiness of the anguished remnants of the most cruel massacre in history;

WHEREAS the natural right of the Jewish people to national existence has received repeated recognition on the part of the nations of the world;

WHEREAS the General Assembly of the United Nations must be deemed to have recognized, on the twenty-ninth of November of the year one thousand nine hundred and forty-seven, the right of the Jewish people in Palestine to independent Statehood;

WHEREAS it has not proved possible to give effect to the intention of the general Assembly as to the manner in which the independent Jewish State shall come into being;

[10] Ibid.

WHEREAS the circumstances resulting in the inability of the Security Council to implement the will of the General Assembly and ... the Special Sessions ... in no way affected the undoubted recognition implicit in its Resolution, of the right of the Jewish People in Palestine to independent national existence;

WHEREAS the Mandatory Power has ceased to exercise the principal functions of government;

WHEREAS the representative organs of the Jewish people in Palestine now in fact exercise the powers of government for the defence of the country against aggression and for providing for the life of the community;

THE JEWISH PEOPLE OF PALESTINE

HUMBLY INVOKING the blessing of Almighty God, the Lord of the Hosts;

Pledging their lives to the cause of the survival and the independence of the Jewish people in Palestine;

REVERENTLY DETERMINED to sanctify the memory of the six million of Jewish martyrs of the Second World War, and of millions of others in the age long history of Jewish martyrdom, by steadfast adherence to the principles of social justice, of international peace, and of respect and equality for all dwellers of our land regardless of race and religion;

SOLEMNLY RE-AFFIRMING their faith in the brotherhood of the Jewish and Arab peoples and their resolve to strive for the friendship of the Arab people in Palestine and of the Arab nations;

GRATEFULLY RECALLING the self-less help of the British nation in laying the foundations of the National Home of the Jewish People;

NOW PROCLAIM that the Jewish Republic within the frontiers approved by the General Assembly of the United Nations is and as of right ought to be an independent State and charge the Provisional Government to assume the rights and duties of government in accordance with the annexed Declaration.

Declaration of the Assumption of Power by the Provisional Government of the Jewish Republic

1. The Mandatory Power has declared its final intention to relinquish the mandate over Palestine on the 15th of May, 1948. On that date the legal sovereignty over Palestine as assumed on behalf of the League of Nations will have come to an end. It was expected that the organs of the United Nations, in pursuance of the authority derived from the last

Assembly of the League of Nations, the General Assembly of the United Nations, and the declarations of the Mandatory Power would assume temporary sovereignty over Palestine with the view to transferring it to the Jewish and Arab states in conformity with the Resolution of the General Assembly of the 29th of November, 1947. That expectation has not been fulfilled. So far as the Jewish People is concerned, the right and duty to effect the assumption of sovereignty must now be brought about by the Jewish people itself.

2. In the circumstances which have arisen as the result of the inability of the Security Council to act upon the Resolution of the General Assembly it is incumbent upon the Jewish people to take the requisite steps for setting up the governmental agencies of the Jewish State as recognized by the United Nations. Those steps must be taken in obedience to the paramount duty to secure law and order within the frontiers of the Jewish State and in the exercise of the fundamental right of self-preservation in face of the armed challenge to the will of the United Nations solemnly proclaimed by the General Assembly.

3. The inherent right of the Jewish people to national self-determination through statehood is independent of any express confirmation by an outside authority. The legal title of the Jewish people to establish a State within the community of nations must be deemed to have been confirmed by the collective decision of the United Nations. Whatever may be the binding legal force of the Resolution of the General Assembly of 29th November, 1947, in relation to individual members of the United Nations, it is indisputable that it constitutes a valid measure of a high organ of the United Nations acting in the full plenitude of its rightful jurisdiction. The resolution of the General Assembly is and will remain a great and beneficent act of international distributive justice. The basic legal and moral factors which underlie it cannot be affected or altered by changes in the political constellation in the relations of states.

4. The Resolution of the General Assembly of 29th November, 1947, provides machinery to the delimitation of the frontiers of the Jewish State by the Palestine Commission and the setting up by that body of the Provisional Council of Government of the Jewish State. These instructions of the General Assembly are in no sense a condition of the recognition of the Jewish State implicit in the Resolution of the General Assembly. Their object was to make provision and to supply the instrument for the peaceful and orderly creation of the new States. But the essential purpose and effect of the Resolution of the

General Assembly of 29th November, 1947, namely, the confirmation of the right of the Jewish people to independent statehood, is in no way dependent on the actual use of the various instrumentalities of peaceful change as envisaged in the Resolution. The Jewish people was – and still is – resolved to lend its full co-operation in order to make possible the assumption of sovereignty by the new States through the methods contemplated in the Resolution. It is equally determined not to allow the failure of these methods to operate as a nullification of the principal avowed purpose of the Resolution of the General Assembly. That purpose must, if necessary, be achieved by the exertion of the Jewish people and by the exercise of its supreme right of self-defense and self-preservation.

5. The Resolution of the General Assembly of 29th November, 1947, refers to the delimitation of the frontiers of the Jewish State, to the setting up of the Provisional Council of Government of the Jewish State, to the date on which the Jewish State shall come into existence, and to the eventual admission of the Jewish State as a Member of the United Nations. No clearer proof is required of the recognition, by a collective act of the organized community of nations, of the existence of the primary condition of statehood of the Jewish people in Palestine. The continued validity of that collective act of recognition of the essential conditions of Jewish statehood cannot be affected by the failure of any particular method chosen for the realization of the primary object of that act of recognition. While, therefore, the Provisional Government of the Jewish State will aim at establishing, as soon as practicable, normal international intercourse with other States through diplomatic, consular, and other agents, it is not intended, in view of the already accomplished act of collective recognition by the United Nations as a whole, that recognition by individual States shall be sought in every case. An effective authority brought into being and maintained in accordance with international law and pursuant to recognition by the international community is entitled to recognition by individual States – assuming that such recognition is necessary. No authority, however temporarily or locally effective, is entitled to recognition if it originates in a defiance and violation of the collective judgment, solemnly and deliberately expressed, of the organized community of States.

6. While, in the light of the avowed intention of the Mandatory Power, the existing legal sovereignty will come to an end on the 15th May, 1948, it is clear that the Mandatory Power has been constrained to

abdicate the normal functions of government. Considerable armed forces, largely recruited from outside Palestine, are in open and savage rebellion against the decision of the United Nations. Unless the law-abiding will of the Jewish people asserts itself against the powers of aggression and destruction, the purpose of the United Nations and the cause of justice may suffer irretrievable harm. For these reasons, the Jewish National Council, in conformity with the Act of Independence of this Date, must assume and hereby does assume the powers of the Provisional Government of the Jewish State.

7. The Provisional Government, acting in co-operation with the Mandatory Power in the period between the date of this Declaration and the termination of the mandate, will assume responsibility for maintaining law and order within the territory of the Jewish State. The Provisional Government will undertake the necessary steps for the assumption by the Jewish State of responsibility, as from the 15th May, 1948, for the protection of nationals of the Jewish State abroad, for regulating the status of the Jewish merchant marine, for the inauguration of diplomatic and consular intercourse, for the conclusion of and adherence to international treaties, and for obtaining admission to the United Nations in conformity with the Resolution of the General Assembly.

8. It will be the duty of the Provisional Government, without prejudice to the sovereign powers of the Constituent Assembly, to take the preparatory steps for ensuring that the Constitution of the Republic shall incorporate provisions for the effective recognition of the following principles: that the law of the Jewish State and its international conduct shall be subordinated to the generally recognized rules of the law of nations; that the obligations of the Charter of the United Nations and of any international treaty or Bill of Rights adopted in pursuance thereof shall form part of the organic law of the Republic; and that the Republic shall adhere permanently and on the sole condition of reciprocity to international instruments conferring compulsory jurisdiction upon the International Court of Justice. It is imperative that among the first acts of the Jewish Republic there shall be the full recognition of the ideas of peace and justice which the Jewish prophets and the apostles of religion have bequeathed to all nations and which, with God's help, will become the true heritage of humanity.[11]

---

[11] The text is available in the Israel State Archives at 366/2/. חצ Online the text can be found at ISA-mfa-NorthAmerica1–0001.4yr on the archive website.

Lauterpacht's draft displays admirable clarity on fundamental topics. It invokes, without shame, the blessings of the "almighty God, Lord of Hosts" where Berenson did not and later drafts would not. The Jewish history evoked is not just the history of the modern *Yishuv* but ancient history, "the torch of its contribution to the spiritual values and to the welfare of mankind."

The text mentions the Holocaust explicitly and plainly, "the most cruel massacre in history." The Jews' right to national existence is a "natural right." Perhaps following the American Declaration, the text affirms that the Jews of Palestine pledge their lives to the cause of survival and independence. Though Lauterpacht's text links Jewish national independence and international law, it also states expressly that "the inherent right of the Jewish people to national self-determination through statehood is independent of any express confirmation by an outside authority."

The text goes beyond these types of references and markers to substantive arguments about the nature of a Jewish state. It expresses the positive character of a Jewish right to a homeland in a more forthright way than many members of the *Yishuv* establishment might have done. Justice requires that the Jews be allowed to establish a state in their independent home. The basis of this justice is not simple nationalism, not the case of Woodrow Wilson for "national self-determination."[12] Rather, the right to a state is instrumental: the Jews are entitled to a state in the first place because they contribute to the spiritual values and the welfare of mankind. The text does not say what these spiritual values are, but it is notable that Lauterpacht's text makes a positive case for the particularity of the Jewish contribution to the human story. Jewish sovereignty has universal interest and importance in this account.

The document is also British – as Lauterpacht had become. And thus it claims that the *Yishuv* gratefully acknowledges "the self-less help of the British nation in laying the foundations of the National Home of the Jewish People." It is certainly true that the Jews benefitted from having Britain as a colonial master as opposed to other potential powers, such as France or Germany. And future Israelis would owe real thanks to their British supporters, from George Eliot and the Earl of Shaftesbury in the nineteenth century through Arthur Balfour and Winston Churchill in the twentieth century.[13]

[12] See Allen Lynch, "Woodrow Wilson and the Principle of 'National Self-Determination': A Reconsideration," *Review of International Studies*, 28, 2, 2002, pp. 419–436.
[13] See Gertrude Himmelfarb, *People of the Book: Philosemitism in Britain from Cromwell to Churchill* (New York: Encounter, 2011).

But there was more to the story. The Jews of the *Yishuv* praising the British nation for its "self-less" help in 1948 would be akin to the Americans of 1776 praising George III and Parliament for selfless help in establishing the thirteen colonies of the United States. Britain had stifled the *Yishuv* actively since the passage of the White Paper of 1939. And, in 1948, it had cast its lot on the Arab side of the war – Jordan was using British matériel and commanders to wage war against the *Yishuv*. And to the last, Britain enforced restrictions on Jewish immigration to Palestine – even to Holocaust survivors living under British military police in Bergen-Belsen in occupied Germany several years after the end of the war. Lauterpacht's text was missing the texture of the *Yishuv*.

THE SPIRIT OF THE UNITED NATIONS

The essence of Lauterpacht's text is neither its invocation of the Jewish right to a homeland, nor its thanks to God or to the British nation. Its central aim is to demonstrate that Jewish independence is in line with the spirit though not the letter of United Nations Resolution 181. It lays out both in broad argument and in legal detail why Resolution 181 is operative and must be followed to its logical conclusion. Lauterpacht's text argues that while subsequent events, including the aggression of Arab neighbors, might have made the letter of that resolution impossible to fulfill, the principled expressed in Resolution 181 remains valid – there should be a Jewish state in Palestine.

Indeed, Resolution 181 is the lynchpin of Lauterpacht's draft. And not by accident. Resolution 181, which set partition of the former British protectorate Palestine into a Jewish state, an Arab State, and a UN-administered free city in Jerusalem with an economic union between all three as UN policy, was at the center of many minds involved in law and diplomacy in the *Yishuv* in the days leading up to independence.[14]

Recall that per Resolution 181, the independence of the Jewish and Arab states was not to occur without the consent of a UN-appointed Palestine Commission. In turn, the Commission was only to grant independence to the states upon their meeting a number of tests. The most important of these was the prevailing of peace between Jews and Arabs. In addition, there were a number of political criteria. The states had to

---

[14] For the text of UN Resolution 181, see https://unispal.un.org/DPA/DPR/unispal.nsf/o/
7F0AF2BD897689B785256C330061D253

elect constitutional assemblies, compose and ratify constitutions, adhere to the ethics of the charter of the UN, participate in an economic union with the other state and with UN administered Jerusalem, and so forth. A timeline for meeting these tests was set out.

This UN Commission was to be powerful. It was to have the power of the purse in the form of the administration of tariffs and allocation of revenues from the tariffs – then a principal form of taxation in Palestine. And moreover, it was to be the body that allowed the Jewish and Arab states to progress from one milestone to the next on the route to independence.[15] Creation of a provisional government, establishment of administrative bodies, of militias, of constitutions – these were all milestones on the road to full independence, and whether these milestones were met was to be judged by the Commission.

UN Resolution 181 had detailed specific borders for the states, delineated a provisional governing council as a political authority, and envisioned an eventual entrance of the two states into the United Nations. Lauterpacht refers explicitly to these criteria to justify Jewish independence and the authority of the new government in his text. The details of Resolution 181 determine many of his choices. Thus, for instance, he declares a "Jewish Republic within the frontiers approved by the General Assembly of the United Nations." The question of whether to mention the borders of the state was to prove highly contentious in the final debates in *Minhelet ha'Am* over the Declaration of Independence. Lauterpacht's text mentions them in order to follow the spirit and text of Resolution 181.

So too, the government will only be "provisional" – for Resolution 181 had set out the establishment of a provisional government as a waystation en route to full statehood upon the setting of a "constituent assembly" to legislate a constitution. The provisional government, in Lauterpacht's text, will maintain the duties laid out by Resolution 181: it will "maintain law and order" and take steps for the protection of nationals at home and abroad, and so on. The document makes clear that the general principles of the path to sovereignty laid out in Resolution 181 will be followed.

And the document explains at length why some of the details and timelines laid out in Resolution 181 were not adhered to by the *Yishuv*:

---

[15] Ibid., UN Resolution, first part.

"It has not proved possible to give effect to the intention of the General Assembly as to the manner in which the independent Jewish State shall come into being." Indeed, "it was expected that the organs of the UN ... would assume temporary sovereignty over Palestine .... That expectation has not been fulfilled."

This failure is no fault of the *Yishuv*'s per Lauterpacht. It is the fault of the enemy armies. The impossibility of adherence to the process of Resolution 181 "in the face of the armed challenge to the will of the United Nations" makes it more essential that the intention of Resolution 181 be fulfilled via Jewish independence outside of the procedures of Resolution 181, he argues.

"The Jewish People was – and still is – resolved to lend its full cooperation in order to make possible the assumption of sovereignty ... through the methods contemplated in the Resolution," the text explains. The Jewish People would like to follow the letter of Resolution 181, however, "the essential purpose ... of the Resolution ... is in no way dependent on the actual use of the various instrumentalities ... as envisaged in the Resolution." Letting the Resolution's intent fail would undermine the United Nations, which must not "allow the failure of these methods to operate as a nullification of the principal avowed purpose of the Resolution .... That purpose must, if necessary be achieved by the exertion of the Jewish ... supreme right of self-defense and self-preservation." Lauterpacht the international lawyer was making his case.

THE VOID

Lauterpacht's emphasis on Resolution 181 might seem odd. As his document explains at length, it had almost immediately been superseded by events on the ground. Resolution 181 was never implemented as planned. The resolution envisioned two states, one Jewish and one Arab, living side by side in peace with economic union, and with a UN administrator of Jerusalem present throughout. The city of Jerusalem was to be the capital of both nations and its holy sites and Old City were to be under the international trusteeship of the United Nations, a kind of urban UNESCO heritage sight policed by blue helmets (though at the time there were no blue helmets and no UNESCO). Of course this vision never materialized.

This seemed remote and implausible by the spring of 1948 to observers on the ground. By March 1948, Henry Gurney in Jerusalem saw that there were no prospects for a UN force in Palestine to enforce a peace:

"Time is now so short that the UN can clearly do nothing, and there will be chaos."[16] The prospect of an easy commerce and peaceable neighborly relations was undercut by war.

By the ceasefire in Winter 1949 that ended the first Arab-Israeli war, Israel's War of Independence, the Kingdom of Jordan would control much of the territory that was supposed to be the independent Arab state of Palestine including its principal cities Ramallah and Bethlehem. Egypt would control Gaza – the territory marked as the Mediterranean port of an Arab state in Palestine.

There would be ceasefire lines, de-facto hard borders between these districts and Israel, instead of the free movement and commerce envisioned in Resolution 181. There would be an Arab blockade of the Jewish state. There would be no Arab state, as neighboring Arab states had appropriated its land. The Jewish state had been founded in full autonomy and independence and not in graduated independence with markers on the path to statehood still to come. Jerusalem would be divided with the holy sites and the ancient city in the east controlled by Jordan and the modern Jewish western districts controlled by Israel.[17] This was certainly not what Resolution 181 had intended.

Lauterpacht saw that Resolution 181 had unraveled. And his text does not circumvent or elide this reality. Though it calls for brotherhood between Jews and Arabs, it also acknowledges that the conditions under which Resolution 181 was passed are no longer operative. This poses a central question. If the facts on the ground had changed so dramatically, and would continue to change, what was the reason for affording such a central place to Resolution 181?

As we will see in Chapter 5, Moshe Shertok would also hearken to Resolution 181, and his reasons largely had to do with diplomatic considerations: he worried that Jewish independence would be poorly received by the powers of the world and in particular by the United States if Resolution 181 was explicitly cast aside. It would seem from the text that Lauterpacht too is focused on this – and that he is also focused on something more.

---

[16] March 25, 1948. *The End of the British Mandate for Palestine, 1948: The Diary of Sir Henry Gurney*, p. 59.

[17] Martin Gilbert, *Israel*, pp. 673–676.

SUBORDINATED TO THE UN

Lauterpacht's text goes further than might have been expected even by the staunchest literalist interpreter of Resolution 181 in its embrace of the role of the United Nations in the formation and declaration of the new state.

Where Resolution 181 envisions that the new Jewish and Arab states will commit to peace and accept "the obligation of the State to refrain in its international relations from the threat or use of force ... or in any other manner inconsistent with the purposes of the United Nations," Lauterpacht subordinates the diplomacy and international relations of the new state to the United Nations: "Its international conduct shall be subordinated to the generally recognized rules of the law of nations."

Where Resolution 181 simply lists many of the principles of the United Nations Charter and demands that the state legislate in accordance with those, Lauterpacht goes further. He writes that "the obligations of the Charter of the United Nations and of any international treaty or Bill of Rights adopted in pursuance thereof shall form part of the organic law of the Republic."

And finally, where Resolution 181 envisions the International Criminal Court adjudicating between the new states and the free city of Jerusalem in the case of disputes stemming from the creation of the states and the end of the mandate, Lauterpacht envisions "compulsory jurisdiction" for the International Court of Justice to which the new state "shall adhere permanently."

In trying to understand Lauterpacht's efforts to embed an extreme version of adherence to international law into the charter of the new state, one need look no further than Lauterpacht's own biography. Lauterpacht was one of the chief theorists of international law in 1948 and an exponent of what has been called "legal internationalism."[18] He clearly believed in the possibility of creating new states: the Jews had an "inherent right" to a state, he wrote. Yet he wished to circumscribe the sovereignty of that state (along with all states) within the internationalist framework that he thought was being born at the UN at Lake Success and at the International Court of Justice at The Hague.

Lauterpacht had arrived at a kind of synthesis of international legalism and Zionism by a twisted path. His middle-class parents, who would

---

[18] James Loeffler, "Zionism, International Law, and the Paradoxes of Hersch Zvi Lauterpacht," https://papers.ssrn.com/sol3/papers.cfm?abstract_id=3313561

perish in the Holocaust, had both been devout and proud Zionists. Though his commitment to the Jewish ritual observance that had been important to his parents slackened somewhat, he maintained the passionate Zionism they had imbued in him in his early life.[19]

While attending a public *Gymnasium* in Lvov, Lauterpacht and like-minded Jewish classmates met regularly to study Hebrew, Jewish history, and the geography of the land of Israel.[20] As a law student in Lvov, he was an active participant in several different Zionist youth organizations, speaking, writing, and organizing conferences and seminars. In November 1917, when the Austro-Hungarian Empire was at war with Britain, Lauterpacht was arrested for arranging a public celebration of the British government's issuance of the Balfour Declaration.[21] The next year, he invited the philosopher and former Lvov resident Martin Buber to address the young Zionists of his home town. Lauterpacht at the time revered Buber as a modern prophet of the Jewish people. At one meeting, he told Buber: "Jesus needed many disciples to spread his ideas amongst the people – so Buber too needs disciples to help him spread his ideas and to materialize them amongst the Jewish people."[22]

As late as 1923, Lauterpacht dreamed of one day making *aliyah* to the land of Israel. Its "future is the future of all of us," he told his in-laws.[23] And yet, his studies took him to England, not Palestine. At University College, London, he led the Zionist section of the Jewish Student Union. In 1924, he spoke at the first meeting of the World Union of Jewish Students, in Antwerp, where he called for "cultural and national co-operation between all the Jewish students throughout the world." In an address to his fellow Jewish students, he spoke of the twin dangers of assimilationism and Bundism, both of which denied the existence of a Jewish people.[24]

In 1925, he would lead a delegation of European Jewish students to attend the founding ceremonies of the Hebrew University in Jerusalem.[25] This was not an easy journey to make. And he still seemed interested in moving to the land of Israel. Around this time, he attempted to get a faculty spot at the Hebrew University, but he abandoned the search when the university could only offer him a part-time position.[26]

In the midst of it all, Lauterpacht became an outstanding student, and ultimately a renowned theorist and practitioner of international law. He

---

[19] Elihu Lauterpacht, *The Life of Hersch Lauterpacht*, p. 10.   [20] Ibid., p. 11.
[21] Ibid., p. 10.   [22] Ibid., p. 21.
[23] Quoted in James Loeffler, "Zionism, International Law, and the Paradoxes of Hersch Zvi Lauterpacht."
[24] Ibid.   [25] Ibid.
[26] Eliav Lieblich and Yoram Shachar, "Cosmopolitanism at a Crossroads," p. 5.

got his doctorate under Hans Kelsen, perhaps the most influential German-language jurist of the twentieth century. Kelsen had rejected all attempts to offer a normative grounding for law, whether natural or divine. The only plausible ground for the legal order, in Kelsen's teaching, was the formal order existing at the time.[27] It is an open question whether the doctrines Lauterpacht espoused are ultimately distinguishable from the conventionalism that Kelsen espoused. And yet, in his own mind, Lauterpacht firmly rejected legal conventionalism in a turn to what became known as legal liberalism and internationalism.

Lauterpacht developed his thinking in England, where he did a doctorate at the London School of Economics, eventually teaching there. He moved to Cambridge in 1937. Throughout the 1930s and 1940s, Lauterpacht continued to offer legal advice to Zionist groups and organizations including the World Jewish Congress and the Jewish Agency.[28] Though it was fortuitous that he happened to be at Lake Success at the same time that Jewish diplomatic efforts there were reaching an apex, his involvement in Israel's founding was not accidental.

And yet, his focus was on his work in the sphere of international law: viewed in light of the events of the Second World War, a sympathetic reader cannot help but see in this work a tinge of the same concerns regarding the rights of those without voice that may have given birth to his Zionism. In his 1945 work, *The International Bill of Rights of Man*, Lauterpacht argued that the locus of law is the protection of the dignity of the individual. This implied a radical check on the sovereignty of the state: "The law of nations and, we may say, the law of nature, by denying, as they needs must do, the absolute sovereignty of State, give their imprimatur to the indestructible sovereignty of 'man.'"[29]

---

[27] Leo Strauss pointed to Kelsen's doctrine as a prime example of the inability of modern legal scholarship to identify tyranny. Under Kelsen's doctrine, the will or command of a dictator would be just as lawful as the "pronouncements" of the powerful body in any other regime. See *Natural Right and History* (Chicago: University of Chicago Press, 1999), p. 42. CF. David Novak, "Haunted by the Ghost of Weimar: Leo Strauss' Critique of Hans Kelsen," in *The Weimar Moment*, ed. L. V. Kaplan and R. Koshar (Lanham, MD: Lexington Books, 2012), p. 344 and Robert Chr. Van Ooyen, "Totalitarismustheorie Gegen Kelsen Und Schmitt: Eric Voegelins 'politische Religionen' Als Kritik an Rechtspositivismus Und Politischer Theologie," *Zeitschrift Für Politik*, Neue Folge, 49, 1, 2002, pp. 56–82.

[28] James Loeffler, "Zionism, International Law, and the Paradoxes of Hersch Zvi Lauterpacht."

[29] Ibid.

In the wake of the Holocaust, which touched Lauterpacht so personally, the emphasis on the "indestructible sovereignty of man" was no mere academic matter. To protect that sovereignty, Lauterpacht looked forward to the day when a confederation of states might emerge. Individual states would retain their legitimacy as units within a broader international system governed by institutions that would mediate conflict and enforce compliance with principles of international law. In 1948, even as Lauterpacht was writing a draft declaration of sovereignty for what would become the state of Israel, he articulated the teaching which would gain him acclaim in legal circles as one of the fathers of contemporary international law: "Sovereignty stops where outrage upon humanity begins."[30]

This effort to create an international set of norms above the state as a check against the violence of the state is in many ways no different in its ultimate aim from conventional Zionism, which sought to establish for the Jewish people a check against the violent world of states. And yet, it is also the opposite of Zionism: Zionism sought safety and peace for Jews via a just state protected by arms and power whereas Lauterpacht's concept of international law sought to constrain the type of state that both the Labor Zionists and the Revisionist Zionists of the mainstream *Yishuv* envisaged.

In the years after Israel's independence until his death in 1961, Lauterpacht would minimize his Zionism and his involvement with Israel. As James Loeffler puts it, Lauterpacht "feared over-identification with the new Jewish state would jeopardize his own role as a protagonist in the new chapter of work in the field of international law."[31] From 1955, Lauterpacht became a judge on the International Court of Justice, and in his public remarks avoided appearing partial to one side or the other in the dispute between the Israelis and the Arabs.[32]

THE SPIRIT OF INTERNATIONAL LAW

In a cruel irony, the very institutions of supra-sovereign authority that Lauterpacht championed would be used against the interests of the State

---

[30] Eliav Lieblich and Yoram Shachar, "Cosmopolitanism at a Crossroads," p. 25.
[31] James Loeffler, "Zionism, International Law, and the Paradoxes of Hersch Zvi Lauterpacht."
[32] Ibid.

of Israel – and never for it.[33] Resolutions would be passed at the UN declaring that "Zionism is racism"; there would be no countervailing resolutions regarding the prejudice suffered by the Jews expelled from Arab lands or for that matter declaring nationalisms less multi-ethnic than Zionism, including Pan-Arabism, as "racism."[34]

The International Court of Justice too has consistently intervened with rulings against the legality of Israeli political decisions, such as deeming a fence built during the Second Intifada to defend Israeli civilians illegal.[35] Again, no similar cases had been heard for instance when Jordan had severed hospitals and universities in northern Jerusalem from western Jerusalem from 1948 until 1967 using a military partition that involved trenches, barbed wire, snipers and all other mechanisms of military blockade.

There have been efforts to bring Israeli political and military figures to trial at the International Criminal Court at The Hague (even as Israel is not a member of that body) but no efforts to bring the airline hijackers of the 1970s, the organizers of suicide bombings against Israeli citizens (both Jewish and not Jewish) in the 1990s and 2000s, or the rocketeers bombarding Israeli civilians at present to justice at these institutions. The institutions of international law, and the "generally recognized rules of the laws of nations," to use the phrase in Lauterpacht's draft of the Declaration, have often been used as narrow political tools against the state of Israel and without the "reciprocity" that Lauterpacht had imagined that multilateral institutions of justice would offer.

PERPETUAL PEACE

The idealized argument of international legal theory is precisely that international norms constrain and push back against the narrow interest of states. As Immanuel Kant wrote in *Perpetual Peace*:

For states, in their relation to one another, there can be, according to reason, no other way of advancing from that lawless condition which unceasing war implies, than by giving up their savage lawless freedom, just as individual men have done, and yielding to the coercion of public laws. Thus they can form a State of nations

---

[33] Gerald M. Steinberg, "The Politics of NGOs, Human Rights and the Arab-Israel Conflict," *Israel Studies*, 16, 2, 2011, pp. 24–54.

[34] Joshua Muravchik, "The UN and Israel," *World Affairs*, November/December 2013, pp. 35–46.

[35] https://news.un.org/en/story/2004/07/108912-international-court-justice-finds-israeli-barrier-palestinian-territory-illegal

(*civitas gentium*), one, too, which will be ever increasing and would finally embrace all the peoples of the earth. States, however, in accordance with their understanding of the law of nations, by no means desire this, and therefore reject in *hypothesi* what is correct in *thesi*.[36]

Kant's argument is that states have no interest in legal constraints even if they might benefit from them. It may be in the interest of the "commercial republics" that "desire peace" to give up the ability to make war. There is a logic that ought to appeal to states to do what citizens of countries of law do, and abrogate the power of war and of enforcement to a higher authority – say a society of states or an "international state." States, however, as they require occasional use of "lawless freedom," simply don't act on this logic.[37]

Lauterpacht's neo-Kantian views reflected the optimistic element of Kant's perspective.[38] In his 1945 work, *An International Bill of the Rights of Man*, Lauterpacht advanced an international bill of rights that he hoped could become the legal standard for all states. In the work's preface he noted that the Second World War had:

Added weight to the conviction that an international declaration and protection of the fundamental rights of man must be an integral part of any rational scheme for world order. However, the idea of an International Bill of the Rights of Man is more than a vital part of the structure of peace. It is expressive of an abiding problem of all law and government .... . It is a problem that cannot be solved except under the shelter of the positive law of an organized Society of States ....[39]

Lauterpacht called his position Kantian: Kant "saw in an international political association of States an essential prerequisite of the performance of that highest function of states [the protection of rights]."[40]

But where Lauterpacht saw supranational constraints as the answer to the problem of the power of the state, Kant saw the state's power as inevitable. For Kant, the prospect of perpetual peace was unserious. He begins *Perpetual Peace* with a joke:

"This Way to Perpetual Peace." We need not try to decide whether this satirical inscription, (once found on a Dutch innkeeper's sign-board above the picture of a churchyard) is aimed at mankind in general, or at the rulers of states in particular,

---

[36] Immanuel Kant, *Perpetual Peace*, p. 136.   [37] Ibid.

[38] Martti Koskenniemi, *The Gentle Civilizer of Nations: The Rise and Fall of International Law 1870–1960* (Cambridge: Cambridge University Press, 2004), p. 366.

[39] Hersch Lauterpacht, *An International Bill of the Rights of Man* (Oxford: Oxford University Press, 2014), p. xxvii.

[40] Ibid.

unwearying in their love of war, or perhaps only at the philosophers who cherish the sweet dream of perpetual peace.[41]

Kant's essay *Perpetual Peace* is rife with absurdities and impossibilities that underline the unlikelihood that the measures which the essay sets forth as prerequisites for perpetual peace might possibly be accomplished. The propositions that make up Kant's scheme for global peace – no national debt shall be accrued with an aim to war, no territory shall be added to any existing state, no standing armies shall be kept – are not just impossibilities, but invitations to war and suffering on the part of the states that practice them.

The examples given in Kant's essay of states that are most intelligent in their practice of the "universal hospitality" which would be the basis of peace in Kant's sketch – China and Japan – are precisely the states that, according to Kant, do not practice universal hospitality. For they have seen that, upon provision of hospitality to rival nations, "oppression of the natives followed, famine, insurrection, perfidy and all the rest of the litany of evils which can afflict mankind."[42]

Kant makes light of the excesses to which an argument for his scheme for perpetual peace inevitably lead him:

It is always possible that moralists who rule despotically, and are at a loss in practical matters, will come into collision with the rules of political wisdom in many ways, by adopting measures without sufficient deliberation which show themselves afterwards to have been overestimated. When they thus offend against nature, experience must gradually lead them into a better track.[43]

Reality collides against schemes for the impossible. A plan for "perpetual peace" must be judged against the impossibility of its implementation.

Kant points out, following Aristotle in the *Nichomachean Ethics*, that all political wisdom is uncertain: In matters of "political expediency – much knowledge of nature is required, that her mechanical laws may be employed for the end in view. And yet the result of all knowledge of this kind is uncertain … ."[44] He points out that statesmen cannot trust treaties with one another: "Still more uncertain is a law of nations, ostensibly established upon statutes devised by ministers; for this amounts in fact to mere empty words, and rests on treaties which, in the very act of ratification, contain a secret reservation of the right to violate them."[45]

---

[41] Immanuel Kant, *Perpetual Peace*, p. 106.   [42] Ibid., p. 140.   [43] Ibid., p. 168.
[44] Ibid., p. 177.   [45] Ibid.

As Kant nakedly states at the start of *Perpetual Peace,* efforts to redeem politics are as hopeless as politics. All roads lead to perpetual peace – they are doomed. In a strange way, that is the hope that Kant attempts to inspire with his writing. If both a rational plan to redeem politics and conventional politics are paths to "perpetual peace," then perhaps there is some chance for incremental redemption of politics via rules and institutions – however unlikely.

CONCLUSION: DASHED IDEALISM

Lauterpacht held Kant's doctrine without regard for Kant's reservations and the provisional character of Kant's conclusion. As Lauterpacht said in an address at Chatham House at the height of World War II:

The disunity of the modern world is a fact; but so, in a truer sense, is its unity. The essential and manifold solidarity, coupled with the necessity of securing the rule of law and the elimination of war, constitutes a harmony of interests which has a basis more real and tangible than the illusions of the sentimentalist or the hypocrisy of those satisfied with the existing status quo.[46]

The status quo, the world of nations, states, and temporary and always shifting alliances, the rapid degeneration of times of fragile peace into brutal war – Lauterpacht hoped that all of these could and should be transcended. This was Lauterpacht's dream.

It is a dream he shared with many others of that war-weary generation which witnessed barbarism and genocide on a previously unimaginable scale. They hoped that a new world could be built. To be sure, in this new world, new states, including the state of the Jews, could be acknowledged and welcomed. But they could be welcomed as additional building blocks in a new confederation aimed at protecting rights and abolishing war.

The history of the first effort to create a federation of states for the aim of perpetuating peace had been an abject disaster. The League of Nations, with its efforts to restrain the powerful amongst the states in order to curtail war, served only to curtail the checking of the rise to power of Nazi Germany. Neither Britain nor France were properly armed in 1936, and so they could not check the rise of Hitler's military state at a time when its deterrence could more likely have been achieved.

---

[46] Quoted in Martti Koskenniemi, "Lauterpacht: The Victorian Tradition in International Law," *European Journal of International Law,* 8, 2, 1997, p. 221.

Limits to standing armies, it turned out, favored those who violated the limit on standing armies – and the most aggressive possible violation at that. The international norms turned out to be nothing other than rules to be gamed. Kant's fatalism, at least from the vantage point of the 1930s, was more justified than his qualified optimism. And his skepticism that plans for perpetual peace could be realized received the strongest possible validation with the collapse of the League of Nations system a brief twenty years after it was created. Indeed the League of Nations system had paved the way to the bloodiest and cruelest war in human history.

These errors were not to be repeated. Despite the hopes of Lauterpacht and many others who shared his views, the United Nations would not be constructed to serve as a limit on the power of states. Instead, it was created as a forum for state competition. The Americans and the Soviets used the UN as a stage and a rallying ground for their various blocks during the Cold War.

This must have been understood by the UN founders – despite the high-minded rhetoric of the UN's founding. It could be seen in the UN's Charter. The UN did not limit the arms of its members or include the type of arms control measures that so thoroughly demilitarized Europe and made Germany's rise in the 1930s possible. The UN's efforts to curtail the spread of nuclear weapons have been in the service of status quo nuclear powers. The UN seeks to disarm those who wish to enter the nuclear club. It does not in effect limit or disarm status quo powers.

There would be no redemption at the United Nations for the oppressed of the world. Although it was hoped that the UN would be a venue to limit savagery and war crimes, it just as often proved to be an avenue to obfuscate and delay intervention by outside powers for those committing war crimes. It would fall to Rwanda's neighboring states to relieve the genocide and not to the Blue Helmets.[47] The Syrian revolution and the violence that it entailed would only come to an end with the efforts of interested states. Great killings would take place in Russia and China amidst the purges of Stalin and the Cultural Revolution of Mao. Neither would motivate the UN to action. Human rights would remain in the domain of states and safety and security would be secured via international war and not international organizations.

This was not how Lauterpacht had seen things from the vantage point of Lake Success in 1948. The suffering and devastation of the Second

---

[47] See Roméo Dallaire, *Shake Hands with the Devil* (Cambridge: Da Capo Press, 2004).

World War had led many to look for something more novel and more certain than the state. Lauterpacht's dream that the new Jewish state would not live in a cruel and turbulent world of warring states, however hopeful, would not prove prescient. The life of the Jewish state, even in 1948, was to take place in a world of warring states. As we will see in the next chapter, there would be no protection or redemption for the Jews of Palestine at the UN in 1948.

PART III

HISTORY

5

Diplomacy

Moshe Shertok's Draft

It was late at night on May 11, 1948, when a rumpled Moshe Shertok (later Sharett) stepped off a small aircraft, likely a well-worn six-seater, accompanied by his daughter Yael, then 17. The slender and unassuming Shertok had just flown to Tel Aviv from New York. There had been stops for refueling along the way, some political business in Paris, and finally a connection in Athens where he was picked up by one of the *Yishuv*'s very few functioning aircraft for a bumpy, dangerous plane ride at low altitude across the Eastern Mediterranean. After this exhausting ordeal, Shertok, probably without a shower or change of clothes, was whisked to a meeting with the "Old Man."

David Ben-Gurion was Shertok's longtime ally in the cauldron of Labor Zionist politics, but also a kind of nemesis and a cause of frequent frustration and befuddlement. The two were a study in contrasts. Shertok had excelled in his legal studies in Britain while Ben-Gurion, eight years Shertok's senior, never graduated from his Istanbul law school.[1] Shertok had mastered the Hebrew language while Ben-Gurion still made grammar mistakes here and there. Shertok was making a name for himself in international diplomatic circles while Ben-Gurion's name barely circulated. And yet there was Ben-Gurion, unassailable and in command of the *Yishuv*. Shertok, on the other hand, was not only in second place on the *Mapai* electoral list; he had to rush from his plane to see the Old Man.[2]

---

[1] On David Ben-Gurion's Istanbul years, see Tom Segev, *A State at Any Cost*, trans. Haim Watzman (New York: Farrar, Straus, & Giroux, 2019), p. 117.

[2] Gabriel Shaffer, *Moshe Sharett: Biography of a Political Moderate* (Oxford: Oxford University Press, 1996), p. 325.

Shertok had been summoned to apprise Ben-Gurion of the diplomatic status of the *Yishuv*'s quest for political independence. For Shertok led the *Yishuv*'s delegation to the United Nations in New York, and the United Nations was the forum that had brought the *Yishuv* to the brink of statehood. Shertok's diplomatic efforts had culminated in the passage of Resolution 181. By the spring of 1948, he was busy heading off efforts to roll back all that Resolution 181 had accomplished – including the much despised Trusteeship Plan. He was the single person best able to inform the *Yishuv*'s leadership of the international diplomatic state of play.

Ben-Gurion likely anticipated that Shertok's news from America would not be positive. Even as the countdown to the final British withdrawal from Palestine advanced steadily, and Ben-Gurion entirely planned to declare independence upon the British withdrawal, it was not certain that a declaration of independence would be met with international recognition or approval. In particular, America's opinion was not known. Shertok was to update Ben-Gurion on events ahead of a marathon meeting of *Minhelet ha'Am*, the de-facto cabinet government of the *Yishuv*, of which Shertok was a part. The session was to be held in Tel Aviv the next morning.

The purpose of the May 12 meeting was to discuss the grave political situation that confronted the *Yishuv* – including the path forward to independence. British troops were to abandon all but a sliver of Palestine three days later, on Saturday May 15, leaving only a tiny rump surrounding the Haifa port to safeguard the last shipments of British matériel.[3] Jerusalem was under siege, and communication between Zionist leadership there and in Tel Aviv was sparse.

Until this point, the War of Independence had been fought principally against Palestinian irregulars. And the *Yishuv* recently had scored some important victories. Over the course of April and the first part of May, *Yishuv* forces had captured Tiberius, Haifa, Jaffa, and the Arab neighborhoods of West Jerusalem.[4] The *Yishuv*, even as it faced setbacks in some areas, generally was holding up well in the struggle.

But the final British departure would almost certainly mean a coordinated invasion by the armies of Jordan, Egypt, Syria, Iraq, and Lebanon. Every member of *Minhelet ha'Am* knew that the outmanned and poorly equipped *Yishuv* was now facing its deepest crisis and its greatest test. And just as importantly, it faced a diplomatic test as the members of the

---

[3] Tom Segev, *One Palestine: Complete*, p. 518.   [4] Benny Morris, *1948*, p. 138.

council struggled to peer into the murk and fog of international politics to discern what the global reaction to the likely expansion of the war on May 15 would be – and vitally, if the *Yishuv* would be able to import the arms it would need in order to meet the invaders on the field of battle.

We do not have a record of the conversation between Shertok and Ben-Gurion on the night of May 11. We cannot know what they talked about. But we do have exhaustive minutes of Shertok's lengthy remarks to *Minhelet ha'Am* the next day. Indeed, the minutes of the meetings in the days leading up to independence read today like a movie script.

Shertok came before his colleagues in a position that no longer exists in the current age of telecommunication. He was an emissary returning back from a vital and delicate mission. He could report to his colleagues his view of the diplomatic situation faced by the *Yishuv*. He possessed all of the information that they lacked: up-to-date news and correspondence with key American interlocutors.

He walked them through the current state of play in Washington and at the UN in New York. There was much confidential information that he had not been able to convey in his official diplomatic cables which were not secure and subject to interception. The Soviets favored independence. The British favored the Arabs. Most ominously, Shertok reported to his colleagues that there were strong forces in the US government opposing Jewish independence.

Shertok explained the lay of the land. There was "a school in the US State Department that won't give up" in its efforts to prevent Jewish independence. It was "trying to cause via arms embargo" an indefinite delay to the creation of an independent Jewish state. "They see disaster" in the declaration of a state "and will do anything to prevent it."[5] These State Department diplomats were maneuvering at the UN to discredit the *Yishuv* and ensure that a declaration of independence would not be recognized.

The meeting minutes contain a steady stream of dramatic presentations: updates on the military state of affairs, accounts of the overall drama unfolding in Palestine, and colorful interventions from the various characters around the table of *Minhelet ha'Am*. Most important for our purposes was a discussion of the text that would be used to proclaim independence. Shertok was a pivotal participant in the discussion. He knew the most about the path to statehood at the UN, and therefore the

---

[5] Protocols of the National Administration, morning meeting, May 12, 1948.

diplomatic finesse that the Declaration might require. Shertok was also a former journalist and newspaperman. His Hebrew was esteemed for its great literary quality.

The briefing books sent out in advance of the meeting had included a version of the draft Declaration produced by Tzvi Berenson with slight alterations made by the Legal Department. Yet another edition, modified again, this time to hold more closely to Berenson's original, was sitting on the meeting-room table.[6] As well, the participants had the draft by Herschel Lauterpacht.

There was some debate regarding what the final text of the Declaration of Independence should say, but the time allotted for discussion was limited and the discourse therefore confined. Two general issues stood out: whether the borders of the state ought to be delineated in the text of the Declaration and the related issue of whether or not the spirit and essence of the document ought to hew to the paradigm for independence set out by the UN.

There was only a vote on the first of these issues – the borders. We will touch on this more in the Chapter 6, but suffice it to say, *Minhelet ha'Am* voted not to mention the borders in detail. On the second matter, the assignment of the authorship of the next draft of the Declaration stands as a kind of vote: *Minhelet ha'Am* assigned the drafting of a declaration of independence to a committee of David Remez, Felix Rosenblüth, Moshe Shapira, Aharon Zisling, and Moshe Shertok. This meant, in effect, that

---

[6] The two texts were on most points the same as Berenson's draft. The differences and edits were caused by a number of running debates in the Legal Department over many of the issues that will be raised in this chapter and the subsequent one: (a) whether the Declaration should mention the state's borders; (b) the degree to which the Declaration should articulate that the state will be "sovereign"; and (c) the correct placement of the word 'democracy' in the text (or whether it should be included at all). The trail of edits and memos includes some surprising suggestions by the Legal Department staff to weaken the commendable egalitarian quality of Berenson's text, but these were largely not incorporated in the texts put before *Minhelet ha'Am*. These issues are thoroughly treated in a memo written by Heinsheimer, Zilberg, and Beham to Rosenblüth. On all of these points, one or the other of the versions of the text on the table of the *Minhelet ha'Am* meeting – either the one that came with the invitation, or the one presented at the meeting – accorded with Berenson's original. This led to the strange result of Rosenblüth demanding that the borders of the state be explicitly laid out in the Declaration even as one of the two versions of the text he presented did not do so. This does not seem to have influenced the political debate. See Yoram Shachar, "Ha'teyotot ha'mukdamot shel hakhrazat ha'atzmaut," pp. 569–581, and see Israel State Archives, 5664/20/ גׄ for the May 9, 1948 memorandum from the Legal Department.

the next draft was to be composed by the studied UN hand Shertok.[7] He had fewer than 24 hours with which to work; the Declaration of Independence would need to be discussed by *Minhelet ha'Am* at the meeting scheduled for the following evening at 6 pm.

The evening meeting of *Minhelet ha'Am* on May 12 ended at 11 pm. Repairing to his sister's family's house on Rothschild Boulevard, Shertok worked late into the night on his draft.[8] On the morning of May 13, Shertok and his four fellow committee members met at the Jewish Agency office to discuss the draft. Some minor stylistic changes were proposed. On the substance: the text added a commitment to the UN's economic partnership plan. The text also asked the world to admit the new state into "the community of nations." And as will become a recurring theme in the debates surrounding Israel's Declaration, the religiosity of the document was debated.

After the committee departed, Shertok stayed alone with a Jewish Agency aide, Moshe Gurari, to incorporate suggestions and tweak the draft further. At this point, the opinion of Ben-Gurion on stylistic matters was solicited and received by telegram and over the phone. Gurari later recalled that the Old Man's editing style led Shertok to bury his head in his hands and wonder aloud: "What do they want from my life?" Ben-Gurion would not let any particular detail rest, and had Shertok revising and re-revising the text. Ultimately, of course, Ben-Gurion would edit the final draft, and Shertok, perhaps out of exhaustion, perhaps out of frustration, would not be involved in formulating the final text.[9] Here is the draft that Shertok ultimately produced for discussion at the May 13 meeting:

Declaration

1) Whereas the Jewish people, which had been exiled by force of arms from its land, *Eretz Israel*, kept its faith throughout the generations of its exile and through the lands of its dispersion, and did not find in all of its wanderings a land in its stead, and never ceased praying and hoping to assemble the diaspora and to renew its freedom in its land;

2) And whereas in every generation and generation the Jewish people strove to return to and possess their homeland, until in recent

---

[7] Protocols of the National Administration, evening meeting, May 12, 1948.

[8] Yoram Shachar, "Israel as a Two-Parent State," *Zmanim*, 2007, p. 40.

[9] See Moshe Gurari, "Galguliya shel megilat ha'atzmaut" ("The Scrolling of the Independence Scroll"), *Davar*, April 24, 1958, and Gurari, "Havlei leidata shel megilat ha'atzmaut" ("The Birth Pangs of the Declaration of Independence"), *Davar*, May 11, 1973.

generations the pioneers of Israel, the migrants under duress and the defenders, were able to immigrate back to their land in large numbers, to redeem its soil and make its wilderness bloom, to revive there the Hebrew Language and to establish there an enduring community ruling over its economy and its culture, defending itself with strength and bravery, bringing the blessing of progress to all the residents of the land, and advancing its soul toward political independence and national sovereignty;

3) And whereas the First Zionist Congress, that gathered in the year 5657 (1897), at the summons of the Jewish State's visionary, Theodor Herzl, proclaimed the right of the Jewish people to national rebirth in its land and founded the World Zionist Congress as the instrument for the realization of this vision;

4) And whereas this right was recognized in the declaration of the British Government of November 2, 1917, which formed the basis for the British Mandate over the land of Israel;

5) And whereas this mandate was sanctioned by forty-two member states of the League of Nations and by the government of the United States, recognizing the historical connection between the Jewish people and the land of Israel and the right of the Jewish people to establish its national home anew in the land of Israel, to immigrate to it and to settle its land;

6) And whereas the persecution that has been visited from time immemorial upon the masses of Israel in different lands, particularly amidst the Holocaust visited upon them in Europe, in which millions of men, women, and children were condemned to slaughter, has proven anew the urgent necessity of a solution to the Jewish problem through a renewal of national independence in their land, so that its gates will be permanently open to all Jews seeking a home, conferring upon the Jewish people the status of a nation with equal rights in the family of nations;

7) And whereas the Hebrew *Yishuv* in *Eretz-Israel* contributed its full share to the struggle of the nations who guarded freedom and peace against the forces of evil and servitude in the Second World War, and by the work of its hands and the blood of its volunteer soldiers, gained the right to be reckoned among the peoples who founded the United Nations;

8) And whereas the survivors of the European inferno, the remnant of Israel, did not desist from immigration to the land despite illegality, hardship and danger, expulsion and blockade, and would not cease

to declaim to the entire world their right to a life of respect, freedom, and honest work in their motherland;

9) And whereas the General Assembly of the United Nations, in its second annual session, after exhaustive research and deep consideration, rendered on November 29, 1947, by a majority of over two-thirds, a decision mandating the establishment of an independent Jewish state in *Eretz-Israel*;

10) And whereas in this decision the General Assembly recommended, before all member states of the United Nations, the acceptance and the implementation of the partition plan of *Eretz-Israel* with economic union, calling on the residents of *Eretz-Israel* to act on their part for the fulfillment of the plan, and requested from all governments of the world to desist from any act likely to damage or delay the implementation of its recommendation;

11) And whereas the recognition of the right of the Jewish people in *Eretz-Israel* to found its independent state, as included in the decision of the General Assembly, is irrevocable;

12) And whereas the British government, which the League of Nations had delegated to oversee the land of Israel, has laid down, from this day forth, the Mandate, and renounces responsibility for ruling over the land;

13) Accordingly we, members of the National Council and representatives of the Zionist movement and the Hebrew *Yishuv* of the country, joyously assembled here and on the basis of the decision of the General Assembly of the United Nations, hereby declare to the Jewish people in the Diaspora and to the world entire, the establishment of a Jewish state in the land of Israel, which shall be called the State of Israel.

14) We affirm that from the hour of the end of the Mandate, tonight at midnight on Shabbat, *vav b'iyar*, 15 May 1948, and until the time of the establishment of permanent institutions of the state according to a constitution that will be ratified by an elected constituent assembly, the People's Council [*Moetzet ha'Am*] will act as the temporary governing council, and its executive body, the People's Administration, [*Minhelet ha'Am*] will be the temporary government of the Jewish state, Israel.

15) We vow that our state of Israel will be based on the principles of freedom, justice, and peace according to the vision of the prophets of Israel; will be open to widespread Jewish immigration; will bestow full and equal social and political rights upon all its citizens

regardless of race or religion; will strive toward the development of the land for the good of all its inhabitants; will promise freedom of religion, conscience, education, and culture; will guard the holy places of all religions; and will adhere to the principles of the Charter of the United Nations.

16) We are prepared to cooperate with the institutions of the United Nations in the fulfillment of the decision of the General Assembly and will work toward the creation of economic union in accordance with the decision. We call on the United Nations to assist the Hebrew people in the building of its nation and its protection, and to accept the State of Israel into the family of nations.

17) In light of the bloody attack being visited upon us we call on the Arab people who live in the Land of Israel to keep the peace, to assume their part in the building of the state that offers them full citizenship, and to enjoy the right that is owed to them to be represented in the high institutions of state, both temporary and permanent.

18) Amidst the current state of combat, we extend a hand of peace and good neighborliness to the surrounding nations and call upon them to desist from their conflict with the Hebrew nation, deserving, like them, a life of freedom and independence in its land, and ready to play its part in a shared effort for progress in the Middle East as a whole.

19) We call the Hebrew *Yishuv* to supreme effort and the enlistment of all its spiritual and material power to stand in battle while building the state and to build the state while standing in battle.

20) To the Jewish nation around the world, we call upon you to stand with the *Yishuv* currently in battle, and to volunteer to help in its vital campaign to realize the dream of so many generations.

21) To the enlightened world as a whole we raise our voices and ask that you stand by the Jewish people in the establishment of its state.

22) And placing our trust in rock of Israel we affix our signatures as witness to the declaration at this session of the provisional council of government, which includes the members of the temporary government, here in the Hebrew city of Tel Aviv, this day, Erev Shabbat, *h' b'iyar*, 14 May, 1948.[10]

---

[10] Copy at Israel State Archives, 5664/20/10 ג.

Moshe Shertok's draft of Israel's Declaration may seem familiar: it echoes many themes that appeared in prior drafts of Israel's Declaration, particularly the draft written by Tzvi Berenson. Shertok's draft describes the yearning of the Jewish people to return to the land of Israel. It builds on the diplomatic events of the post WWI-era to invoke a legal right to the creation of a "national community" for the Jews of Palestine. It characterizes the state in many of the same terms as Berenson had: a state open to Jewish immigration, at peace with Arab neighbors, with equal rights for all its residents irrespective of creed, and seeking for its citizens "freedom, justice, and peace in the spirit of the prophets."

There are of course notable differences. There is less labor Zionism and more political Zionism in Shertok's draft than in Berenson's. Theodor Herzl is in and the language of A. D. Gordon is out. The new state has a name: the State of Israel (a subject discussed in Chapter 6). The Diaspora enters the picture – Shertok calls on the Diaspora for support.

Perhaps most notably, Shertok omits Berenson's claim that the state should be democratic. Shertok leaves in the decisive element that Berenson had introduced with regard to the character of the state, an element which implies democracy and more than democracy: the state "will align itself with the principles of the Charter of the United Nations."

And here we come to the underlying theme that Shertok sought to introduce in his draft. Shertok wrote with a view toward an international audience, and in particular, toward American statesmen. At the time, the position of the United States and its willingness to recognize a new Jewish state was up in the air. Among the principal issues raised by American statesmen – including Secretary of State George Marshall, arguably the most powerful diplomatic voice in the United States other than President Truman – was that the path to statehood envisaged by UN Resolution 181 was in tatters.

Resolution 181 had called for a UN-administered commission to preside over geographic Palestine divided into separate Arab and Jewish polities under a UN Commission for the ensuing decade.[11] This plan was entirely implausible by May 1948. And therefore, if the UN process was derailed, so too might the path to Jewish statehood be thrown off course.

Shertok hoped to tip the sentiment of the relevant decision makers in the international arena, and particularly the United States, toward favoring the creation of the Jewish state. He thought that meant ensuring

[11] UN Resolution 181, https://unispal.un.org/DPA/DPR/unispal.nsf/o/7F0AF2BD897 689B785256C330061D253

that Jewish independence occurred at least optically within the rubric of the UN process that had so far achieved Britain's impending withdrawal.

To that end, Shertok's draft stresses the *Yishuv*'s scrupulous accordance with Resolution 181. And it emphasizes, perhaps somewhat surprisingly, the *Yishuv*'s membership in the Western Alliance that fought and defeated the Axis during the Second World War. This is part and parcel of an appeal to the Western nations and above all to the United States to recognize the new state and give it international legitimacy.

The significance here is that the United States was seen by the *Yishuv* as a much less reliable supporter of Jewish independence than the other large and relevant global powers. By means of its representative at the United Nations, Andrei Gromyko, Russia had conveyed that it would not stand in the way of the creation of a Jewish state.[12] Britain, for its part, was abandoning Palestine, bringing with it all of its war matériel while leaving matériel and even soldiers in British bases in Jordan and Egypt. Britain's lot was de facto cast against the success of the Jewish enterprise, but paradoxically, not against Jewish independence.[13] The United States was the great question mark.

The most important US diplomatic actors were either on the fence or lined up against the prospect of Jewish independence. The State Department was opposed to supporting the *Yishuv*. The newly formed Department of Defense was opposed. And the President's opinion, although believed to favor Jewish independence, was ultimately unknown, and seemed to be constrained by the views of his cabinet.

In any case, all relevant actors in the American administration, Truman included, believed that the international diplomatic framework for Palestine ought to run through the UN. Shertok thus understood, given the seeming breakdown of the Resolution 181 process, that he was fighting an uphill battle to win the backing of the United States for the declaration of an independent Jewish state.

THE ARGUMENTS ACCEPTED BY NATIONS

The argument of Shertok's text thus relied heavily on international recognition of the Jewish right to statehood, both in the past and at the UN.

---

[12] Gabriel Shaffer, *Moshe Sharett*, pp. 304–305.

[13] The best, if not always perfectly accurate, account of the waning days of the British Mandate remains that of Arthur Koestler, *Promise and Fulfillment* (New York: Macmillan, 1983).

The text opens with the Balfour Declaration and Britain's promise to support a Jewish "national home" in geographic Palestine. It argues that the British Mandate, sanctioned by the 42 founding member states of the League of Nations, along with the nonmember United States, similarly affirmed this right.[14] And of course it invokes Resolution 181, which, Shertok writes, approved the creation of a Jewish state "after exhaustive research and deep consideration."

The text culminates in a declaration of independence that is less than declaring actual independence. It is a declaration of the formation of a state under the auspices of the UN:

The National Council and representatives of the Zionist movement and the Hebrew community of the country, joyously assembled here and *on the basis of the decision of the General Assembly of the United Nations* [emphasis added], hereby declare to the Jewish people in the Diaspora and to the world entire, the establishment of a Jewish state in the land of Israel.

In a similar vein, Shertok's text is scrupulous in adhering to the Resolution 181 framework: the governing council is a provisional or temporary government, the principles of the state are those of the UN Charter, and so on. The text even asserts that "we are prepared to cooperate with the institutions of the United Nations in the fulfillment of the decision of the General Assembly and will work toward the creation of economic union in accordance with the decision." After all, cooperation with the UN was the essence of statehood in Resolution 181.[15]

The focus on the demands of statecraft and diplomacy in a declaration of independence is not without precedent. A declaration of independence is a supremely political act that has a bearing on both domestic politics and foreign relations. It is necessary that the author of a declaration of independence consider foreign policy. Famously, not only does the American Declaration submit its particular grievances against the King of Great Britain to a "candid world"; it also speaks of a "decent respect for the opinions of mankind" when it makes its theoretical argument for

---

[14] See Patrick M. Cottrell, "Lost in Transition?: The League of Nations and the United Nations," in *Charter of the United Nations: Together with Scholarly Commentaries and Essential Historical Documents*, ed. Ian Shapiro and Joseph Lampert (New Haven, CT: Yale University Press, 2014), pp. 91–106.

[15] See Yoram Shachar, "Israel as a Two-Parent State," pp. 40–43, for a further discussion of the similarity between Shertok's text and the text of Resolution 181.

the natural equality of human beings upon which the American project is said to rely.[16] Shertok too writes for "enlightened opinion" in his own interesting locution.

What is notable about Shertok's draft in contradistinction to the US Declaration is Shertok's attempt to navigate the minutiae of international diplomacy *without* an attempt to alter the landscape of foreign affairs. However much a new state is accepted and approved by great powers, it is precisely as something new (or renewed) – as a force that is disruptive. Shertok's draft was missing this crucial dimension. He emphasized the nondisruptive character of the birth of a Jewish state and argued that the state would fit within all relevant political and legal norms and the procedural drift of Resolution 181. It would be for this reason, in the logic of Shertok's diplomacy, that the nations of the world would support the creation of Israel.

In what follows we will examine further Shertok's rationale for adhering so closely to Resolution 181 in his draft of Israel's Declaration of Independence. But for now, suffice it to say that his choice poses an obvious question: Why did he care so much about Resolution 181? It had, after all, almost immediately been superseded by events on the ground – the war between the *Yishuv* and the Arabs, the failure of the UN to establish a viable commission to supervise partition, the list could go on. The British were at that point almost entirely withdrawn from Mandatory Palestine. The Zionist Actions Committee had publicly declared that there would be a provisional or temporary government of the *Yishuv* upon the withdrawal of Britain. And *Yishuv* public opinion, as Shertok would relate to various American interlocuters, demanded independence.

Shertok was well aware of all of this. In Lauterpacht's case, the decision to emphasize the importance of UN Resolution 181 had a deep intellectual and ethical motivation: Lauterpacht's excessively optimistic wish for a world peace enforced by the UN. This is unlikely to have motivated Shertok. He was a political Zionist to his core. There is nothing to indicate that he held the ability of the UN to protect the *Yishuv* in high esteem.[17] Indeed, Shertok might well have been prepared to declare independence irrespective of what the UN or, for that matter, the United States decided.

[16] See Jeremy Rabkin, "American Independence and the Opinions of Mankind," in *Law without Nations* (Princeton, NJ: Princeton University Press, 2005), pp. 233–270.
[17] Gabriel Shaffer, *Moshe Sharett: Biography of a Political Moderate*, p. 310.

And yet, despite the fact that a war had preempted the vision of Resolution 181, the optimistic and perhaps even naïve vision of a peaceful UN-administered multi-state arrangement in geographic Palestine was what the cold-blooded realists at the US State Department and Department of Defense envisioned through the winter and the early spring of 1948. These were the consequential men with whom Shertok believed that his draft of the Declaration of Independence had to contend.

THE SOLDIERS AND THE STATESMEN

Shertok had been hard at work advocating for American and international support for Jewish independence at the United Nations since February 1947. In New York, Shertok was already widely recognized as the de-facto foreign minister of the *Yishuv*. He initially had been dispatched to the United Nations to advocate against British Foreign Secretary Bevin's proposal that England maintain a five-year trusteeship period over Palestine – a path which would have forestalled the creation of a Jewish state.[18]

What is called the Bevin Plan came to naught; Britain decided to submit the "Palestine Question" to the UN instead.[19] Shertok was then tasked with both the planning and execution of the Zionist strategy at the UN, where he led a team that included Americans Aba Hillel Silver, Lionel Gelber, and Cy Kenen, as well as Nahum Goldmann, David Horowitz, Abba Eban, Walter Eytan, Michael Comay, Gideon Ruffer, Moshe Toff, Menachem Kahany, and Eliahu Epstein. These efforts ultimately led to UN Resolution 181 and a path to statehood, albeit under UN auspices.[20]

Shertok's work in those months had brought him face to face with Secretary of State George Marshall, famous today both as the Chief of Staff of the American Army in World War II and for the Marshall Plan to revive the European economy and cement an anti-Soviet bloc in Western Europe after the war.[21] Marshall was at the time principally concerned with his European initiative, and he saw the Palestine issue through that prism.

---

[18] On the Bevin Plan, see H. Levenberg, "Bevin's Disillusionment: The London Conference, Autumn 1946," *Middle Eastern Studies*, 27, 4, 1991, pp. 615–630.

[19] Michael J. Cohen, *Palestine and the Great Powers* (Princeton, NJ: Princeton University Press, 1982), p. 208.

[20] Gabriel Sheffer, *Moshe Sharett*, pp. 242–246.

[21] Forrest C. Pogue, George C. *Marshall*, vols. 3–4 (New York: Viking, 1986).

The documentary record shows that Marshall was concerned about the Palestine Question only insofar as it touched on three more vital issues: the organization of an anti-Soviet alliance, his plan to galvanize that alliance in Europe via economic rebuilding, and the impact it would have on Soviet expansionism in the Middle East. Viewed in that light, American backing of a Jewish state seemed potentially costly, dangerous, and needlessly antagonistic of important allies in the Middle East whose oil would power the hoped-for European economic recovery.

Perhaps unbeknownst to Shertok, Marshall had made exactly this case at a meeting of the National Security Council in February 1948. Marshall had presented a paper to President Truman drafted by no less than George Kennan, also the anonymous author of the famous article "The Sources of Soviet Conduct," which drew the realpolitik lines of the Cold War for American readers. Kennan's paper on the issue of Palestine had been endorsed by numerous senior State Department officials. It argued:

Any aid to the establishment of a Jewish state . . . would be construed by the Arabs as a virtual declaration of war against the Arab world . . . . We would be threatened with . . . cancellation of air base rights, commercial concessions, oil pipeline construction, and . . . a serious impediment to the success of the European Recovery Program, which is dependent on Middle Eastern Oil.[22]

Secretary of Defense James Forrestal, also present at that meeting, added to Marshall's concerns. He predicted that America might have to commit over 100,000 troops to Palestine in the event of Jewish independence.[23] Even as State Department officials argued that Jewish independence would give the Soviets an inroad to the Arab world, Near East specialist Loy Henderson of the State Department feared that "the Jews might in fact ally themselves with the Soviets."[24]

The American intelligence community largely supported the thrust of Kennan's assessment. The CIA had earlier presented its doubts as to whether the Jews of Palestine could withstand a successful assault from the combined forces of the Arab states. In a memo from November 1947 that Kennan likely saw, CIA analysts had presented their assessment of the situation:

---

[22] George Kennan Memorandum, January 20, 1948, https://history.state.gov/historicaldocuments/frus1948v05p2/d10
[23] Ibid.
[24] Ibid., Clark Clifford characterized Henderson as "openly anti-semitic." Clark Clifford, *Counsel to the President* (New York: Random House, 1991), p. 4.

The Jewish forces will initially have the advantage. However, as the Arabs gradually coordinate their war effort, the Jews will be forced to withdraw from isolated positions, and having been drawn into a war of attrition, will gradually be defeated. Unless they are able to obtain significant outside aid in terms of manpower and matériel, the Jews will be able to hold out no longer than two years.[25]

According to most experts, American recognition of the Jewish state seemed foolish. Marshall did not want to involve America with an undefined Jewish state, population: around 600,000 Jews, without leaders (Marshall did not know of Ben-Gurion's existence on Earth until May 12, 1948), without a formal army, and besieged by the 30 million Arabs who sat on half the world's oil. It seemed to the State Department that the Arabs could conceivably tilt to the Soviets – as indeed Egypt, Syria, and Iraq later would.[26]

Such was the prevailing view among most of the foreign policy elite of the United States in the winter and spring of 1948. This had led the United States to cast about for alternatives to Jewish statehood, arriving at what became known as the United Nations "Trusteeship Plan" which aimed to defer the declaration of independent Jewish and Arab states.[27] Whether US policy would continue to support the creation of a Jewish state or if instead the US would advocate for its indefinite delay had become unclear.

The main actors in the US State Department were hard at work undercutting the initial policy of American support for the creation of independent Jewish and Arab states under UN administration. The debate was not simply theoretical. Concrete actions were undertaken. The Department of State made a diplomatic and bureaucratic end-run around President Truman to try to defer partition.

In late February 1948, the State Department had attempted to compel Truman to advocate the Trusteeship Plan through a formal request. The President had neither agreed to nor rejected the overture, thinking it politically expedient to keep his options open and, one imagines, attempting to avoid alienating Marshall. Truman had told Marshall that he approved of his efforts to prevent an escalation of Arab-Jewish violence "in principle." But the president insisted "that nothing should be presented to the Security Council that could be interpreted as a recession

[25] "The Consequences of the Partition of Palestine," November 28, 1947, in *The CIA Under Harry Truman*, ed. Michael Warner (CIA: 1994).
[26] "No message had been sent to Mr. Ben-Gurion, and I did not even know that such a person existed," George Marshall, Memorandum of Conversation, May 12, 1948, https://history.state.gov/historicaldocuments/frus1948v05p2/d252
[27] Martin Gilbert, *Israel*, p. 165.

on our part from the position we took in the General Assembly."[28] The
position taken in the General Assembly had been that the United States
continued to endorse Resolution 181.

The President subsequently either sat on or rejected numerous efforts by
the State Department to get him to endorse the Trusteeship Plan. Truman
refused to accept the text of a speech endorsing trusteeship that was proposed
by American UN Ambassador Warren Austin and outright rejected a proposed letter drafted for him to send to British Prime Minister MacMillan that
would have seen him proposing the Trusteeship Plan to the British.

The State Department officials at the UN were not deterred or out-
foxed by Truman's bureaucratic obfuscation. They took Truman's ambiguity as an opportunity to advocate for the Trusteeship Plan on the floor
of the UN. On March 19, acting on instruction from Marshall, Austin
attempted to begin a process that would see the UN override Resolution
181. He said:

The United States fully subscribes to the conclusion ... the Security Council should
take further action by all means available to it to bring about the immediate
cessation of violence and the restoration of peace and order in Palestine .... My
Government believes that a temporary trusteeship for Palestine should be established under the Trusteeship Council of the United Nations to maintain the peace.[29]

This statement was calibrated to imply that the criteria of Resolution
181 had not been met. There had to be peace in order to implement
partition and peace was not at hand. Austin's initiative sought to rally UN
members and necessitate a UN trusteeship over Palestine.

Truman later claimed to have been livid upon learning of the State
Department's maneuver. His daughter Margaret in her biography of her
father would claim that the State Department "pulled the rug" from
under him and that Truman had never committed to the State
Department's plan. The documentary record, as it exists, corroborates
this point, with Clark Clifford's notes implying that the President's strategy was to remain open to the Trusteeship Plan in conversation with the
State Department but not in fact to advance it. Truman's Administrative
Assistant Charles Murphy claimed that Truman's instructions had been
deliberately "garbled by the State Department." Margaret Truman

---

[28] Cited in Michael J. Cohen, "Truman and the State Department: The Palestine Trusteeship
Proposal, March 1948," *Jewish Social Studies* 43, 2, 1981, pp. 170–171.
[29] Austin address at UN Security Council, March 19, 1948, https://history.state.gov/
historicaldocuments/frus1948v05p2/d105

claimed that her father felt as though the State Department, via bureau-cratic maneuver, had "cut his throat."[30]

The most telling exchange is found in a memorandum of a telephone call between Truman and Marshall on March 20. The President called Marshall and told him to reverse the position Austin had taken at the UN in favor of the Trusteeship Plan. Marshall was to muddy the waters and insist that trusteeship had been advanced only as a possible temporary measure until partition could be effected.

Marshall, himself as adept a diplomat and bureaucratic infighter as any other, held a press conference and did what Truman told him to do. But then he added that he found Austin's recommended course at the UN to be "the wisest," adding that a potential trusteeship would be temporary.[31] Truman's ability to control this rebellion of the clerks and even Secretary Marshall at that point seemed limited. The damage had been done.

To nuanced observers of US diplomatic discourse, it could have seemed as though it was tenable that the UN Partition Plan would not come into effect. This state of affairs was apparent to both the leadership and the populace of the *Yishuv*. Commenting on Jewish attitudes in Palestine that March, the American Consul General in Jerusalem wrote in a telegram that "most feel United States has betrayed Jews interests [for] Middle Eastern oil and for fear Russian designs."[32]

Shertok had personally come face to face with this perspective both at the United Nations and in conversations with US officials including Marshall throughout the winter and spring of 1948. On February 21, Shertok spoke with Under Secretary of State Robert Lovett, who questioned him about why the *Yishuv* had not made peace overtures to the Arabs in light of the war raging in Palestine. From the point of view of the State Department, the lack of such peace overtures and the likelihood of military escalation required a revisiting of US Palestine policy.

Writing to Lovett the next day, Shertok expressed the "greatest alarm" that a new effort of "conciliation" (i.e. the cancellation of the Jewish

---

[30] See the FRUS editorial note at https://history.state.gov/historicaldocuments/frus1948v05p2/d106

[31] Quoted in "Marshall, the United Nations, and Palestine," George C. Marshall Foundation, www.marshallfoundation.org/library/digital-archive/statesman-chapter-20-marshall-the-united-nations-and-palestine/

[32] Robert Macatee to George Marshall, March 22, 1948, Foreign Relations of the United States, March 22, 1948, https://history.state.gov/historicaldocuments/frus1948v05p2/d114

statehood promised in the Partition Plan) might be undertaken. Such a move, according to Shertok, would:

... come as a reward for the campaign of violence now being conducted against that Resolution and encourage the forces of defiance to redouble their efforts once the peace move had failed, as it must fail. It would completely shatter Jewish confidence in the United Nations authority and fortify extreme councils among Jews.[33]

Less than a month later, on March 13, Shertok, along with his Jewish Agency colleague, the American Abba Hillel Silver, were summoned to a meeting with representatives of the permanent members of the Security Council (Britain boycotted). At the meeting, they were grilled about the plausibility of partition.

According to the report of the meeting by Austin, Shertok had stood his ground in the face of pressure: "All essential elements of the plan are essential ... ." Shertok had said, "The combination of essential elements make up the irreducible minimum acceptable to the JA [Jewish Agency]. This includes statehood, sovereignty, territory, control of immigration, a seat in the UN."[34] As for the Arabs, Shertok thought that "nothing less than complete subversion of the [Partition Plan] would satisfy them."[35] Shertok's defiance here did not yield immediate fruit. And by March 19 when Austin undertook his notorious end run around Truman's policy – Shertok and his colleagues called it "Black Friday" – the situation had come to seem even more dire.[36]

The Trusteeship Plan, of course, never gained anything remotely close to the traction it would have required. Britain would not relent on its plan to leave Palestine to its fate on May 15 – the plan for withdrawal was too far along by mid-March. As Lovett acknowledged on April 23, the 50,000 American troops that he believed might need to be deployed to Palestine to keep the peace (in contrast to the 100,000 troops he had earlier told Truman would be required) were "still not an actuality."[37] And yet, the State Department remained adamantly opposed to a declaration of independence for a Jewish state until the moment this became no longer possible – when Truman recognized the new state and its

---

[33] Moshe Shertok to Robert Lovett, February 22, 1948, https://history.state.gov/historicaldocuments/frus1948v05p2/d53
[34] J. L. Austin to George Marshall, March 13, 1948, https://history.state.gov/historicaldocuments/frus1948v05p2/d91
[35] Ibid.   [36] Gabriel Sheffer, *Moshe Shertok*, p. 304.
[37] Robert Lovett to James Forrestal, April 23, 1948, https://history.state.gov/historicaldocuments/frus1948v05p2/d177

provisional government just after Israeli independence was declared on May 14.

On May 5, an aide to Dean Rusk, then a director at the State Department, met with Shertok and Abba Hillel Silver in order to urge the *Yishuv* to accept an immediate and "unconditional" ceasefire in Palestine. The goal of this proposed ceasefire, Shertok later noted, was not actually "the end of the war, but ... cancelling the founding of a Jewish state at this time."[38] This was not accompanied by a promise that America would support a Jewish state sometime afterward.[39]

Then, on May 8, 1948, Shertok met with Secretary Marshall. At the meeting, Marshall conveyed to Shertok that the State Department remained opposed to any unilateral Jewish declaration of statehood. As Shertok remembered it, Marshall had said:

If we, [the Jews] succeed [in establishing a state], well and good. He [Marshall] would be quite happy; he wished us well. But what if we failed? He did not want to put any pressure on us. It was our responsibility and it was for us to face it. We were completely free to take our decision, but he hoped we would do so in full realization of the very grave risks involved.[40]

In the case of failure, Marshall said, the Jews could not count on any support from the United States. In light of recent successes by the *Yishuv* in battles with the local Arabs in Palestine, Marshall, speaking as an "experienced general," told Shertok not to "trust your commanders especially since they are drunk with victory at the moment."[41] This was the message Shertok was given before his flight back to Tel Aviv.

THE PANIC AND THE CALM

Shertok recounted at length Marshall's "friendly" parting warning at a crucial marathon meeting with his *Minhelet ha'Am* colleagues, in Tel Aviv, four days later. "Marshall and his advisors," said Shertok, "view the situation here as a disaster. They believe all options to prevent independence are kosher."[42]

---

[38] Protocols of the National Administration, morning meeting, May 12, 1948, p. 48.

[39] Gabriel Sheffer, *Moshe Sharett*, p. 302.   [40] Ibid., p. 324

[41] Moshe Sharett interview with Eliezer Whartman, "Interviews with Signers of the Israeli Declaration of Independence," c. 1961, Israel National Library, 2= 2007 A 8945, p. 187.

[42] Protocols of the National Administration, May 12, 1948, Morning meeting, p. 48.

The US State Department's campaign to prevent or undermine Jewish independence had been extensive and would continue to be so. This campaign had featured a number of elements. First, an arms embargo had been put in place by the United States against Palestine. Theoretically this was meant to restrict the flow of arms to all parties, both Jews and Arabs, in keeping with UN policy. But Britain had already supplied arms to its Arab clients throughout the region. And America zealously pursued its embargo.[43] On the very day that Shertok met Marshall, Austin told Harold Beeley of the British Foreign Office that the two countries should enact a joint blockade off the Palestinian coast to restrict weapons smuggling into Palestine.[44]

There were also active efforts to prevent Jewish Americans from moving arms to Palestine, and State Department memos went so far as to attempt to address technicalities used by American Jews purchasing American arms via foreign shell corporations.[45] The commitment of the US government to an arms embargo was such that it would be maintained even after the Declaration of Independence.[46] Indeed, the embargo against Israel would be maintained until the early 1960s.[47]

Second, the State Department had in place draconian policies to prevent Americans from enlisting to fight on behalf of the *Yishuv*. Special counsel to President Truman Clark Clifford opposed the ban on the enlistment of Americans in the cause of Jewish independence. Perhaps speaking for Truman, he argued that "American citizens were not barred from joining the British Air Force or the Chinese Flying Tigers in the last war."[48] Despite Clifford's logically compelling point, the ban stayed in effect.[49] Had this ban been strictly enforced, it might have been crippling. Of the 193 pilots

---

[43] Shlomo Slonim, "The 1948 American Embargo on Arms to Palestine," *Political Science Quarterly*, 94, 3, 1979, pp. 495–514.

[44] Ibid., p. 509.

[45] See Boaz Dvir, *Saving Israel* (New York: Rowman & Littlefield, 2020).

[46] Michael Ottolenghi, "Harry Truman's Recognition of Israel," *The Historical Journal*, 47, 4, 2004, p. 984.

[47] From 1962, America permitted the supplying of arms to Israel via West Germany. After some backsliding in the wake of the Six Day War, the decisive change in American policy did not occur until 1968, when Lyndon Johnson, with support from Congress, approved the sale of top-of-the-line American phantom fighter jets to Israel. See John Golan, *Lavi* (Lincoln: University of Nebraska Press, 2016), p. 14.

[48] Clark Clifford memorandum, March 6, 1948, https://history.state.gov/historicaldocuments/frus1948v05p2/d78.

[49] On Clifford's support for the Zionist cause, see John Acacia, *Clark Clifford: The Wise Man of Washington* (University Press of Kentucky, 2009), p. 104; on Americans serving in the War of Independence, see Amy Weiss, "1948's Forgotten Soldiers?: The Shifting

who flew for Israel in the War of Independence, over half were Americans who chose to ignore the law.[50]

Extreme financial sanctions were threatened. One unnamed interlocutor told Shertok that "[w]e won't let the Jews wage a war that we don't want with our dollars," and that a general dedollarization and banning of acceptance of dollar transactions from the entire Middle East could be brought to bear. This kind of an arrangement would hardly have penalized Egypt, Jordan and Iraq – all states expected to attack the *Yishuv* and all states whose main foreign exchange transactions were conducted in British Pounds. But it would have been perilous for the Jewish state.[51]

The opponents of Jewish independence were not above accusing Jewish Americans of holding dual loyalties. Speaking to the Washington press corps in off-the-record comments, Marshall had stated firmly that there was no American geopolitical rationale for supporting Jewish independence. Such support was based on what Marshall had told the press were "political threats" that were not "on a plane of integrity" and to which he "would not bend."[52] As Lovett would put it, supporting a Jewish state was a "very transparent attempt to win the Jewish vote" and it would be "injurious to the reputation of the President."[53]

And so it followed that a public opinion campaign to emphasize the Jewish dimension of the American policy of supporting Jewish statehood was not beneath Shertok's various government interlocutors. Reporting to *Minhelet ha'Am* upon his return from America on May 12, Shertok stated that there were credible rumors that the State Department would attempt to use American Jews as pawns in an effort to prevent the creation of a Jewish state. The Department of State, Shertok warned, could disseminate allegations of Jewish "terrorism," "illegal weapons purchasing," and "illegal immigration."

A campaign of shaming could take place in the pages of the popular mass media, such as the *The New York Times,* in which trumped up or exaggerated details of Jewish violence in Palestine might shame the Jews

---

Reception of American Volunteers in Israel's War of Independence," *Israel Studies,* 25, 1, 2020, pp. 149–173.

[50] Benny Morris, *1948*, p. 85.

[51] Protocols of the National Administration, May 12, 1948, morning meeting, p. 47.

[52] Remarks to press February 27, 1948. Quoted in *Papers of George Catlett Marshall,* vol. 6, ed., Larry Bland, Mark Stoler, Sharon Stevens, and Daniel Holt (Baltimore: Johns Hopkins University Press, 2013), p. 387.

[53] Memorandum of Conversation, George Marshall, May 12, 1948, https://history.state .gov/historicaldocuments/frus1948v05p2/d252

of America and compel them to turn away from the Zionist cause.[54] Favorably disposed senators, like Senator Lehman of New York, could be pressured into reversing their pro-Zionist positions to advocate against Jewish independence – as in fact occurred.[55] Shertok feared that such an anti-independence whisper and press campaign would lead to a "large wave" of anti-Semitism in America.[56] And of course, such a campaign would not only cause psychological damage. American Jews had been a vital source of finance for the *Yishuv* as it sought to defend itself and build up its military forces.[57]

The conclusion of the story, and the failure of Marshall, Lovett, and the Foggy Bottom crew, is well known. Truman would overrule the generals and the foreign policy experts. Eleven minutes after David Ben-Gurion proclaimed a Jewish state in Palestine, the United States recognized his government as "the de facto authority of the new State of Israel."

One commonly proffered explanation for Truman's decision is that an intensive lobbying campaign – one even more intensive than the effort to hijack American policy initiated by the State Department – had successfully cajoled or pressured him to side with the cause of Jewish independence.[58] Truman's former partner in a Missouri haberdashery, Eddie Jacobson, had famously been prevailed upon by two New York-based Jewish activists to contact the president and implore him to meet with Zionist leader Chaim Weizmann on March 18, 1948. This was the culmination of more than a year of nonstop efforts whereby everything from campaigns of letters to visits from the New York Senate delegation had been brought to bear on Truman.[59]

This account fails to do Truman justice, for in retrospect we know that Truman saw things more clearly than Marshall: Marshall's concerns were misplaced, his geopolitical reasoning too limited and ultimately wrong. Though war ensued between Israel and its neighbors, American GI's were

---

[54] Protocols of the National Administration, May 12, 1948, Morning meeting, p. 50.

[55] Duane Tananbaum, *Herbert Lehman: A Political Biography* (Albany: State University of New York Press, 2016), p. 289.

[56] Protocols of the National Administration, Morning meeting, May 12, 1948, p. 50.

[57] See Derek Penslar, "Rebels without a Patron State: How Israel Financed the 1948 War," in *Purchasing Power: The Economics of Modern Jewish History*, ed. Rebecca Kobrin and Adam Teller (Philadelphia: University of Pennsylvania Press, 2015) pp. 171–191.

[58] See John Snetsinger, *Truman, the Jewish Vote, and the Creation of Israel* (Stanford: Hoover Institution Press, 1974).

[59] Ian J. Bickerton, "President Truman's Recognition of Israel," *American Jewish Historical Quarterly*, 58, 2, 1968, p. 178.

not summoned to protect Israel. The Jewish state emerged victorious over the Arab armies by the strength of its own arms, and the American-Saudi alliance survived. The Marshall Plan continued and European homes were heated with Arabian oil that winter. Even the Bolshevism of the Israeli Labor movement had been a myth: Czechoslovakian arms shipments to Israel ended in December because, as a diplomatic telegram would read, Red Army efforts "failed to create an indoctrinated cadre of the Israeli army."[60]

On May 12, 1948, Special Counsel to the President Clark Clifford had stood before President Truman, Marshall, and Lovett. He had been charged by the President with presenting the case for recognizing Israel, contra Marshall. Truman had earlier told Clifford, an accomplished trial lawyer and Democratic Party political operative, "You know how I feel. I want you to present it just as though you were making an argument before the Supreme Court . . . . I want you to be as persuasive as you can possibly be."[61]

Clifford had already presented his personal view to Truman in a March 6, 1948, memo: America ought to recognize the Jewish state for geostrategic reasons. Clifford argued that an American about-face at the UN, contra-Jewish Palestine, would be more damaging to American alliances and American interests than any insult that could be made to the oil states: "The Arabs need us more than we need them ... they must have dollars, and can only get dollars from the United States . . . . The Arab leaders would be committing suicide to accept Russian orientation."[62]

Clifford thought that the Saudi complaints were mere posturing. He would not allow the United States to flip-flop at the UN and "appear in the ridiculous role of trembling before threats of a few nomadic desert tribes." Clifford asked, "Why should Russia ... treat us with anything but contempt in light of our shilly-shallying appeasement of the Arabs?"[63]

This culminated in Clifford's realpolitik dismissal of Marshall at the May 12 meeting: "Trusteeship, which State supports, presupposes a single Palestine. That is unrealistic. Partition into Jewish and Arab Palestine has already happened. Jews and Arabs are already fighting each other from territory each side presently controls."[64] Clifford explained

---

[60] Penfield to Acting Secretary of State, December 8, 1948, https://history.state.gov/historicaldocuments/frus1948v05p2/d816
[61] Clark Clifford, *Counsel to the President*, p. 6.
[62] Clark Clifford to Harry Truman, March 8, 1948, https://history.state.gov/historicaldocuments/frus1948v05p2/d79.
[63] Ibid. [64] Clark Clifford, *Counsel to the President*, p. 11.

that war and independence were an inevitability, and US policy needed to be based on those realities.

Marshall exploded and argued true to form: "Mr. President, I thought this meeting was called to consider an important and complicated problem in foreign policy. I don't even know why Clifford is here. He is a domestic adviser, and this is a foreign policy matter." Lovett was bolder still. He said that recognizing Israel "is obviously designed to win the Jewish vote, but in my opinion, it would lose more votes than it would gain." Clearly, according to Marshall, since the recognition of Israel was unmerited in light of "international considerations," the President was "making foreign policy in light of domestic considerations."[65] Marshall closed the meeting by hinting that he might resign over the policy.[66]

Truman in his memoirs would offer a summary of Marshall's misjudgment:

I'd recognized Israel immediately as a sovereign nation when the British left Palestine in 1948, and I did so against the advice of my own secretary of state, George Marshall, who was afraid that the Arabs wouldn't like it. This was one of the few errors of judgment made by that great and wonderful man, but I felt that Israel deserved to be recognized and didn't give a damn whether the Arabs liked it or not.[67]

Above Marshall and the State Department employees stood a President who knew more than them, who saw further than them, and whose geostrategic judgment was stronger than theirs. The foreign policy professionals may not have seen things that way. They had been trained, at least to some extent, by way of America's institutions for understanding foreigners and foreign ways. They had surely taken overseas postings and developed networks among foreign dignitaries in the United States. Almost all had served oversees in the World Wars. Most were members in good standing of America's foreign policy clubs. (There was not yet a school of American "international relations"; that would only come into being in the 1950s.)

And yet, in history's gaze, their views were obviously in error and short sighted – and almost comically absurd. Loy Henderson had traveled in and studied the Middle East. Austin had a storied career in the Department of State already. Marshall had led the US Army. Of course, all of this is impressive.

But it cannot compare with Truman's experience at that point. He was after all the same president who had successfully concluded not only

---

[65] Ibid., pp. 16–24.   [66] Ibid.   [67] Ibid., p. 64.

World War II in Europe, but perhaps more impressively World War II in the Pacific. He had ordered the atomic bombing of Hiroshima and Nagasaki. He was drawing up the borders of Europe. The buck stopped with him on the biggest geopolitical matters of the day, as the sign on his desk famously said.

Perhaps Henderson had met Middle Eastern dignitaries. Truman had faced off against Stalin. Truman had already experienced more geopolitical decision making than nearly any other American human being in the twentieth century, and had met with great success. Only FDR had made more consequential choices. The knowing expertise of the Middle East hands and even of Marshall seems quaint relative to Truman's experience.

Shertok understandably was not near to this. His understanding of the geopolitical reality confronting the *Yishuv* was limited to what he knew of Marshall and whatever appreciation Shertok had gained of American public discourse during his time there. And Shertok was understandably committed to the UN process. It had brought the *Yishuv* to within a hair of some kind of political independence.

But Truman, who would make the ultimate decision, was focused on the effectual truths of strategy, politics, national foundings, and statehood. Above the UN process stood diplomatic and political realities. Truman – and as we will see, David Ben-Gurion – swam in those seas. The State Department officials, and along with them, their *Yishuv* interlocutor Moshe Shertok, were focused on the procedures and the details.

CONCLUSION

The pressures that confronted Moshe Shertok as he took his leave from the meeting of *Minhelet ha'Am* on May 12 were enormous. He had been assigned to rewrite the Declaration of Independence, and he did so with a full appreciation of the political and diplomatic gravity of the initiative. Berenson, Beham, and the Legal Department workers who had taken earlier cracks at writing a declaration of independence knew that they wrote for posterity and perhaps for a demanding boss back at the office. But they did not have the full weight of the US State Department and the pressure of potential military boycotts and wars upon their shoulders. They were oblivious to the high diplomatic maneuvering in which Shertok was engaged. And surely they were unaware of the cohesion of the campaign against Jewish independence underway in Washington.

Shertok had little else on his mind. As the shepherd of the diplomatic achievement of Resolution 181, he was understandably focused on seeing it through to its end. He was aware that Truman could override the State Department. And he was not wrong.

But by the same token, the independent state Truman envisioned was the one dictated by the UN partition plan. Clark Clifford, the keen supporter of Zionism, later recalled that he had told Eliahu Epstein on May 12 that the "new state [must] claim nothing beyond the boundaries outlined in the UN resolution of November 29, 1947, because those boundaries were the only ones which had been agreed to by everyone, including the Arabs, in any international forum."[68]

Epstein, based in Washington, was unaware of the deliberations over the borders of the state that would take place in Tel Aviv over the days leading up to independence. Epstein had thus himself assented to this request, confirming that the Jewish state would indeed stick to the UN plan. After Israel had declared independence, Epstein wrote to President Truman that the independent state of Israel had been declared "within frontiers approved by the [UN] General Assembly of the United Nations."[69]

This, as we will see, was not so. But as Truman's account of the matter lays bare, irrespective of whether Epstein's message was born of ignorance or chicanery, its substance ultimately did not matter. There would be no revocation of US recognition of Israeli statehood. The test of statehood would be on the battlefield.

Presenting his account of the political configuration in America at the May 12 meeting of *Minhelet ha'Am*, Shertok asked the key question regarding the threats and warnings from the State Department: "Has the matter [to undercut Jewish statehood and independence] been weighed carefully and has it become the official policy in Washington ... or should this be seen as the effort of a small school of people in the State Department?" Shertok offered an answer at some length:

Our group of friends in Washington – like Ben Cohen, Oscar Gass ... who may not be senior officials, but do have an opportunity to know what's happening, their opinion is: "don't worry." But with all due respect to them, I need to point

---

[68] Quoted in Martin Kramer, "The May 1948 Vote that Made the State of Israel."
[69] Eliahu Epstein to Harry Truman, May 14, 1948, https://history.state.gov/historicaldocuments/frus1948v05p2/d266

out their fundamental limitation. They are not privy to all the details. To them everything comes down to the question: who is in charge?[70]

Shertok understood that there was a political dimension that could exceed procedure. But ultimately, he was too wrapped up in the procedural process he himself had initiated. He could see the forest for the trees, but he was also more familiar with the trees. Even as he exercised his diplomatic and political perspective, his months spent wading through the details dragged him back down to them.

And so, the draft of the Declaration of Independence that he produced overnight reflected his position on the matter. Working through the late hours and into the morning, the former journalist Shertok harnessed not only his old skills of writing to deadline but also his newfound knowledge of the world of international diplomacy at the nascent United Nations. He ensured that the text of the document lined up with the scheme that Resolution 181 set in motion.

He believed that the Jewish state faced two prospects. The first option was independence declared along the lines of Resolution 181 even if the substance of independence would be quite different – the facts on the ground guaranteed that a new state would immediately be at war and in its essence a state in full. Perhaps it might have to wait for international recognition. Perhaps it might have to follow some procedural aspects of Resolution 181. Surely it couldn't be seen to deviate from them.

The alternatives – explicit statements regarding independence that implied a scuttling of Resolution 181 – ran the risk of scuttling the prospect of a Jewish state along with them. At least this was Shertok's fear. Deviation from Resolution 181 could have meant that no major states would recognize a newly declared Jewish state. And a lack of recognition could have meant an ongoing blockade, the possible arrival of foreign forces, and thus a risk of political catastrophe.

It may have been a limitation of the prior drafters of the Declaration not to see things through Shertok's diplomatic prism; but it was equally a limit of Shertok's vision that he had difficulty seeing much else. For Jewish independence would prove to be much more than Shertok's text envisioned. It would be a full independence – the declaration of a state subject to the vicissitudes of the world. It would be sovereign by necessity. In practice there

---

[70] Protocols of the National Administration, morning meeting, May 12, 1948, p. 54. Shertok was referring to Benjamin V. Cohen, a key legislative architect of the New Deal and adviser to Truman, and Oscar Gass, the economist who went on to be an economic advisor to Israel.

would be no economic union, no overseeing boards, no United Nations troops, no internationally-mandated frontiers. Independence would be total, and it would be won finally in war and not in the halls of the UN.

One may wonder whether Shertok's meticulous efforts to satisfy the preexisting criteria betray a lack of understanding of the fundamentally disruptive character of founding of the state – or indeed of any state. The act of founding requires not indeed ignorance, but deliberate disregard, of some crucial established modes of operation. In the founding of the state, the only modes that mattered would be created by the state. In the ordinary course of politics, hewing to established norms and laws is essential. But at moments of sovereignty, the crucial decisions stand outside the established orders.

It may not have seemed that way to Shertok – but it seemed that way to Truman and, as we will see, to David Ben-Gurion. Diplomacy is essential. But the diplomatic process has its limits.

6

Politics and Law

Debating the Declaration

Politics would triumph over both diplomacy and law in the drafting of Israel's Declaration of Independence. *Minhelet ha'Am* reconvened on May 13, the day that Shertok completed his draft of the Declaration, and a discussion of the text was on the agenda. Time was short. Independence would be declared on May 14 in advance of the Jewish sabbath that evening. Shertok had written through the night of the May 12 into the morning of May 13. The leadership of the *Yishuv* had to weigh in. There were decisions to make regarding its Declaration of Independence.

Shertok's text was roundly rejected. On essentially every matter of importance, David Ben-Gurion would override Shertok. Ben-Gurion went on to effectively take over the production of the final text. Shertok had believed that the Declaration of Independence had to address four main open questions: (1) whether to simply declare a state or to declare a state within the framework of the United Nations process; (2) whether to declare an independent government or a provisional government within the framework of the UN process; (3) whether to delineate the country's borders; and (4) the extent to which Jewish history and tradition were to find their way into the text.

Shertok made decisions on all of these issues. He was for declaring a state within the UN process. He was thus also for a provisional government, if with some hair-splitting distinctions. He had been for delineating the borders in accordance with the UN's plan, though this was overruled even before he set out to write his draft. He was against tying the state's founding document deeply into the arc of Judaism's texts, even if his writing was replete with Jewish signifiers. These were Shertok's opinions. None of these opinions would stand.

Shertok presented his draft of the Declaration to *Minhelet ha'Am* at a meeting held on May 13, fewer than twenty hours after a committee consisting of Shertok and four fellow drafters had been nominated to compose the final document in the first place. Shertok had worked through most of the night and assembled the final text only after both presenting it to the other members of the committee in the morning and then taking feedback from Ben-Gurion. He brought a text based on these writing sessions and deliberations to a meeting of *Minhelet ha'Am* that was held the next evening.[1]

Shertok's drafting committee must have worked under tremendous pressure. The scope of the undertaking and the time constraint made things hard enough. But on top of that, the members of the council had varied and even rival perspectives. David Remez was a Labor Zionist trade union leader with little life experience beyond those circles. Felix Rosenblüth was a German lawyer with extensive training and experience studying under Germany's leading legal minds, but he was very much that: a German lawyer whose political judgment was literalist and legalistic. It was Rosenblüth who had been charged with producing a declaration of independence in the first instance – a process he had delegated first to Beham, then Beham and the fledgling team at the Legal Department, next to Berenson, and then back to the Legal Department under his own guidance. Moshe Shapira was the leader in Israel of the now all-but-lost world of moderate socialist modern orthodox Zionism called *ha'Poel Mizrahi*. His interests and worldview were decidedly religious, if moderate, and his political instincts were oriented toward issues of ethics and procedural fairness. Aharon Zisling was a far-left member of a union of labor parties to the left of the one that David Ben-Gurion had consolidated. He would later become an outspoken critic of Israel's military policies, advocate for Arab rights, and a defender of the already-decaying socialist planned economy.[2] And Shertok, of course, was one of the most powerful leaders of the *Yishuv* and the Labor Party, its principal diplomat in the United States, and a famous journalist. He would eventually become Israel's second prime minister.

Their levels of comfort with diplomacy and law varied. Their literary abilities and interest varied. Their reading in political thought was

---

[1] See Ariel Feldstein, "One Meeting – Many Descriptions: The Resolution on the Establishment of the State of Israel," *Israel Studies Forum*, 23, 2, 2008, pp. 99–114.
[2] Benny Morris, "The Harvest of 1948 and the Creation of the Palestinian Refugee Problem," *Middle East Journal*, 40, 4, 1986, pp. 671–685.

generally low and focused on labor Zionist works with the exception of the legalist Rosenblüth. Most of all, with the exception of Shertok, their experience of world affairs was limited to the select issues that had confronted the *Yishuv*. And Shertok's schooling in global diplomacy had occurred mainly at the United Nations and in his days working with Chaim Weizmann in London. The five ultimately followed the path that had already been laid out for them and produced a draft of the Declaration fully in keeping with Berenson and Lauterpacht's work, if geared to meet Shertok's diplomatic agenda.

The reception of their document thus could not have been what any of them, and above all Shertok, would have expected. The repudiation of the text was scathing. Upon Shertok's presentation of the text, it was criticized from nearly all sides, including, to some degree, by Shertok's fellow members of his drafting committee. The critiques covered all four of the major issues raised above as well as an additional one: the missing discussion in depth of the rights of the citizens – which ought to be at root the basis of the state.

The reasons that Ben-Gurion used at the May 13 meeting in order to himself take over the drafting of the Declaration were stylistic and religious. There was broad dissatisfaction among the members of *Minhelet ha'Am* with Shertok's use of the legal formula "and whereas" to begin each of his paragraphs – this despite the fact that Ben-Gurion had, when canvassed for his opinion earlier that day by Shertok, preferred that Shertok use "whereas" instead of the prefix "being that."[3] There was also a debate over the use of the term "rock of Israel" to describe God in the document.

But the essence of the critique of Shertok's draft lay in other areas: on matters of deep substance pertaining to independence and political founding. In what follows, this debate is pieced together based on the primary transcripts of the meetings of *Minhelet ha'Am* on May 12, when Shertok received his assignment, and on May 13, when his work was presented. At these meetings, views and positions were presented by Ben-Gurion and others in debates which bring out the most important matters at the foundation of the state.

---

[3] See Moshe Gurari, "Havlei leidata shel megilat ha'atzmaut," *Davar*, May 11, 1973. Years later, Shertok would still express frustration at the removal of this formula from the final document – perhaps disguising a more general bitterness about Ben Gurion's takeover of the process. See his interview with Eliezer Whartman, in "Interviews with signers of the Israeli Declaration of Independence," c. 1961, Israel National Library, 2= 2007 A 8945, p. 187.

NO INDEPENDENCE WITHOUT A STATE

The UN was a particular point of controversy in the founding of the state of Israel. In declaring independence, was the *Yishuv* obligated to adhere to the letter and spirit of Resolution 181 and, in general, to the UN as a source of legitimacy and political authority? To what extent would the new state have to part ways with the legal and political reality that had been proposed by the UN, and to what extent did it have to commit to work toward attaining it? How had the beginning of the war in Palestine between the Jews and the Arabs, the withdrawal of Britain from much of Palestine's territory over the prior five months, Britain's imminent final withdrawal on May 15, and the failure of the UN to implement the terms of Resolution 181 after November, necessitated a new calculus?

This set of questions had been foremost in the minds of Herschel Lauterpacht as well as Moshe Shertok as they drafted their texts. The scholarship of the drafting of Israel's Declaration of Independence tends to emphasize the debates surrounding: (1) whether to explicitly mention the name of God in the Declaration and (2) whether the text should delineate the borders of the state.[4] Yet the question of the United Nations process and a potential departure from it was the foremost practical issue that *Minhelet ha'Am* had to face as it assessed the Declaration in its final meetings before the formal end of the British Mandate.

After all, the council had to ask itself: What exactly are we doing? Are we declaring independence, or following a UN process? Are we creating a new state, or following a UN process toward the creation of a state? The issue of the UN was central and not merely exigent. It was the major question addressed in Shertok's draft. And accordingly, it occupied the vast majority of the time allotted for debate. It also held great weight in principle: it went to the core of the question of what kind of state the Jews were to found.

Minhelet ha'Am was strongly divided over how to proceed. One camp followed the logic of Moshe Shertok's draft and argued that it was best to declare a state in what they termed the "framework" (lit. "enclosure" – *misgeret*) of the United Nations, thereby committing the state, at least in theory, to the terms of independence and political logic that the United

---

[4] See Martin Kramer, "The May 1948 Vote That Made the State of Israel," April 2, 2018. Also see Avi Shilon, "Ben-Gurion's Pragmatic Approach to Borders," *Mosaic*, April 23, 2018. https://mosaicmagazine.com/response/israel-zionism/2018/04/ben-gurions-pragmatic-approach-to-borders/, cf. Yoram Shachar, "Yomano shel Uri Yadin" ("Uri Yadin's Diary"), *Iyunei Mishpat*, 3, 1991.

Nations had set forth the prior November.[5] Though the British Mandate was set to expire on May 15, the United Nations had specified October 1 as the date in which this new political arrangement would come into place. And so, if the *Yishuv* were to follow the letter of the United Nations resolution, a declaration of independence in May would only be a provisional declaration of independence; the new entities specified by the UN were only supposed to come into being in October 1948.

Shertok's draft did not declare provisional independence. However, it also did not proclaim its opposite. His draft is ambiguous. In meetings with his colleagues, he opposed the explicit ascription of sovereignty (*ribonut*) to the new state. He meant to skirt the issue by declaring a state within the "framework of the United Nations," in his phrase. This tactic would, if not push the politics and law of the state into the Resolution 181 process, at least leave that avenue open even as its culmination had grown exceedingly doubtful.

Shertok had elaborated on this position at a meeting of the *Mapai* leadership on what must have been a very busy May 12 – he composed his draft of the Declaration that night. The meeting had been called so that the *Mapai* party could authorize Ben-Gurion's course of declaring independence. Shertok was mustered to persuade the few wobbly *Mapainiks*. The logic: if Shertok, who could see both sides of the issue, was for independence, then the vacillating among the party faithful could well be won over by him for decisive action.

"There will be no delay," Shertok told his fellow party members. *Yishuv* leadership had listened to all American diplomatic proposals, no matter how unreasonable they had seemed, he explained. It was appropriate to listen and hear out the other side. However, there could be no compromise on independence itself. The state would be declared in two days, Shertok noted resolutely. Shertok was absolutely committed to declaring independence.[6]

At the same time, Shertok remained noncommittal on the kind of independence to be declared: "*Minhelet ha'Am* is deliberating. It will undoubtedly make a decision tonight or tomorrow morning. I have no doubt the answer will be positive [i.e. in favor of a state]. But I cannot say exactly what the form of the state will be." At least for Shertok, the matter of whether or not to abandon the Resolution 181 framework had not yet been settled.

---

[5] Protocols of the National Administration, May 12, 1948, evening meeting, pp. 105–114.
[6] Protocols of *Mapai*, May 12, 1948, Labor Party Archives, 2-023-1948-49.

Of course, as Shertok knew well, war and diplomatic reality had made the UN path nearly untenable. The Arab rejection of partition meant that there was no partner for partition. The beginning of total war between the Jews and Arabs on its face did not respect the careful procedural and territorial markers envisioned by the United Nations. The British had departed, leaving in their wake a void. In practice, with the withdrawal of the British, the *Yishuv* would rule itself. And so, as Shertok's argument went, if the UN path was dead, why not pretend that it was in place for another few months and gain a recognized state in the process?

Perhaps unsurprisingly, the camp that called for a Declaration very much in line with the legal process of the United Nations was led at the meetings of *Minhelet ha'Am* by by Felix Rosenblüth. At the May 12 evening meeting, before Shertok wrote his draft, Rosenblüth had nicely illustrated the problem as follows:

Should the declaration be in the framework of the decision of the United Nations or [merely] on its background and basis. I am in favor of keeping it in the framework .... We stand on the basis of the new fiction that today is more than a fiction: the decision of November 29, 1947 stands.[7]

No one could argue that the UN or Resolution 181 could be ignored; all recognized that the UN resolution that approved the partition of Palestine had immense political and legal relevance for Jewish independence.

By the same token, no one could argue that it was in effect: it was clearly "a fiction." The question was whether to place the declaration of the state within the framework of the UN decision or merely to acknowledge that the United Nations decision had given some form of sanction to the creation of a Jewish state.

The former was a far more strict proposition, both legally and politically. It could theoretically commit the *Yishuv* to the terms of Resolution 181. Merely asserting that the state would be declared on the "basis" or "background" of the United Nations and its decisions was an entirely different matter. That maneuver could and would imply some general agreement with the idea of the UN Partition Plan, and certainly acknowledge the legitimacy of the UN approval of Jewish sovereignty. Why would one avoid stating that the UN had recognized an independent Jewish state?

In terms of the political dynamics within *Minhelet ha'Am*, Rosenblüth was naturally in favor of the literalist approach, albeit with important

---

[7] Protocols of the National Administration, evening meeting, May 12, 1948, p. 105.

qualifications. Reviewing Lauterpacht's Declaration, Rosenblüth had argued at the evening meeting on May 12 that it "was also based on the declaration of the United Nations."[8] Joining him in this opinion was David Remez, the heavyweight trade unionist who had founded *Mapai* along with David Ben-Gurion. Commenting on Shertok's draft in the meeting on May 13, Remez supported it fully: there was almost "nothing to remove" from it.[9] Eliezer Kaplan, who would go on to be the first finance minister of the state, concurred, arguing that the Declaration should clearly state that "we are prepared to cooperate with the UN in fulfilling the UN plan" for the region.[10]

Aharon Zisling, who had also worked on the draft with Shertok, voiced his approval of its general tenor, though, as we will see, he was the principal anti-theological voice in the room when it came to the effort to remove the reference to God, "the rock of Israel," at the text's conclusion. His opposition did not end there. Zisling also expressed mild reservation to locating the sovereignty of the state within the United Nations framework. "Get rid of the reference to the United Nations," he said, after Shertok had read his draft out loud to his fellow committee members. "The rights of the Jewish people are not dependent on a decision of the General Assembly."[11]

Though Shertok would budge a little over the next day, he was extremely wary about departing from the framework of Resolution 181. Before he wrote his draft, he said to *Minhelet ha'Am*:

We can't simply appeal to the United Nations to recognize [the new state], when we haven't fulfilled the conditions that the United Nations imposed upon us .... I suggest we declare independence in two stages. First, we declare the independence of the governing bodies of the state. These bodies, which can then fulfill the conditions of the United Nations, will present the case [for independence] to the United Nations.[12]

The draft that Shertok wrote would not go so far as to explicitly propose a "two stage" independence. But this comment is highly revealing of how concerned members of *Minhelet ha'Am* were when it came to fulfilling the terms of Resolution 181. Shertok even floated delaying independence until an economic union with the Arab state could be shown to exist and an international Jerusalem could be enforced.

---

[8] Ibid.   [9] Protocols of the National Administration, May 13, 1948, p. 125.
[10] Protocols of the National Administration, May 12, 1948, evening meeting, p. 105.
[11] Protocols of the National Administration, May 13, 1948, p. 124.
[12] Protocols of the National Administration, evening meeting, May 12, 1948, p. 111.

As we know, the political world envisioned by Resolution 181 – an international Jerusalem, an economic union, and a self-governing Arab state – never came close to becoming a reality. Waiting for it thus could have precluded independence. Shertok's focus on the details of law and diplomacy in Washington made him hesitant to depart from the United Nations plans and procedures even as he knew that the UN scheme was inoperative.

Felix Rosenblüth, though not as close to the diplomatic details as was Shertok, sought a coherent legal rationale for Jewish sovereignty: a logical bridge between the decision of the UN taken the previous November and the proclamation of the *Yishuv* taken that May. The latter decision (independence), in this framework, had to logically follow the former (the UN granting a legal right to independence).

There was, however, a subtle distinction that Rosenblüth the keen legalist had identified in Lauterpacht's draft text – a difference which separated Lauterpacht's approach from Shertok's. Lauterpacht's text had laid out a novel argument that cut to the essence of the matter. It argued that the UN decision of November 1947 on the validity of an independent Jewish state could "not be revoked" even as the specific procedural aspects of that decision were no longer operable. The United Nations provisions for the organization of an international Jerusalem, and peace between the Jews and Arabs, may not have been maintained despite their explicit mention in Resolution 181. But, Lauterpacht argued, the failure to meet the details of Resolution 181 did not invalidate the overarching principle of Resolution 181. Resolution 181's *aim* was to create a Jewish state and an Arab state. The big picture was what mattered.

That, of course, was not Lauterpacht's final word. He desired to limit Jewish sovereignty by placing it under the evolving doctrine of international law and the bodies that might enforce it. Yet, even as he held this doctrinaire position, he never insisted that the details of Resolution 181 remained binding. Perhaps he justified this by thinking that the spirit of international law – in this case the spirit of Resolution 181, which clearly called for the creation of a Jewish state – ought to prevail over the letter of international law because he believed that there exists a fundamental spirit of international law consisting in independence and mutual respect for nations under a United Nations. Be this as it may, Shertok and other members of *Minhelet ha'Am* were more doctrinaire than Lauterpacht. They insisted on meeting the letter and not just the spirit of Resolution 181.

ENTER BEN-GURION

It took the practical wisdom of David Ben-Gurion to expose the severe limitations of this literalist point of view and to suggest an alternative. Ben-Gurion, master of the *Yishuv*, Israel's Prime Minister from 1948 until 1963 with only a short interregnum, would have over his life moments both of strategic and tactical brilliance as well as myopia and misjudgment. When we consider his version of Israel's Declaration in Chapter 7, we will delve further into Ben-Gurion's statesmanship. Suffice it to say for now that in these final meetings surrounding independence, Ben-Gurion's prudence was unrivalled, essential, and the sufficient condition for the founding of the Jewish state as it in fact transpired.

Over the course of the meetings on May 12 and 13, Ben-Gurion demolished the argument that independence should only be declared in the framework of UN Resolution 181 – whether in its letter or its spirit. Through magnificent political and rhetorical maneuvering and management of these meetings, he argued that declaring a state on the strict basis of the UN resolution made no sense either from a legal or a political point of view.

From a legal point of view, Ben-Gurion could rely upon Rosenblüth's exposition of Lauterpacht's text for its assertion of the right of the Jews to declare independence. Before Shertok wrote his draft, Rosenblüth argued that the text of the Declaration of Independence should unabashedly proclaim a sovereign independent state – as the UN had promised:

Lauterpacht says, which makes sense, that on November 29 it was indisputably decided that the Hebrew people have a right to found a state. This wasn't even contested, even as in the meantime there have been difficulties and attempts to make the thing fail. In his opinion, we have the right to [proclaim a state], which by all rights the UN executive committee was supposed to do. This theory we have to accept.[13]

Rosenblüth saw that the spirit of the UN Resolution recognized the *right* of the Jewish people to proclaim independence. This could be a useful debating point. After all, Rosenblüth was arguing, the UN had failed to uphold the details. The UN was supposed to guarantee Jewish independence. And yet, says Rosenblüth, they have not done so. Indeed, the UN has in some ways through its actions undermined its own proclamation. It prevented the *Yishuv* from arming itself even as the *Yishuv* faced war prosecuted by the Arabs of Palestine with state backing from Palestine's neighbors. And so, the details of UN Resolution 181 were not operative.

---

[13] Ibid., p. 106.

Ben-Gurion would go further and argue that the details of Resolution 181 were irrelevant. Yet the principle of international recognition of the rights of the Jewish people was worth accepting and recognizing for Ben-Gurion. For who among the decent nations wanted to argue against the formation of a state for the Jews just three short years following the Holocaust and six short months after such a state had become an aim of the UN itself? Ben-Gurion may have had a "decent respect for the opinions of mankind," but here he was to teach his colleagues a lesson: sometimes the details of those opinions are not germane to the matter at hand.

The crucial issue for Ben-Gurion was not the fulfillment of this or that condition set out by the Resolution 181 – conditions which, as we saw, were not and would never be fulfilled. It was to declare a state. This was, he strenuously argued, to be a state in the simplest and most naïve sense: a polity that, *ipso facto*, is responsible for the things that states must in their nature be responsible for. Rosenblüth was obsessed with the idea of declaring a *sovereign* state explicitly, even as he wanted to declare it in the context of the UN process. He believed, from his legalist perspective, that the word "sovereignty" was the key factor. He was supported in this view, almost to a fanatical degree, by the Young Turks in the Legal Department Heinsheimer, Zilberg, and Beham, who together had talked themselves into imagining that the absence of the word 'sovereignty' from the Declaration of Independence would preclude actual sovereignty.

Ben-Gurion eventually grew fed up with this hair-splitting – he had been dealing with it over the preceding weeks, and the old arguments never seemed to go away. As far as he was concerned, a state is by definition sovereign. Indeed, in Ben-Gurion's mind, the fact that *Moetzet ha'Am* and *Minhelet ha'Am* were operating, and their decisions were recognized as legitimate, was perhaps evidence enough that the state was about to come into being. The British were well along in their withdrawal and the final departure to the port in Haifa of the Mandatory Authority's last vestiges was scheduled in 24 hours. The vacuum was being filled by the institutions of the *Yishuv* and its military forces. A state was already in a sense in existence. Ben-Gurion had to help it emerge fully and irrevocably.[14]

---

[14] See Ben-Gurion's comments at the first meeting of the *Minhelet ha'Am*, Protocols of the National Administration, April 18, 1948, p. 6.

SOVEREIGNTY AND THE UN PROCESS

There was no doubt that a Jewish state of some kind would be declared when the Union Jack came down for the last time that May. But what kind of state would it be? Uri Heinsheimer of the Legal Department raised the issue in his diary on April 29: "Nothing is decided. There is still no clear decision in the Council of 13 whether to declare a state immediately or a regime of partial independence."[15] This was the issue at hand in the final meetings of *Minhelet ha'Am*: not whether to declare a state, but whether to declare a state within the UN's framework of "partial independence" or a state simply.

David Ben-Gurion sought to call for independence, as, he thought, the *Yishuv* already had nearly achieved in practice. In order to guarantee that independence, the state had to decisively break away from the United Nations process which might have promised something less than independence. As he put in the meeting on May 12:

I say: we should not state "in the framework of the decision of the UN" but rather "on the basis of the decision of the UN"; we should not discuss sovereignty or lack of sovereignty, but rather discuss a state. We must approve the term: "the State of Israel." To announce: from this moment onwards the State of Israel is established. We have to decide upon the government and if we're announcing its establishment. I propose that we not proclaim "the government of the Jews" but rather "the government of the state," and should the state be named Israel, "the government of the State of Israel."[16]

A state inherently possesses, in Ben-Gurion's telling, all sovereign powers. There was no import to writing about "a sovereign state" or "a non-sovereign state." What mattered was in fact declaring a state without tying it to the UN or Resolution 181.

Perhaps the legalisms of the United Nations process might theoretically have mattered had they been necessary in order to bring a state into being. But the UN process had already died. What mattered was what course of action the *Yishuv* would take. It is worth quoting Ben-Gurion's comments on the subject at the May 12 meeting further:

We have to found a government. We do rely, and we'll say this in the declaration, on the declaration of the United Nations. But in the UN [declaration] there were two things. A) A solution to the question of the land of Israel: a Jewish

---

[15] Heinsheimer's diary has been reproduced in *Sefer Uri Yadin (The Uri Yadin Book)*, ed. Aharon Barak (Tel Aviv: 1990), p. 18.

[16] Protocols of the National Administration, evening meeting, May 12, 1948, p. 107.

state, an Arab state, and economic union. B) A specific procedure for the coming into being [of these]. That procedure has proven counterfeit and is not now in existence. And since it is counterfeit it does not oblige us. But the core of the matter – the emergence of a Jewish and also the emergence of an Arab state – this does bind us. And if the UN does call for an economic union, then the boundaries of this will be obligatory for us. And if this stops us from capturing a manhole [beyond our boundaries] we won't capture it. But the procedure failed. It was not cancelled by us, but because the United Nations had no power to implement it.[17]

Ben-Gurion was actually willing to concede quite a lot to the authority of the United Nations here. He states explicitly that the *Yishuv* would be bound to what he calls "the solution" of the question of the land of Israel; that solution involved the creation of a Jewish state, an Arab state, and an economic union. He even was willing to grant that the UN might theoretically determine borders should it intervene in the war already raging either militarily or diplomatically. Partition of the Land of Israel as a route to Jewish statehood was an important political plank for his party – and one which stood in stark contrast to the Revisionists.[18] Just as Ben-Gurion had accepted the partition plan in 1937, assenting to Chaim Weizmann's famous willingness to accept a state "the size of a table-cloth," Ben-Gurion was far from absolutist here.

And yet, Ben-Gurion saw through the UN. His acceptance of the UN process was contingent: it was contingent on the UN holding up its end of the bargain. The UN had not done this. The UN process had proven "counterfeit." As Lauterpacht himself had seen, the lack of fulfillment of the process meant that the *Yishuv* was not bound to it. The crucial matter, the only matter, said Ben-Gurion, was thus for the *Yishuv to declare a state on its own terms*. It is no surprise then that in his own comments on Shertok's draft, Ben-Gurion suggested deleting the mention of partition altogether: "Why is that incumbent upon us?" he asked his colleagues.[19]

Ben-Gurion received crucial help from Golda Meyerson (later Golda Meir, Israel's fourth Prime Minister). Meyerson had just returned from a secret meeting with King Abdullah of Jordan. She had attempted to persuade the Hashemite monarch not to invade the Jewish state.

---

[17] Protocols of the National Administration, May 13, 1948, p. 113.
[18] For a review, see Itzhak Galnoor, "The Zionist Debates on Partition (1919–1947)," *Israel Studies*, 14, 2, 2009, pp. 74–87.
[19] Protocols of the National Administration, May 13, 1948, p. 113.

Meyerson had bad news to deliver on this front. The king could not be swayed.[20]

Meyerson had an uncanny ability to see to the essentials in questions. Responding to David Remez, who on May 12 said that the *Yishuv* "must act as if the UN decision was still operative," Meyerson cut to the heart of the issue:

> This isn't useful to us. We have to go all the way. We can't zig-zag now. Something [the UN Commission that would implement Resolution 181] was supposed to emerge on April 1. And it didn't. There was supposed to be a UN Commission here. There wasn't, and there won't be. And so, we are declaring independence. We are, ourselves, of necessity, declaring the foundation of the state. And if we do this – we must go all the way.[21]

These shrewd remarks reveal some of the common sense that was to typify Meyerson's long and successful career in Israeli politics and international diplomacy. She lacked an interest in the niceties of international law. Her deliberate disregard of legal process here let her see the issue for what it was. Politically speaking, Resolution 181 had lost all ability to compel. It may have maintained a certain nominal or formal right, but it had lost all power. The procedures themselves had no moral worth. They were mere procedures. And so, with the UN failing to live up to its end of the bargain, it fell to the Jews to determine their own political reality.

That political reality would be determined by the declaration of a state that was not limited by UN fiat: "The core of the matter is declaring independence – the meaning of this is that the world is asked to recognize this... The politically salient fact is: 'we declare that the state has arisen,'" said Meyerson.[22] In short, a full and complete state, like all other states. It is perhaps not surprising that the two politicians then serving on *Minhelet ha'Am* who would go on to the greatest subsequent political success were also the ones who saw the issue of independence most astutely.

NO STATE WITHOUT A GOVERNMENT

Just as Ben-Gurion would steer the committee toward a declaration of a state outside the UN process, so too would he insist that the *government*

---

[20] See Francine Klagbrun, *Lioness: Golda Meir and the Nation of Israel* (New York: Shocken, 2017), p. 323.

[21] Protocols of the National Administration, evening meeting, May 12, 1948, p. 110.

[22] Ibid., p. 113.

of the state be recognized as an actual government, without any qualifications. Shertok, we recall, had desired to avoid using the word "sovereignty" [*ribonut*] with respect to the state for fear of running afoul of the procedures of the United Nations. He had also wanted to appoint a provisional government that would become permanent once the state became permanent. This was, after all, what the Zionist Actions Committee had ruled, and at the time, Ben-Gurion had agreed.

By mid-May, Ben-Gurion reasoned, it was possible and in fact necessary to go further. Ben-Gurion, again supported by Meyerson, rejected the half-measure of "provisional government." Ben-Gurion sought rather to ensure that *Minhelet ha'Am* would evolve into the temporary holder of the state's permanent executive power and *Moetzet ha'Am* would be the temporary holder of its permanent political office. The government could be described acceptably as "temporary" insofar as it was to be elected democratically, and thus, at some point in the future, when hostilities and emergency had abated sufficiently to allow some political deliberation and national repose, elections would be held to legitimate the members of the bodies that would lead the state.

But the governing bodies at the declaration of the state were only to be temporary insofar as there would be plans to supplant them by better conceived and more thoroughly legitimated ones later. And of course, Ben-Gurion expected that there might be a constitution which could even overhaul the governing bodies of the state. In this sense, some of the institutions *as then constituted* might be temporary. But the idea that rulers of the state would be sovereign was to be "permanent."

In a lecture delivered in 1919 immediately following the defeat of Germany in the First World War, the German sociologist Max Weber famously quoted Soviet Revolutionary journalist and leader Leon Trotsky in order to define the state. "What is a 'state'?" Weber asked:

Sociologically, the state cannot be defined in terms of its ends . . . . There is scarcely any task that some political association has not taken in hand, and there is no task that one could say has always been exclusive and peculiar to those associations which are designated as political ones . . . . "Every state is founded on force," said Trotsky at Brest-Litovsk. That is indeed right . . . . Today, however, we have to say that a state is a human community that (successfully) claims the monopoly of the legitimate use of physical force within a given territory. Note that "territory" is one of the characteristics of the state.[23]

---

[23] Max Weber, "Politics as a Vocation," (1919) trans. H. H. Gerth and C. Wright Mills, http://fs2.american.edu/dfagel/www/class%20readings/weber/politicsasavocation.pdf

In Weber's account, a state has no delineable purpose. The state is simply instrumental. One state aims for the flourishing of the populace under just laws of independent individual freedom with reasonable and popularly checked curtailments thereof; another aims for unlimited conquest under a religious banner; a third aims to cement the ongoing tyrannical rule by a single family. These aims may not be equal in their moral ranking. But the state, on Weber's terms, is not the right term to use in order to understand these moral differences. The state, as an idea, according to Weber, stands neutral on moral questions.[24] Where it is not neutral is with respect to the permanent sovereignty of its institutions.

The early days of the State of Israel would reflect Ben-Gurion's understanding of these criteria. By the standards of other movements of national independence and revolution, there was little in the way of struggle for supremacy in the proto-state of Israel among the residents of the *Yishuv*. There were limited political assassinations during the run-up to the creation of the state, most notably of Shertok's predecessor as head of the Political Department of the Jewish Agency, Chaim Arlosoroff, who was killed by unknown assailants in 1933.[25] And there would be a campaign in which Labor Party-aligned military forces joined with the British Mandate authorities in an effort to disarm and arrest the right-wing militias in what became known as "La Saison." But there were not to be other prominent political assassinations of Israelis by Israelis until the killing of Prime Minister Yitzhak Rabin by a fanatic, acting on his own, in opposition to the Oslo Accords.

The most famous instance of battle over the monopoly of the use of force in the early state shows the degree to which the early state had been consolidated.[26] Ben-Gurion was to order the attack on the Revisionist party's *Altalena* ship (named for Revisionist Party's founder Ze'ev Jabotinsky's pen-name which was also *Altalena*) traveling from Europe bearing arms for use by the new state. Ben-Gurion feared the arms would

[24] Cf. Philipp Lottholz and Nicolas Lemay-Hébert, "Re-Reading Weber, Re-Conceptualizing State-Building: From Neo-Weberian to Post-Weberian Approaches to State, Legitimacy and State-Building," *Cambridge Review of International Affairs*, 29, 4, 2016, pp. 1467–1485.

[25] Pierre M. Atlas, "Defining the Fringe: Two Examples of the Marginalization of Revisionist Zionism in the 1930s," *Israel Studies Bulletin*, 9, 2, 1994, pp. 7–11.

[26] On the Altalena as a "Weberian moment," see Nathan Yanai, "Ben-Gurion's Concept of *Mamlahtiut* and the Forming Reality of the State of Israel," *Jewish Political Studies Review*, 1, 1/2, 1989, pp. 151–177.

be channeled directly to units composed of Revisionist Party soldiers generally fighting under Revisionist Party commanders. Thus, after the ship had disembarked refugees aboard as well as a portion of the arms it was carrying into the custody of the state, Ben-Gurion had the ship bombarded with Revisionist Party leader and future Prime Minister Menachem Begin, and many remaining weapons, still on board. The commander leading the bombardment was none other than future Prime Minister Yitzhak Rabin.

There were numerous dead. Historical accounts generally describe the event as leading Israel to the edge of a civil war. But the words of the Revisionist Party leader Menachem Begin in the wake of the bombardment show that civil war was far from breaking out:

It was extremely hard to order our men to restrain their natural instinct for revenge, but I had to do it, because we are Jews! ... Do we not know from history what civil war does to a nation? Do we not know that generations pass before a nation at war with itself can ever heal? Therefore, I say to you tonight, a curse on him who preaches civil war. Let his hand be cut off before he raises it against another Jew. There will never be a civil war in Israel – Never![27]

There had been a sovereign state in the Weberian meaning already in existence by the Spring of 1948. Why wouldn't Ben-Gurion and his counsel declare one?

At the evening meeting of May 12, before Shertok wrote his draft, Ben-Gurion thus urged the use of the term "government" in the Declaration. Shertok had wanted to use the term "council of state" but wanted to avoid the term "government."[28] Ben-Gurion, along with Meyerson and, in this instance, David Remez and Rosenblüth, saw things differently. "We have to found a government. It's empty otherwise," said Ben-Gurion.[29] Golda Meyerson similarly rejected Shertok's avoidance of the term government: "It's not possible that we won't appeal to the United Nations to recognize [the state]. But to prevaricate and hesitate won't help us. It seems to me that the world is waiting for a [declaration]. If there's a declaration – it's upon us to do the thing all the way."[30]

---

[27] Quoted in Yehuda Avner, *The Prime Ministers* (Jerusalem: Toby Press, 2012), pp. 79–80.
[28] Protocols of the National Administration, evening meeting, May 12, 1948, p. 108.
[29] Ibid., p. 113.   [30] Ibid., p. 111.

NO BORDERS

The test of a sovereign state rests on borders. As Weber said, the state exercises "monopoly on the use of force *within a given territory*." Ought the new state's declaration of independence delineate those borders? On this matter, as the others, attitudes largely followed opinions related to the question of the Resolution 181. For if one accepted that the state was a state within the framework of the United Nations – that meant the borders specified in Resolution 181.

That rationale explains why Shertok advocated declaring specific UN-approved borders in the Declaration. Felix Rosenblüth agreed with Shertok, stating that it was "impossible not to mention borders" – that is, impossible because the borders were a key feature of the UN resolution.[31] Bechor Sheetrit, the lone Sephardi member on *Minhelet ha'Am* and a future minister of police, held that borders had to be mentioned since "the Arabs have to know whether they fall under the sovereignty of the Jewish state or not."[32]

Ben-Gurion saw further than his colleagues. First, he understood that there was no practical reason for a state to delineate its borders upon independence because its borders were liable to change with time. Showing a simply superior grasp of history, he referred to the American experience. He said:

This is a declaration of independence. There is, for instance, the Declaration of Independence of the United States. There is nothing therein on territorial arrangements. There's no need, no law for this. I read in the law books that a state is composed of a territory and peoples. Every state has borders ... but we're not obligated to state what the boundaries of the state are.[33]

The United States was founded in a situation of territorial uncertainty: there was no certainty with respect to what borders the United States would ultimately encompass. The Thirteen Colonies had been invaded. There were other British North American territories. Some of the colonies' allegiance to Britain remained strong after independence. Even during the War of Independence of the United States, there were efforts to incorporate Quebec into the new state.[34]

Shortly after the founding of the United States, there would be expansion westward. Treaties and wars would bring Louisiana, California, and even Alaska and Hawaii into the American union. This could not have

---

[31] Ibid., p. 107.   [32] Ibid., p. 109.   [33] Ibid., p. 112.
[34] Eliot A. Cohen, *Conquered into Liberty* (New York: Free Press, 2012).

been anticipated at independence. And it also was not relevant. For both the territory in which the American state could expand and the force of the state could change. Moreover, the area over which America's laws and ethos would extend itself would grow even without the force of the state. The colonists and the laws would themselves extend the force of the state. Ben-Gurion saw much to learn for Israel from the American example.

There was also no procedural reason for the *Yishuv* to follow the UN's decrees. For the UN had done nothing to enforce them:

> Why shouldn't we state them [the borders of the state]? Because we don't know [what they are]. If the United Nations upholds the borders – we won't fight against the UN. But if the UN is not involved in this manner, and war is made against us, and we defeat them, and we conquer the Western Galilee and the secondary road to Jerusalem – all of this will be part of the state if we have the strength. Why should we hamper ourselves?[35]

Ben-Gurion expressed a simple fact. The UN had done nothing to enforce the partition borders, and in fact, had the left the *Yishuv* vulnerable to attack. The UN had declared partition borders that neither the Arabs nor the Jews fully favored. This was of course the essence of compromise: a deal in which no side fully gets what it wants. But the Arabs had reacted to this compromise via armed opposition to the borders.

The Arab residents of Palestine had blockaded Jerusalem and attacked some of its outlying *moshavim* and *kibbutzim*. This was an error on their part. As the *Yishuv's* militia struck back, it pushed back the Arab militias across most fronts. Even before independence, Arab enclaves in most of the major cities had fallen. The *Yishuv,* though by no means yet victorious, was holding up well in the Galilee. Only in the Jerusalem sector and on the Jordan River's west bank, where the Jordanian Arab Legion, trained, armed, and commanded by the British, could support the Arab military initiative, did the local Arab militias stand strong.

Ultimately the Arab war to overturn the UN partition backfired. The armistice lines at the conclusion of the war dramatically reduced the size of the Arab territory and left that territory, moreover, in the hands of the Jordanian and Egyptian armies and not of Palestinian Arabs. This would all materialize later. But Ben-Gurion anticipated this. He was strategically confident: "Why should we hamper ourselves?"

[35] Ibid., p. 113.

He also saw to the more abstract essence of the matter. There was no reason to mention the borders controlled by the state because those borders were to be determined by military conflict. Some of the territory allocated to the Jewish state, which was to include some of the earliest Labor Zionist settlements as well as newer ones such as Masuot Yitzhak, had already fallen or were about to fall to the Arab armies in bloody conflict.[36] Other territory that was to have been part of the Arab state in the UN's plan had fallen to Jewish forces. The military situation was highly fluid. Any claims to borders by treaty had been overtaken by events.

There was also the basic folly of the idea of natural partition by geography. There were no natural or even logical borders that could partition the land. For the land's demographic and urban makeup was entirely novel *and* interwoven. No natural barriers separated the largest Jewish and Arab residential blocks. The scope of what natural barriers existed – mountains, rivers, deserts – was laughable. The mountains were hills, the rivers were streams, the deserts enclosed the country but did not separate its populations.

The populations also did not lend themselves to easy segmentation. In 1890, before the most significant waves of Jewish immigration, the total population of Palestine was around 532,000. By the eve of independence there were close to two million.[37] The arrival of Western capital along with the founding of the *Yishuv* in the nineteenth century and then the British Mandate in 1917 had attracted not only Jewish immigration en masse from Europe and Russia, but as well Arab immigration from Lebanon, Syria, and Iraq. Many of the migrants moved to the cities. The largest cities, Jerusalem, Tel Aviv-Yafo, and Haifa, were mixed cities.

As a result, there was no clear and proper allocation of them. There had been at least three major plans for the allocation of Palestine's land, from the Balfour Report's vague promise of a "Jewish home in Palestine," to the Peel Commission's segmentation of the land into Arab and Jewish blocks, to the UN Partition Plan. The Peel Commission had set off a cottage industry of local experts drawing partition maps. Their efforts were earnest. But they confronted an implacable reality of intermingling.[38]

---

[36] David Ohana, "Kfar Etzion: The Community of Memory and the Myth of Return," *Israel Studies*, 7, 2, 2002, pp. 145–174.

[37] Arieh Avneri, *Hetyashvut ha'yehudi ve'ta'anat ha'nishol (The Claim of Dispossession)* (Efal, Israel: Yad Tabenkin, 1982), p. 11.

[38] See Meron Benvenisti, *Sacred Landscape*, trans. Maxine Kaufman-Lacusta (Berkeley: University of California Press, 2002).

One can only imagine the difficulties that specifying the ultimate borders of the state would have imposed upon the future State of Israel. The constraints that this would have placed on future Israeli politicians would have been such as to perhaps endanger the state. How could one possess territories that the state ultimately possessed even in 1948 – such as western Jerusalem – while at the same time declaring in one's founding document that one had no right to them? Ben-Gurion saw, clearly, that this was a political matter, not a legal one. Ultimately, the question of the borders was put to a vote. It was resolved to omit the precise borders by the barest of majorities: 5–4.

Ben-Gurion went beyond consideration of the exigencies of the *Yishuv's* situation and even beyond a consideration of the political options that would open to the new state during the first fifty years of its life. Ben-Gurion looked into the nature of politics. His ultimate insight into the matter of borders was philosophical. It came in an exchange with Rosenblüth. Rosenblüth believed that the borders had to be mentioned *as a matter of law*. Ben-Gurion understood that law would be made by the founders of the state.

Rosenblüth: We can't help but mention the borders [in the Declaration].
Ben-Gurion: Anything is possible. If we decide we're not mentioning borders, we won't mention them. There's no *a priori* requirement [that we do so].
Rosenblüth: It's not an *a priori* but it's a matter of law.
Ben-Gurion: Law – that's something that is made by men.[39]

Rosenblüth says that law is *a priori* – that law comes before politics. Ben-Gurion inverts this construction and goes above it: law might be prior to action, but law is made by man – making man prior to law.

This is the essence of political founding: the creation of new modes and orders for government and a disordering of the world in order to accommodate a new ordering of the world. Political founding is always new. Abraham, the Mishnah relates, departed from Ur Kasdim and set out to Canaan in order to found a new tribe.[40] In doing so, the Mishnah adds, Abraham had to destroy his father's gods – his father's collection of idols. Abraham arrived and, Genesis relates, received prophecy of new laws and a new rhythm of life. The Talmud claims that Abraham was given by God a new schedule of prayer. Moses, as related in Exodus, murdered the Egyptian slave master and unleashed mortal plagues on Egypt in order to

---

[39] Protocols of the National Administration, evening meeting, May 12, 1948, p. 107.
[40] James Diamond, *Maimonides and the Shaping of a Jewish Canon*, p. 76.

lead Israel into the wilderness where it could receive an entirely new law-giving. So that Britain could live under the Magna Carta, the Barons and Lords first had to compel King John with arms so that he would arrive at Runnymede. And as Ben-Gurion explained, the American Declaration of Independence was itself a supersession of law even as it was undertaken in the name of a higher law.

MATTERS OF PRINCIPLE

Ben-Gurion thus established the basis for what *Minhelet ha'Am* was to do through his critique of Shertok's draft. Ben-Gurion meant for *Minhelet ha'Am* to go all the way. It was to rise to the level of a founding council. Ben-Gurion would be the leader of the council and the founder. He would build something entirely new.

But what was he to build and establish? On this front the debate was surprisingly shallow. The critique of Shertok's draft carried out by his fellow committee members concerned the legal, diplomatic, and political positions it staked out. There was not much on the subject of the state's constitution and essence.

But there was not nothing. Shertok's draft presented, following previous draft texts, a normative account of the basis of the state and the rights it was meant to guarantee. Alas, at the meeting of *Minhelet ha'Am* on May 13, with the Mandate ending just two days later, there was shockingly little debate on normative matters. Rights, equality, duties of citizenship, the constitution of the state – none of these subjects meaningfully arise in the meeting minutes.

What was to be the character of the Israeli regime? There were certainly assumptions about this in the various drafts of the Declaration. Though many founders of Israel shared a common background, there were stark religious and political differences between them. And yet, they did not spend the final years before independence thinking through and debating these issues. Perhaps this was luckily the case; unity at that moment was necessary. But it also meant that the official position of the state on many normative matters would remain murky for years to come – often indefinitely.

Some issues of principle were discussed. The most famous of these was the debate over the name of God, referred to as "rock of Israel" (*Tzur Yisrael*) in the text. This formulation would have been known to almost the entirety of the council from the Jewish prayer service. In their youths, even the irreligious among them would have at some point recited "rock of Israel, rise in aid of Israel" in the daily and Sabbath prayers immediately prior to the *Amidah*, the centerpiece of the Jewish prayer service. (The phrase also appears, less prominently, in the Book of Psalms.) Shertok had retained the phrase "rock of Israel," which was used as early as Beham's draft, in the text that he composed. As we will see in Chapter 7, there was debate surrounding the inclusion of this term, with some finding it insufficient and others excessive.

There was also the business of the name of the state, which first appears in Shertok's draft. It was not, on the face of things, an intuitive choice. When David Ben-Gurion announced that the name of the state would be "Israel," more than a few attendees at the Tel Aviv Museum were surprised. They were not alone. Postage stamps printed in advance of the ceremony had been labeled *"doar ivri"* (Hebrew mail), since the name of the state was not yet determined.[41] As Martin Kramer has noted, the diplomats of the *Yishuv* lobbied the Truman Administration for recognition of the "Jewish state" – since they too did not know what the name of the state would be. Clark Clifford, sympathetic to Zionist aspirations, later noted: "The name 'Israel' was as yet unknown, and most of us assumed the new nation would be called 'Judaea.'"[42]

Debate over the name of the state took place at the end of the marathon evening meeting of the *Minhelet ha'Am* on May 12 – before Shertok set to work. The minutes leave a record of only a brief exchange on this subject. But they indicate that the name was introduced by David Ben-Gurion, who spoke first in this section of the evening's proceedings: "We have decided that the name of the state will be Israel. And if one says 'state' – then 'state of Israel … .' One can merge this [name] with every construct: the army of Israel, the community of Israel, the people of Israel," said Ben-Gurion.[43]

According to the minutes, the name was voted upon immediately after Ben-Gurion's assertion that the name of the state had already been decided. Seven voted in favor. The opposition votes were not recorded, but without suggesting an alternative, Aharon Zisling stated that "I am against a name that will compel every Arab to bear a name that he must revolt against."[44]

[41] Martin Gilbert, *Israel* (New York: Harper, 1998), p. 187.
[42] Quoted in Martin Kramer, "Why the Name Israel?" April 27, 2020. https://martinkramer.org/2020/04/27/1948-why-the-name-israel/
[43] Protocols of the National Administration, evening meeting, May 12, 1948, p. 119.
[44] Ibid.

Other possibilities then circulating included Judea, Zion, and *Eretz-Yisrael*. The minutes do not indicate that any of these were proposed. According to Ze'ev Sharef, the first two possibilities were rejected on territorial or geographic grounds. Zion could not be used because "Zion is the name of a hill overlooking the Old City of Jerusalem" and "Judea is the historical name of the area around Jerusalem, which at that time seemed the area least likely to become part of the state." *Eretz-Yisrael* had seemed too religious and to imply territorial maximalism.[45]

The name Israel won out for lack of a better alternative – it was received without enthusiasm at the time. Ze'ev Sharef recorded this impression:

It was Mr. Ben-Gurion who first suggested "Israel." It seemed strange at the beginning, and the proposal was received coolly. But members tried pronouncing "Israel Government," "Israel Army," "Israel citizen," "Israel consul" to see how it sounded. Most were unenthusiastic, but there were only 48 hours left and much urgent work to be done, and the matter was put to a vote. Seven of the ten members present [at the *Minhelet ha'Am* meeting] voted for "Israel."[46]

While the name had its critics, Walter Eytan, who had been one of Shertok's deputies in New York, captured the essence of its suitability:

The moment the name was proclaimed, everyone realized instinctively that it could in fact have been no other. The children of Israel, the people of Israel, the land of Israel, the heritage of Israel – all these had existed, in reality and metaphysically, for so many thousands of years, they had exercised such influence on the evolution of mankind that the state of Israel was their logical consequence and conclusion.[47]

And, of course, *am Yisrael,* the people of Israel, was accepted as a principal label for Jews through the ages.

Much of *Minhelet ha'Am* was largely satisfied with Shertok's "archeology" of Israel: his rendition of the genesis, history, and the basis of the Jewish state. Recall that Shertok's history of Israel started with the exile of Israel following the destruction of the Second Temple and skipped rather quickly to the early twentieth century and the Second *Aliyah* – without explicit mention of Judaism, though with literary allusion to it.

David Remez defended Shertok's historical use of Zionist and Jewish history: "The writer of the draft," said Remez to his colleagues, "succeeds in conveying the historical connection [of the Jews to Israel], and says a

---

lot to every man and every nation. It says a lot about the passion with which we are building our state."[48] Aharon Zisling rejected suggestions to shorten Shertok's rather long text: "It might be possible to shorten it, but I wouldn't take it to the point of changing its fundamental structure. For future generations, and even today, our justification for founding has a political rationale, both external and internal ... .The structure of [Shertok's draft] is beautiful and contributes to the goal."[49] This was, of course, Shertok's position as well.

Surprisingly, the sole rabbi in the room, Aryeh Leib Fishman (Maimon), suggested that much of the first part of Shertok's draft dealing with the justification for independence be cut out: "It is said in the Jerusalem Talmud," he told his colleagues, "that 'what is clearly brought to light brings many evils.'"[50] According to the rabbi, it was perhaps not necessary for the text to explicitly present justifications for why a state was being founded. Mordechai Bentov, a Mapam Party organizer and journalist, concurred: "[Chaim] Weizmann said once, that our tragedy is that we always have to justify ourselves. In my opinion, we do not have to justify ourselves and our rights."[51]

Others, however, sought a more capacious moral justification for Jewish sovereignty than Shertok had presented. Bechor Sheetrit castigated Shertok for beginning with the history of the Jewish people rather than theological justification: "The Declaration begins from the banishment of the people from its land. But until the exile there was something – there was a people that ruled with religion and tradition. And it's impossible not to mention our book of books. Epicureanism amongst the people in Israel began not that long ago."[52]

Shapira and Fishman agreed with Sheetrit's desire to mention our "book of books" as well as the name of God in the document. As Shapira said, in a moving speech:

We are signing this document not only in the name of the Jewish settlement in the land of Israel but in the name of twelve million Jews in all the lands of the Diaspora. And I can't disguise my opinion that this historic text should include the name of God. One can be irreligious. But it cannot be that we do not mention the heavenly name. I'm prepared to conduct a survey of all the *Epikorsim* in the

---

[48] Protocols of the National Administration, May 13, 1948, p. 125.   [49] Ibid., p. 124.
[50] Ibid.   [51] Ibid.
[52] We have translated the Hebrew *epikorsim* literally. The Talmudic meaning of "Epicurean" could range from hedonist to heretic to materialist to student of foreign texts. Ibid., p. 126.

world – we'll see if this is a mistake .... . Jews are dying every day with *Shema Yisrael* on their lips. I would have wanted for it to say "God of Israel" and not merely "rock of Israel." But we can compromise.[53]

Fishman defended Shapira's suggestion by invoking the international history of declarations of independence: "I still haven't seen an important world declaration, excepting that of Russia, in which the name of God is not mentioned."[54] For his part, Zisling wanted to remove the connotation of belief in God implicit in the formulation "out of trust in the rock of Israel":

I don't see [*Tzur Yisrael*] as appropriate. I agree to some wording that makes mention of the foundations of Jewish belief. I do not need to quarrel. However, it is not necessary to force me, and those like me, to declare "I believe."[55]

This question had already been a contentious one for the members of Shertok's drafting committee earlier that morning. Shapira then had suggested that the text should elaborate on *Tzur Yisrael*, adding to it so that it would read: *Tzur Yisrael ve'goalo*. The addition of *gaolo*, which translates as "redeemer," would unmistakably mark the text as affirming an active role for God as the redeemer of Israel.

This suggestion had incensed Zisling, who insisted he would not be able to sign a declaration that included this phrase.[56] Zisling remained unsatisfied with the religious compromise regardless. Ben-Gurion, as we explain in Chapter 7, would lean to the side of religion, mentioning both the "book of books," in Sheetrit's formulation, and keeping *Tzur Israel* in the final document.

THE RIGHT OF RIGHTS

It is important to note that the critics seeking a more morally capacious document did not offer specific suggestions at these pre-independence meetings – beyond, of course, wanting more or less, and more direct or indirect, mention of God. It is surprising but true that the text's enumeration of rights and responsibilities was barely discussed. Again, it was David Ben-Gurion who, to a large degree, rose above this debate and its relatively petty quibbles. And he did so because he saw the issue of the Declaration politically – and saw that Shertok's effort to adhere to diplomatic persuasion, though perhaps acceptable in parts, would not be sufficient.

---

[53] Ibid., p. 125.   [54] Ibid., p. 127.   [55] Ibid.
[56] Moshe Gurari, "Havlei leidata shel hahrazat ha'atzmaut," May 11, 1973.

Mordechai Bentov, under fire for his decision to cut out early segments of Shertok's draft dealing with the Jewish justification for sovereignty, recast his objection in moral terms.

This is a document for the ages. In a hundred years children will learn it by heart. And therefore it doesn't have to be a document with legalistic paragraphs but about human rights ... . Our historical rights are drowning in the number of paragraphs. I don't find in these paragraphs the expression of the natural rights of our people to live freely in our homeland.[57]

Bentov wanted less legalism and more human rights. He is one of only two people to point out that the idea of inherent natural rights is absent from the document. And it is very unlikely that he knew that the concept had been eliminated after one of the primary texts of natural rights, the American Declaration of Independence, had been the basis for the first draft of the Declaration.

The other person to raise the issue of rights, notably, was Ben-Gurion. Ben-Gurion argued that Shertok's draft had said that the state will bestow rights upon its citizens. This is a bad formulation, said Ben-Gurion. The state will rather recognize rights. Rights "belong" to the people, he noted. They do not come from the state.[58] This pregnant insertion would matter, and we will discuss it further in Chapter 7.

But in general, Ben-Gurion tried to steer the debate to the political question at hand. First and foremost, the Declaration had to accomplish a pressing task: declare independence in a clear, unambiguous fashion. But this would entail, in his view, some normative content. It is again worth quoting Ben-Gurion's intervention:

I am a pragmatist in these matters. We don't have to write a declaration that school children will learn by heart in a hundred years. It has to be a document that includes deep Zionist justification, inclusive and comprehensive also for Jews – because there are still many Jews who are wavering – and also to non-Jews that are not haters. There's no room in it for judicial justification – it has to determine political reality.[59]

It would be hard to find a statement as revealing of Ben-Gurion's great strength as the political leader of Israel. In this statement, he set forth clearly and decisively the politically necessary conditions for declaring independence.

---

[57] Ibid., p. 125.   [58] Ibid., p. 123.   [59] Ibid., p. 126.

CONCLUSION: DETERMINING POLITICAL REALITY

A declaration of independence, the very act of founding a country, had to, in Ben-Gurion's intelligent phrase, *"determine political reality."* The detailed discussions of Resolution 181 were casuistry and almost irrelevant to the task at hand. A new country is a break with old political reality. At one moment you are ruled by others, and now you are no longer. What political choices can one make to best set the course for the country to succeed politically? To be sure, the country will need laws. But just as Plato's *Laws* is secondary to his *Republic*, the laws of a really existing country, too, can only take shape in line with the character of the regime that is established. Shertok's Declaration was, at the end of the day, in need of deep revision because it was merely judicial.

But Ben-Gurion might also seem to have missed an important point, almost contradicting himself. While the document, Ben-Gurion said, would "determine political reality," it also needed not "be recited by school children in a hundred years" to quote his reformulation of Bentov's poignant remark. It would seem, as we will see in Chapter 7, that Ben-Gurion knew better. He knew that if the document were to establish a new political reality, it would also, inevitably, be both recited by school children in a century, and, what's more, become a founding document cited by politicians, lawyers, and judges in a century as well.

And of course, Israeli children today know about Ben-Gurion's Declaration. Americans study their Declaration of Independence because of the strength and soundness of its principles – principles that stand above and ultimately help rectify American life.[60] Ben-Gurion's dismissal of the likely future significance of the document may have been in part rhetorical. He did, after all, take control of the writing process. And his document, as discussed in the next chapter, does present a moral account of Jewish sovereignty, which, if limited in some ways, was far more presentable than what his colleagues had come up with.

But perhaps his minimization of the theoretical dimension of the task helps explain what we will see as some of the limitations in his draft. Solon famously left Athens for 10 years after giving the Athenians their laws. Washington ruled for two terms and refused a lifetime appointment as president. Ben-Gurion articulated a doctrine called *mamlichtiyut* that

---

[60] Ralph Lerner, "Lincoln's Declaration – And Ours," *National Affairs* (Winter: 2011). www.nationalaffairs.com/publications/detail/lincolns-declaration-and-ours

permitted him and his party to basically rule with limited constraints beyond elections for the first quarter-century following the establishment of the state.[61]

Ben-Gurion was aware that the text of the Declaration of Independence would likely stand for and shape the regime beyond the political moment at hand. But he was aware of other things too. The political moment at hand was essential. Nothing could be done unless that moment was seized in an intelligent way.

Ben-Gurion saw that the document had to stand above the second-order disputes in which his colleagues were engaged. This implies, contrary to Ben-Gurion's debating point, that he also saw that it had to set out principles and ideas that would mean something for generations. It had to accomplish simple independence above and beyond what many on the council seemed willing to risk. And it had to mean something to the generations.

At the conclusion of debate on May 13, Ben-Gurion appointed a final committee of three to "polish," "sharpen," and "refine" Shertok's text.[62] He would be on that committee. In reality, this meant he himself would write a new final version. That this was necessary is apparent based on the debate over Shertok's draft text.

Ben-Gurion was clairvoyant regarding the practical question at hand. He was a maximalist on the question of ensuring that the Declaration of Independence of Israel would create a new state that was totally new. A reader of the classics of political thought, Ben-Gurion sensed this even as many of his colleagues got lost in the minutiae of the moment. On the second question, which Ben-Gurion saw too, namely the legacy of the Declaration and its importance not only in creating a state, but in shaping a state, Ben-Gurion would labor through the night.

[61] Herodotus, *The History*, trans. David Grene (Chicago: University of Chicago Press, 1988), 1:29.
[62] Protocols of the National Administration, May 13, 1948, p. 127.

7

Natural and Historical Right

David Ben-Gurion and Israel's Declaration

"By virtue of our natural and historic right and on the strength of the resolution of the United Nations General Assembly, we hereby declare the establishment of a Jewish state in Eretz-Israel, to be known as the State of Israel." This sentence forms the center of the Declaration of Independence of Israel. Recited by David Ben-Gurion on May 14, 1948, it announced the creation of the first Jewish state in the land of Israel since the fall of the remnants of the Judean Kingdom in 133 CE.

Interpreted in light of the preceding drafts of the Declaration of Independence, it also offers a window into the deepest matters at play in the founding of Israel. And consideration of those issues leads even further afield: to the nature of states and politics. The formulation that declares Israel's independence itself poses questions that must be answered. What are natural rights? What are historical rights? How are they related to the founding of a state? Why does Israel claim a natural and historical right to come into being as a new state?

The inner meaning of Israel's Declaration of Independence is wound up in the decisions that David Ben-Gurion made as he composed its final text. His choices as he wrote and edited – what would be retained from prior drafts, what would be excised, and what he thought needed to be added – present an intellectual tour of the most important political and intellectual questions on the eve of Israel's Independence.

This transforms a study of the text of the Declaration from interpretation into an archeological excavation using a long-lost blueprint of the essentials of Zionism. Through understanding the matters of first-order importance to the founders of Israel at its foundation, it is possible that we may come to understand topics that are of first-order importance to us today. The history of ideas is unique in that it is a history of something outside of history: ideas.

David Ben-Gurion wrote on May 13 as he prepared the Declaration of Independence that he would recite the next day. The document that he composed bears an obvious likeness to the drafts that came before his. He based his work directly on Shertok's draft written the night before – the final text of the Declaration of Independence of Israel could be mistaken for an edited version or annotation of Shertok's draft. This makes perfect sense. Ben-Gurion had but a few short hours to produce an essential document on a tight deadline. He thus focused on reworking Shertok's text. Words and often entire paragraphs are if not identical, at least syntactically similar.[1]

In basing his text off of Shertok's writing, Ben-Gurion implicitly was following the work of Tzvi Berenson and the rest of *Minhelet ha'Am*'s legal team as well as Herschel Lauterpacht's draft. For Shertok drew heavily upon them, and thus, in using Shertok's text, so too did Ben-Gurion. And likewise, his text reflects the comments of his colleagues on *Minhelet ha'Am* amidst their debates and quite possibly during a meeting on the night of Ben-Gurion's final editing. One might thus fall into the error of thinking that there is a neat collective effort that brings together Ben-Gurion and those who came before him. The final text of the Declaration of Independence of Israel can be seen as the culmination of a communal drafting process – a story of collaboration to create a seminal text in Jewish history.

It is not so. In nearly all decisive respects, Ben-Gurion produced a document that was different to its predecessor drafts with the exception of the work of Mordechai Beham – the lone draft of importance that Ben-Gurion did not see. Beham had drawn upon the idea of natural rights, the concept of state autonomy in a violent world, and the unique history of the Jewish people in formulating his draft Declaration. No one else until Ben-Gurion attempted this. Ben-Gurion tried to bring the focus of the Declaration of Independence more directly and explicitly toward the themes of natural rights, state sovereignty, and Jewish history as he saw them.

The debate at *Minhelet ha'Am* and the work done by Shertok expressed a preference among the leadership of the *Yishuv* for a document arguing that the Jews of Palestine had fulfilled their part of the bargain of UN Resolution 181 and thus were entitled to declare some form of independence.

---

[1] Cf. David Ben-Gurion interview in Eliezer Whartman, *Interviews with signers of the Declaration of Independence*, 1961, p. 5. Ben-Gurion claims, modestly, that he merely "edited" Shertok's draft.

Ben-Gurion's aim was higher than the aim of his colleagues. He understood that by declaring independence, the leadership of the *Yishuv* was departing from the world of legal and formal rights. The argument of the Declaration thus had to cut to the essence of things and rise above Resolution 181. It had to articulate deeper ideas. The changes that Ben-Gurion made to the Declaration reveal an effort to shape the state that he had fought so hard to build. He needed to shape it in the proper direction.

Foremost on Ben-Gurion's mind on the night of May 13 was conducting the war, managing the generals, and ensuring that heavy weapons would arrive for the soon-to-be-outgunned *Haganah*.[2] Even as Ben-Gurion worked on the text of the Declaration, he also confronted a military situation that, as he wrote in his diary that evening, was "approaching catastrophe."[3]

Knowing that time was short and that the work was hard, Ben-Gurion still did his best on the Declaration of Independence. The substantial differences between his work and the prior drafts show it to be the case that he indeed, as he put it while speaking to *Minhelet ha'Am*, tried to imbue the text with the deep "Zionist and Jewish" justification that it deserved.[4] Accomplishing this elevated task had been no easy matter for the various politicians and bureaucrats that had come before David Ben-Gurion. And their work had not met his standard. To articulate the essence of the ideas that animate a nation defined and indeed created by its ideas is on its face a monumental undertaking.

It is thus necessary to draw out the differences between what Ben-Gurion wrote and what had been in the prior drafts of the Declaration in order to shine a light on the essential themes of the final document. Here is the final version of Israel's Declaration, the product of David Ben-Gurion's efforts.

[1] ERETZ-ISRAEL was the birthplace of the Jewish people. Here their spiritual, religious and political identity was shaped. Here they first attained to statehood, created cultural values of national and universal significance and gave to the world the eternal Book of Books.

---

[2] Eliezer Whartman, "Interviews with the Signers of the Declaration of Independence," p. 6.

[3] David Ben-Gurion Diary, May 13, 1948, trans. Tuvia Friling and S. Ilan Troen, "Proclaiming Independence: Five Days in May from Ben-Gurion's Diary," *Israel Studies*, 1998, 3, 1, p. 183.

[4] Protocols of the National Administration, May 13, 1948, p. 126.

[2] After being forcibly exiled from their land, the people kept faith with it throughout their Dispersion and never ceased to pray and hope for their return to it and for the restoration in it of their political freedom.

[3] Impelled by this historic and traditional attachment, Jews strove in every successive generation to re-establish themselves in their ancient homeland. In recent decades they returned in their masses. Pioneers and defenders, they made deserts bloom, revived the Hebrew language, built villages and towns, and created a thriving community controlling its own economy and culture, loving peace but knowing how to defend itself, bringing the blessings of progress to all the country's inhabitants, and aspiring towards independent nationhood.

[4] In the year 5657 (1897), at the summons of the spiritual father of the Jewish State, Theodore Herzl, the First Zionist Congress convened and proclaimed the right of the Jewish people to national rebirth in its own country.

[5] This right was recognized in the Balfour Declaration of the 2nd November, 1917, and re-affirmed in the Mandate of the League of Nations which, in particular, gave international sanction to the historic connection between the Jewish people and Eretz-Israel and to the right of the Jewish people to rebuild its National Home.

[6] The catastrophe which recently befell the Jewish people – the massacre of millions of Jews in Europe – was another clear demonstration of the urgency of solving the problem of its homelessness by re-establishing in Eretz-Israel the Jewish State, which would open the gates of the homeland wide to every Jew and confer upon the Jewish people the status of a fully privileged member of the comity of nations.

[7] Survivors of the Nazi holocaust in Europe, as well as Jews from other parts of the world, continued to migrate to Eretz-Israel, undaunted by difficulties, restrictions and dangers, and never ceased to assert their right to a life of dignity, freedom and honest toil in their national homeland.

[8] In the Second World War, the Jewish community of this country contributed its full share to the struggle of the freedom- and peace-loving nations against the forces of Nazi wickedness and, by the blood of its soldiers and its war effort, gained the right to be reckoned among the peoples who founded the United Nations.

[9] On the 29th November, 1947, the United Nations General Assembly passed a resolution calling for the establishment of a Jewish State in Eretz-Israel; the General Assembly required the inhabitants of Eretz-Israel to take such steps as were necessary on their part for the implementation of that resolution. This recognition by the United Nations of the right of the Jewish people to establish their State is irrevocable.

[10] This right is the natural right of the Jewish people to be masters of their own fate, like all other nations, in their own sovereign State.

[11] ACCORDINGLY WE, MEMBERS OF THE PEOPLE'S COUNCIL, REPRESENTATIVES OF THE JEWISH COMMUNITY OF ERETZ-ISRAEL AND OF THE ZIONIST MOVEMENT, ARE HERE ASSEMBLED ON THE DAY OF THE TERMINATION OF THE BRITISH MANDATE OVER ERETZ-ISRAEL AND, BY VIRTUE OF OUR NATURAL AND HISTORIC RIGHT AND ON THE STRENGTH OF THE RESOLUTION OF THE UNITED NATIONS GENERAL ASSEMBLY, HEREBY DECLARE THE ESTABLISHMENT OF A JEWISH STATE IN ERETZ-ISRAEL, TO BE KNOWN AS THE STATE OF ISRAEL.

[12] WE DECLARE that, with effect from the moment of the termination of the Mandate being tonight, the eve of Sabbath, the 6th Iyar, 5708 (15th May, 1948), until the establishment of the elected, regular authorities of the State in accordance with the Constitution which shall be adopted by the Elected Constituent Assembly not later than the 1st October 1948, the People's Council shall act as a Provisional Council of State, and its executive organ, the People's Administration, shall be the Provisional Government of the Jewish State, to be called "Israel."

[13] THE STATE OF ISRAEL will be open for Jewish immigration and for the Ingathering of the Exiles; it will foster the development of the country for the benefit of all its inhabitants; it will be based on freedom, justice and peace as envisaged by the prophets of Israel; it will ensure complete equality of social and political rights to all its inhabitants irrespective of religion, race or sex; it will guarantee freedom of religion, conscience, language, education and culture; it will safeguard the Holy Places of all religions; and it will be faithful to the principles of the Charter of the United Nations.

[14] THE STATE OF ISRAEL is prepared to cooperate with the agencies and representatives of the United Nations in implementing the resolution of the General Assembly of the 29th November, 1947, and will take steps to bring about the economic union of the whole of Eretz-Israel.

[15] WE APPEAL to the United Nations to assist the Jewish people in the building-up of its State and to receive the State of Israel into the comity of nations.

[16] WE APPEAL – in the very midst of the onslaught launched against us now for months – to the Arab inhabitants of the State of Israel to preserve peace and participate in the upbuilding of the State on the basis of full and equal citizenship and due representation in all its provisional and permanent institutions.

[17] WE EXTEND our hand to all neighbouring states and their peoples in an offer of peace and good neighbourliness, and appeal to them to establish bonds of cooperation and mutual help with the sovereign Jewish people settled in its own land. The State of Israel is prepared to do its share in a common effort for the advancement of the entire Middle East.

[18] WE APPEAL to the Jewish people throughout the Diaspora to rally round the Jews of Eretz-Israel in the tasks of immigration and upbuilding and to stand by them in the great struggle for the realization of the age-old dream - the redemption of Israel.

[19] PLACING OUR TRUST IN THE "ROCK OF ISRAEL," WE AFFIX OUR SIGNATURES TO THIS PROCLAMATION AT THIS SESSION OF THE PROVISIONAL COUNCIL OF STATE, ON THE SOIL OF THE HOMELAND, IN THE CITY OF TEL-AVIV, ON THIS SABBATH EVE, THE 5TH DAY OF IYAR, 5708 (14TH MAY, 1948).[5]

On the face of things, the final version of the Declaration evokes and even sticks to the previous drafts of the Declaration. It begins by invoking Jewish history and the building of the *Yishuv* as all others had done. It engages with the legal argumentation surrounding United Nations Resolution 181. It declares a state and describes the principles of the state. It culminates in a call to the nations of the world to recognize and support

---

[5] The official English translation from Israel's Ministry of Foreign Affairs, accessible here: www.mfa.gov.il/MFA/Peace+Process/Guide+to+the+Peace+Process/Declaration+of +Establishment+of+State+of+Israel.htm

the new state. It reaches out to Israel's Arab residents and neighbors in peace. And the text ends with the invocation of *Tzur Israel*, "rock of Israel," as a stand-in for the name of God.

Entire paragraphs of the Declaration's final text should be familiar at this stage in the book. As in Shertok's text, the Jewish people "never ceased to pray and hope" to return to the land and restore their political freedom. In Israel the pioneers made "the deserts bloom" and "revived the Hebrew language." Using the formulation that Berenson inserted into his draft from Rubashov's work, the final text proclaims that the new state will be governed by "principles of freedom, justice, and peace as envisaged by the prophets of Israel." Roughly two-thirds of the text may be said to be either a reproduction of or largely based on Shertok's draft.

There are of course stylistic differences between Shertok's text and Ben-Gurion's which are immediately evident. Ben-Gurion removed prefixes such as "and whereas . . ." from the document's clauses (even though Ben-Gurion may have instructed Shertok to use them). Shertok had used words and phrases evocative of the Jewish tradition to imbue a sense of *Yiddishkeit*, locutions such as *"be'khol dor va'dor"* (from generation to generation), which recalls the Passover *Hagadah* ("In every generation and generation, every man must see himself as though he had himself left Egypt"). Ben-Gurion dropped this and almost all other similar allusions. Jargon terms such as "the Jewish problem" were removed.[6] Years later Shertok was still resentful of Ben-Gurion's editing, which, he said, deprived the document of its "logical basis" and "inner drama."[7]

Ben-Gurion maintained the language regarding "full and equal social and political rights" which belong to "all . . . citizens regardless of race or religion." "Freedom of religion, conscience, education, and culture" are assured. Ben-Gurion added that the state would not discriminate on the basis of "sex," making equality of the sexes a founding principle of the Jewish state. Of course, Rubashov had included this in the Zionist Actions Committee's text creating the provisional government too. In addition to freedom of religion, conscience, education, and culture, the final draft also included an assurance of freedom of "language" – an addition made at the council review of the final draft on May 14.[8]

---

[6] For an optimistic contemporaneous account of the Jewish problem in the American context, see Alvin Johnson, "The Jewish Problem in America," *Social Research*, 14, 4, 1947, pp. 399–412.

[7] Eliezer Whartman, "Interviews with the Signers of the Declaration of Independence," p. 186.

[8] Ze'ev Sharef, *Three Days*, p. 279.

To the extent that the debates surrounding the drafting of Israel's Declaration have been discussed in the wider cultural sphere, it has generally been to build a mythology around the inclusion of the oath upon the "rock of Israel" at the text's conclusion.[9] Following what David Ben-Gurion himself said in the council meetings and in later private letters, it has been proposed that "rock of Israel" was an ingenious compromise position taken at the last moment.

And yet, *Tzur Yisrael* was in the Declaration from the very beginning. Having seen the American Declaration's reliance on "divine providence," Mordechai Beham had replaced it with the reliance of the Jews on the Rock of Israel.[10]

One reason for the emphasis placed on this formulation is that discussion of it occupied a great amount of *Minhelet ha'Am*'s time in the days leading up to Israel's independence – certainly more time than Ben-Gurion thought the issue deserved. In *Minhelet ha'Am*'s discussion of Shertok's draft text, the issue of the invocation of God had already come to the fore. On May 13, Ben-Gurion had closed debate on the issue by insisting that *Tzur Israel* would remain in the text.

The debate was not over. Late that evening, Ben-Gurion hosted the atheist *Mapam* party member Aharon Zisling and the Rabbi Yehuda Leib Fishman at his house to discuss the work. Along with Moshe Shertok, these two had been delegated, after the review of Shertok's draft, to produce a final text. Likely upset by the reception of his work, Shertok did not join the other two at this late-night visit to the home of the Old Man.[11]

Ben-Gurion later recalled that both accepted Ben-Gurion's text but argued vociferously over the question of *Tzur Yisrael*. Rabbi Fishman suggested *"Tzur Yisrael v'gaolo"* ("rock of Israel and his redeemer"), a more religious formulation that evokes the blessing of redemption in the daily prayer service – and a possibility that he had raised earlier with Shertok. Zisling protested against the mention of redemption, and in general objected to the whole phrase.

Ben-Gurion himself popularized this account later in life, disseminating letters and making other public pronouncements on the issue. In a letter to historian Alex Bein in 1972, Ben-Gurion wrote:

---

[9] See, for instance, Daniella Kolodny, "Why Israel's Independence Led to an Argument over the name of God," *The Jewish Chronicle*, April 16, 2018. www.thejc.com/judaism/features/why-israel-s-independence-led-to-an-argument-over-the-name-of-god-1.462387

[10] See Yoram Shachar, "Jefferson in Tel Aviv."

[11] Moshe Gurari, "Havlei leidata shel megilat ha'atzmaut," *Davaar*, May 11, 1973. See also, Protocols of the National Administration, May 13, 1948, p. 127. It is also possible that Shertok was not present in order to work on the English rendition of the text.

I explained that Rav Fishman and his associates could interpret the words "with trust in *Tzur Yisrael*" to mean "trust in God," and Zisling and his associates could interpret it to mean ... "the strength of the Jewish people." There followed an argument that lasted two hours, and in the end they accepted my argument.[12]

The fact of the matter is that two hours were not enough. Zisling did not let the matter go. There was a final meeting before independence held the next day at 1 pm with the full representative body of the *Yishuv*, the 37-member *Moetzet ha'Am*, to approve the text of the Declaration of Independence. Zisling again brought the issue of "rock of Israel" to the fore:[13]

We do not intend to limit someone's freedom of conscience .... We know how to respect values and beliefs. But on the other hand let's not force anyone of us to articulate "I believe" who does not have that belief in his heart or in his conscience. Every one of us will believe as he believes ... . It's possible that the expression "rock of Israel" could be included in this declaration, and in that case that wouldn't wound us. But don't compel "I believe" on us.[14]

Ben-Gurion was clearly less than thrilled to have to revisit the topic. But his answer to Zisling was decisive:

It seems to me that we all believe, everyone in his own way and according to his own understanding. There is one good thing, among the other good things in Judaism, and that is: "this do," and "this do not do." How to believe – about this we are not commanded. Every one of us believes in *Tzur Yisrael* in his own way and according to his own understanding. There is – and I bring my belief and feeling both on a Jewish and human level – nothing injurious and nothing coercive when we put our faith in *Tzur Israel*. I know what the *Tzur Israel* that I have faith in is. Surely my friend on the right knows in whom he believes, and I also know how my friend on the other side believes in it.[15]

This was to be the final word on the issue. Using his power as the convener of the meeting, Ben-Gurion ensured that the phrase would not be voted upon. An oath upon *Tzur Israel* was to stay in the Declaration. A materialist could see the Rock of Israel as a "what," either a material thing or a principle. A traditional believer could see the rock of Israel as an active God who intervenes in history.[16]

---

[12] Letter from David Ben-Gurion to A. Bein, November 13, 1972, www.zionistarchives.org .il/AttheCZA/Pages/BenGurion.aspx

[13] On the division of powers between the *Moetzet ha'Am* and the *Minhelet ha'Am*, see Jonathan Fine, *A State Is Born* (Albany: State University of New York Press, 2018), p. 98.

[14] Protocols of the National Council, May 14, 1948, p. 17.   [15] Ibid., p. 20.

[16] A third possibility still is the understanding of this in terms of synthesis. As James Diamond has written, "On the one hand, the Bible metaphorically alludes to Abraham

This entire episode shows Ben-Gurion's tremendous political and even bureaucratic tact. Though most members of *Moetzet ha'Am* were irreligious, nearly all, and doubtless Ben-Gurion, would have recognized the phrase *Tzur Yisrael* from the prelude to the culminating prayer in the *Shacharit* service, the *Amidah*. In the Hebrew language, itself reborn from the Hebrew of the Jewish religious tradition and the *siddur*, the phrase *Tzur Yisrael* has an obvious meaning.

Perhaps the phrase appealed to Ben-Gurion's belief that he had a philosophic understanding of the nature of God. Ultimately, Ben-Gurion knew that God had to be in the document. As Rabbi Fishman had said at the previous day's meeting, all world constitutions, excepting that of the Soviet Union, invoked the name of God. A declaration of independence for a people who, as Israel's Declaration begins, wrote the "book of books" would be an unlikely exception to this rule.

There is also a glaring omission from the prior drafts in the final text. Berenson's text had spoken of a "Jewish, free, independent, and democratic state." Shertok had removed that phrase. Ben-Gurion left it that way. Neither the word "democracy" nor any of its cognates, appears anywhere in the final text.

This fact has both interested and troubled observers.[17] Berenson, later interpreters have argued, used the phrase to signify that the state's Jewish and democratic aspects could not be in tension.[18] Shertok, perhaps, thought democracy need not be directly mentioned since democracy was connoted by his reference to the principles of the UN Charter (which Ben-Gurion also includes) and Resolution 181, which called for elections.[19] Ben-Gurion saw no need to include the word "democracy." His articulation of the "social and political rights" guaranteed by the state would be sufficient.

---

as a rock (Isaiah 51:2), depicting him as the founding model for Israel's moral and spiritual life. On the other, those verses comparing God to a rock suggest God's role, not as a parochial legislator but as the 'first cause' of all of existence." James Diamond, "Maimonides and Medinat Yisrael," *Jewish Review of Books*, April 28, 2020. https://jewishreviewofbooks.com/articles/7486/maimonides-and-medinat-yisrael/

[17] See Chapter 8 for an extensive discussion of this theme. Israeli politics and especially the Supreme Court has developed the view that the "fundamentals" of the Declaration are democratic even as the word democratic does not appear in the final text.

[18] Berenson, as he himself later recalled, was adamant that "democracy" be included in the Declaration, and was disappointed that it was not so. Cf. Elyakim Rubinstein, "The Declaration of Independence as a Basic Document of the State of Israel," *Israel Studies*, 3, 1, 1998, pp. 195–210.

[19] Christopher C. Joyner, "The United Nations and Democracy," *Global Governance*, p. 337. The UN Charter itself does not mention democracy, though it has been said to express "democratic aspirations."

DISTINCTIONS WITH A DIFFERENCE

These are the differences that jump off the page and which have received the bulk of scholarly attention. But there are more subtle and important differences. Somehow this standard account does not do justice to the ambition and scope of Ben-Gurion's effort. Nor is it consistent with the critique of the prior drafts that Ben-Gurion had leveled during the meetings of *Minhelet ha'Am* which we reviewed in Chapter 6.

The "central debate," as Ben-Gurion recalled in 1961, "was whether to say in the Declaration that the state was to be founded within the parameters of the General Assembly of the United Nations or not. I was very much against [declaring a state within those parameters]."[20] This was the key issue on May 12 and 13. There was no consensus. Shertok and Ben-Gurion simply disagreed – and Ben-Gurion, supported by Golda Meyerson, won out.

Shertok and council allies had only wanted to declare a state "in the framework of Resolution 181" (quoting Shertok, in the debate of May 12), while Ben-Gurion wanted to declare a state and a government simply. This was the first major issue that Ben-Gurion had to address in his amendments to the text.

Second, the previous drafts had lacked something indescribable but essential. They had been noble efforts. Yet, even if the text, to use a phrase that had caught Ben-Gurion's fancy during the debate, needed not be of such quality as to be "recited by school children" – it in fact did need to be of adequate quality so as to be recited by school children. Ben-Gurion seemed to have thought this even though he never said it, and indeed said the opposite. For Ben-Gurion in his redrafting tried to amend the text to include more elemental and fundamental arguments.[21]

---

[20] David Ben-Gurion Interview, Eliezer Whartman, "Interviews with the Signers of Israel's Declaration of Independence," p. 5.

[21] Ben-Gurion also might have been thinking about America's Declaration of Independence. He had expressed an in-depth familiarity with its text and even its nuance during the debate of Shertok's draft. And his understanding of America and appreciation for the importance of its texts seems to have run deep. He had, after all, spent part of World War I locked in the New York Public Library on Fifth Avenue working on a polemic justifying the *Yishuv*'s growth but also reading itinerantly and, in all likelihood, deeply. He would have understood that the Declaration of Independence of Israel would inevitably play an important part in the structure of the state. He knew that future generations, would turn to it as a representation of the *raison d'être* of the newly born state. See Tom Segev, *A State at Any Cost*, p. 132.

On these two decisive issues – what to do and why to do it – Ben-Gurion went his own way. He attempted to find a novel grounding for the state of Israel in different principles than those which the others had raised. And he declared a state simply without any of the provisos or conditions that had hampered or constrained Berenson, Lauterpacht, and Shertok.

BEN-GURION'S DEPARTURE

Ben-Gurion's text does two things that no previous draft, other than Mordechai Beham's effort, had done: it declares the founding of a state on the strength of "natural and historic rights" and it offers an argument from principle about what those rights are.

The three preceding drafts – those of Lauterpacht, Berenson, and Shertok – had focused their arguments elsewhere. Berenson's and Shertok's declarations proclaimed a state which comes to be by way of the UN's Resolution 181 process. Lauterpacht declared a state subject to international law under a global confederacy.

In contrast, Beham had turned to three main intellectual sources: the ideas of natural rights of citizens to life, liberty, and the pursuit of happiness found in the American Declaration of Independence; the argument of the English Bill of Rights regarding the ancient and indubitable rights of the English people to live freely; and the ideas embedded in the Bible and its promise of the land of Israel to the children of Israel in order that they might do the sacred work of the Bible.

Just as he had kept things simple in justifying the state, sticking to well-worn and time tested arguments, Beham's thought regarding national statehood had taken the naïve and simple position of the American Declaration of Independence: all states are by their nature completely independent and rely on their own arms in the cruel political world.

Ben-Gurion attempted to go down a different path from Beham in writing about the "natural and historical rights" of the Jewish people: he turned to the intellectual-moral accomplishments of the people of Israel in antiquity. Ben-Gurion wrote of Israel and the Jewish people: "Here their spiritual, religious and political identity was shaped. Here they first attained to statehood, created cultural values of national and universal significance and gave to the world the eternal Book of Books." This legacy of spiritual accomplishment, in the argument of Ben-Gurion's text, stands as one part of "the natural and historical right" upon which the state is established.

Ben-Gurion also explained Israel's right to establish itself as a state in terms of *realpolitik*: "The right of the Jewish people to establish their State is irrevocable ... this right is the natural right of the Jewish people to be masters of their own fate, like all other nations, in their own sovereign State."

"Here they wrote the Book of Books" and "the natural right to be masters of their own fate." These are the two main arguments of Ben-Gurion's Declaration of Independence. We will take up the "natural right to be masters of their own fate" first.

NATURE AND STATES

Ben-Gurion radically altered the actual declaration of the state. The final text of the Declaration proclaims the founding of a new sovereign state finally and irrevocably. Shertok's text had declared the establishment of an "independent state as included in the decision of the General Assembly [of the UN]." Shertok's formulation was deliberately ambiguous. It could be taken to mean both that the new state would be entirely independent (an "independent state") *and* that the new state would be established according to the blueprint laid out in UN Resolution 181, making the state less than independent and subject to regulation by and indeed dependence upon the UN ("as included in the Resolution of the General Assembly"). Shertok had understood this ambiguity as one of the chief features of his draft.

Ben-Gurion introduced an absolutely novel formulation to replace Shertok's:

This recognition by the United Nations of the right of the Jewish people to establish their State is irrevocable. This right is the natural right of Jewish people to be masters of their own fate, like all other nations, in their own sovereign State.

The right of the Jewish people to establish a state is cast as nothing less than the reality of being subject to the whims of fate – and having a responsibility to do something about it.

Ben-Gurion's departure from Shertok's text continued into the Declaration's ultimate paragraph – in which a state is declared. Shertok's text declares the state's establishment as follows: "Accordingly we ... solemnly assembled here and on the basis of the decision of the General Assembly of the United Nations, hereby declare to the Jewish people in the Diaspora and to the world entire, the establishment of a Jewish state in the land of Israel, which shall be called the State of Israel." In Shertok's account, the basis of the state is simply the decision of the UN. The clause declaring the establishment of the state justifies itself on the basis of the UN and the UN only.

This would not be the case for Ben-Gurion. The final text of the Declaration reads: "By virtue of our natural and historic right and on the strength of the resolution of the UN General Assembly, [we] hereby declare the establishment of a Jewish state in Eretz-Israel."[22] Ben-Gurion's text introduces the idea of the natural and historical right of the Jews to establish a state, and puts the Resolution of the UN in a subordinate position to natural and historical rights.

It must be said that Ben-Gurion's text was not seen this way by all parties. From the heart of the Legal Department came a note of dissatisfaction. Uri Heinsheimer (Yadin), who had worked with Mordechai Beham, expressed in his diary deep disquiet when he heard Ben-Gurion's Declaration: "It was a great disappointment for me. A heavy depression came over me."[23] The ceremony in Tel Aviv, according to Heinsheimer, had not matched the weight of the historical moment. Ben-Gurion's recitation of the Declaration, wrote Heinsheimer, cuttingly, "was more like a speech in a Zionist *moshav*."[24]

The principle source of Heinsheimer's dissatisfaction was that Israel's Declaration had not gone far enough in asserting sovereignty. An assistant of Felix Rosenblüth's at the Legal Department, and one of the legal experts who worked on the Declaration's text from Beham's draft through to Berenson's, Heinsheimer likely received first-hand reports of the meetings of *Minhelet ha'Am*.

On May 12, he wrote in his diary: "Someone important is hesitating, thinking it may not be necessary to declare an independent state, but rather just a state – without independence. This time even Rosenblüth was strong. He objected to the lukewarm version and insists on a clear, unambiguous declaration of independence."[25] Though he may be

---

[22] There is an interesting distinction between the Hebrew and English texts – both official – of Israel's Declaration. The Hebrew text reads "ובתוקף" or "on the strength of our natural and historical right" while the official translation reads "by virtue of our natural and historic right." And moreover the Hebrew text continues "ועל יסוד" or "on the basis of the declaration of the General Assembly" while the English edition reads "and on the strength of the declaration of the General Assembly . . . ."

[23] Yoram Shachar, "Yomano shel Uri Yadin," ("Uri Yadin's Diary"), *Iyunei Mishpat*, 3, 1991, p. 542.

[24] Ibid.   [25] Ibid., p. 544.

referring to Shertok, the context of his diary more strongly implies that Heinsheimer here is referring to Ben-Gurion.

With the benefit of hindsight, Heinsheimer's view seems confused. While the work of the Legal Department, expressed most clearly in the draft of Tzvi Berenson, did indeed declare a "sovereign" (or "independent" – depending on one's preferred translation) state, it also explicitly called for a state within the framework of UN Resolution 181, with its borders determined by the UN resolution as well. The state was to be both sovereign and subordinate in a strange act of legal gymnastics. Ben-Gurion was not hesitating with respect to declaring a state. On the contrary, he believed that the declaration of a nonindependent state was impossible.

Heinsheimer came to his pessimistic conclusion because, in his view, what the Israeli legal community would come to call the "operative" clause of the Declaration, the middle paragraphs in which the state is actually proclaimed, does not mention the words independence (*atzmaut*) or sovereignty (*ribonut*). It says: "[W]e ... hereby declare the establishment of a Jewish state in *Eretz-Israel*, to be known as the State of Israel." According to the legalistically-minded Heinsheimer, the absence of the word sovereignty from this paragraph could lead one to assume that the state was neither fully independent nor sovereign.[26]

Heinsheimer attributed what he saw as the ambiguity in the Declaration's central paragraph to the frustrating character of David Ben-Gurion. As he wrote about Ben-Gurion further in his diary:

The wonder and frustration of it all is the combination in one man of vision and prophecy, weighing philosophy and mysticism on one hand with, on the other hand, cold logic, outstanding realism and impressive understanding of details. One minute he develops his all-encompassing thoughts on the relationship between the Jewish people and the state of Israel, and in the next minute he asks Sharett, "what will be the details of the divorce proceedings?" He asks Rosen and the rest of the professionals complex legal questions and proceeds to debate the fine points with them – and successfully so. And all marked by the force of his personality.[27]

Heinsheimer missed the forest for the trees. The words "independent" and "sovereign" did not need to appear in Ben-Gurion's "operative clause" for two reasons. First, Ben-Gurion believed they were implied in the very idea of a state. Ben-Gurion was so very far from being lukewarm

[26] Ibid., p. 543.   [27] Ibid., p. 551.

on sovereignty that he refused to countenance the idea that a state could be anything but sovereign.

Second, the driving theme of the final text of the Declaration on the whole is that the Jewish nation will now be "masters of its own fate" in its own "sovereign state." Indeed, this was the natural right by virtue of which the state was declared: "by virtue of our natural and historical right." Heinsheimer had not seen the importance of this formulation. His legal mind had missed the fact that Ben-Gurion had shifted the text from being a legal document with an operative clause and transformed it into a reasoned textual argument.

Ben-Gurion's logic ran deep. There was no need to use the word sovereign in the so-called operative clause in any case. A state is not sovereign or independent by virtue of what it calls itself. The Soviet Republics were nominally independent. Today, the states in Russia's orbit are called the Commonwealth of Independent States. States are independent because they win independence. Sovereignty is not granted or recognized but achieved. Ben-Gurion knew that the sovereignty of the new state would be determined in practice, not in diplomatic language.

And of course, as Ben-Gurion wrote the final version of the Declaration, the *Yishuv* was already subject to the whims of fate. Locked in brutal war, the costs of sovereignty were being borne by the *Yishuv* even without its prerogatives. Whether they wished to be or not, the *Yishuv* leaders were "as masters of their own fate" – as we all are. For we may not wish for sovereignty and responsibility. Yet there is no fleeing either. The *Yishuv* was on the verge of independence. How could it not take matters into its own hands? Ben-Gurion had been on a multi-decade mission to declare a state. It can even be fairly said that the foundation of an *independent* state for Jews was the single-minded purpose of Ben-Gurion's entire life.[28]

THE RIGHT MAN AT THE RIGHT TIME

David Ben-Gurion was born David Gruen in Plonsk, a Polish city in the Russian Empire, in 1886. His father had been active in *Hovevei Zion* (Lovers of Zion), the Zionist movement most popular in Eastern Europe.

---

[28] The biographical material is based largely on the excellent Ben-Gurion biography by Tom Segev, *A State at Any Cost*. Also see Anita Shapira, *Ben-Gurion: Father of Modern Israel* (New Haven, CT: Yale University Press, 2014) and Shabtai Teveth, *Ben-Gurion: Burning Ground* (New York: Random House, 1989).

Young Gruen was intellectually curious and his poetic letters to his childhood friends show his literary and intellectual enthusiasms.

Despite this, he struggled as a student to win admission to technical colleges and even relied on a variety of chicaneries to ultimately gain access to institutions of higher learning in Warsaw and, later in life, in Istanbul. By the time he was 18, on account of his rabble-rousing labor organizing, sometimes at pistol point as legend would have it, he may have seemed to be on the way to becoming one of the early twentieth century's dangerous young men.

Gruen found purpose, however, through the rough and tumble world of Zionist activism. He became involved in *Po'alei Zion*, the Zionist workers' movement. Settling in Palestine in 1906 after a series of disappointments in Poland, Gruen almost immediately, following a brief career as a day laborer, threw himself into the world of political and union organizing.

David Gruen became Ben-Gurion, adopting the name of a first-century rebel against Roman rule over the Jews. This period of his youth featured his most intense self-guided reading in philosophy, science, politics, literature, and world religions.

Wanting to learn the laws of Turkey to further the cause of Jewish statehood in then-Ottoman Palestine, Ben-Gurion studied law in Istanbul but did not graduate. During World War I he spent two years in New York as a Zionist activist, writing a book on the Jewish labor movement in Palestine. He also married a Russian-born American Jew named Paula Munweis.

His career took off after the war. Ben-Gurion, along with other aspiring Zionist leaders, had joined the British military's Jewish Legion in an effort to build a military basis and military argument for a Jewish state. Stationed in Egypt, Ben-Gurion became close to Berl Katznelson, a leader of the Israeli workers movement.

Upon his return to Palestine, Ben-Gurion, with Katznelson's support, worked to unite the various labor factions into a single party. In 1919, the Zionist Social Union of the Workers of the Land of Israel party (*Ahdut ha'Avodah*) was formally created. By 1930, after another merger, *Mapai*, the forerunner of the Labor Party that would rule Israel until 1977, was born. Ben-Gurion's expert ability to hold together union business through the *Histadrut* labor union and transform it into political power allowed him to ultimately become the de-facto leader of the *Yishuv*, and, indeed, its prime minister-in-waiting.[29]

---

[29] Neil Rogachevsky, "The Man Who Willed a State," *Mosaic*, July 1, 2020.

Ben-Gurion's life reflected the idea of creating a state at any cost, in the words of his biographer Tom Segev. This commitment precluded any ideological fixation on the prospective borders of the state. At various times, Ben-Gurion seemed to offer contradictory messages. In the summer of 1947, before the United Nations had approved the Partition Plan, Ben-Gurion reminded his colleagues that the first convention of the old *Ahdut ha'Avodah* movement which he had led in 1919 demanded the establishment of a Jewish state in all of the land of Israel. "I still believe that to this day," he said. After the partition was approved, he said the Jewish state would have to hold back opponents of partition who were dreaming of "our undivided homeland."[30] He was able to be at once a maximalist and a pragmatist on the question of borders.

Ben-Gurion's contradictions both masked and revealed a deeper consistency. He understood the nature of states: "The borders of the land under Jewish rule – from the time of the judges to Bar Kohba – changed all the time .... In ancient times the boundaries of Jewish independence retreated and advanced in accordance with constant political change."[31] The borders of states are never truly fixed because states are human constructs and human constructs exist in a world of change. Indeed, as the largest construct of human beings, the histories of cities or states, which come and go, demonstrate that humans exist in the world of generation and corruption, a world without permanence, the world of change.[32]

Borders were negotiable. Details were negotiable. A state was nonnegotiable. Ben-Gurion knew from his experience as a Polish Jew that it is certainly possible to exist in the world without political sovereignty. However, to live in a civilization without sovereignty subjects one to the cruel turns of fortune. In the belief in a sovereign state for the Jews, Ben-Gurion never wavered.[33]

When it came down to it, in 1948, Ben-Gurion maintained maximum flexibility on the question of borders but implacable commitment to declaring a state. On May 9 he was pessimistic about the balance of

---

[30] Tom Segev, *A State at Any Cost*, p. 406.   [31] Ibid.

[32] See Xenophon, *Hellenika*, Book I, trans. John Maricola (New York: Anchor, 2010).

[33] Cf. Dmitry Shumsky, *Beyond the Nation-State: The Zionist Political Imagination from Pinsker to Ben-Gurion* (New Haven, CT: Yale University Press, 2018). Shumsky cites examples where Ben-Gurion displayed a tactical and prudential flexibility regarding possible political outcomes for the *Yishuv*. This does not, however, negate the overwhelming evidence that independent Jewish statehood was his lodestar and ultimate goal.

forces between the *Yishuv* and the Arab nations. "At this moment we do not have the necessary strength to withstand a possible invasion," he said.[34] Yigal Yadin, the *Yishuv*'s military leader, would say much the same thing on May 12.

But despite that canny military observation, Ben-Gurion did not plan to delay. History had presented an opportunity that could not be missed. And so he would risk going to war without the heavy weaponry the *Yishuv* needed, including European airplanes. He was confident that matériel would begin to arrive in the country within days. Risks had to be run.[35]

Just as Ben-Gurion had recognized that borders are "always changing," he also grasped that opportunities to assert one's influence over the ebb and flow of events – the British departure from Palestine was surely one such opportunity – are exceedingly rare. This opportunity had to be seized, despite the risks, despite the potential cost in human life, to decisively change Jewish history.

MASTERS OF THEIR OWN FATE

The preamble of the text in all three editions of the Declaration seen by Ben-Gurion – Berenson's, Lauterpacht's, and Shertok's – had dwelled on the cruelties of exile and the horrors of the Holocaust. There was a rich Zionist literature built on analysis of the vicissitudes of life without a state. Ben-Gurion simply got to the essence of the matter.

In doing so, he articulated a simple truth that lay at the center of Zionist thought. The Zionist activist Max Bodenheimer expressed this same idea at the First Zionist Congress in Basel in 1897: "The entire misery of the Jewish people since the loss of national independence consists in the fact that it did not possess, and as an insignificant minority could not possess, sufficient power to acquire sovereignty as a state."[36] Fate would always find you. That was nature. The world could not be kept at bay.

---

[34] Tom Segev, *A State at Any Cost*, p. 421.

[35] Tom Segev, *A State at Any Cost*, p. 422. On Ben-Gurion's decision making in wartime, see Eliot A. Cohen, *Supreme Command: Soldiers, Statesmen, and Leadership in Wartime* (New York: Free Press, 2002).

[36] Quoted in Michael J. Reimer, *The First Zionist Congress*, proceedings (Albany: State University of New York Press, 2019), p. 217.

Ben-Gurion's formulation did not speak of a natural right to a state. Rather, it was a natural right of the Jews to be "masters of their own fate," to give it a go. In Shertok's draft, the UN was the master of the fate of Israel. Not in Ben-Gurion's. One can almost say that Ben-Gurion here channels Niccòlo Machiavelli in the *The Prince*. There Machiavelli writes that fate (*fortuna* in his inimitable phrase) "is like a violent river .... And though ... like this, it is not as if men, when times are quiet, could not provide for it with dikes and ditches."[37]

The vicissitudes of life cannot be eliminated, but fate can be constrained and even mastered. The best that can be said of fate is that, to the limited extent it can be mastered, it is "won more by the impetuous than by the cautious."[38] Humanity cannot with assurance master its own fate in fact, but the best and the least that we can do is to try. Israel would try. It had no choice. The choice had been made for it.

This way of thinking was strongly opposed by many central and respected participants in Jewish life. The stark statement in the Declaration stands in contradistinction to one of the enduring beliefs articulated by diasporic Judaism: the belief in deliverance in a world to come. This messianic belief was in fact anti-messianic. It precluded false messiahs. Pinsker's "auto-emancipation" could be seen as a promethean usurpation, no different from the false messiahs of prior centuries who led bands of enthusiasts to ruin.[39] Rabbi Chaim Soloveitchik (1853–1918), a leading light of turn-of-the-century Judaism, distinguished jurist, founder of the Brisker method of Talmud study, and the standard-bearer for Jewish jurisprudence and thought in his generation stated the matter plainly: "The people of Israel should take care not to join a venture that threatens their souls, to destroy religion, and is a stumbling block to the house of Israel."[40] Zionist Rabbi Samuel Mohilewer explained the outlook of his rivals: They "brusquely declared that the national idea conflicts with the messianic idea of religion."[41]

---

[37] *The Prince*, trans. Harvey Mansfield (Chicago: University of Chicago Press, 1998), p. 98.
[38] Ibid., p. 101.
[39] See Gershom Scholem, *Sabbatai Ṣevi: The Mystical Messiah, 1626–1676* (Princeton, NJ: Princeton University Press, 1973).
[40] Quoted in Adam Zachary Newton, *The Fence and the Neighbor* (Albany: State University of New York Press, 2001), p. 233. See also, Allan L. Nadler, "Religious Movements in Nineteenth- and Twentieth-Century Eastern Europe," in *The Modern Jewish Experience*, ed. Jack Wertheimer (New York: New York University Press, 1993), p. 165.
[41] Quoted in Michael J. Reimer, *The First Zionist Congress*, p. 207.

Of course, this view was to change as Israel emerged. A few short decades later, Rabbi Joseph B. Soloveitchik, Chaim Soloveitchik's grandson and a leading figure in post–Second World War Jewry, embraced the Jewish state as a vital node in Jewish life. His views were explicitly Zionist and he celebrated what he saw as the nearly miraculous rise of Israel as an extraordinary and welcome development for the Jewish people which contributed to their revitalization in the wake of the Holocaust. He was proudly Zionist and helped the classical world of Torah embrace the modern project of Zionism.[42] After the Second World War, the Haredi world made its peace with Zionism and the state of Israel even as many communities within it live a life apart from its mainstream institutions.[43] This was one of the revolutions that would come about as the Jews became "masters of their own fate" in the new state.

The acculturated Jewish world too had its tensions with the Jewish national project. Many feared that Zionism drew into question the loyalties of the increasingly assimilated Jews of the emancipated Western countries in the eyes of their countrymen. Zionism was risky. Many Jews in the wealthy and politically liberal countries did not want to associate with the political actions and ethical compromises that Zionism would have to make as the *Yishuv* was built.[44]

This view also found its way into the *Yishuv*. There was a learned class in the elite of the *Yishuv* that was opposed to the creation of a Jewish state out of a combination of trepidation and high-mindedness. Judah Magnes, the American-born president of the Hebrew University, had since 1930 led the effort to found a binational government in Palestine. As late as March 1948, as war raged in Palestine, he went to the US to rally Jewish support there for the Trusteeship Plan – the very plan that Shertok, and by extension the *Yishuv*'s leadership, labored day and night to undercut and avoid.[45] The Hebrew University's most celebrated

---

[42] Reuven Ziegler, *Majesty and Humility: The Thought of Rabbi Joseph B. Soloveitchik* (Jerusalem: OU Press, 2012).

[43] Another exception remains some among the relatively small and eccentric Satmar sect, whose twentieth-century leader, Rabbi Joel Teitelbaum, maintained an ardent anti-Zionism retained by his followers. Before the founding of Israel, Teitelbaum pronounced the desire for political sovereignty absent messianic intervention a heresy: "If they [the Zionists] establish government and [acquire] freedom on their own before the appointed time, this is forcing the end which is a heresy," he said. See Zvi Jonathan Kaplan, "Rabbi Joel Teitelbaum, Zionism, and Hungarian Ultra-Orthodoxy," *Modern Judaism*, 24, 2, 2004, p. 171.

[44] Walter Laqueur, "Zionism and Its Liberal Critics, 1896–1948." *Journal of Contemporary History*, 6, 4, 1971, pp. 161–182.

[45] Ibid., p. 16.

philosopher, Martin Buber, provided more abstract arguments for the political diagnosis of the university president. In the words of one Buber scholar, the Jewish thinker did not support the creation of a Jewish state "because he denied all validity to structures of authority instituted by the state, society, or religion. The only viable foundation of communal life is dialogue and exchange between persons."[46]

Zionism was already in the process of overturning these views. The Declaration, when it proclaimed that the Jews would be "masters of their own fate ... in their own sovereign state," finished the job. It articulated the argument for an active role for the Jewish people in their own fate. Transcendental values of thought and spirit required and were even enhanced by active participation in the steering of one's own fate. There had been no shortage of opponents to this view in Ben-Gurion's Jewish world. His Declaration of Independence made the starkest argument against them: the argument for the necessity of sovereignty.

The argument for sovereignty too had its hallowed place in the Jewish cannon. Ben-Gurion was continuing in the tradition of others who had written on this subject even before Zionism had risen. Maimonides' *Mishneh Torah*, 9:2 includes an account of messianic times. They constitute "Deliverance from the oppression of wicked regimes . . . . Sovereignty will be re-established in Israel, and there will be a return to Israel ... and the heart of the kingdom will be in Zion."[47] Nature, in this messianic era, will continue on as it always has. He writes: "One should not think that the customary way of the world will be abolished or that there will be any change in nature, rather the world will go its customary way."[48] The aim of a revived Jewish state, in his account, is not "to rule the entire world, and not the subjugation of the nations."[49] It is rather the creation of a just state that lives under a just law.[50]

---

[46] Freddy Raphaël, "Le Sionisme de Martin Buber," *Esprit,* 38, 2, 1980, p. 79.

[47] See *Mishneh Torah,* 9:2 www.sefaria.org/Mishneh_Torah%2C_Repentance.9.2?vhe= Torat_Emet_363&lang=bi

[48] Ibid. For a full explication, see James Diamond, "Maimonides and Medinat Yisrael." Cf. Theodor Herzl, cited above: "Certain matters we might organize better [in a future Jewish state] than we did in the old society, but in general, everything will remain the same." Benzion Netanyahu, *The Founding Fathers of Zionism* (Jerusalem: Gefen, 2012), p. 70.

[49] *Mishneh Torah* 12:4, www.sefaria.org/Mishneh_Torah%2C_Kings_and_Wars.12.4? ven=Laws_of_Kings_and_Wars._trans._Reuven_Brauner,_2012&lang=bi

[50] *Mishneh Torah* 12:4. *Mishneh Torah,* Maimonides' distillation of Jewish law into a multi-volume text, culminates in an articulation of the laws of kingship and politics. In a complex hermeneutic, a king of Israel is commanded in the Bible, "when he sitteth upon the throne of his kingdom, that he shall write him a copy of this law ('*mishneh Torah*') in

The state, in this conception, is simply a vessel for a people. It seeks to be a just vessel so that the people may conduct themselves well. Which brings us to Ben-Gurion's effort to explain why the state of Israel had a natural and historical right underlying its establishment beyond the natural right of the Jews to be masters of their own fate. And that is found in the remarkable new introductory paragraph that Ben-Gurion wrote for the Declaration whose essence is the phrase: "Here they wrote the Book of Books."

BY VIRTUE OF OUR NATURAL AND HISTORICAL RIGHT

The culminating sentence of Ben-Gurion's Declaration invokes the creation of the State of Israel "by virtue of our natural and historical right." There is a "natural right" and a "historical right." The natural right that the text refers to is "the natural right to be masters of our own fate" which we just discussed. The historical right to which it refers is the historical justification of the state found at the beginning of the Declaration of Independence – the only historical argument for the creation of the state provided in the Declaration's text.

Like all of the prior drafts of the Declaration of Independence of Israel, the final text invokes the antiquity of the Jewish people's presence in the land of Israel. Berenson, Shertok, and Lauterpacht had all included such histories. Berenson had written of a "right of the unbroken historical and traditional connection of the people of Israel to the land of Israel." Shertok had written of an unjust and forced "expulsion" of the Jews from Israel and a longing "in every generation and generation" to return.

Ben-Gurion's account of the antiquity of the Jewish presence in the land of Israel, his historical account, goes further. It takes a fascinating turn, one with no real parallel among the preceding drafts, and one which points to an argument that is not historical:

ERETZ-ISRAEL was the birthplace of the Jewish people. Here their spiritual, religious and political identity was shaped. Here they first attained to statehood, created cultural values of national and universal significance and gave to the world the eternal Book of Books.

---

a book out of that which is before the priests the Levites. And it shall be with him, and he shall read therein all the days of his life." This second Bible or '*mishneh Torah*,' is the king's guide to governance. That is how Maimonides conceived of his codification of Jewish law.

Ben-Gurion's text argues not only that the Jewish people were born in the land of Israel, but as well that their "spiritual, religious, and political identity was shaped" in Israel. Why would the formation of a people's spiritual, religious, and political identity matter? Why would their formation of an identity in the past provide a rationalization for the foundation of a state in the present? The logic seems flawed.

Indeed, so too, it thus stands to reason, Shertok's and Berenson's invocations of the ancient residence of the Jews in Palestine does not add up to a coherent argument for the founding of a state in present times. The residence of the Jews in Israel in antiquity might be a fact. But what title or meaning does that ancient fact provide in the present?

To put the matter more starkly: there is always a precedent historical claim to any given historical claim, an older history, a prequel. History does not on its own provide an ability to rank historical claims. There is no ultimate original or beginning that does not end in *reductio ad absurdum*. The objective search for the original ends in the subjective acceptance of plurality and the inability to refer to an objective or original value.

In 1948, this was obvious on its face. There was Arab history and there was Jewish history. Each mattered on its own terms. But to consider only those two would have been only to begin to look at the nineteenth- and twentieth-century histories of the land. In the sweep of history, there were Turks, Romans, Greeks, and beyond. The history of the Canaanites would have been integral to the Canaanites, and so on. Once something has become historical, its relevance only applies to its historical context. It has always been known that different notions of justice obtain in different nations in different historical periods.[51]

This very contingency of history seems to have entered into the logic of the text that Ben-Gurion composed. It caused him to reach for a more profound historical right than a mere historical claim. Ben-Gurion's text does not stop at describing the historical spiritual formation of the Jewish people. The text goes beyond this intellectual dead end by grasping toward the universal.

The relevance of the Jewish spiritual formation is described as being of "universal significance." The Jews created "cultural values of national and universal significance." What the Jews did in Israel in antiquity, the text argues, mattered not only for the Jewish people but for all people. It

---

[51] Leo Strauss, *Natural Right and History* (Chicago: University of Chicago Press, 1999), p. 10.

mattered for the whole of mankind, the text argues, because the Jews "gave to the world the eternal Book of Books."

The Declaration's text reaches to the wisdom that lies at the kernel of not just Jewish ideas but indeed even Christian and Muslim ideas, not to say the ideas at the bedrock of both Western and Islamic civilization. If those ideas remain important, the text argues, then it is also vital that the political and social development of the people who are the carriers of those ideas must continue – so that those ideas shall not perish from the Earth and their torch be carried ahead. In this we see an echo of Lauterpacht's argument that the Jews are the "torch-bearers" of values that are of universal significance.

This argument represents the text's effort to transcend what might be thought of as the inherent limits of historical right even as the text refers to this argument as a "historical right." The idea of historical right – not Ben Gurion's invocation of it, but the idea simply – demands an objective or scientific historical account of a phenomenon's origins in order to ground action or thought in the present.

The text of Israel's Declaration seeks to go beyond that type of historical right through its invocation of the ideas of "universal significance" exemplified by "the book of books." It tries to offer principles that are outside of time and the reader may judge if the principles – the principles of the Book of Books – are operative or of significance.

The text, however, does not meditate on what those ideas are. It seems to leave them at a vague level. The text points to the general universal *principles* of the Jewish people. It understands that these principles are an essential aspect of the coming to be of the state. The state's people have been galvanized by those principles to endure as a people even without a state; and the state is thus being founded in some respects so that those principles might endure and continue their journey. Regarding what these principles are, the text is silent.

None of this is to say that the text argues for a theological state, a state whose essence is the practice of or devotion to the letter of the Book of Books. On the contrary, the very manner in which Jewish ideas are raised in the text of the Declaration in its essence undercuts any such claim.

The Declaration proclaims that the Book of Books was written in the land of Israel. Surely the books of the Judges, Kings, and Prophets were likely composed there. However, believers do not believe that the entirety of Bible was written in Israel. On the contrary, the Book of Deuteronomy describes its own composition across the Jordan River, outside the land of Israel.

The *Mishnah Avot,* or *Ethics of the Fathers,* is a bedrock work of Jewish ethics and understood as a divine scripture of importance secondary only to the Bible. It begins: "Moses received the Torah from Sinai and passed it to Joshua."[52] Moses did not enter into the Land of Israel. The Pentateuch and indeed the entire Torah, according to the *Mishnah* and to itself, was not written there. The Declaration sets the authorship of the Bible in Israel in a kind of deliberate departure from Jewish tradition and religious belief.

The clearest explanation for this departure is that the text of the Declaration purposefully leaves the realm of traditional Judaism and settles instead into the language of what is called cultural or spiritual Zionism. Cultural or spiritual Zionism was a formulation created by Zionist theoretician and activist Ahad Ha'am to describe the nature of the Jewish people's contributions of "universal significance" to the human story. In Ahad Ha'am's writing, Jewish religion is but a part of Jewish culture. The overriding Jewish culture is characterized by the introduction to the world of particular ideas as ways of life: fairness, supremacy of reason, elevation of the spiritual at the expense of the material, elevation of the ethical above the practical.

Ahad Ha'am sees all of these ethics as finding their most significant expression in the teachings of the Hebrew Bible. "So long as the Bible is extant, the creative power of the Jewish mind will remain undeniable," he wrote.[53] To Ahad Ha'am, the core teaching of the Bible is: live life according to strict morality and righteousness. Heeding the call of the prophets, the people of Israel, in this telling, are meant to demonstrate to all mankind through their actions how an ethical life might be lived and a just society built.[54] And Ahad Ha'am believed that his formulation was universally recognized: "Almost everybody recognizes the moral genius of the people of Israel," he wrote.[55]

Ahad Ha'am not only saw the Bible as a source of wisdom but also as a specific cultural product from a specific time, "the embodiment of the spirit of our nation *in a bygone era.*"[56] As history advanced, the Jewish

---

[52] www.sefaria.org/Pirkei_Avot.1?lang=bi
[53] Ahad Ha'am, *The Spiritual Revival,* trans. Leon Simon (London: The Zionist, 1917), p. 7.
[54] See Leon Simon, Introduction, *Ahad Ha'am, Selected Essays* (Philadelphia: Jewish Publication Society of America, 1912), p. 16. See also, Allan T. Levenson, "In Search of Ahad Ha'am's Bible," *The Journal of Israeli History,* 32, 2, 2013, pp. 241–256.
[55] Quoted in Anita Shapira, "Herzl, Ahad Ha-'Am, and Berdichevsky: Comments on Their Nationalist Concepts," *Jewish History,* 4, 2, 1990, p. 63.
[56] Quoted in Allan Arkush, "Biblical Criticism and Cultural Zionism Prior to the First World War," *Jewish History,* 21, 2, 2007, p. 124.

people, Ahad Ha'am theorized, though inspired by the Bible, would inevitably and necessarily develop or create new cultural products reflective of what he called their "national genius." In modern times, Ahad Ha'am counseled not a return to Rabbinic religion or the Bible but for the creation of a renewed national literature, written in the national language of Hebrew, that might rival and surpass other "national literatures."[57]

The English version of the Declaration uses the phrase "created cultural values" to describe the ideas encapsulated in the phrase proclaiming that the Jews in Israel "gave to the world the Book of Books." The Hebrew, in a more interesting turn of phrase, reads "*yatzar nekhasei tarbut*" – created cultural "goods" or "assets" and in Biblical Hebrew "treasures" or "bounty." (The word for "values" – *erekhim,* which translates directly as "measures" or "values" – is not used.)[58] This language, in echoing Ahad Ha'Am's idea of the Bible as a cultural treasure, seeks to find a timeless principle on which to hang the purpose of the Jewish state's founding. But in reducing the idea of universal principles to mere cultural artifacts, it seems to accomplish only part of what it set out to do.

Israel's Declaration grasps for a timeless distillation of Jewish ideas to act as the nation's founding principle. Did it accomplish this task? It would be difficult to find a community in Israel which would be happy to give an account of itself in Ahad Ha'Am's terms, that is to say, which sees itself as continuing to advance and evolve the universal values created by the ancient Hebrews in the Book of Books but which, Ahad Ha'Am believed, require updating today.

Ben-Gurion saw a need to ground the state in a universal argument. He called this a "historical right" but he meant much more. He settled on an allusion to the intellectual paradigm of spiritual or cultural Zionism – a middle way between purely religious and purely political or secular Zionism. It does not omit of the religious by the secular nor does it allow for the domination by the religious of the secular. The doctrine itself does not render unto the state that which is the state's, nor does it allow religion to control the state.

This compromise pleases no one. The state will always be in deliberate, purposive, conscious, and willful violation of some religious law or another; and some religious accommodation or another will always consciously and willfully restrict secular freedoms, sometimes in the form of an inconvenience and sometimes in the form of a deep alteration of life.

---

[57] See Ahad Ha'am "The Spiritual Revival."
[58] Hersch Lauterpacht had also used similar language in his Declaration text.

Practically, there was a certain merit in seeking a compromise between these two outlooks, even as it is a compromise in tension with each side's core beliefs. It provides a practical *modus vivendi* as well as a *modus operandi* for the state itself. It articulates a place for the state to serve as a Jewish state while delineating a practical freedom for the state. The state is not hamstrung or even responsible to the strictures of Jewish law or to any particular definition of being a Jewish state. The military will conduct itself on Shabbat. But the state will remain a Jewish one. Holidays are Jewish holidays, the weekend will occur over Shabbat. This is modern Israel.

If it is an incomplete compromise, then it is a compromise whose articulation is understandable: it was articulated by Ben-Gurion himself the night prior to the declaration of independence. He saw the problem. Indeed, the problem was plain to see. It had been raised in the debate of *Minhelet ha'Am*. To recall a quote from Bechor Sheetrit, "Until the exile there was something – there was a people that ruled with religion and tradition. And it's impossible not to mention our book of books. Epicureanism amongst the people in Israel began not that long ago."[59] It seems too uncanny that Sheetrit's locution, his reference to the book of books, found its way into the final text. Perhaps this comment had lodged itself into Ben-Gurion's mind too.

Ben-Gurion did his best to find a solution to a complex question. What is a Jewish state? His effort points at once to a vital political question for the state of Israel at its birth and to a question that remains open to this day. It would not be the only question that Ben-Gurion articulated but left open.

INHERENT VERSUS BESTOWED RIGHTS

The third major intellectual change that Ben-Gurion introduced into the Declaration could seem minor and simply grammatical. And indeed, it is small, partial, and nowhere near being fully articulated. It is a nod, but one with far-reaching theoretical implications. It takes the form of a tiny edit made by Ben-Gurion with regard to the discussion of political and social rights.

---

[59] See footnote 52 in the previous chapter.

All of the drafts of the Declaration, from Berenson's onwards, had included sections articulating the idea that the citizens of the state would live in freedom and equality. The final text would read:

[The State] ... will be based on freedom, justice and peace as envisaged by the prophets of Israel; it will ensure complete equality of social and political rights to all its inhabitants irrespective of religion, race or sex; it will guarantee freedom of religion, conscience, language, education and culture; it will safeguard the Holy Places of all religions; and it will be faithful to the principles of the Charter of the United Nations.

This was very close to the prior texts. Berenson's draft had said: "One law will apply to all residents regardless of race, religion, language, or sex." Shertok had gone beyond Berenson's legal nominalism to speak of rights. He had written that the state "will *bestow* (*ta'anik*) full and equal social and political rights upon all its citizens regardless of race or religion."

Both Berenson and Shertok had likely sought, in accordance with their own principles as well as the strictures of UN Resolution 181, to imply that the state would ensure civil equality. And their texts were very close to Resolution 181's language on the matter. Per Resolution 181, the new states, Jewish and Arab, were to grant: "Persons equal and non-discriminatory rights in civil, political, economic and religious matters and the enjoyment of human rights and fundamental freedoms, including freedom of religion, language, speech and publication, education, assembly and association."

Ben-Gurion does not seem to have had any objections to Shertok's list of rights and freedoms. His past included passionate advocacy in defense of all of these rights as would his future. Ben-Gurion did, however, take particular issue with one word in Shertok's formulation. Shertok's draft said that the state "bestowed" equal rights upon the citizens. Ben-Gurion disagreed. He articulated his critique in the debate over that draft on May 13.

Immediately upon Shertok's presentation of his draft text, Ben-Gurion had pounced. He offered copious revisions. Perhaps he had prepared them while reading Shertok's briefing materials during a lull or boring moment in the proceedings of the *Minhelet ha'Am* that day. Possibly he had thought of them while mulling over the text that morning. We do not have a transcript of exactly what Ben-Gurion said – there were many revisions and the minute-taker simply listed them. It is possible that the revisions were proposed at great length in a speech; it is likewise possible that they were merely listed like copy edits as they appear in the minutes. We will never know.

The record shows that after recommending the removal of a number of "flowery words" from Shertok's draft, Ben-Gurion offered a pointed critique of Shertok's conception of rights. The minutes read: "Paragraph 15 – '[the state] shall ensure [or "make manifest" – "*te'kayem*"] equality of rights. Not 'ensure.' They belong [to the people]." And so the minutes show Ben-Gurion making a succinct case: the state does not grant or bestow rights upon citizens. Rights are inherent. They belong to the people.[60]

When Ben-Gurion took over the drafting process, he did not neglect to address the point that he had made during the debates. On the matter of rights, the final text of the Declaration indeed reads: "[the state] will *ensure* [*te'kayem*] complete equality of social and political rights to all its inhabitants irrespective of religion, race or sex; it will guarantee freedom of religion, conscience, language, education and culture . . . ."

Ben-Gurion had only changed one word. The state went from "granting/bestowing" rights in Shertok's text to "ensuring" rights in the final edition's English translation. The Hebrew - *te'kayem* - is even stronger. A better translation of *te'kayem* might be to "instantiate" rather than to "ensure." To instantiate is to give a pre-existing idea presence in the world.[61]

The implication of Ben-Gurion's change is that the state is neither the master of rights nor the creator of rights. It rather makes manifest in practice the rights that all human beings inherently possess. There is a doctrine underlying this account of civil rights: it is Blackstone's doctrine that rights exist before or above the state as ideas or guiding thoughts that may orient or guide political choice. It is the doctrine of natural or inherent rights.[62] By replacing Shertok's "grant/bestow" with "ensure/make manifest," Ben-Gurion edged toward reorienting the state on the question of rights. He moved Israel's Declaration in a more liberal direction.

---

[60] Protocols of the National Administration, May 13, 1948, p. 123.

[61] See *Republic*, Books V–VII on the notion that ideas could be present and thus somehow "guide" material things in the world. Medieval Hebrew commentaries on Plato and Aristotle tended use the root word *kayam* to mean the instantiation of an intellectual pattern in the material world. We are grateful to Professor Yehuda Halper of Bar Ilan University for clarifying the meanings of these terms in medieval Jewish philosophical writing.

[62] Cf. William Blackstone, *Commentaries*, "Right of Revolution," https://press-pubs .uchicago.edu/founders/documents/v1ch3s3.html

The Jewish tradition famously articulates the doctrine of natural or inherent rights; the kings of Israel and Judah in the Bible are all subject to the law and punished for violation of the law.[63] This model is an archetype for the English system whereby the royals are subject to the law that they enforce.[64] On the question of *civil* rights and equality of rulers and ruled with regard to civil rights, Judaism in many ways is the progenitor of what has come to be known in the English world as the idea of equality under the law.

Ben-Gurion has long had a largely justified reputation as a statist in politics. He rarely worried about limiting or dispersing power or passing laws that would constrain the freedom of action of the executive.[65] As author of the Declaration, Ben-Gurion saw through the theoretical incoherence of the statist position on *civil* rights. A state does not bestow civil rights because a state is made up of individuals. And some individuals, whatever their positions of authority, do not bestow civil rights on other human beings. Civil rights either belong to all citizens equally or they belong to none.

MORE THAN A JEWISH AND DEMOCRATIC STATE

The final pivotal decision that Ben-Gurion made in composing the ultimate text of the Declaration was perhaps one that he had not realized that he had made, and surely a decision that, even if it was conscious, may not have seemed particularly pregnant at the time.

The text of the second draft, composed by the Legal Department and Tzvi Berenson, had proclaimed that the Jewish state-to-be would be "a free, independent, and democratic state." Shertok had omitted that aspect of Berenson's text from his draft, probably because he assumed that the state's attributes of freedom and democracy were connoted by his draft's commitment to the principles of Resolution 181 which called for elections, the rule of law, and so on.

---

[63] See discussion, above, on the *Mishneh Torah* on the just king according to the Maimonidean idea of "*mishneh torah*." See also David Polish, "Rabbinic views on Kingship – A Study in Jewish Sovereignty," *Jewish Political Studies Review*, 3, 1–2, 1991, pp. 67–90.

[64] See Saul Olyan, "Zadok's Origins and the Tribal Politics of David," *Journal of Biblical Literature*, 101, 2, 1982, pp. 177–193.

[65] Mitchell Cohen, "Labor Zionism, the State, and Beyond: An Interpretation of Changing Realities and Changing Histories," *Israel Studies Review*, 30, 2, 2015, pp. 1–27.

Ben-Gurion, in revising Shertok's text, emphasized the independence of the state but, like Shertok, did not write that the state would be democratic. Ben-Gurion had read Berenson's draft as had all of the members of *Minhelet ha'Am* who received a copy of it as part of their briefing package for the discussion of the drafting of the Declaration. We know that Ben-Gurion even read those documents with care indicated by his mastering of the subtleties of the texts.

We can of course only guess at Ben-Gurion's potential rationale for omitting the word "democracy." The easiest guess would be to say that it was irrelevant: the *Yishuv* was already democratic. During the period of the British Mandate, votes were conducted by universal suffrage for membership on the Assembly of Representatives.[66]

There is also a less charitable interpretation, though one that does not pass any muster upon closer inspection. The erroneous interpretation runs as follows. To claim that the state would be "democratic" would be to imply that the state would be a democracy for all – not just for the Jews of the *Yishuv* but for Arab residents of Palestine now falling under Israel's government. And perhaps Shertok and Ben-Gurion did not wish for this – so the argument goes.

This argument is incoherent and fails on two fronts. First: Arab citizens would in fact vote immediately upon the foundation of the state. Two Arab parties won election to Israel's first Knesset. Suffrage would be extended to Arabs living in territories under military law as those territories entered the realm of civil law.[67]

Second, the immediate election of Arab parties to the Knesset is of a piece with the text of the Declaration. All texts of the Declaration, including Shertok's and Ben-Gurion's, emphasized the extension of political rights to the Arab residents of the new state. The interpretation that claims that the omission of the characterization of the state as being "democratic" was a deliberate effort to deny political rights to minority groups seems implausible.

An alternate explanation is that Ben-Gurion had other more important things to say about the nature of the state. The text of the Declaration is replete with descriptions of the state. The state is a "sovereign state," a state "of the Jewish people" who are taking on the "natural right" to be "masters of our own fate." It is a state declared "by virtue of our natural

---

[66] Meir Chazan, "Israel Goes to the Polls: The Road to Elections for the Constituent Assembly, 1948–1949," *Israel Studies Review*, 31, 2, 2016, pp. 80–100.
[67] Ibid.

and historical right," drawing on the legacy of the Jews' authorship "of the Book of Books." It is a state "open for Jewish immigration and for ingathering of the Exiles." It is a state "that will foster development of the country for the benefit of all its inhabitants" and will "be based on freedom, justice, and peace as envisaged by the prophets of Israel." It is a state that will make manifest the political and social rights of all its citizens with no discrimination based on "religion, race, or sex," guaranteeing "freedom of religion, conscience, language, education, and culture" and safeguarding all religions' holy places and being "faithful to the principles of the Charter of the United Nations." It is impossible to imagine that such a state does not choose leaders via elections. But elections are just a small element of it its attributes.

There is no shortage of description of the content of the regime of the new state in the Declaration. The description alas defies simple categorization. The description points to essential ideas at the root of the state: the state would combine Jewish ideas and the Jewish legacy, meet the *realpolitik* need for the power and organizational strength of a state, and safeguard classical and early modern ideas of civil rights and mid-twentieth century ideas of social rights.

Ben-Gurion had ensured that these essentials were in the Declaration. There would be a truly sovereign state so that the Jewish people might be "masters of their own fate." There was a consciousness of the state as the vessel for the ongoing cultivation of the Jewish nation and its ideas flowing from the principles of the Jewish world. And there would be a modern liberal state characterized by the protection of individual liberties and the provision of modern social goods. This combination says much more than could be encapsulated in the word democracy.[68]

THE PATHS NOT TAKEN

There were many paths not taken in the Declaration of Independence. The state could have been characterized principally by the classical liberal ideas of the American Declaration of Independence as Beham had attempted. It could have been characterized by a Lockean conception of raw power and ownership via expansion and possession as Berenson had somehow argued. It could have been a Jewish and democratic state as

---

[68] For a different review of the topic, see Ruth Gavison, "Jewish and Democratic? A Rejoinder to the 'Ethnic Democracy' Debate," *Israel Studies*, 4, 1, 1999, pp. 44–47.

Berenson too had written. It could have been, as Lauterpacht had dreamed, a Hebrew Republic under universal United Nations law. It could have been a partially born state as part of a UN convention as Shertok believed would be necessary at least in writing. It could have been a trusteeship of the United Nations policed by American arms as Shertok had feared the Americans might try to impose. These are just some of the possibilities that are raised by the process of drafting and consideration of the options that were weighed at the time of the writing of Israel's Declaration of Independence.

The drafting process, instead of pointing to an intention to take any of those paths in the ongoing building of the state, points to the fact that these various paths were abandoned, consciously in most cases, and the state instead set out to combine the concepts of inherent rights, political power and sovereignty, and the legacy of the Jewish world. It is a state whose intellectual conception draws on ideas from various well-known schools of thought but cannot be said to be a state characterized in its essence as belonging to or being of any of those particular sets of ideas. The Declaration of Independence of Israel set a new state out on a path that was entirely new based on ideas that were to combine into something entirely new.

What must be said is that these underlying ideas were not fully articulated in the Declaration of Independence. The characterization of the Jewish essence was incomplete. The account of liberal principles and freedoms needed further reflection and sharper elaboration. Only – and perhaps pivotally – the idea of sovereignty reached its entire and mature articulation in the Declaration's text.

The reasons that the drafting process resulted in an at-best partial outcome are not hard to find. The obvious explanation for the partiality and incomplete character of the Declaration's meditations upon and explications of some of the core ideas that it addresses is the shortness of time that the drafters confronted. Both Shertok and Ben-Gurion had only hours in which to complete a monumental task.

It was never clear to Ben-Gurion that he had succeeded on all fronts. In later life, he tended to focus on the tangible importance of the Declaration of Independence as opposed to its intellectual content. In a 1949 speech discussing the pros and cons of writing a constitution for Israel (an initiative which he opposed), he addressed the possibility that a constitution would articulate a nation's first principles.

He opposed such an undertaking for two reasons. It would divide the young nation over intellectual squabbles. And second, the task would require greater thinkers than the Knesset had to offer: "I do not see that we have time to deal with declarations," Ben-Gurion told the Knesset Committee on the Constitution. "This is a matter perhaps for men of humane learning."

Ben-Gurion's considerations on the issue led him to raise the possibility that the principles of Israel's Declaration were not as expansive as the principles of other declarations of independence – say of the French Declaration of the Rights of Man of 1789:

What about a constitution in the sense of a solemn declaration of known principles but without the ability to compel. There are many such constitutions in the world in which are written perhaps fine things. However, they are intangible because they lack the ability to compel. For instance in France, the constitution speaks of equality, fraternity, but has no ability to compel, and if one man is in fact not equal to another, nothing happens. It's just a nice formulation. If that's our intent, we already have something like this: the Declaration of Independence. At the time [in May 1948] it was necessary to state that we were independent because until that moment we were under foreign rule. And it was not necessary only to state that we were independent; we also spoke about principles, about the vision of the prophets, about equality, and about freedom. Perhaps it is the case that it is possible to improve the style. But I am skeptical that we would produce a document very different from the document we have. The value of this document is that it founded the state. Today a professional writer could sit down and do the work with a more ornamental style. Maybe some flourishes could be added. But it would not change this: the privilege of the Declaration is that it expresses the transfer from foreign rule to independence. Not every day does one pass from foreign rule to independence. Just once – well, I pray it's just once.[69]

The real and practical importance of the Declaration of Independence was: its declaration of political independence. In this Ben-Gurion took great personal pride. Its other aspects perhaps could have been improved. And in any event, they were not the essence of the issue.

When in 1961 a journalist asked the aging Prime Minister to reflect upon the Declaration and its meaning, Ben-Gurion at first demurred, telling the interviewer to read the narrative account written by the general secretary of *Minhelet ha'Am*, Ze'ev Sharef. Ben-Gurion had no soul-warming or heartening thoughts to offer.

Pressed further, he said that "I would not now add anything nor would I change anything." He further maintained that, happy though he had

---

[69] David Ben-Gurion, "Speech to the Knesset's Committee on Constitution, Law, and Justice," July 13, 1949, trans. Neil Rogachevsky, *Mosaic*, March 10, 2021, https://mosaicmagazine.com/observation/israel-zionism/2021/03/against-court-and-constitution-a-never-before-translated-speech-by-david-ben-gurion/

been to declare independence, he had been especially preoccupied with the "impending invasion" and the weapons that "had not yet come into our hands."[70] These comments certainly reflect his main preoccupations at the time. But in his minimization of the Declaration we can adduce that, somehow, Ben-Gurion was not perfectly satisfied with the document he revised and rewrote on the night of May 13, 1948.

THERE WAS SUPPOSED TO BE A CONSTITUTION

It is important to remember that the drafters of the Declaration did not believe that they were *truly* out of time. For there was to be a constitution, and its drafting would have provided a new opportunity to consider foundational political matters in more depth and with more leisure and to arrive at a more final understanding on all of the key issues. All of the drafts of the Declaration had called for the production of a constitution and this was both because it seemed like a good idea, but also because it was mandated by Resolution 181.

The deadline established by the UN for a Constitution was supposed to be October 1, 1948 – the same deadline the UN had allotted to see whether the new states were in compliance with the process for achieving independence that Resolution 181 had outlined. With this in mind, but not wanting to mention this rationale in the text, the final language of the Declaration thus committed the new state to produce a constitution.

October 1 came and went, and with the war still ongoing, no constitution had been legislated. However on January 25, 1949, with the War of Independence largely over, Israelis went to the polls for the first time to elect a "Constituent Assembly."[71] It is an often forgotten fact that the chief purpose of the first elected government of the state was to be the drafting of a constitution.

It was not to be. In short order, by February, the "Constituent Assembly" became the "Knesset" – Israel's permanent legislature. The Constituent Assembly never drafted a constitution but merely a "transition law" which offered some very general rules regarding the presidency, legislature (Knesset), and procedures of government. The renaming of the Constituent Assembly as the Knesset removed the last connection between

---

[70] Eliezer Whartman, "Interviews with the Signers of the Declaration of Independence," pp. 2–6.

[71] Samuel Sager, "Israel's Dilatory Constitution," *The American Journal of Comparative Law*, 24, 1, 1976, pp. 88–89.

the country's new legislative body and the constitutional purpose for which it had initially been assembled.[72]

This had two important implications. First, it meant that the unfinished work of the Declaration would not be completed. There would be no additional formal and official articulation of what it meant for Israel to be at once a state whose principles and wellsprings were a liberal framework of rights, a realpolitik view of power and the state, and its status as the *Jewish* state. Neither the relationship between these ideas nor the further development and sharpening of these ideas would happen in any formal setting.

Even as the work of thinking about the nation's first principles would not continue in a constitutional or other official framework, the Declaration was left as the *only* document from the founding period of the state that sought to define the nature of the state and the overall priorities and principles that ought to underlie its jurisprudence and ultimately government.

As there was no constitutional convention or effort to otherwise elaborate the architectonic principles of the state, the Declaration of Independence, with its ambiguities and its uncertainties, and one should add, its lack of official standing as a legal document for these purposes, would have to suffice as an intellectual bedrock of the state's legal and political institutions.

The absence of a constitution was not necessarily disapproved of by Israel's leadership. Over the first year of the Knesset's sitting, the writing of a constitution still remained on the list of prospective business for the Israeli government. But it was clear that this was now but one item of business amongst many in a functioning legislative body, and certainly not the central one.[73] The Knesset created a "Constitution, Law, and Justice Committee" tasked with working toward the production of a constitution, and its business was widely debated.[74] But little came of it.

By the end of 1949, the opinions of the Israeli leadership were hardening against the adoption of a formal constitution. David Ben-Gurion was foremost in moving in this direction. As he told coalition partners before the formation of the very first government:

---

[72] Ibid., p. 89.
[73] Nir Kedar, *Ben-Gurion ve'hahuka (Ben-Gurion and the Constitution)* p. 39.
[74] Samuel Sager, "Israel's Dilatory Constitution," p. 93.

I do not favor that we deal now with the writing of a constitution for the country. We have no time for this now. We have to build houses for immigrants. A constitution we will make when we're a bit more comfortable. But in this matter I'm bringing my private pragmatic opinion, and I don't know whether it'll be accepted by my colleagues. The English are still living without a constitution – and it's not too bad for them. [The] issues [we face] will not wait. they are urgent ... we have to work at a fast tempo. Things won't be perfect, but we can fix them with the passage of time. A law isn't something eternal. If we're convinced in a year that we were mistaken – we can fix it.[75]

The need to "focus urgently on the matter at hand" would become Ben-Gurion's rhetorical line against a constitution, and he would use it again and again. That November, Ben-Gurion said that a constitution was not an immediate priority for a country doubling its population in four short years and in need of infrastructure to accommodate the new citizens.[76] His preferred solution was to have the Knesset pass certain "basic laws" – better translated as "fundamental laws" or "foundational laws" – that would serve constitutional purposes. These could be passed quickly and deal with the fundamentals of government such as the make-up of the Knesset, the army, and so on.

This was the path that the Knesset would in fact take, and leave the dynamic articulation of the country's principles up to future generations. It would be for successive generations to find the way, and to themselves consider and articulate the state's principles.

[75] Quoted in Nir Kedar, *Ben-Gurion ve'hahuka*, p. 40.   [76] Ibid., p. 41.

PART IV

LEGACY

8

The Laws of Israel and the Declaration of Independence

The legacy of the Declaration of Independence went on to exceed the most expansive ambitions of its authors. The Declaration's drafters had thought that they were writing a document whose appearance would change the fate of the Jewish people and whose text would be judged by the standards of history. This was already quite ambitious. David Ben-Gurion had ensured that the document would create a state, that it would be the "Declaration of the Establishment of the State of Israel." At the ceremony at which the Declaration was read, Ben-Gurion referred to the Declaration for what it was: "the Declaration of Independence." A state would be established, and its fate would be determined in the realm of states.

Ben-Gurion, in writing a declaration of independence, had aimed for more than just a declaration of independence. He attempted to articulate the unique Jewish legacy and mission. And he had made the point, in his role as editor, that the document ought to articulate more clearly the nature of social and political rights, though to this he had devoted much less time and attention. Indeed, the text of the Declaration discussing these matters had mainly been left in a form designed to accord with UN Resolution 181. Some small distinctions had been drawn, some words removed, others added. But the work had been left unfinished.

There is no doubt that the Declaration of Independence weighs heavily in the national life of Israel. The footage of Ben-Gurion reading the Declaration at the Tel Aviv Museum is ubiquitous in Israeli letters and culture. It is enlisted by voices across the political spectrum.[1] The museum

---

[1] See the recent volume, Israel Dov Alboim, ed., *Megilat ha'Atzmaut em Talmud Yisrael* (*The Declaration of Independence with an Israeli Talmudic Commentary*) (Rishon Lezion: Yedioth Aharanoth, 2019).

on Rothschild Boulevard where it was read aloud in 1948 is now dedicated to the commemoration of the Declaration of Independence. Though not yet a national shrine like America's Independence Hall in Philadelphia, it is a regular stop for groups of Israeli schoolchildren and soldiers and a popular destination for tour-groups visiting from abroad.

Ben-Gurion's words declaimed on that Friday afternoon in 1948 are as a matter of course known by most Israelis; if they are not always recited by schoolchildren, they are certainly familiar to schoolchildren. Israel's principal basic civics textbooks all celebrate the Declaration and as a bedrock text of Israel's national life. For instance, *Being Citizens in Israel: In a Jewish and Democratic State*, published by the Ministry of Education, presents a long summary of Israel's Declaration in its first pages and extols the Declaration's importance for the political life of the state.[2]

The Declaration of Independence, as Mordechai Bentov had imagined, indeed became a part of the national culture of Israel. His vision was exact. It is a text that is literally, as he had speculated at the May 13, 1948, meeting of *Minhelet ha'Am*, read by schoolchildren. And it is even more than that. It has become an important text in Israel's legal edifice. This makes the Declaration of Independence more than merely a declaration of independence.

America is the land of life, liberty, and the pursuit of happiness. American citizens might all know the hallowed words of the American Declaration of Independence. But the American Declaration's situation in the corpus of American law is less definite than its central place in the national mind. There is legal interpretive power to America's Declaration. Its principles are used at times to interpret the nature and spirit of America's laws. But there is no decisive doctrine for its use. There are scholars who make the case that the Congress's authority to make laws and enact constitutional amendments emanates from the Declaration of Independence.[3] But no courts unambiguously articulate it.

The closest that there is to a standard doctrine for the use of the American Declaration in American law is *interpretive*. "It is always safe," said Justice Brewer in *Gulf, Colombia, and Santa Fe Railways* v. *Ellis*, "to read the letter of the Constitution in the spirit of the Declaration of

---

[2] *L'heyot ezrachim b'yisrael* (*Being Citizens in Israel*), textbook available for digital download through https://ecat.education.gov.il/

[3] See Harry V. Jaffa, "What Were the 'Original Intentions' of the Framers of the Constitution of the United States?," *Seattle University Law Review*, 351, 1987.

Independence."[4] The American Declaration, following the ideas of Abraham Lincoln, represents the cherished principles of the nation.[5]

Israel's Declaration has a similar status in Israel's legal cosmos. Israel's courts, and particularly the Supreme Court of Israel, have articulated a doctrine of the place of the Declaration of Independence of Israel which sees it not as law, but as a vital source nonetheless: to be counted amongst the sources of *principles* that animate the spirit of the laws and as the grounding for the legitimacy of Israel's government.

In what follows, we present a sketch of the legal legacy of Israel's Declaration of Independence. We take a historical approach to the analysis of the status that the Declaration holds in Israel's legal and arch-legal/constitutional framework, drawing on the work of Israel's leading legal minds and showing how they have understood the Declaration and the use they have made of it.[6] This chapter is not meant as a legal work, but rather a study of the use of Israel's Declaration – the history of the legal use of Israel's Declaration of Independence.

THE SUPREME COURT AND THE DECLARATION

The first principle regarding the place of the Declaration in Israel's legal framework is that the text of the Declaration is *not* itself law. It is rather an expression of the spirit of the law. The first notable appearances of the Declaration in Israel's legal system came shortly after the declaration of

---

[4] *Gulf, Colo. & Santa Fe Ry. v. Ellis*, 165 US 150, 160 (1897). Quoted in Charles Cosgrove, "The Declaration of Independence in Constitutional Interpretation: A Selective History and Analysis," *University of Richmond Law Review*, 32, 1, 1998, pp. 143–144.

[5] See Harry V. Jaffa, *A New Birth of Freedom: Abraham Lincoln and the Coming of the Civil War* (Lanham: Rowman & Littlefield, 2000).

[6] See especially Aharon Barak, "haNasi Agranat: Kol Ha'am – Kolo shel Ha'am" ("President *Agranat: Kol Ha'am* – The Voice of the People"), in *Writings*, Volume 1, 2000, Aharon Barak, "Megilat ha'atzmaut ve'haKnesset k'reshut mechunenet" ("The Declaration of Independence and the Knesset as a constituent assembly"), *Hukim*, 11, 2018, https://law.huji.ac.il/sites/default/files/law/files/42-ktavim_01_29.pdf; Elyakim Rubinstein, "The Declaration of Independence as a Basic Document of the State of Israel, *Israel Studies*, 3, 1, 1998, Benjamin Aksin, "Ha'khraza al ka'mat ha'medina" ("The Declaration of the Founding of the State"), in *Sefer ha'yovel l'Pinchas Rosen,* ed. Haim Cohen, 1962, Tzvi Berenson, *Sefer Berenson,* ed. Chaim Berenson and Aharon Barak (Navo, 1997), Yitzhak Zamir ed. Sefer Klinghoffer, Israel Law Faculty: Jerusalem, 1993. For a Marxist approach, see Uri Zilbershied, "The Legal and Political Development of the Israeli Declaration of Independence: A Victory of the Bourgeois Democratic Conception," *Democratic Culture*, 12, pp. 7–58.

the state. The 1948 case of *Ziv* v. *The Tel Aviv Administrator* (*Gubernik*) saw the court express the view that:

> The Declaration ... comes only to establish the fact of the founding of the state and its establishment for the purposes of its international legal recognition. It articulates the vision of the nation and its "I believe" [translated also as "basic credo"]. But it does not contain any constitutional law that adjudicates practical rules on particular issues, particular decrees, various laws, or annulments.[7]

This short paragraph begins the legacy of the Declaration in Israel's legal framework. It lays out three basic principles:

(1) The Declaration's purpose is the establishment of the State of Israel.
(2) It is not itself a source of practical law and cannot be used to argue that old law is annulled and replaced by the Declaration.
(3) It is the articulation of the "vision and basic credo" of the state.

The argument that the Declaration is not a source of law in-and-of-itself was advanced in another early and landmark Supreme Court case, *al-Karbutli* v. *Minister of Defense* (1948), in which the court emphasized that the Declaration's standing as a law pertained to its declaration of the state's independence – and that was it. The Declaration was not to be misinterpreted to be the constitution of the new state. It was rather a document which announced the creation of the state and called for a constitution to be written in the future. The Declaration "carries the weight of law with respect to establishing the fact of the legal establishment of the state: and yet the Court did not accept the claim that this document brings into being a constitution."[8]

The essence of *Ziv* v. *The Tel Aviv Administrator* was to establish a place for the Declaration in Israel's legal landscape without teasing out all of the implications of that place. The essence of the *al-Karbutli* case was to emphasize that the Declaration could not be seen as a constitution. It is worth noting some of the implications of the *Ziv* and *al-Karbutli* rulings. The two cases limited the legal use of the Declaration by explaining what it is not. It is not a law beyond its establishment of the state. It is not a constitution. But in

---

[7] *Ziv* v. *Tel Aviv Administrator* (*Gubernik*) (1948). The archive of Israeli Supreme Court rulings is available at www.nevo.co.il. In many cases we have translated the text ourselves. We have also relied on translations available through Yeshiva University's Cardozo Law School's excellent "Versa" project on the Israeli Supreme Court available at https://versa.cardozo.yu.edu/

[8] *al-Karbutli* v. *Minister of Defense* (1948).

defining the Declaration using these negatives, it also delineated the possibilities of what the Declaration could be: (1) "a vision and credo" and (2) a legal document situating broad authority in the state and its government. Both of these definitions would offer wide legal possibilities.

The articulation of what the Declaration could positively be – the account of the Declaration's legal presence, and not the spheres from which it was absent – gained an important formulation in the case of *Kol Ha'am* v. *Minister of the Interior* (1953) in which the newspaper *Kol Ha'am* protested government intervention in its business for publishing matter deleterious to the public interest. The Court there ruled that:

The set of laws according to which the political institutions of Israel are established and operate, testify that it is a state whose foundations are democratic. So too, the matters that are raised in the Declaration of Independence – and in particular the matter of the basing of the state "on the foundations of freedom" and the assurance of freedom of conscience – their meaning is that Israel is a country that promotes freedom. Although the Declaration "does not contain any constitutional law that adjudicates practical rules on particular issues, particular decrees, various laws, or annulments" (*Ziv*), it does, in the sense that it "articulates the vision of the nation and its credo" (*Ziv*), obligate us to pay attention to the matters raised in it, when we come to interpret and give meaning to the laws of the state . . . .[9]

Here the Court gave voice to the view that the basic principles of the state of Israel are democratic. It means by this that Israel's institutions are democratic, the body of law that it has passed is in its spirit democratic, and that "the matters that are raised in the Declaration of Independence" make clear that the State of Israel "promotes [or loves] freedom." The Court stresses that it is obligated on the basis of the judgment in *Ziv* to pay attention to the matters raised in the Declaration "to interpret and give meaning to the laws of the state."

This judgment is seen as one of the landmark cases in Israeli legal history because of its implications and broad influence: it has a vital place in the establishment of freedom of speech and of the press in Israel.[10] But it is perhaps just as or even more important for the introduction of a legal doctrine in which the principles of the Declaration are taken as the spirit of the laws. These principles are defined (1) as being democratic, and (2) used as an edifice on which to build a broader understanding of Israel as a democracy. The *Kol ha'Am* case gave judicial birth to Israel's democratic spirit.

---

[9] *Kol Ha'am* v. *Minister of the Interior* (1953).
[10] See Aharon Barak, "haNasi Agranat: Kol Ha'am – Kolo shel Ha'am," p. 581.

Aharon Barak, Justice on the Supreme Court from 1978 until 1995 and then its President until 2006, and the individual most credited with the codification of Israel's system of Basic Laws, argued that *Kol Ha'am* paved the way for the courts to avail themselves of the nation's *principles* in jurisprudence:

Judge Agranat posited the normative framework obligating the courts in the interpretation of the laws to the foundational principles of the regime . . . . He widened the circle beyond the Declaration of Independence ... . This broadened circle, premised upon and widened beyond the Declaration, expanded to include "the foundational principles upon which the rule of law is built" ... universal principles in all democratic states ... discernable from the unwritten constitution of ours.[11]

Courts, in this view, must be governed by a normative framework based on foundational principles. These foundational principles in the case of Israel, Barak notes, could be gleaned from many sources, but two could be particularly helpful: "The body of law and the Declaration of Independence. From these sources, Judge Agranat learned about the democratic character of the state. And from this democratic character, he derived the existence of a freedom of speech."[12] The key phrase codifying the logic underlying this legal reasoning in Agranat's decision in the *Kol Ha'am* case is, to Barak, the following: "The law of a nation can be learned through the *aspaklaria* [mirror or aspect] of its national way of life."

This legal doctrine has many sources, but one shines through: the thought of Hans Kelsen (1881–1973), the Jewish-Austrian jurist who expounded a theory of legal positivism or conventionalism. Kelsen looked to culture to establish national principles and moralities. The laws created by human beings, in Kelsen's formulation, could only be judged by the standards human beings established for themselves – the evolving standards of the community.[13] As Leo Strauss, quoting Kelsen, highlighted in a well-known footnote, Kelsen's doctrine placed the law outside the realm of absolute standards, searching instead for relative or changing community standards.[14] Using this framework, Justice Barak adopted the Declaration of Independence as a reflection of the standards and ideas

---

[11] See Aharon Barak, "haNasi Agranat: Kol Ha'am – Kolo Shel Ha'am," p. 583, quoting from *Lubin v. The Municipality of Tel Aviv* (1956).

[12] Ibid., p. 586.

[13] Clemens Jabloner, "Hans Kelsen," in *Weimar: A Jurisprudence of Crisis*, ed. Arthur J. Jacobson and Bernhard Schlink (Berkeley: University of California Press, 2000), pp. 67–109.

[14] Leo Strauss, *Natural Right and History* (Chicago: University of Chicago Press, 1999), footnote, p. 4.

of Israel, and cast it as a principal source for understanding and uncovering Israel's national or Kelsenian way of life.[15]

The invocation of the principles of the Declaration in legal argument continued in the years following *Kol Ha'am*. In *Streit v. the Chief Rabbi* (1963) the court applied the doctrine of *Kol Ha'am* explicitly. The court argued that it would "hold the Israeli legislator always to the standard that he or she did not intend to do damage, by way of legislation, to the foundational principles of equality, freedom, and justice that are evident in all enlightened and just states."[16]

The Court pointed out that legislators were unlikely to intend to legislate in a manner such that the laws themselves resulted in outcomes "that stand contrary to the Declaration of Independence of Israel and the UN's Universal Declaration of the Rights of Man." In making this argument, the Court maintained its prior precedent that the Declaration is not a constitutional document (and, needless to say, the UN Universal Declaration is not either). But, it asserted, the "Court will henceforth regard the Israeli legislator as one who does not intend, by a constitutional act, to violate the principles of equality, liberty, and justice" as expressed by these documents.[17]

This use had other precedents. In *Peretz v. Kfar Shmaryahu* (1962), the Court was asked to decide whether the managers of an event hall had acted wrongly by declining to allow non-Orthodox Jews to worship there in a non-Orthodox service. To be sure, the Court ruled mainly on the basis of other facts and principles. But in *obiter dictum* it added that the principle of religious freedom invoked in the Declaration ought to shine as a beacon too: "The Declaration of Independence guarantees freedom of religious observance to all citizens of the state, and even if it did not intend to guarantee the citizen the right to legal claim ... its principles should be raised as a beacon in the darkness of every administrative body in the country."[18]

During these years, the Court broadened its reading of the Declaration. It was not only the "freedom and equality" invoked in the Declaration that deserved attention. Statements about the character of the state in the Declaration had normative force too.

---

[15] See Aharon Barak, "Megilat ha'atzmaut ve'haKnesset k'reshut mechunenet," p. 15.
[16] *Streit v. The Chief Rabbi* (1963).
[17] Quoted in Elyakim Rubinstein, "The Declaration of Independence as a Basic Document of the State of Israel," *Israel Studies*, 3, 1, 1998, p. 200.
[18] Ibid., p. 201.

In *Yeredor v. Chairman of the Central Election Committee* (1965), the Court was asked to decide on whether it was appropriate that the Central Elections Committee of the state had forbidden a political party, The Socialists' List, from fielding candidates for the national election. The party had been banned on the grounds that its "initiators deny the territorial integrity of the State of Israel and its very existence." In this instance, the Court upheld the ban on the party. Supreme Court President Agranat wrote:

There can be no doubt – as clearly attested by what was declared upon the proclamation of the founding of the state – that not only is Israel a sovereign, independent, freedom-loving state that is characterized by a regime of rule by the people, but also that it was founded as "a Jewish state in the Land of Israel."[19]

In other words, the Declaration's characterization of Israel as a Jewish state in the Land of Israel encapsulated a normative reality just as did its invocation of principles of freedom and justice. In this case, Agranat in effect balanced between normative principles. As he noted, the Declaration had invited Arab residents to "participate in the upbuilding of the state" on the "basis of full and equal citizenship." This promise had to be kept; Arab citizens of Israel have a sacrosanct right to vote and participate in the political process.

But the Declaration also strongly expressed the principle that Israel was to be a viable Jewish state. As Agranat put it: "The question whether or not to act towards the destruction of the state and the end of its sovereignty cannot be on [the] agenda [of the Knesset] at all, inasmuch as the very presenting of this question contradicts the will of the people residing in Zion, its vision and its credo."[20] Here Agranat refers to the vision and credo finding expression in the Declaration of Independence.

This case presents a revealing portrait of the President of the Court weighing two sets of principles articulated in the Declaration to judge the legitimacy of parliamentary procedures. It demonstrates how, fewer than 20 years after the founding of the state, the Declaration had already been turned into a source for the articulation of the principles of the state on the most fundamental matters.

It is important to note that the Declaration has never been claimed as an exclusive source for norms guiding the interpretation and application

[19] *Yeredor v. Chairman of the Central Election Committee* (1964), See https://versa.cardozo .yu.edu/opinions/yeredor-v-chairman-central-elections-committee-sixth-knesset
[20] Ibid.

of Israeli law or underlying Israeli society. On the contrary – it's one of many. In 1950, the Court had referred to the importance of some unwritten principles that every "enlightened democratic system of government" had to uphold.[21] There are many other wide-ranging sources for normative relevance: other legal systems, legal theory and, as Justice Barak argued, the voice of "enlightened public opinion."[22] This offers a hybrid use for the Declaration: both as a source from which to glean the nation's consensus, and also as a source from which to appeal to principles that meet the standards of enlightened judgment.

While the Declaration grew in importance and stature over the years, there were some voices who expressed reservations. As early as 1964, one of the young state's preeminent scholars of political constitutionalism, Benjamin Aksin, expressed reservations about the evolving use of the Declaration in Israel's jurisprudence. While the Declaration certainly had normative relevance, Aksin denied that the so-called credo, the catalogue of social and political rights near the end of the Declaration, had preeminent normative weight.

In Aksin's view, legally speaking, the most important part of the Declaration was the assertion of "sovereignty" in the middle of the Declaration – the actual declaration of the state.[23] And Aksin, more politically-theoretically minded than many of the judges, did not tie himself into knots searching for a legal authority by which Israel declared independence. According to Aksin, the Declaration was made on *political* rather than legal grounds. Had the Jews lost the War of Independence, then the Knesset would not have held the authority it ultimately gained. And thus, in establishing its sovereignty, the provisional government of Israel established its authority to issue such a declaration.[24]

In Aksin's interpretation, the Declaration, with the exception of the operative language declaring the state, calling it Israel, declaring a government, and so on, was in the form of a *preamble* akin to the preamble to the American Declaration of Independence. This was as true of the latter part of the declaration as the former.

The essence of the preamble, per Aksin, was to offer the grounding and justification of Jewish sovereignty. Aksin seems to have been uniquely aware of the origins of Israel's Declaration in the American Declaration,

---

[21] See Shimon Shetreet, "Reflections on the Protection of the Rights of the Individual: Form and Substance," *Israel Law Review*, 12, 1, 1977, pp. 32–67.

[22] Cf. Gideon Sapir, *The Israeli Constitution* (Oxford: Oxford University Press, 2008).

[23] See Benjamin Aksin, "Ha'khraza al ka'mat ha'medina."   [24] Ibid.

both quoting from the American Declaration and mentioning Mordechai Beham by name.[25] He had a non-Kelsenian view of the grounding of the state.[26] He thus saw the role of the Declaration differently than many of his contemporaries and successors.

The professor Aksin's somewhat muted and polite dissent notwithstanding, the role of the Declaration in Israeli jurisprudence would only increase. As Justice Aharon Barak explained from the bench of the Supreme Court in *Schnitzer* v. *Military Censor* (1989):

The Declaration of Independence is not the only source from which one can learn about the basic values of the state. For example, the Supreme Court refers from time to time to the "basic principles of equality, freedom and justice, which are the legacy of all advanced and enlightened states" (Justice Cohen in H. C. 301/63 [15], at p. 612) and to "basic rights which are not recorded in texts, but emanate directly from the character of our state as democratic and freedom-loving" (Justice Landau in H. C. 243/62 [16], at p. 2414).[27]

And yet, among the sources for principles, Barak continued, the Declaration remains one of the most important: "The nature of the basic principles can be learned from different sources, one of the most important of which is the Declaration of Independence, 'which constitutes a legal charter that expresses the nation's values.'"[28]

Justice Landau's inclusion of the turn of phrase "democratic and freedom-loving [or 'promoting']" to describe the Israeli state solved a problem for the Supreme Court. The word democracy does not appear in the final text of Israel's Declaration. It notably appears in the draft of Tzvi Berenson – later a justice on the Supreme Court. To remedy this, from its very beginnings, the Supreme Court has expressed and repeatedly emphasized the notion of Israel as a democratic state – with democracy understood substantively rather than merely procedurally. *Kol Ha'am* was the landmark case in developing this line of reasoning. But there was still need for further articulation of Israel's essence as a substantive democracy.

This was clarified and given further assertive power when language proclaiming Israel's democratic essence was incorporated into the text of

---

[25] Ibid., p. 52.

[26] Aksin's more political-theoretical approach to the founding of states can be seen in his work *Torat ha'mishtarim* (*The Idea of Regimes*) (Jerusalem: Hebrew University Student Union Press, 1964).

[27] *Schnitzer* v. *Military Censor* (1989), https://versa.cardozo.yu.edu/opinions/schnitzer-v-chief-military-censor

[28] Ibid.

the Basic Laws passed in the 1990s. These explicitly called Israel a democratic state.[29]

The state's democratic character, and the role of judges as guardians of democracy, has remained a strong point of emphasis for the Court in recent times.[30] By combining an emphasis on democratic norms, and with recourse to the Declaration as a "legal charter that expresses the nation's values," the Supreme Court of Israel has built for itself a potent arsenal of normative language to interpret the practices of the state, the procedures of the Knesset and the governing bureaucracies, and, finally, the constitutional Basic Laws of the Knesset.

THE DECLARATION AND THE BASIC LAWS

The idea that the Declaration could be a vital source representing the national consensus on principles was fully established in the state's early years. From the late 1980s, the Supreme Court took a decisive step in giving the Declaration a firmer place as a major source conferring legitimacy on the Knesset as a body that can pass a constitution or constitutional laws (the Basic Laws), and thus, by the same token, making the Declaration a vital text for the constitutional system of Basic Laws.

This judicial evolution was decisively prepared in *Mizrahi* v. *Migdal Cooperative* (1995), another one of the most famous cases in Israeli legal history. After having served on the Supreme Court for 17 years as a Justice, Aharon Barak was now its President – the Israeli equivalent of Chief Justice. In the *Mizrahi* case, the Supreme Court, for the first time, articulated a doctrine by which a Knesset law could be unconstitutional by virtue of it having violated the idea of fundamental rights contained in the Basic Laws. In so doing, the Court established the status of the Basic Laws as supra-legislative and constitutional in nature.[31]

The specific question faced by the Court was whether the fundamental rights of creditors had been violated when the Knesset, in the wake of a

---

[29] See the texts of the Basic Laws Human Dignity and Liberty (1992), and Freedom of Occupation (1994), https://m.knesset.gov.il/Activity/Legislation/Documents/yesod3.pdf, https://m.knesset.gov.il/Activity/Legislation/Documents/yesod1.pdf

[30] See Barak's extensive argument on behalf of the role of judges as guardians of democracy in *Movement for Quality Government* v. *Knesset* (2006). Also see Aharon Barak, *The Judge in a Democracy* (Princeton, NJ: Princeton University Press, 2006).

[31] *Mizrahi* v. *Migdal Cooperative* (1995). https://versa.cardozo.yu.edu/opinions/united-mizrahi-bank-v-migdal-cooperative-village

severe economic crisis, had passed a law forgiving the debts of certain borrowers who had incurred large losses.

While the Court ruled on narrow grounds in favor of the borrowers, it took advantage of the case to lay down the following logical argument: (1) the Knesset possessed, and continued to possess, the power to pass Basic Laws; (2) the Basic Laws had Constitutional authority; and (3) Basic Laws could be used to strike down other legislation and thus limit the legislative freedom of the Knesset in the future.

The Court's argument was that the Knesset possessed the authority to legislate Basic Laws since the Knesset was founded as the Constituent Assembly of Israel. Before having been called the Knesset, the governing body of Israel had in fact been called a "Constituent Assembly" the purpose of which was to prepare a constitution for the state. This was in line with United Nations Resolution 181, which, it is to be recalled, had demanded the drafting of a constitution as a condition of recognizing the sovereignty of new states in Palestine.[32]

Justice Barak argued that the constituent power invested in the first Knesset was transferred to future Knessets. The constituent power is "continuous" until a full constitution is complete.[33] As a consequence, the Knesset of Israel continues to be in essence the Constituent Assembly of the state. As Barak explains it, the Knesset has a dual function. It passes the Basic Laws in its capacity as a constituent assembly and it passes normal laws in its capacity as a workaday legislature.[34]

From where is the ultimate authority of the Knesset as a "constituent assembly" derived? The scholar Aksin had given a political response to this question. The governing bodies of the *Yishuv* had succeeded in establishing themselves by political means – by a mix of force and persuasion in the midst of the War of Independence. The members of *Minhelet ha'Am* and *Moetzet ha'Am* had been legitimated both via election to predecessor bodies and by the proclamation of the Zionist Actions Committee. That legitimacy would be enhanced by the election of the "Constituent Assembly," soon to be the first Knesset.[35]

Justice Barak takes a different tack. We read in his decision in *Mizrahi* that the ultimate source of the Knesset's authority derives from the fact that it reflects the "national consciousness" as well as the legislative

---

[32] Aharon Barak, "Megilat ha'atzmaut ve'haKnesset k'reshut mechunenet," p. 17.
[33] Ibid.   [34] Ibid.   [35] Cf. Benjamin Aksin, "Ha'khraza al ka'mat ha'medina," p. 55.

history of Israel.[36] The Israeli consciousness has decided to conduct its political business through it. And one learns about the role of a "constituent assembly" in Israeli consciousness through the clear call to convene one in the Declaration.[37]

Justice Barak's argument about the Declaration and the Knesset in *Mizrahi* was not uniformly accepted. Justice Mishael Chesin disputed whether the constituent powers that the first Knesset had clearly possessed were transferrable to future Knessets. He argued: "When the Constituent Assembly – the first Knesset – completed its term without adopting a constitution, the Knesset's right to adopt a constitution in accordance with the Declaration of Independence ceased." Chesin also raised doubts about whether the Basic Laws actually possessed such clear and decisive constitutional status.

And yet, Barak's argument clearly won out. And the implications were vast. Justice Shlomo Levin expressed the guiding principle in his concurrence:

The Basic Laws constitute chapters of the Israeli constitution. The framers of Israel's Declaration of Independence intended that legislation be effected on two parallel levels: a constitution to be adopted by the constituent authority, which would express the fundamental human rights on the basis of the vision of Israel's prophets, and the regular, day-to-day legislation to be conducted by the legislature. The Declaration of Independence indicates that the source of the Knesset's authority to adopt a constitution is its constituent power. The fact that there have been delays in the process of adopting a constitution since the election of the Constituent Assembly does not change or influence the source of the legislature's authority in advancing constitutional legislation. Constituent power continues to exist until the task of adopting a constitution is completed.[38]

In *Mizrahi*, the Declaration is given not only relevance as a source of principles, as it had possessed virtually from the beginning of Israel's legal history; it also gained normative value as a justification for the Knesset's drafting of a constitution or the equivalent of a constitution – that is, the

---

[36] *Mizrahi v. Migdal Cooperative* (1995). https://versa.cardozo.yu.edu/opinions/united-mizrahi-bank-v-migdal-cooperative-village

[37] See Aharon Barak, *Megilat ha'atzmaut ve'haKnesset k'reshut mechunenet*. For a review of Barak's sources in legal theory for his idea of constituent power see his "Al tafkidi ke'shofet" ("My Work as a Judge"), *Law and Government*, 7, 2003. Also see Martin Loughlin, "The Concept of Constituent Power," *European Journal of Political Theory*, 13, 2, 2014, pp. 218–237. Of course, there may be an absolute normative basis for the use of the Knesset to legislate (a basis derived from its implicit reasonableness or justice); and there may be a political basis (a basis derived from the Knesset's power).

[38] Ibid.

Basic Laws. The Declaration, expressing the "national consciousness" of the people, per the court, had delegated constitutional drafting authorities to a Constituent Assembly which became the Knesset. The Declaration's principles, as Levin put it, could thus be crucial tools for enlivening the Basic Laws. Levin went still further, arguing that the Declaration pointed the country toward a constitution that would express "fundamental human rights on the basis of the vision of Israel's prophets."

Over the course of the 1980s and 1990s, the Declaration of Independence surely came to be seen as an important interpretive lighthouse, a mystical *"urim v'thumim"* that judges could use to divine the meaning of both ordinary laws and practice as well as the Basic Laws.[39] Though the role of the Court was decisive in this respect, one should note that support for this idea did not derive exclusively from the bench.[40]

Beginning especially in the 1990s, the idea was integrated into the very structure of the Basic Laws that the Knesset itself drafted and passed. Indeed, it is unclear whether the decision in *Mizrahi* could have occurred absent the fact that two then-recently-passed Basic Laws had themselves invoked the Declaration.

"Basic Law: Human Dignity and Liberty" (1992) and "Basic Law: Freedom of Occupation" (1994) both assert that the source for understanding the rights of man *"in Israel"* (emphasis added) is the Declaration of Independence: "The fundamental rights of man in Israel are based on the recognition of the dignity of man, the sanctity of human life and human freedom, and these rights will be respected in the spirit of the principles in the Declaration of the Establishment of the State of Israel."[41] The project of entrenching the normative status of the Declaration was joined by the Knesset, which passed the Basic Laws. Of course, leading jurists played a major role in crafting these Basic Laws.[42]

---

[39] *Klal Insurance Enterprises* v. *The Minister of the Treasury* (1994). On the uses of *Urim* and *Thumim* in judgment, cf. Ibn Ezra commentary on Exodus, 28. www.sefaria.org/Ibn_Ezra_on_Exodus.28.31?lang=bi

[40] A good example from the realm of politics: After conquering the Old City of Jerusalem in the Six Day War, Israel proclaimed that it would preserve access to the holy places of all religions in "faithful preservation of the principles laid down in Israel's Declaration of Independence." See Meron Benvenisti, *City of Stone*, trans. Maxine Nunn (Berkeley: University of California Press, 1996), p. 99.

[41] The full texts of the basic laws are available here: https://m.knesset.gov.il/Activity/Legislation/Documents/yesod3.pdf, https://m.knesset.gov.il/Activity/Legislation/Documents/yesod1.pdf

[42] On the process of the composition of the basic laws of this period, see Uriel Lind, *Hukei Ha'yesod shel medinat yisrael* (Yosef Sapir Research Center, 2011).

From *Mizrahi* onward, the Supreme Court could and did invoke the Declaration as a source of principles and a rooting for their invocation. Prominent, of course, were cases involving rights. In *Movement for Quality Government* v. *the Knesset* (2006), the Supreme Court considered the legality of the Tal Law, which had formalized the process of deferment of military service for religious students, a practice that had gone on mostly informally since the beginning of the state. An NGO petitioned the court to end the practice.

While the Court, on narrow and restricted grounds, declined to completely overturn the Tal Law at that time, it indicated that the exemption of religious students could in the future run afoul of the Basic Law: Human Dignity. As the Court put it:

[The] grant of a swift deferment – which over the years transforms into an exemption from military service – for thousands of persons eligible for military service based only on reasons of study in a yeshiva constitutes harm to the equality of everyone in the majority group who is subject to military service. The distinction among persons designated for military service based on a religious worldview is discrimination without any relevant difference.[43]

In his decision, Justice Barak clarified that his interpretation of the nature of equal dignity was rooted in the Declaration:

The Declaration of the Establishment of the State determines that the state of Israel "will ensure complete equality of social and political rights to all its inhabitants irrespective of religion, race or sex . . . ." These words certainly must influence the interpretation of rights and including [more capacious] aspects of equality beyond the protection [of individuals from humiliation].[44]

In 2012, with Justice Dorit Beinisch now President of the Supreme Court, the Court ruled by a majority of 6–3 to overturn the Tal Law, mainly on the grounds that it violated the principle of equality.[45] The drafting of Haredi students remains a radioactive political issue.

In *MK Gal-On* v. *The Attorney General* (2012), the Court ruled on the constitutionality of the Citizenship and Entry to Israel Act (2003), which held that residents of the West Bank or the Gaza Strip were not

---

[43] Quoted in Ruth Levush, "Israel Supreme Court Decision Invalidating the Law on Haredi Military Draft Postponement," Law Library of Congress Report, March, 2012. www.loc.gov/law/help/il-haredi-military-draft/israel-haredi-military-draft-postponement.pdf

[44] *The Movement for Quality Government* v. *Knesset* (2006) quoted in Aharon Barak, "Megilat ha'atzmaut ve'haKnesset k'reshut mechunenet," p. 28.

[45] Ruth Levush, "Israel Supreme Court Decision Invalidating the Law on Haredi Military Draft Postponement," March, 2012.

automatically eligible for Israeli citizenship if they married Israeli citizens. In a divided ruling, the Court upheld the law. In his dissent, Justice Edmond Levy went perhaps further than anyone had before in invoking the importance of the Declaration in Israeli law:

A distilled expression of the constitutive narrative of Israel is provided by the phrase "Jewish and democratic state," which constitutes the keystone of our constitutional law. The Declaration of Independence, from which I quoted at the beginning of my opinion, provides the outline for the character of the foundational infrastructure of the Israeli nation. The late Justice Haim Herman Cohn wrote of this declaration that it had been "raised to the level of the 'manifesto' of the state, in other words, a value unsurpassed by any other, values upon which the founding fathers promised to base the state."[46]

Justice Levy, in his dissent, argued that the Declaration is more than one source of principles for interpreting the spirit of Israel's laws. It is the central one. It is the "value unsurpassed by any other ... upon which the founding fathers promised to base the state." And, reasoned Levy, the Declaration's promise of equality, also expressed in the Basic Laws, rendered the Citizenship and Equality Act unconstitutional.[47]

It is not a surprise that cases involving equality and rights, and the Basic Laws which set those out, have seen an appeal to the principles of the Declaration. But the principles of the Declaration have also been invoked in cases related to procedural questions or questions related to other Basic Laws.

Of course, the boundaries between procedural and normative matters is not so clear. When in 2003, in a flashback to *Yeredor* discussed above, the Court was asked to determine whether the *Balad* Party political candidate Ahmed Tibi had justly been denied the ability to stand for election to the Knesset, the Court interpreted the matter on the basis of the Basic Law: Knesset (1958) and the ideas of rights in the Declaration. (In this case, unlike in *Yeredor*, the Court overturned the decision of the Central Elections Committee; Tibi was permitted to appear on the *Balad* electoral list.[48])

It is not the purpose of this chapter to catalogue every major Israeli Supreme Court case in which the principles of the Declaration have been invoked as a portion of the legal scaffolding that make up the reasoning of the Court. In addition to the cases we have cited, there have been significant cases involving the equality of men and women, freedom of

---

[46] See *Gal-On* v. *Attorney General* (2012), https://versa.cardozo.yu.edu/opinions/gal-v-attorney-general-summary

[47] Ibid.　　[48] *Central Elections Committee* v. *Ahmed Tibi* (2003).

language, religious freedom and freedom of worship, freedom of language, and even the constitutionality of political decisions like the withdrawal from Gaza.[49]

Rather, the aim is to illustrate the following: Whether it was the intent of the authors of the Declaration or not, the Declaration has indeed come to be seen as vital text drawn upon to discuss the ethics and principles of Israel.

As of this writing, there is one further turn in the ongoing evolution of the use of the Israeli Declaration in Israeli law. Until now, the principles of the Declaration have been used to establish the ethical grounding of Basic Laws and as a plank in the elevation of the Basic Laws to constitutional status. Now there is a move toward using the Declaration not merely to establish the standing of the Basic Laws and to interpret them, but also to judge whether the Basic Laws passed by the Knesset are themselves consistent with the nation's principles. Once one has accepted the principle that the Declaration is the source for the legitimacy of the Basic Laws, this is not a difficult leap. Why, given this premise, should the Basic Laws not conform to the Declaration's principles – or at least not stand in too great a tension with them?

In *The Academic Center for Law and Business* v. *Knesset* (2017), the Court offered a view on Basic Law: Freedom of Occupation. The Deputy President of the Supreme Court Justice Elyakim Rubenstein said:

Similarly, in my eyes, that in the field of principles there is in Israel a place for the 'eternity' of fundamental legal principles. For example, foundations like the Jewish basis – and the Democratic basis – of the state according to the Declaration of Independence and the Basic Laws regarding rights, or damage to the heart of human rights.[50]

The argument is that all laws must adhere to supra-constitutional principles, and amongst those, the principles of the Declaration and those of the Basic Laws concerning rights hold a special place.[51]

This raises the matter of contradictions between those principles and principles in new Basic Laws. While he has not explicitly endorsed using

---

[49] See, for instance, On the equality of men and women, *Shakdiel* v. *Minister of Religious Affairs* (1988), *Miller* v. *Minister of Defense* (1995); on freedom of language see, *Adalah* v. *Tel Aviv* (2002); on the constitutionality of the Gaza withdrawal see *Regional Council, Coast of Gaza* v. *Knesset* (2005).

[50] Quoted in Aharon Barak, "Megilat ha'atzmaut ve'haKnesset k'reshut mechunenet," p. 33.

[51] Ibid.

the Declaration's notion of equal rights as a means for the Court to challenge the recently passed Basic Law: The Jewish State (2018), Justice Barak has posed the possibility openly.[52] Were that to occur, it would represent a certain culmination of the role of the Declaration in Israeli judicial history as the tensions amongst its framing of key issues would be brought directly to the fore.

THE SUPREME COURT ON THE CHARACTER
OF THE DECLARATION

We have seen the evolution of the Supreme Court of Israel's use of the Declaration of Independence in interpreting the law of the land in Israel. We have yet to clearly lay out, however, what view of the Declaration the Court has largely followed. For the Court has evolved its own understanding of the structure of the Declaration and its decisive aspects. When President Smoira said in 1948 that the Declaration contained the "basic credo" of the state, he did not at the same time present a complete interpretation of the structure and meaning of the Declaration. He did not elaborate the credo. This took shape over time.

The Court's view of the Declaration has been ably summarized by Aharon Barak, who has done more than anyone to shape the Court's use and understanding of the Declaration. As Barak explains, the Declaration consists of three parts:

Part 1) "History and Ideology." The beginning section compromises the ideological pronouncements at the beginning of the Declaration (the land of Israel as the birthplace of the Jewish people through the recitation of the historical markers pointing toward the present moment).

Part 2) The "Operative" Section. The middle part of the Declaration. The assertion of the authority of the governing bodies as provisional governing bodies of the state, the responsibility of these bodies to conduct elections, and the responsibility of the government to draft a constitution.

---

[52] Ibid., pp. 31–34.

Part 3) The "I Believe [Basic Credo] and Vision" section. The articulation of social and political rights and the state's dedication to the idea of freedom, justice, and peace in the spirit of the prophets of Israel.[53]

In addition to this view of the structure of the Declaration and the nature of its contents, the Court has consistently stressed – and especially in recent times – the Declaration's role in setting out Israel's nature as a democratic state. Though the word 'democratic' does not appear in the Declaration, the principles [*ekronot*] are democratic, as Justice Barak said in 2019, echoing the *Kol Ha'am* case.[54]

This is not the entirety of the relevance of the Declaration, however. Justice Barak explains that judges in the past had attributed differing normative weight to various parts of the Declaration – and particularly emphasized the "credo" contained in the final third of the Declaration. According to Barak, though, the entire Declaration has normative weight. In particular, Barak stresses the second part of the Declaration as expressing the "national consciousness" of Israel that its representative body would also be a "constituent assembly" with the rightful authority to pass a constitution or constitutional laws – that is, the Basic Laws.

Barak's innovation, what looks like it may be his ultimate judicial revolution with respect to the Declaration, is the assertion that the "Basic Laws" that the Knesset can pass – on authority given to it by the Declaration – cannot contradict the ideas and principles expressed in either the "history and ideology" or moreover the "I believe/vision/credo" section of the Declaration. By this logic, the Supreme Court might very well have the authority to rule against a Basic Law if its content is too heavily in tension with higher principles articulated in what the court defines as the country's national consciousness. This would obviously be unlikely to apply to those Basic Laws passed in the 1990s which themselves allude to the principles of the Declaration of Independence.

But what of other Basic Laws? What if the recent Nation-State Law, which holds Israel to be the nation-state of the Jewish people, is interpreted by a Supreme Court Justice to be contrary to the spirit of equality

---

[53] Aharon Barak, "Megilat ha'atzmaut ve'haKnesset k'reshut mechunenet," p. 10. Cf. Benjamin Aksin, who accepted the tripartite division but refuses Barak's later separation of parts 1 and 3 into "history and ideology" (part 1) on one hand and "credo" (part 3) on the other. He saw both as intimately linked and equal in status as a preamble.

[54] Quoted in tweet by Amit Segal, December 21, 2019.

in the Declaration – however unlikely that might be given that the Declaration refers throughout to Israel as the Jewish state? These are momentous questions in Israeli public life – and their moment is likely to increase in the years ahead.

Disregarding the question of whether the Court could, or would, declare a Basic Law invalid, the fact remains that judges have had to deal with the reality that, under their interpretive framework for the Declaration, the text seems to contain different principles that may clash with one another. How, then, should different parts or principles of the Declaration be balanced?

In *Central Elections Committee* v. *Tibi* (2003) cited above, for instance, the Court had to consider two different fundamental principles. Had the candidate's equal rights been violated when the Elections Committee had revoked Tibi's right to stand for election? Or, on the other hand, was there was a violation of the "basic credo" of the state as "Jewish and Democratic"?

In such circumstances, the judge must judge. The judge must "balance" or weigh principles against one another. This is a notion that Justice Barak articulated from his earliest days on the court. In *Ressler* v. *The Ministry of Defense* (1988), Barak wrote:

In the absence of legislative guidance, the Court must turn to the fundamental values of the nation, to its "credo" (as the Declaration of Independence was called by President Smoira), or to its "national way of life" and to "the sources of national consciousness of the people in whose midst the judges reside" (M. Landau, "Rule and Discretion in the Administration of Justice"). In doing so, the court will consider the outlooks "accepted by the enlightened public" (Justice Landau). At times the judge will find that, for one reason or another, those sources do not afford sufficient guidance. In such situations it will be incumbent upon the judge to exercise his discretion *(see* H. L. A. Hart, *The Concept of Law).* This task is at times difficult . . . .

True, the exercise of judicial discretion in this situation is difficult, but despite the difficulty the judge must exercise it. The lack of sufficient guidance as to "the fundamental principles of the system" and the national "credo" is likely to influence the substance of the choice, but this does not make the choice impossible. In such a situation the judge must consider all values and interests, and he must give them the weight he thinks best reflects their meaning in his society.[55]

---

[55] *Ressler* v. *Minister of Defense* (1988), https://versa.cardozo.yu.edu/opinions/ressler-v-minister-defence

The judge must find "balance" (*izzun*) between the various contesting principles including those reflected in parts of the Declaration. The judge must consider the "values and interests" of the society, outlooks "accepted by the enlightened public," and the meaning of the principles as they are understood by the society at the time. This doctrine leaves judges to weigh principles in light of a reading of current conventions of enlightened opinion and an assessment of the values and interests of society. It leaves derivation of principles in the hands of judges.

A PROPER WEIGHTING FOR THE DECLARATION?

The long-unfolding efforts by the Justices of the Supreme Court of Israel to build a constitutional framework out of the Basic Laws with the Declaration as one of the normative sources in its background speaks to an effort to define core principles of political right and justice for the state. As we saw, the work of articulating the political and national principles of the state had been left unfinished in the Declaration and at the time of independence. And a written constitution, which was supposed to follow, did not follow.

It was thus necessarily left to others to fill in what Ben-Gurion had tried to articulate without full success. In the founding of Israel, we saw how the arch-political mind of David Ben-Gurion triumphed over the more legalistic minds around him. The story of the role of the Declaration in Israeli jurisprudence is a story of the role that legal systems inevitably play following moments of high politics. By means of the interpretation of the Declaration (though certainly not exclusively by these means), the Supreme Court has decisively shaped the understanding of laws in Israel especially regarding the rights of citizens. It has done so in response to a genuine void present at the founding of the state. The state requires a capacious normative understanding of itself.

From Smoira in 1948 onwards, the Court has held that the Declaration expresses the "basic credo" of the state – with the vision particularly contained in the promise of the state to instantiate the social and political rights of all citizens. The necessary implication is that the drafters of the Declaration saw themselves as seriously expressing a "credo" – a fundamental vision of the state.

There is no question that the Declaration represents a basic credo in precisely one domain – on the question of sovereignty. Ben-Gurion expressed the credo that the Jewish state was to be an independent sovereign state without ambiguity, and that it would rise or fall in the world of states. This was the "natural right" that Declaration of Independence declared. It was by virtue of that natural right that the state was founded.[56]

The Declaration also represented a partially mature credo with respect to its articulation of the state as a *Jewish* state. The justification of the state in the Declaration is Jewish history. It elevates Jewish history to universal history; it interprets Jewish history as advancing the universal ideas of the Jewish texts. The aim of advancing Jewish ideas and their universal meaning is seen as the aim of the Jewish people. The universal significance that the Declaration attributes to the Jewish legacy is the universal significance of the state. The aim for universals in the particular history of the Jewish people elevates the historical justification of the state. This is the *historical* right on which the state is founded: on the merit of Jewish principles. But this doctrine is not fully articulated in the Declaration. And neither are the principles themselves articulated. The Declaration's treatment is at best partial and subject to further questions.

The domain of rights, which the Court emphasizes above all others, has the most partial treatment in the Declaration. The list of social and political rights had its genesis in Rubashov's text written for the Zionist Actions Committee. That was channeled and further articulated by Tzvi Berenson. Shertok melded that language not so as to express the state's normative aims, but rather, to meet a political and diplomatic need. Shertok was likely focused on showing international authorities that the state-to-be was living up to its side of the bargain in the UN Resolution 181.

It is worth quoting in full the requirements of the United Nations for the new states to be created in Palestine in 1948 with respect to the question of rights. The new states, according to the United Nations had to:

Guarantee to all persons equal and non-discriminatory rights in civil, political, economic and religious matters and the enjoyment of human rights and fundamental freedoms, including freedom of religion, language, speech and publication, education, assembly and association.[57]

---

[56] It is notable that the lawyers drafting the text did not see it this way. See Yoram Shachar, "Yomano shel Uri Yadin" ("Uri Yadin's Diary"), *Iyunei Misphat*, 3, 1991, cf. Benjamin Aksin, "Ha'khraza al ka'mat ha'medina" ("The Declaration of the Founding of the State").

[57] The text of Resolution 181 at: https://unispal.un.org/DPA/DPR/unispal.nsf/o/7F0AF2BD897689B785256C330061D253, Also see, Yoram Shachar, "Israel as a Two-Parent State," *Zmanim*, 2007.

Resolution 181 had not restricted itself to this catalogue of social and political rights. It had included a whole section explaining how the new states had to safeguard rights in holy places: "Existing rights in respect of Holy Places and religious buildings or sites shall not be denied or impaired," according to chapter 1 of Resolution 181. The Resolution further proposed rules specifying economic union between the states. The full title of Resolution 181 is "Plan of Partition with Economic Union." And thus Israel's Declaration committed to "take steps to bring about the economic union of the whole of *Eretz-Israel*."

In short, much of the language and many of the specific recommendations that appear in Resolution 181 find their way into Israel's Declaration. The Declaration incorporated UN language into the Declaration for two reasons. First, because its authors probably agreed with much of it, and surely would not have found much with which to disagree. The debates around the ratification of the Declaration see more rights being added than Shertok had initially inserted. The idea that the Declaration should include a list of rights was only endorsed and augmented. *Minhelet ha'Am* liked the ideas and believed in them.

More significantly, however, Shertok, in inserting the language related to the criteria in Resolution 181, was trying to gain legitimacy and recognition for the state. And it was thought by many, especially by Shertok, that the language of the United Nations Resolution was the way to accomplish this aim.

Shertok reached for this language not out of any explicit and overriding agreement with the principles of the United Nations but for purely instrumental reasons – to persuade the powers of the world that the new state was deserving of international support. It seems unlikely that Shertok believed he was articulating the "basic credo" of the state when he included these words.

For his part, David Ben-Gurion believed that a sort of basic credo for the state was needed. He attempted to insert it through his introduction and his invocation of natural and historical rights that stand at the state's foundation. His credo addressed the universal significance of the Jewish experience. This went in two directions. There was the universal significance of the ideas of the Jews: the universal significance of the Book of Books. And there was the Jewish learning of the universal lessons of statecraft and politics: the Jews had learned and had to believe that they needed a state, for they had been taught the world's cruel lessons.

On the matter of political rights, however, Ben-Gurion generally relied on the previously inserted boilerplate language. He understood that rights are inherent and fundamental and changed the language of the Declaration to reflect this. But he did not exert other effort with respect to the locutions, forms, and ultimately the rationale for those rights.

This could well be because he ran out of time. There is more editing of the beginning of the document than its end. In the final meetings before independence, Ben-Gurion did not quarrel much with efforts to amend this part of the text, nor with the absolute last-minute addition of freedom of "language" as a right. This was suggested in the meeting of the full *Moetzet ha'Am*, and Ben-Gurion accepted it immediately, perhaps to avoid debate and move things along.[58] The inclusion of a "freedom of language," of course, brought the text's catalogue of rights further in line with the demands of the United Nations.

While the United Nations Resolution was a major source for the catalogue of rights in Israel's Declaration, the statements about the character of the state and its purposes do not stem exclusively from there. The Declaration's insistence on a state that would be governed in line with the "vision of the prophets of Israel" is of course not language from the United Nations. It comes from Rubashov's text. Berenson, having read that text, and likely believing Rubashov, who was higher up the *Mapai* chain of command than Berenson, might be involved in further drafting of the Declaration, included a variant of Rubashov's phrase in his work.[59]

This language had therefore been in Israel's Declaration from almost the beginning of the drafting process. It is quite a beautiful sentiment. It leaves much open, however. Berenson, following Rubashov before him, had combined democracy and the principles of the prophets of Israel in a unique formulation. Yet the formulation raises obvious questions: It is difficult to find agreement regarding the definition of principles of prophetic justice. And the text does not elaborate on the meaning of this formulation.

The Declaration also maintains ambiguity on fundamental questions of state and society. It does not express a view on the relationship between social and political rights or positive and negative rights, which often, in their very nature, clash with one another. It also has little to say about the democratic substance of the Jewish state. The Declaration, again following Resolution 181, asserts that there will be elections. Elections are procedural. And their presence certainly has some substantive implications for the political culture of a nation. It would have been impossible to imagine the *Yishuv* accepting a method of nominating leaders other

---

[58] Ze'ev Sharef, *Three Days*, p. 279.
[59] See Yoram Shachar, "Ha'teyotot ha'Mukdamot shel megilat ha'atzmaut," p. 549.

than through a democratic procedure, and the state of course today conducts its political nominations through the mechanisms of elections. But the conception of the state as a democratic one requires more building and more work than the Declaration provides. This has been augmented by the passage of Basic Laws and by the Court's building of an edifice of jurisprudence supporting it. And the work continues.

The Supreme Court has relied on the contention in the Declaration that Israel is a Jewish state. But this goes only so far. The Declaration does unambiguously assert Jewish sovereignty and independence. And this is made manifest by the "in-gathering of the exiles." Given the Declaration's clarity on this matter, it would be very hard indeed for a Court to invoke the Declaration if it ever tried to argue that the Law of Return is unconstitutional. But it would be excessive to argue that these arguments were fully baked at the time of the Declaration's publication. The Declaration's ambiguity on these questions leaves the matter open.

However much it has been judicially influential, the enterprise to spin out a coherent judicial philosophy from the Declaration of Independence is therefore subject to enduring *aporia*. Corresponding to this difficulty, the Declaration thus retains a central but highly ambiguous place in the state of Israel today.

In 2013, Israeli parliamentarian Ruth Calderon tabled a motion to legislate the Declaration of Independence of Israel as a Basic Law – that is, to complete the process of turning the Declaration into a document with official constitutional status.[60] The effort gained some support within her *Yesh Atid* party. But it ultimately came to naught. One could easily imagine similar efforts in the future.

In an interview, Calderon explained her rationale: the legislative and political confusion about the character of the state. "I think it is the one most important challenge in Israeli legislation today," Calderon said. "The question of what is the identity of the state, and what are the values; [the problem of] a constitution, or the lack of a constitution" – these were the dilemmas that Calderon aimed to solve.[61] The Declaration, in Calderon's view, provides a way to entrench the principle of equality in Israel while at the same time reinforcing the "Jewish and democratic" character of the state.

---

[60] See Ruth Calderon and Simon Rabinovitch, "On the Declaration of Independence as a Basic Law and the Meaning of a Jewish Nation State," in *Defining Israel*, ed. Simon Rabinovitch (New York: Hebrew Union College Press, 2018), p. 323.

[61] Ibid.

Nearly 75 years after the founding of Israel, it is natural and inevitable that political and legal minds have turned to the Declaration of the Establishment of the State of Israel for guidance on the fundamental questions of law and politics that lie at the foundation of the state. And the Declaration is indeed a rich source for reflecting on these questions. In terms of concrete guidance regarding doctrines of rights, however, Israel's Declaration poses as many questions as it answers.

Conclusion

Sovereignty, the Jewish State, and Principles of Political Right

The place of the Declaration of Independence in the subsequent national life of Israel points not only to the lasting importance of the text, but as well to inevitable uses that such a text will be put to. It is a founding text. Implicitly, its uses would be vast.

Israel's Declaration of Independence had three main goals. The most obvious one: the declaration of a state, a development that opened a new chapter in the history of the Jewish people. It also attempted to give definition and color to the term "Jewish state" – a more complicated endeavor than it might seem. And finally, Israel's Declaration of Independence manifested the first stirrings of an effort to define the principles of political right that would later animate the state.

These three aims can be distilled to three themes: sovereignty, a Jewish state, and principles of political right. The Declaration was written to address pivotal questions on all three fronts.

This book has explored how these questions were addressed by studying the drafts of Israel's Declaration of Independence. It has done so because these issues remain alive today. The definition of a Jewish state, the principles that should animate Israel's government and jurisprudence, and even the manner in which Israel should conceive of its sovereignty remain *the* issues of interest in Israel today.

Israel's Declaration of Independence settled the issue of sovereignty. There would be a state, and it would be declared without provisos. Ben-Gurion's argument won out in *Minhelet ha'Am*. And his political calculus was validated: independence was proclaimed and respected. The state of Israel was declared and recognized immediately by the United States. This concluding chapter will narrate this final episode in Israel's journey to independence.

The Declaration of Independence, however, was less clear when it came to its two other principal themes. The drafts of the Declaration show the founders of Israel working to define the meaning of the Jewish state and giving thought to the matter of principles of political right – but not arriving at a full articulation of either of them. As the Declaration was being composed, these issues were less settled and final.

Of course, there is copious thinking on these latter two subjects in the Declaration of Independence. The state declared is a "Jewish state." It is a Jewish state insofar as it is the state of the people who wrote "the Book of Books" and who "kept faith with [the land] throughout their Dispersion and never ceased to pray and hope for their return to [the land]." It is a state for Jews, who are invited to immigrate to Israel. It is a state that guarantees the rights of all who live there, whether Jewish or not Jewish, even adding the language of the principal minority, Arabic, as an official language. It offers a capacious and forward-looking way of thinking about simultaneously being a Jewish state and a state that upholds the dignity of all of its citizens.

It is a state for the entire Jewish people, around the globe, who are called on to support it. It is a Jewish state founded in a Hebrew city and called Israel. It is Jewish, Hebrew, and Israeli. The Jewish state's material is outlined: it is composed of Jewish people who share citizenship with non-Jewish people, in a land of Israel with no fixed territory, living in a new Hebrew modernity with Hebrew cities. It bridges the Jewish past, present, and future.

The proximate cause that has brought the Jewish state into being is outlined in the text: the persecution of the Jewish people, their need for a homeland, and their rallying and efforts to build a thriving and robust community to alleviate these burdens. And the reason why a state is the vessel through which these matters might be addressed was clearly expressed by David Ben-Gurion: the Jews would be masters of their own fate in their own sovereign state.

There are efforts to clarify the point at which the state aims – the essence of being a Jewish state. The people who "wrote the book of books" have a "historical right" that is really an ethical imperative to continue their mission. Their particular story must have a universal significance. The text sees that a Hebrew-speaking nationalism is not enough to explain the Jewish state and cannot do it justice. Hebrew-speaking nationalism cannot explain 1,800 years of Jewish exile without a Hebrew language. David Ben-Gurion looked for an explanation for this. But finding the right formulation proved too daunting a task for the Declaration even as its final text aimed to articulate one.

This speaks to the legacy of the Declaration of Independence both as an unambiguous declaration of unambiguous independence and also as a more ambiguous guide to the direction that the state would take.

There is no question that the drafters of the Declaration thought about the ideas and principles that were to give life to the state and which would characterize life in the state. All drafts of the Declaration featured language about the state's political essence, and many, including the final text, tied its political essence to its Jewish essence.

The formulation that was articulated in the draft produced by the Legal Department of the *Yishuv*, led by Tzvi Berenson, said of what it had already called "the Jewish state" that "the state will be a democratic state, open to Jewish immigration, a state of freedom, justice, and peace in the spirit of the vision of the prophets of Israel and the father of political Zionism, Theodor Herzl, loyal to the principles of the charter of the United Nations."

The text tried to imagine a hybrid of political principles: democracy, the prophets of Israel, peace, freedom, and justice, Jewish immigration, Theodor Herzl, and the United Nations. This combination of ideas is extremely complex and contains many implicit contradictions to work through.

This text, understandably, would be radically modified. Moshe Shertok would remove the phrase "the state will be democratic." The text citing the prophets of Israel as the source of the spirit of the state's laws would ultimately read: "The State of Israel will be based on freedom, justice and peace as envisaged by the prophets of Israel." There would be additions to the text. It would continue on to list other civil and political rights that the state would make manifest – largely in line with the demands of UN Resolution 181 that the Jewish and Arab states created in Palestine should manifest certain characteristics.

This points to the ambiguity of the text's efforts to formulate ideas of political right. There were many ideas. They had not been distilled. Some were employed in order to meet external criteria that would almost immediately prove irrelevant. Some were cherished but perhaps not fully deliberated convictions. Some were simply true. The Supreme Court would come to see this aspect of the text as an articulation of a "vision and basic credo," literally, the "I believe," of the nation. But this vision and credo had not been fully articulated when the text was finalized, and the ideas continue to require rethinking and completion.

The text of the Declaration, read in light of its drafts, sheds light on the three core principles of the state: sovereignty, the idea of the Jewish state, and principles of political right. But the drafts also shed light on alternative ways that these principles can and must be further considered.

SOVEREIGNTY

The Declaration's central achievement is its upholding of the principle that right and necessity compel the Jews to establish a sovereign state in the land of Israel. Summed up as a "natural right" that the Jews must take up to be "masters of our fate ... in our own sovereign state" by Ben-Gurion, this argument is made in the Declaration with absolute clarity.

Readers of the final text of the Declaration today, used as they are to living in a world where the independence of the Jewish state is an established fact, can miss its significance and its break with all that came before it. But independence required great courage. It was a departure from alternative routes. Independence looked to many like it would come about on the basis of rules, laws, and order: on the basis of UN Resolution 181. Ben-Gurion took risks and disregarded the rules. It seemed to many at the time as a choice to take the hard road.

Acclaimed Israeli novelist Shai Agnon put the matter succinctly:

"Of course I wanted a Hebrew State, but if I had been asked at the moment of the proclamation of the state whether to declare independence or not – I would have demurred. And it's clear to me that no one else amongst us would have finished the job. Ben-Gurion, who I had previously erroneously underestimated, wasn't intimidated – he did it. The masses of Israel wanted a Hebrew state, but the men of action amongst us – not every man of action brings the action to completion..."[1]

Of course, Ben-Gurion's hard road was to prove to be the right one. On May 14, 1948, short hours after Israel's Declaration of Independence was read out in Tel Aviv, the United States recognized Israel. President Truman's official statement did away with Resolution 181 in two sentences: "This Government has been informed that a Jewish state has been proclaimed in Palestine and recognition has been requested by the Provisional Government thereof. The United States recognizes the Provisional Government of the new State of Israel."[2] The decision validated Ben-Gurion's insights and decisions – mostly.

In the days leading up to May 14, President Truman had already begun to consider recognizing the inevitable Jewish declaration of independence. Truman convened a May 12 meeting with Secretary of State George Marshall, Undersecretary Robert Lovett, Presidential Special Advisors

---

[1] Quoted in Mordechai Naor, *Yom ha'shishi hagadol* (*The Great Friday*), p. 196.
[2] Press Release Announcing US De Facto Recognition of the State of Israel, May 14, 1948 available at www.archives.gov/milestone-documents/press-release-announcing-us-recognition-of-israel

Clark Clifford and David Niles, and various other State Department and White House staffers. The ostensible purpose was the president's "serious concern as to what might happen in Palestine after May 15." State Department position papers had been prepared on the subject suggesting various diplomatic maneuvers to resuscitate UN Trusteeship of Palestine.[3]

The President was not especially interested in these proposals. He would initial and thus authorize them, but simultaneously work against them. Truman's ulterior motive in calling the meeting seems to have been for Clifford to raise the possibility of recognizing a Jewish state imminently.

The May 12 meeting began with Marshall and Lovett speaking for some time about how ill-advised it would be for the Jews to declare independence. Suddenly, whether by chance or by the wiles of Clifford, a phone call was made to the President's office relating a United Press Service report. It claimed, quoting Marshall's memo recalling the events, that:

Following two interviews with me by Mr. Shertok the latter had flown to Tel Aviv bearing a personal message from me to Mr. Ben Gurion, who was styled in the press despatch as the forth-coming President of the Jewish State. The despatch likewise was reported as saying that Shertok had informed me of the intention of the Jewish Agency to establish a sovereign state on May 16.[4]

Of course, Marshall continued, nothing of the sort had happened. "In actual fact, no message had been sent to Mr. Ben Gurion. I did not even know that such a person existed." Marshall seems to have thought that David Ben-Gurion was named first-name Ben, second-name Gurion. "Furthermore," Marshall added, "Shertok had not told me of any intention to establish a Jewish State on May 16."[5]

Following the dramatic reception of the phoned-in press report, Clifford presented a compelling and straight-forward argument against Lovett and Marshall. "The actual partition of Palestine had taken place 'without the use of outside force.'" Marshall and Lovett's argument that war in Palestine and US recognition of a Jewish state could draw the United States into a Middle Eastern quagmire had already been invalidated by events on the ground.[6]

Moreover, Clifford added, given that partition was happening on its own through war, a Jewish state inevitably would be declared immediately upon the departure of the British. And therefore, Clifford suggested (again quoting Marshall's memo):

[3] Memorandum of Conversation by the Secretary of State (Marshall), May 12, 1948, https://history.state.gov/historicaldocuments/frus1948v05p2/d252
[4] Ibid.   [5] Ibid.   [6] Ibid.

The President, at his press conference on the following day, May 13, should make a statement of his intention to recognize the Jewish State, once the provision for democratic government outlined in the resolution of November 29, had been complied with, which he assumed would be the case. The proposed statement would conclude: "I have asked the Secretary of State to have the Representatives of the United States in the United Nations, take up this subject in the United Nations with a view toward obtaining early recognition of a Jewish State by the other members of the United Nations."[7]

Clifford's remarks indicate two things: first, that the President was not at all blindsided by discussion of recognizing a Jewish state and doing so preemptively. Indeed, Clifford, as Truman's Special Advisor, was more often than not making the arguments to others that Truman, for one reason or another, did not want to give voice to himself. It's reasonable to view Clifford as a stalking horse for Truman. He likely was acting as one.

Second, and most interesting of all, the White House understood that Resolution 181 was no longer operative but still wanted to pay it lip service. If, as Clifford explained, the Jews and Arabs were at war and "actual partition had taken place," it was impossible to imagine that the peaceful partition scheme that Resolution 181 called for would come into effect. This was an implicit acknowledgement that UN Resolution 181 was already dead, and Clifford clearly expressed his knowledge that it was on its way to being buried.

On the other hand, here was Clifford saying the recognition of a future state ought to be contingent on "the provision for democratic government outlined in the resolution of November 29 ... [having] been complied with, which he assumed would be the case." That is to say, recognition would be granted to a new state in contravention of Resolution 181 so long as the political optics of recognition did not stray too far from Resolution 181.

Behind the scenes, the State Department team that was arguing against Clifford's case for preemptive recognition of a Jewish state already understood that Resolution 181 would be inoperative at midnight on May 15. Hardheaded legal thinkers that they were, Lovett and company may have been arguing for upholding the UN process, but, for that very reason, they had to acknowledge that UN Resolution 181 was a dead letter. A May 11 State Department legal opinion had concluded that "[t]he Arab and Jewish communities will be legally entitled on May 15, 1948 to proclaim states and organize governments." The logic was straightforward: there would be no other political authority after the British Mandate over Palestine came to an end because no UN Trusteeship had been established.[8]

---

[7] Ibid.   [8] Ibid.

To recognize, or not to recognize? That would be a political question: "The United States will be free to recognize the existence of any new states . . . . Whether it should do so is a matter of executive discretion which may be decided upon the basis of the political interests of the United States."[9]

Clifford had not seen the State Department legal memo at the time of the May 12 meeting. Lovett offered to send it to Clifford. Lovett may have hoped that its legal logic would deter the President from recognizing Jewish independence preemptively, why rush if there would be an avenue to Jewish independence in some short days? And Lovett must have thought that there was some outside chance, minimal as it was, that Ambassador Austin and the State Department team could achieve Trusteeship on the floor of the UN in the meantime.

Upon reading the memo, the lawyer Clifford would have certainly come to the same conclusion as the State Department crew: there was no conceivable legal reason to pay any attention to Resolution 181. It would be possible for the Jews to declare independence the moment that the British Mandate ended. Perhaps it would still be preferable to lock-in recognition of a Jewish state in advance of May 15. But the legal memo showed that there would be nothing to stop the President from recognizing Jewish independence when the clock struck midnight on the British Mandate.

There would, at that juncture, however, still be a PR reason to pay lip service to UN Resolution 181. It was the politically astute thing to do. The UN framework had the buy-in of all of the relevant political actors, particularly Marshall and team. Clifford met Lovett on May 14 and talked through the relevant issues after lunch – likely after 1 pm in Washington and thus three hours after the Declaration of Independence had been read in Tel Aviv.[10]

Clifford explained that President Truman had been impressed by two arguments following the May 12 meeting. The first: preemptive recognition of a Jewish state would have brought few benefits. "By stating in advance of any request from the Jewish Agency that he would recognize the state, it would place this country in the position of being a sponsor and increase responsibility."

More than that, Clifford continued, "The boundaries were unknown and the President would be putting this country in the position of buying a pig in a poke without knowing who the Government was or

---

[9] Memorandum by the Legal Advisor (Gross) to the Under Secretary of State (Lovett), May 11, 1948, https://history.state.gov/historicaldocuments/frus1948v05p2/d247

[10] Memorandum of Conversations by the Under Secretary of State (Lovett), May 17, 1948, https://history.state.gov/historicaldocuments/frus1948v05p2/d283

anything about it." Finally, there was a UN special session sitting and deliberating the Palestine issue. There was no reason to pre-empt it.[11]

There was, however, a second and even more impressive argument that had struck the President. Clifford explained that:

At six o'clock Friday night there would be no government or authority of any kind in Palestine. Title would be lying about for anybody to seize and a number of people had advised the President that this should not be permitted. The President had decided to do something about recognizing the new state if it was set up but that he would agree to wait until the request had been made and until there was some definition of boundaries.

The legal memo that Austin had sent to Clifford left its mark. Lovett explained in his own memo recollecting the lunch that Clifford had internalized "the legal paper that I had provided him with."[12]

And Clifford had acted on it. Clifford went on to tell Lovett that a request to recognize an independent Jewish state was forthcoming: "The White House had been informed that an appeal would be made for immediate recognition by the new state, which had been proclaimed that morning." The new state "proposed to live within the conditions of the November 29 General Assembly resolution and to restrict its claim to the borders therein defined."[13]

Clifford knew all of this because he had set the stage for the request for recognition. On May 13, Clifford had telephoned Eliahu Epstein (later Eilat), then the Jewish Agency Representative in Washington DC, who would soon see his title change to Representative of the Provisional Government of Israel and then Minister of the Government of Israel – all in four short days. Clifford had a message for Epstein. He needed to be prepared to submit a letter to the President announcing Jewish independence so that the President could recognize the new state immediately at midnight on May 15 – 6 pm on May 14 in the United States. That was the good news.

The message came with a political warning: "It was particularly important that the new state claim nothing beyond the boundaries out-lined in the UN resolution of November 29, 1947, because those bound-aries were the only ones which had been agreed to by everyone, including the Arabs, in any international forum."[14] The proposal had to be as easy as possible for Clifford to get past the State Department and the President's other opponents. The PR spin had to be that the Jewish state

---

[11] Ibid.   [12] Ibid.   [13] Ibid.
[14] Martin Kramer, "The May 1948 Vote That Made the State of Israel," *Mosaic*, April 2, 2018.

was acting with eminent reasonableness and there was no conceivable rationale for delaying recognition of Jewish independence.

Epstein did what Clifford asked. The letter he sent to Truman reads as follows.

My Dear Mr. President: I have the honor to notify you that the state of Israel has been proclaimed as an independent republic within frontiers approved by the General Assembly of the United Nations in its Resolution of November 29, 1947, and that a provisional government has been charged to assume the rights and duties of government for preserving law and order within the boundaries of Israel, for defending the state against external aggression, and for discharging the obligations of Israel to the other nations of the world in accordance with international law. The Act of Independence will become effective at one minute after six o'clock on the evening of 14 May 1948, Washington time.

With full knowledge of the deep bond of sympathy which has existed and has been strengthened over the past thirty years between the Government of the United States and the Jewish people of Palestine, I have been authorized by the provisional government of the new state to tender this message and to express the hope that your government will recognize and will welcome Israel into the community of nations.[15]

This letter served as the basis for Truman's recognition of Israel just after 6 pm on May 14 in the United States and a bit after midnight in Israel.

Much has been made since Epstein's letter came to light of a seeming contradiction between it and the actual Declaration of Independence. Epstein wrote that the state was declared "within frontiers approved by the General Assembly of the United Nations in its Resolution of November 29, 1947." The Declaration of Independence of Israel says nothing about borders. The basic argument is that Epstein engaged in chicanery.

The simplest response to this is that it is extremely unlikely that Epstein even knew that the Declaration of Independence did not mention the borders of the state. The debate on the issue occurred late at night on May 12 in Israel. Shertok's draft was only available on May 13. This was in the pre-email age. It is unlikely that Epstein, on May 13, when he likely drafted the letter, would have had the faintest idea regarding what Shertok's text said. It is impressive enough that he knew that the state was called Israel.

But there is a deeper point to be made. The criticism of Epstein – the view that he acted duplicitously – is based on a simple misreading of Epstein's words, the meaning of the Declaration of Independence of

---

[15] The Agent of the Provisional Government of Israel (Epstein) to President Truman, May 14, 1948, https://history.state.gov/historicaldocuments/frus1948v05p2/d266

Israel, and finally the political context of Clifford's request – and by extension Truman's. Truman and Clifford both knew that Resolution 181 was dead at this point. There was a war raging in Palestine and it was about to get worse. Borders change amidst wars. Everyone knew that. Truman recognized the Jewish state despite that fact. As Clifford explained to Lovett, Truman had a simple reason not only to recognize the state, but to do so forthwith: not only justice, but simple necessity, demanded that a state be declared not least to avoid rival claims to sovereignty over Palestine.

Epstein's letter made this point. It said that the state was "proclaimed" within the frontiers of Resolution 181 as indeed it was out of necessity. Those were the frontiers of the state at the moment of independence. The state, as Ben-Gurion had said during the debates in *Minhelet ha'Am*, would honor them if other parties did too. The sad reality was that those frontiers immediately began to change amidst war, compelling the new state into action to defend itself. As Epstein also said, the new government would be responsible "for defending the state against external aggression."

The Declaration of Independence as proclaimed in Tel Aviv that morning DC time had neither affirmed that Israel would live by Resolution 181 nor its opposite. It had simply declared a state. Of course, it did not reject Resolution 181. The Declaration of Independence in fact said that "[t]he State of Israel is prepared to cooperate with the agencies and representatives of the United Nations in implementing the resolution of the General Assembly of the 29th November, 1947." The state was not prejudiced against Resolution 181. But if Resolution 181 was not to be implemented, as it had not been and was not to be, what more could the new state do?

In effect, Ben-Gurion's declaration and Epstein's letter were the perfect combination. If the Truman administration required PR, Epstein provided it. And if the substance of the matter was that the Jewish state's fate would be determined by the facts on the ground, as Clifford also knew, then Epstein's letter had to be written on behalf of a Declaration of Independence akin to Ben-Gurion's.

The demands of the American political process were for a letter like Epstein's. But the demands of reality in Tel Aviv were for a Declaration like Ben-Gurion's. The navigation of America's complex in-group ideological politics would be a necessary element in the process of independence. But the decisive element for the *Yishuv* would be the political acumen of its leadership and the military resources and stamina of its people. Ben-Gurion's Declaration of Independence charted the wisest course.

When the subject of the Declaration would come up in later years, Ben-Gurion would emphasize that sovereignty was the fundamental contentious issue at the moment of the founding. In a 1961 interview, he stated pointedly: "The central debate was whether to say in the Declaration that the state was to be founded within the parameters of the General Assembly of the United Nations or not. I was very much against [declaring a state within those parameters]."[16]

Ben-Gurion, in a practical manner born of the consequences that his choices would inevitably put in train, understood completely what an independent state would require. He was more than willing to run the associated risks and navigate the related complexities. This was because he also understood what having an independent state was for.

To be independent required taking the reins of fortune as far as possible and charting one's own course. It meant acknowledging one's existence in the world of states from which there seems to be no escape but which at least allows one the chance, by no means guaranteed, of survival and of flourishing.

This perspective accepts that success cannot be guaranteed. Political decay and decline are part of political life. But these principles and this same logic explain the need for an independent state. As Ben-Gurion wrote in his diary on May 14, "our fate is in the hands of the armed forces." Sovereignty proclaimed was insufficient without sovereignty defended. Yes, sovereignty brought with it a flag, a recognized body to govern domestically and represent the Jewish people internationally, and a military force to protect that sovereignty. The thinkers and writers who had come before Ben-Gurion in the story of Zionism had understood this in theory.

But none had to choose to pull the trigger and unleash the forces that come with sovereignty. To take the risks and invite both the potential and the danger, the greatness and the risk: this burden rested with Ben-Gurion, and he bore it. He knew that his people needed it. And so they went for it.

As things would turn out, both Israel and the United States would ignore borders drawn up before the war that had been launched against the Jews. Marshall, Lovett, Austin, and others continued to campaign

---

[16] David Ben-Gurion Interview, Eliezer Whartman, "Interviews with the Signers of Israel's Declaration of Independence," p. 5.

against Israel, attempting to forestall "de jure" recognition of the government (the initial recognition was "de facto"). But even in this they failed. De jure recognition was conferred immediately following Israel's first elections on January 25, 1949 – as Clifford had said that it would be in Truman's office on May 12, 1948. This occurred after Israel's borders had changed over the course of seven months of war. The borders were not an issue either for Truman or the American people.

Ben-Gurion's Declaration proclaimed that there was a "natural right of the Jewish people to be masters of their own fate, like all other nations, in their own sovereign State." With that proclamation, and of course the victory in the War of Independence that ensued, sovereignty was achieved. There was a Jewish state, free to succeed, free to fail, but free as far as states in the world can be.

A JEWISH STATE

Nearly all of the men and women who were involved in the founding of Israel thought that sovereignty, though necessary, was not sufficient in itself. The state to be created, as the Declaration announced, was to be a Jewish state. In the debate over the final text of the Declaration, no one, neither the Communist Party member Meir Vilner nor the fervent left-wing atheist Aharon Zisling, objected to this phrase. And all of the drafts of Israel's Declaration described the state using the word "Jewish" – whether referring to the state of the Jewish people or the Jewish state.

Yet there was not consensus or even much discussion regarding the meaning of this phrase. How should the institutions of the state and its laws relate to the intellectual, moral, and religious world of Judaism? The debate over whether and how to invoke the name of God in the Declaration which took place in *Minhelet ha'Am* indicates that Jewish issues remained of tremendous importance to the *Yishuv*'s leaders. And yet, they barely debated or even considered what they meant in their establishing of a Jewish state.

Of course, all of the drafts of Israel's Declaration contained Jewish allusions and language. Zalman Rubashov wrote that "the Jewish State which the nation of Israel will establish in the land of its inheritance will be a state of justice and freedom." Herschel Lauterpacht wrote of a "Jewish Republic" guided by the vision of "the Jewish prophets." Tzvi Berenson described an "unbroken chain" of connection to the land of Israel on which the "Jewish state" would be founded. Mordechai Beham and Harry Davidowitz, in their inimitable way, simply quoted the King

James version of Deuteronomy: "Whereas this holy land has been promised by the Lord God to our [ancient Jewish people] fathers, Abraham,
Isaac, and Jacob, and to their seed after them."

Perhaps the most nuanced effort on this front was Moshe Shertok's.
Shertok's tone and language was religious: "From every generation to
generation" the Jews longed to return to their land. But even as his
rhetoric evoked Jewish tradition, Shertok's draft offered limited guidance
on the meaning of calling the state a Jewish state.

Shertok's draft did notably point out the ambiguity involved in thinking of Israel as a Jewish state. The text says that it was signed in the
"Hebrew city" of Tel Aviv. It is a text pronouncing the independence of a
Jewish state but the state is not named Judah. It is called Israel. This
ambiguity might compel one reader to conclude that the founders of Israel
wanted to distinguish their Hebrew future from a Jewish past. It could
compel another to think that they sought to return to their Hebraic
origins in the Bible – Moses was identified as an *Ivri* in contrast to the
Egyptians.[17] These reflections raise the open definition of the term
"Jewish state."

It fell to David Ben-Gurion to try to address the complex question:
What is a Jewish state? Like Mordechai Beham, Ben-Gurion began at the
beginning with an invocation of the Bible. But any honest account must
conclude that Ben-Gurion did not adequately express how Judaism should
inform the politics or the life of the Jewish state in the Declaration. At
most, his text succeeded in avoiding the excess of theocracy on one hand
and the similar excess of total secularism and materialism on the other.
This ambiguity, the unresolved character of the meaning of a Jewish state,
is very much alive. It is perhaps the central tension of modern Israel.

A RADIO BROADCAST

In contrast to Ben-Gurion and the other drafters of Israel's Declaration of
Independence, there were Zionist leaders who were more comfortable
and indeed adamant about expressions of Judaism in the politics of the
state. One obvious example is Menachem Begin, in 1948 the leader of the
Irgun paramilitary group.

Entering the Knesset in 1949, he soon became leader of the opposition,
leading the *Herut* party that later morphed into *Likud*. He held this

---

[17] See Yoram Shachar, "Israel as a Two-Parent State."

position until becoming prime minister in 1977. That was far off in 1948. With the establishment of Israel on May 14, Begin came out of hiding.

The British authorities had sought him since World War II for his role in leading what he would call "The Revolt" against British government in Palestine. On the evening of May 15, after the end of Sabbath, Begin went to the secret radio station of the *Irgun* in Tel Aviv to broadcast a message to his followers on the occasion of independence.

Begin's principal practical aim was to inform his supporters as well as his opponents in the mainstream Zionist movement that the Revisionist movement he led would accept the authority of the newly-established government:

> The *Irgun Zvai Leumi* is leaving the underground ... now we have a Hebrew rule in part of our homeland. And as in this part there will be Hebrew law – and that is the only rightful law in this country – there is no need for a Hebrew underground. In the state of Israel, we shall be soldiers and builders. And we shall respect its government, for it is our government.[18]

With this statement, Begin announced that his Jewish underground would come in from the cold.

Yet Begin in this address, which he apparently worked on for some weeks, and which evokes the Declaration of Independence read a bit more than 24 hours earlier, attempts to do more than this. He presents his own reflections on the founding of the state of Israel.

Begin's radio address cannot be seen as a draft of Israel's Declaration. It was not subject to approval, edits, or compromise with others, as political declarations inevitably are. What makes it notable is that Begin himself addresses, in his own way, what we have called the three central themes of Israel's Declaration: the question of sovereignty, the role Judaism in the state, and the rights of citizens. Begin's treatment of these issues is of course different from Ben-Gurion's, but also shares some surprising similarities. The similarities and differences are both enlightening.

On the question of sovereignty, Begin's speech shares much in common with Israel's Declaration of Independence and reveals a sort of common front between the two leaders of Israel's first two major political factions on the question of sovereign independence. Ben-Gurion rejected declaring a state within the framework of the United Nations process and insisted

---

[18] "Menachem Begin's Broadcast to the Nation," May 15, 1948. *Menachem Begin Heritage Center* publication. Excerpts of this speech also appear in his memoir, *The Revolt* (Jerusalem: Steimatzsky, 1977).

on a sovereign state. Begin had the same view but was less politic and more strident.

Nowhere is the United Nations or its resolution mentioned, though Resolution 181's dictates, particularly regarding borders, are disparaged. The departed British are referred to only as "oppressors." As Begin puts it in his Biblical phrasing: "The State of Israel has arisen. And it has risen 'only thus' – through blood, through fire, with an outstretched hand and a mighty arm, with sufferings and sacrifices." Much like Ben-Gurion did in Israel's Declaration, Begin speaks of a sovereign state reliant on itself and its force of arms for survival.

There was of course a key difference. Ben-Gurion maintained flexibility on the question of borders. Begin here asserts rigidly and stridently that the day of independence is only phase one. The ultimate goal, in the telling of the 35-year-old Begin, is the "restoration of the whole land of Israel to its God-covenanted owners." He went further: "Whoever does not recognize our natural right to our entire homeland, does not recognize our right to any part of it."

Were this statement to have been included in the actual Declaration of Independence, it might have been just as damaging and self-defeating as the insistence on independence only within the borders of the United Nations. For borders of states are changing all the time. Israel, for instance, conquered the Sinai Desert in 1967, which Menachem Begin returned to Egypt in the 1979 peace treaty when he was Prime Minister of Israel. This vital difference between Ben-Gurion and Begin shows the contrast between ruling and opposition, statesmanship and faction. It sheds light on the responsibilities of leadership.

On the matter of religion, the differences between the Declaration and Begin's address jump out. Begin's address, more so than any draft of the Declaration, is replete with references to Jewish liturgy as well as scripture. He, too, invokes "*Tzur Israel*," but draws out what he sees as the miraculous and covenantal implications in that invocation: "Although our suffering is not yet over, it is our right and our obligation to proffer thanks to *Tzur Yisrael* for all the miracles that have been done, as in those times."

Begin's invocation of Jewish themes goes beyond this proud and open prayer of benediction (notably the same blessing was made upon the recitation of the Declaration one day prior), as well as his invocation of the miracle of the Maccabees ("as in those times"). He also attempts a kind of distillation of the principles of Judaism insofar as they will be instantiated in a Jewish state.

The Declaration had invoked "cultural treasures" and "the teachings of the prophets." Begin was more concrete.

"Remember you were strangers in the land of Egypt" – this supreme rule must continually light our way in our relations with the strangers within our gates. "Justice, Justice, shall you pursue" will be the guiding principle in our relations amongst ourselves.

Begin highlights two quintessential Jewish principles that should, in his telling, influence the politics of the state of Israel. The first: remember that you were strangers in the land of Egypt. This passage is taken from Deuteronomy, 10:19. This passage has a special resonance: it is a formulation of the phrase "remember that you were a slave in Egypt" that is found later in Deuteronomy as well. In both cases, the phrase is tied to respecting the downtrodden, appearing in a list of charitable commandments: "Love the stranger, for you were once strangers." Retribution for the actions of the father is not to be visited on the sons; the poor are not to be disciplined for taking the leftovers of the harvest; kidnapping and enslavement are capital crimes.[19]

The second principle articulated by Begin comes by way of the famous invocation "justice, justice, shall you pursue." Judaism demands a politics devoted to the pursuit of justice. The community of the land of Israel will not be a community of individuals pursuing only individual, idiosyncratic ends. Rather, the national life of Israel must be a life in pursuit of justice. Begin draws out the implications of these principles:

And within our homeland, justice shall be the supreme ruler, the ruler over all rulers. There must be no tyranny. The Ministers and officials must be the servants of the nation and not their masters. There must be no exploitation. There must be no man within our country – be he citizen or foreigner – compelled to go hungry, to want for a roof over his head or to lack elementary education.

Begin's remarks here are certainly self-interested. He wishes to ensure the continuing existence of his own political party. The *Irgun* and Revisionist movement viewed themselves as stifled and repressed by the leaders of mainstream Zionism. The ministers of the state-to-be, according to Begin, could not by justice rule in a high-handed fashion.

---

[19] The precepts in the two sections of Deuteronomy are similar, but described with slight variances in language in the two sections of the same book – a seeming repetition but of course with slight variances. The commentator Ibn Ezra alludes to the strangeness of the repetition. The reader of the text sees in the two formulations the core of the political hermeneutic of the Jewish teaching.

There is no doubt that he is arguing for pluralism for the sake of the perseverance of his party.

But it would be an error to read it only thus. Begin is also making a substantive point about the nature of government in a free country. Public service serves the public. The ruler faces the same rules as the ruled. This is the formulation in the laws of kingship codified by Maimonides and mentioned above. It is the principle of English government: one law for king and citizen. The Jewish formulation goes further. The text of Deuteronomy strives to ensure that no man goes hungry by commanding liberality toward the poor. In the modern age of abundance, this can extend to assurance that each has a roof, food, and elementary education.

Begin attempts to define the character of the politics of the state in terms of what Judaism teaches about political arrangements and justice. And these lessons include ministerial representation and social solidarity that extends to the provision of the essential needs of all. Even passing familiarity with the history of Israel indicates that these principles, at the best times, have indeed been a major part of the life of Israel – and an elevating and ennobling part of that life.

On the question of rights, Begin states that "the government must protect human and civil rights, without discrimination and favoritism. It shall safeguard the principles of justice and freedom and our house shall shine with brotherly love." Begin's writing here, in a strange way, recalls the work of Mordechai Beham. Beham had turned to Philadelphia. Begin here almost turns to Paris.

One hears echoes of liberty, equality, and fraternity phrased in the language of the Bible. Begin's formulation combines an emphasis on justice as the pursuit of the common good with liberty and the protection of rights. Needless to say, this introduces many theoretical problems in need of further elucidation. How is the pursuit of justice understood in terms of social solidarity to be reconciled with individual liberty? What is the appropriate balance between the two? It would be too much to ask resolution of this in Begin's speech. Yet Begin somehow saw that a modern Jewish state would have to combine these two ideas.

Both the ruling party and the opposition saw a need to try to infuse the founding moment with Jewish ideas. Begin attempted to distill the political essence of Judaism and the principles of the Jewish state. Begin was concrete. The principles he mentioned do not exhaust or even encapsulate the essence of the political teaching of Judaism. But they represent a foray into this terrain.

It is a difficult counterfactual to consider whether Begin's ideas, under the pressures that the leaders of the *Yishuv* faced, would have had been able to resonate with other members of the *Yishuv* leadership. The faction and enmity between the parties was too thick to possibly imagine a fruitful collaboration. In that way, Begin's independence speech, at the very least, points to the difference between Philadelphia in 1776 and Tel Aviv. In Philadelphia, characters as different as Thomas Jefferson, John Adams, and Benjamin Franklin collaborated on a Declaration of Independence. Not so in Israel in 1948.

THE DECLARATION'S PRINCIPLES OF POLITICAL RIGHT

The final major theme addressed in the Declaration is that of the notion of principles of political right: the character of the state with respect to the civil rights of its citizens. This topic has taken on immense importance for the evolution of Israel jurisprudence – and thus, for the evolution of the politics of Israel. The discourse on rights in the Declaration takes place principally in its thirteenth paragraph. There the Declaration states:

The state of Israel will be open for Jewish immigration and for the Ingathering of the Exiles; it will foster the development of the country for the benefit of all its inhabitants; it will be based on freedom, justice and peace as envisaged by the prophets of Israel; it will ensure complete equality of social and political rights to all its inhabitants irrespective of religion, race or sex; it will guarantee freedom of religion, conscience, language, education and culture; it will safeguard the Holy Places of all religions; and it will be faithful to the principles of the Charter of the United Nations.

It is this catalogue of rights that the Supreme Court of Israel has established as the "basic credo" of the state.

The drafting process did not prioritize this aspect of the Declaration. The debates over Shertok's draft and Ben-Gurion's draft in *Minhelet ha'Am* and *Moetzet ha'Am* – i.e. the central debates among the state's founders – prioritized how the Declaration should position itself vis-à-vis the UN resolution and other related diplomatic concerns; whether to specify the borders of the state in the Declaration, a matter related to questions of international diplomacy; and whether or not to invoke the name of God in the text.

There were other minor issues too. The Communist Meir Vilner demanded a denunciation of imperialism. The Revisionist Herzl Vardi asked politely whether he could only sign the Declaration partially since his political faction remained opposed to any invocation of the UN process at all. These issues attracted more attention at the pre-Declaration meetings than debate over the character of rights.

The most meaningful intervention on this subject occupied less than a sentence in the committee's review of Moshe Shertok's draft – according, at least, to the records we have in the minutes. This was David Ben-Gurion's assertion that the state should instantiate or make manifest (*te'kayem*) the citizen's rights rather than *ensure* or bestow them as Shertok had written; the state, according to Ben-Gurion, did not possess the rights to bestow. Rights belong to the people, said Ben-Gurion – a point he integrated into Israel's Declaration.

Whether it was a simple oversight or not, Moshe Shertok's draft had promised nondiscrimination on the basis of race or religion but not on the basis of sex, which the UN had indeed indicated. What motivated Ben-Gurion in this respect is not clear. But he did fortunately decide that the idea of equality between men and women belonged on the list and added it back.

There were other interventions in the committee discussions of the Declaration on the question of rights. Meir Bentov, discussing Shertok's draft and reversing an earlier preference for no discussion of rights, finally argued that greater explication of the nature of rights was necessary: "This is a document for the ages. In a hundred years children will learn it by heart. And therefore it doesn't have to be a document with legalistic paragraphs but about human rights .... I don't find in these paragraphs the expression of the natural rights of our people to live freely in our homeland."

And, of course, at the final pre-Declaration meeting of *Moetzet ha'Am*, at which the definitive text of the Declaration was debated and approved, the *Mapai* politician Meir Grabovsky insisted that "freedom of language" – which had been left out by Ben-Gurion – would be included in the list of rights.[20] *Moetzet ha'Am* voted to approve this suggestion. The list of guaranteed rights of Israelis was added in a manner that is pluralistic and showed great thought for the various peoples of the new country.

On the whole, though, the discussion of rights as they appeared in the drafts of Shertok and then, in somewhat modified form, in the final version produced by David Ben-Gurion, were not widely debated – neither by the proto-cabinet *Minhelet ha'Am* nor the proto-parliament *Moetzet ha'Am*.

---

[20] Protocols of the National Council, May 14, 1948, p. 15.

The account of rights in the Declaration certainly has its sources – the principal one perhaps being Resolution 181 and the kinds of rights the new states that it would create had to guarantee. Of the early drafters, Tzvi Berenson seemed to have been the most interested in the political character of the state with respect to rights. He wrote of a "democratic" state and one devoted to "freedom, justice, and peace in the spirits of the prophets of Israel." And of course, he followed the text composed by Zalman Rubashov – who was clearly interested in these matters too. Shertok dropped the word democratic. No one discussed or debated the meaning of the prophetic spirit.

One cannot resist comparing the paucity of debate on the character of rights in Tel Aviv in May, 1948 with the extended debate over them in Philadelphia in July, 1776. When Thomas Jefferson recalled his Declaration late in life, he looked particularly to the American Declaration's doctrine of rights which, he said, was drawn from "Aristotle, Cicero, Sidney, Locke, etc."[21] The drafting of the American Declaration of Independence was conducted explicitly within the frame of political thought.

And the debate over the question of rights in Jefferson's Declaration was extensive. Jefferson's rough draft gained approval from colleagues in a drafting committee that included Benjamin Franklin, John Adams, Roger Sherman and Robert Livingston in addition to Jefferson himself. Adams would later claim that "I do not now remember that I made or suggested a single alteration."[22] But Jefferson's colleagues in the Continental Congress altered a great deal of Jefferson's text. Jefferson had written:

We hold these truths to be sacred & undeniable; that all men are created equal & independent, that from that equal creation they derive rights inherent & inalienable, among which are the preservation of life, & liberty, & the pursuit of happiness; that to secure these ends, governments are instituted among men, deriving their just powers from the consent of the governed.[23]

After what must have been stormy debate in the halls of the Continental Congress, the Congress approved the following for the crucial second paragraph of the American Declaration of Independence:

---

[21] Thomas Jefferson to Henry Lee, May 8, 1825, https://founders.archives.gov/documents/Jefferson/98-01-02-5212

[22] John Adams to Timothy Pickering, August 6, 1822, https://founders.archives.gov/documents/Adams/99-02-02-7674

[23] Thomas Jefferson's Rough Draft available at www.loc.gov/exhibits/declara/ruffdrft.html

We hold these truths to be self-evident, that all men are created equal, that they are endowed by their Creator with certain unalienable Rights, that among these are Life, Liberty and the pursuit of Happiness. – That to secure these rights, Governments are instituted among Men, deriving their just powers from the consent of the governed.[24]

The differences here are subtle but important. They suggest significant debate in Philadelphia over the nature of rights. Are the truths better understood to be "sacred and undeniable," as Jefferson initially wrote, or as "self-evident," as was finally decided? Do rights come from an "equal creation," as Jefferson wrote, or are men "endowed by their Creator" with rights, as the Congress edited? Are life, liberty, and the pursuit of happiness better understood as "ends," as Jefferson had written, or as "rights?"

These changes suggest that reflection on rights was not merely the privilege of Jefferson, Adams, or Franklin in Philadelphia. The founders of the United States paid serious attention to finding the suitable words to express their ideas regarding the nature of rights and the purposes of government.

The record shows that David Ben-Gurion had, at least to some degree, been considering the American Declaration of Independence, perhaps even consulting its text. In the cabinet meeting the day before independence, he noted perspicaciously that the American Declaration had not specified the borders of the country. Ben-Gurion asked: Why should Israel's?

It should thus not come as a surprise that Ben-Gurion, writing the final text of Israel's Declaration, expressed thought regarding the nature of fundamental political rights. He insisted that rights are not a creation of the state but rather inhere to people; the state can only instantiate or ensure rights. In making this change, Ben-Gurion had shifted the orientation of the state toward the protection of inherent rights.

Yet, fundamentally, Ben-Gurion's final text does not depart very far from that of his predecessors. Israel's Declaration states that the new country will make manifest "complete equality of social and political rights to all its inhabitants irrespective of religion, race, and sex," and will "guarantee freedom of religion, conscience, language, education and culture." Resolution 181 had insisted that new states must guarantee "all persons equal and non-discriminatory rights in civil, political, economic and religious matters and the enjoyment of human rights and fundamental freedoms, including freedom of religion, language, speech and publication, education, assembly and association."

---

[24] American Declaration of Independence available at www.archives.gov/founding-docs/declaration-transcript

Israel's Declaration of course diverges from Resolution 181. It says nothing about freedom of publication. Indeed, many aspects of Resolution 181 were simply ignored. But the Declaration's reliance on Resolution 181 and its catalogue of rights is apparent. The extent to which the discourse in Israel's Declaration relies on the text of UN Resolution 181 throughout its text is an important conclusion of this book – and one which has not been generally recognized.

Resolution 181 had insisted on the state safeguarding of the holy places; Israel's Declaration says Israel will guarantee this. The UN had approved the states with "economic union," and Israel's Declaration, while not committing directly to this union, states that the country "will take steps to bring about the economic union of the whole of *Eretz-Israel.*" Ben-Gurion had fought his colleagues to liberate the state from the limitations on sovereignty in the UN process and he had succeeded. But when it came to cursory or rhetorical measures, the final text continued to pay extensive lip service to Resolution 181.

The ambiguities in the Declaration on the matter of rights has become one of the central ambiguities of political life in Israel. The jurists of Israel have taken on the responsibility to weigh and prioritize questions regarding competition between rights. In so doing, they have often looked to the Declaration, and particularly its catalogue of rights, which, they have claimed, represents the "basic credo" of the state.

Yet Israel's Declaration does not offer clear guidance or a fully articulated theory of the nature of rights.

It is no small irony that the clearest exposition on the character of rights in the drafting of the Declaration came from a young man, on the lowest end of the governmental totem pole, a man far removed from the dilemmas facing the leaders of Israel whose names are remembered by posterity. With help from Rabbi Harry Davidowitz, Mordechai Beham turned to the core texts of Anglo-American political thought to argue that the modern Jewish state should be devoted to the protection of the equal inherent natural rights of individuals – that protecting life, liberty, and the pursuit of happiness should define the purpose of government. He had added that these rights were ancient and indubitable. He combined the American Declaration and the English Bill of Rights.

He had turned to the clearest political conceptions of respect for the sanctity of the individual and the political salience of that sanctity. The ingeniously formulated distillations of John Locke, the American Founders, and the English Bill of Rights had served the English speaking world so well.

At the time of the creation of Israel, in 1948, as the world stood but short years from the terrors of the Second World War, the power and the virtue of these doctrines was plain to see. The English-speaking states and their empires, the United States, Great Britain, Canada, and Australia, were the only modern countries of note that had neither adopted despotism, withered before it, or made their accommodations with it.

And what is more, their commercial societies had succeeded in standing up to Germany's mass-production machine. It was the United States that had bailed out the Soviet Union, even as the Soviet Union suffered the heavy sledding in lives and matériel from then onwards.

The United States had defeated Germany on the European front and Japan in the Pacific. It had harnessed the atom. And it had done so while its millions lived in prosperity. The durability and wisdom of the Anglo-American political order had been, so to speak, proven on the battlefield.

From the vantage point of 1948, why would anyone have even been interested in Weimar legal theories? They had wilted in the 1930s, standing incapable of articulating a coherent doctrine to defend German society from its worst depredations. Of what relevance could the political orders of France or Central Europe have been? These countries' political orders, it turned out, were vulnerable to violent upheaval and worse. The divided governments that they produced and the ultimately illogical principles that they attempted to combine had not been able to unite society in simple defense of itself. The result had been paralysis and collapse to an invader that intended to enslave and destroy them.

Life, liberty, the pursuit of happiness; the rights of the individual; limited government focused on democratic supervision of the power of the representative and the strong state rather than the balancing of ideologies and general wills. The political ideas of the English republics were predominant by 1948. They were obviously ascendant. Beham saw it. On a certain level, even without understanding it, everyone alive had to see it.

Beham as well seems to have intuited that these could not be the only goals of a Jewish state. Turning to the text of the Bible, Beham tried to distill a Jewish ethical message that could justify and orient the politics of the state.

The Jews of the 1920s could have perhaps persuaded themselves that they could build a state that was not Jewish – that the state that would come to be might only incidentally contain Jews. The more naïve among the Jews of the *Yishuv* might have imagined that a new world order of peace and brotherhood policed by the United Nations would obviate the need for a Jewish state. Post-nationalism already had its beginnings amongst those blaming the nation-state for the devastation of World War II. For them, the difficulty of building a Jewish state in defiance of Arab opposition could not be reconciled with the moral trade-offs that such action entailed. In a world in which the principle of self-determination and respect for others was to be tantamount, how could the demands for self-determination by two rival parties be reconciled?

These questions tortured many and led them to shy away from the idea of a Jewish state. The authors of Israel's Declaration and its drafts had no such trepidation. In 1948, there was no question that the Jews needed a state, and that any state that the Jews would create would be, inevitably, a Jewish state. There was thus no reason for half-measures. Beham sensed what the situation actually called for: a marriage between the political doctrines of the English-speaking world with the experience and ideas of the Jewish world.

This was not to occur. The founding and success of Israel is in many senses a modern miracle, an event unthinkable over the course of 1,800 years of Jewish history that amazingly happened in the 1,855th. It is a miracle that owes itself to Zionism: its theorists and its supporters, but especially and moreover to the efforts of the Jews who immigrated to and built the *Yishuv* and the unique statesmen who were able to steer it to independence. They had built an economy, bodies of social organization, a government, and an army. They had reconstituted the Hebrew language and revived it. They had built a small country by 1948, and that country proved itself in war.

That country had been built under the shadow of the British Empire and with the help and support of a Jewish diaspora in America that was the largest Jewish community thriving outside of Israel in 1948. But though the world of the *Yishuv* might superficially have had these connections to the English world, its roots, and particularly the roots of its generation of founding leaders, were elsewhere.

The world of natural and inherent rights of the citizens, of ancient and indubitable rights – this was not their world. The Jewish civilization that had ranged from Odessa to Brisk to Berlin to Baghdad to Tunis was their principal origin. They were refugees from this world. They had left that world before its destruction to go to Jerusalem and Tel Aviv and Haifa and the swamps and hills of the Galilee and Judea. They endeavored to escape Jewish history by fleeing to ancient Judea and Dan. They consciously tried to leave the old behind. They inevitably brought it with them. The Jewish state that was founded could not have been anything else.

It is one of the enduring mysteries that the state of Israel was created at a time when the political ideas of the English-speaking countries had proven themselves so thoroughly, and indeed the country of Israel was carved out of the British Empire, and yet the political institutions of the new state of Israel were created with limited likeness to those of either the United States or Great Britain.

At a moment when the institutions of political organization of Western and Central Europe had been shown to be of limited value, and when those of the parliamentary constitutional republics of the English world had proven so ascendant – the latter left little mark on the political development of Israel at its origin. One of the unique examples of an effort to learn from and incorporate the lessons of America and England in the political birth of Israel is found in the record of Mordechai Beham's draft of Israel's Declaration of Independence. He had asked how the ideas of the Jewish people and the political principles that had been distilled by the tradition of English political thought could fit together. This effort was discarded by the legal bureaucracy of the *Yishuv*. They did not understand it.

In his own way, David Ben-Gurion, as final author of the Declaration, tried to reconcile principles of political right and the ideas and tradition of Judaism. He knew that in founding the Jewish state he should have recourse to fundamental ideas. The foundations of the state would be intellectual. He reached for natural and historical rights. He founded the state on the basis of what he called natural and historical rights. These were the rights to be masters of one's own fate and the call to direct one's fate toward good works – the works that are pointed to in the history of the Jewish people and their ideas.

A distillation of what this would mean in practice was left for posterity. The work was incomplete. We learn of its central importance from Israel's Declaration of Independence and its drafts. A declaration of independence is just a beginning. Even as it has a foundation, a political structure is not like a physical structure. Its foundations are only metaphorical. It is rather the case that political bodies rest on the ideas that constitute them. And ideas, as they are always accessible, call to being always accessed. Even if they are not articulated at one moment, the ideas persevere and remain, waiting to be articulated anew in every generation.

Afterword and Acknowledgments

This book was first conceived by Dov Zigler in the mid-2000s. It was catalyzed by the rediscovery of Mordechai Beham's draft of the Declaration of Independence by Professor Yoram Shachar of IDC Herzliya. Professor Shachar produced clean manuscripts of Beham's work, published them, compiled along with them other drafts of the Declaration of Independence derived from a variety of sources, and traced the historical path of their authorship and strands in the text. Absent Shachar's work, this book might never have been written.

The compilation of the drafts of the Declaration of Independence of Israel had pointed to new questions about the founding of Israel. There had been many military histories of the War of Independence of Israel. There were accounts by both witnesses to history and historical actors. Excellent scholarly accounts drawing on vast materials had been published. And over the course of the 1980s, 1990s, and 2000s, revisionist accounts broadened the understanding of events beyond those initial and partial efforts. All contributed deeply to filling out the picture of Israel's War of Independence and Israel's path to independence. The ongoing declassification of state materials allowed for a closer view of the decisions that were made on the battlefield and in the halls of power. The deep efforts to conduct social history added the necessary color to a view of the war – mainly from the Israeli side, it must be said, with many earnest efforts to tell the Arab side of the story too, if none that have been fully satisfying.

Despite all of this, the initial public appearance of the first draft of the Declaration of Independence more than 50 years after it was composed, and in the wake of dozens of serious works written on the period surrounding independence, pointed to an issue of vital importance hiding in plain sight. What was the political history and moreover the intellectual history of the founding of Israel? What was the history of Israel's declaration of independence as well as its Declaration of Independence? How, why, to what end, and aiming toward what had Israel's independence been declared? What was the political theory of Israel's independence? These questions are not just academic. They bring other questions to the fore. Israel is not that old. The unearthing of the political path that led to its founding and the political ideas that animated it would have resonance beyond the founding era.

This book is an effort to shine a light on the questions raised by a study of the textual, political, and intellectual history of the Declaration of Independence. There were many surprises along the way. We had believed that we were setting out to write a book that would draw into contrast the first draft of Israel's Declaration and its final draft. Put in the most crude terms, at the beginning of this literary and research journey, this book seemed likely to take the form of a battle of the drafts: Ben-Gurion vs. Beham, natural rights vs. Labor Zionist ideology. Instead, it was the similarities between the starting point and the end point – and the contrast with the middle – that astonished us, enlightened us, and raised to our attention the main themes of this book. It turned into a study of the point at which the text started to the point at which it concluded.

In our study of the drafting of the Declaration of Independence and our effort to situate it, we have been aided along the way and motivated by the works of those who came before us. Some central participants in events of those days kept good notes or wrote up their reflections later. These figures – particularly Ze'ev Sharef, Moshe Gurari, Tzvi Berenson, and Uri Heinsheimer (Yadin) – provided vital context as well as insights into an historical story and a theoretical subject about which much more will surely be said in the years ahead. Along with all present and future scholars of the founding of Israel, we are in Yoram Shachar's debt for first shining a light on the primary drafts.

The writings, memoirs, and public speeches of David Ben-Gurion, despite or because of their laconic tone, proved to be of remarkable and surprising value. We began this project with natural admiration for Ben-Gurion as a founder of Israel. But we were also skeptical about the public image he had created in his later years: the Bible study groups with scholars, the yoga-like meditation, the occasional references to celebrated intellectuals of the past – we assumed this had to be hype generated by a statesman attentive to his legacy and his image. His hype worked. We came away thinking that he was indeed a real and profound reader of the copies of Thucydides and Plato's *Laws* that he bragged about carrying around.

And, of course, there is the writing and notes of Mordechai Beham, the young lawyer, in many ways the other hero of this book. The story of Beham in the library of Rabbi Davidowitz, however it may actually have gone, deserves to be long remembered. Davidowitz is probably a hero too.

The efforts of the participants in this drama helped give birth to an extraordinary historical corpus which, to our delight, has been improving all the time. The writings of Tom Segev, Nir Kedar, and Benny Morris on Ben-Gurion, the British Mandate, and the War of Independence have been vital. The writing on the period surrounding independence, which happily is now growing all the time, has guided us even where we have departed from it. Aharon Barak, Ariel Feldstein, Elyakim Rubinstein, Ilan Troen, Tuvia Fruilling, Dov Elboim, Martin Kramer, and Mordechai Naor deserve special mention.

The archivists of the Israel State Archives and Central Zionist Archives should be commended for preserving, digitizing, and rendering accessible many key documents related to Israeli independence and the Declaration of Independence. The pace of this work has picked up in recent years, and thanks to the labors of the archivists new discoveries are being made and will surely continue to be made in the years ahead.

The reader will not find in this book an in-depth account of the politics of Palestine's Arab community or its reflections in the spring of 1948. This is to be regretted, as it should be the subject of many works. We believe there is a great book to be written about deliberations at the highest levels of Arab society in 1948 on topics such as sovereignty, religion and state, political rights, and other subjects that are treated from the Israeli perspective in this book. It is a book we would very much want to read.

Over the course of our own frequently interrupted but never abandoned study of Israel's Declaration, we benefited enormously from conversation, advice, and encouragement from friends, teachers, and colleagues in the United States, Israel, and around the world. Their contributions and encouragement will be of enduring appreciation. Needless to say, anything blameworthy in this book is our responsibility. But we cannot take credit for it without acknowledging the generosity of others.

We are in special debt to Professor James Diamond of the University of Waterloo, whose wisdom and generosity of spirit have guided us since the beginning. His mastery of texts modern and ancient, and his combination of his perspective with his practical sense, makes us lucky to count him as a friend, mentor, and in the fullest sense, *moreh*.

Rabbi Professor Meir Soloveichik, rabbi of Shearith Israel and director of the Straus Center for Torah and Western Thought at Yeshiva University, has been an extraordinary backer of this project and well-spring of provocative thoughts and insights as well as friendship. To Soly we also owe particular thanks for highlighting the importance of Menachem Begin's radio address of May 15, 1948.

Allan Arkush, a rare expert in Israeli history and political philosophy, was unfailingly generous, providing us with specific historical and theoretical comments and general insights about political theory and modern Israel.

Very early drafts of this text were reviewed and encouraged by Michael Oren, Fouad Ajami, Yitzhak Lifshitz, and Eliot Cohen when this was but a (very lengthy) academic seminar presentation and book proposal in 2008 and 2009. Fouad is remembered with the greatest fondness.

This book is a journey through Israel's founding, but it is also a journey through the world of political philosophy as it relates to Israel's founding. The journey takes place in the text, footnotes, within the book's plan, and occasionally between the book's lines. The various contributors to this journey receive due mention. Interested readers will know where to find the appropriate references.

Seth Jaffe, Neal Kozodoy, Roger Hertog, Stu Halpern, Yehuda Halper, Leon Kass, and Asaf Hadany made insightful and probing comments on earlier drafts of chapters. Dan Polisar in particular offered a keen eye and critical questions that motivated us to dig deeper and hopefully see more in the texts.

We thank our editor at Cambridge University Press, Beatrice Rehl, for her enthusiastic reception of the project and expert guidance through the field of academic publishing. Likewise Kaye Barbaro, Matthew Rohit, Jessie Epstein, and the rest of the team at Cambridge University Press have provided expert aid and advice for which we are grateful.

Our friends and mentors deserve great thanks for discussing (and in some cases reviewing) the text during our many years meditating on both the Declaration of Independence of Israel and its intellectual context. Stanley Rosen, Peter Berkowitz, Kenneth Green, James Ceaser, Leon Kass, Eli Pffeferkorn, Yossi Shain, Hal Waller, Harry V. Jaffa, David Goldman, Reuven Brenner, Julius Krein, Tom Velk, Todd Fox, Glen Feder, Reihan Salam, Amiad Cohen, Uriel Lind, Yehuda Halper, and Rotem Sella deserve particular mention. In writing Chapter 7, on the use of the Declaration in Israeli legal history, we benefited from excellent research assistance by Atar Porat and Yossi Sella.

Neil Rogachevsky is delighted to acknowledge many colleagues and students at Yeshiva University, which carries on that great and humane learning of a kind that typifies the world of Judaism at its best. At Yeshiva's Straus Center for Torah and Western Thought, I feel fortunate to have worked with Meir Soloveichik, Stu Halpern, Dov Lerner, Chaya Sima Koenigsburg, and Shaina Trapedo on what has been an exhilarating and indeed unique educational enterprise. Yeshiva has allowed me to teach at the intersection of Israel studies and political thought. In the classroom, I have rarely failed to learn from student contributions. Special thanks to Michael Weiner, Yehuda Goldberg, Dovid Schwartz, and Mendel Uminer.

While writing this book I was happily associated with the Foundation for Constitutional Government, a wonderful institution dedicated to perpetuating the study of constitutional subjects of a kind we have advanced here. Thanks to Bill Kristol, Andy Zwick, and Susan Hamilton who were unfailingly generous with encouragement during the long slog and a source of helpful ideas and suggestions.

Across a winding journey in writing and academics, spanning several countries and conventional disciplinary boundaries, I have accumulated more intellectual and moral debts that I can relate. I must mention the following names here: Seth Jaffe, Alex Orwin, Alan Rubenstein, Cheryl Miller, Sam Goldman, Eliora Katz, Liel Liebovitz, Geraldo Vidigal, James Cameron, Charlie Laderman, Jonathan Leaf, Liz Skeen, Casandra Silva Sibilin, Shani Yannay, Haviv Rettig Gur, Nola Weinstein, Clif Mark, Joanna Baron, Andy Fleming, and Eva-Maria Kuhn. Also I must thank the team at the great web journal *Mosaic* – especially Neal Kozodoy, Jonathan Silver, Andrew Koss, and Dan Kagan-Kans – for giving me the opportunity to write about Israel and expecting nothing less than the best I could do, every time. My family has been nothing if not supportive all along the way.

Dov Zigler would like to acknowledge the many people who put him on an intellectual collision course with a study of the political foundations of Israel. There are more than I can name here. But one, Fouad Ajami, deserves particular notice. He conspired with Natan Sharansky to steer a young graduate student to Israel in 2007, thus setting this journey in train. Ajami was a scholar of intellectual history of the first order. He had taken his own entirely different journey. He was the most unlikely of people to have encouraged mine.

My grandfathers Dov Laufer and Salo Zigler and grandmothers Tzipora Laufer and Etty Zigler are written into this book in more ways than I can explain here. Their visions and dreams persevered despite confronting the harshest cruelties of fate. I hope I can honor but a small portion of the spirit that they maintained and endowed to their precious children and grandchildren, not least my parents Mark and Sally Zigler and my sisters Rina and Aliza. I also thank my parents for their careful reading and considered views, and particularly my father for his keen eye and editorial acumen.

My father and mother-in-law, Drs. William and Gisela Schecter, were both a source of encouragement and advice. I benefited greatly from our evening discussions of the history of Israel, Zionism, and beyond while watching the waves of the Pacific Coast on countless visits. What more could a son-in-law ask for?

I have left my wife and children to the end because a special thanks is owed to them. I am beyond grateful for my wife Anna's profound perspective, even keel, kindness, generosity, motivating spirit, companionship, friendship, love, beauty – and indulgence of this project. She is extraordinary in every way and thus, no surprise, has been an essential participant in the writing of this book. She has welcomed the additions of Mordechai Beham, Moshe Shertok, Golda Meyerson, and especially David Ben-Gurion into our ongoing conversation with grace and interest. There were moments when Anna was interviewing presidents of foreign countries, my work schedule in financial markets was intense, our children blessedly numbered three though the oldest was but four – and yet, Anna had nothing other than encouragement for the writing of this book. There are no words for this kind of support. All that can be said is: thank you.

Our children Sophia, Salo, and Elijah are a source of inspiration. Their understanding that Abba and Neil were writing a book, their curiosity about its contents and mysteries, their zeal to learn about it, and their passion to figure out how to write books themselves are sources of energy, perseverance, and creativity. This book is in many ways theirs.

And to the reader from both of us: hopefully this is just the beginning.

Appendix: Address by Zalman Rubashov (Shazar) to the Zionist Actions Committee, April 12, 1948

THE DECLARATION OF THE FOUNDING OF THE GOVERNMENT

The Zionist Action Committee, the highest body of the World Zionist Organization, in declaring today our decision to found the highest authority of our sovereign independence in the land, sees the need and obligation to turn to all cultured nations of the world, to the representatives of the United Nations, and to all of the dispersed of Israel in the diaspora and proclaim:

Great has been our subjugation. The Holocaust of Israel openly proved what can be expected for our people so long as it is sentenced to live, in every place in the world, the life of a minority dependent on the benevolence of foreigners. Our growing success and the roots we are planting in our homeland are proving how great will be the salvation for the dispersed of our people and for the wilderness of our land in the absence of the foreign hand arresting our pace. The menacing danger to our people has not subsided. And the blessed, hidden gates of our land are still locked.

And now come the last days of the Mandate. On the 15th of the month of May, the United Nations will receive again from the hands of the government of Britain the valued bond that had been entrusted to it by the League of Nations twenty-eight years prior and whose terms it did not succeed in fulfilling. The unwillingness of the government of the Mandate to fulfil its obligation strengthened and grew and turned over the last ten years into the cornerstone of its policy in the East. Instead of helping with the immigration of Jews to their national home, it locked the gates in the face of our beleaguered people at the hour of the greatest tragedy in the life of our people in the diaspora. It blockaded our immigrants and enlisted far-off powers to sentence them to a life of danger and devastation; it left our land destitute and chose for her ally our fiercest rivals, they who were among the allies of our greatest enemy – the enemy of all mankind. The hand that locked the gates of the land to our distressed brothers, for whose rescue the national home in the land of Israel was designated with the agreement of all nations, instead opened the gates to the passage of marauding infiltrators who invaded and aimed to prevent the fulfillment of the decision of the nations – and to implement here that which the Satan of the world had devised but not completed. And before laying down its trust, the Mandatory government continues to degrade our capacities and to abandon to chaos that which we cultivated and multiplied through assiduous labor over the course of generations. The land of our hoped-for redemption stands, in contrast, woefully, before us as a crucible for the remnant of Israel.

And hence we say, at last, on behalf of the World Zionist Organization, and with the agreement of all the House of Israel: with the end of the disappointing rule of the Mandatory government, the rule of foreigners in the land will end. The nation will claim its inheritance and establish its political independence.

The Jewish state – as envisioned by the father of political Zionism Dr. Theodor Herzl and the great object of the Hebrew nation in all its generations of dispersion – has now turned into a lifeline to our people wherever they are dispersed and a fateful obligation for our land and all its inhabitants.

Authorized representatives of the nations of the world that researched, and considered, and again researched the matter from all aspects were not able, in the final analysis, to bring to light any other effective solution to the question of our people in its diaspora and the question of the future of our country other than that which planted its flag and in fact has been realized in the Zionist movement of rejuvenation. Again and again, good people of conscience and leaders of liberation movements around the world promised their help. And the General Assembly of the United Nations, after weighing the matter in detail, in a ruling supported by more than two-thirds of representatives of nations that are a part of it, returned to this solution, sanctioned by international law. The judicial authority of this decision cannot be denied, and its moral authority will forever hold. And now the hour of its implementation has come. With the end of the days of the British mandate the government of the Jewish state shall arise.

And the Jewish state that the Jewish nation will found in the land of our inheritance will be a state of justice and of freedom, of equality for all its residents, without respect to religion, race, sex, and land of origin, a state of the ingathering the exiles and the blossoming of the wilderness, a state of uprightness and understanding, and the vision of the prophets of Israel will illuminate the way for us.

To the Arabs of the Hebrew state and to our surrounding neighbors we call out today – in the midst of the bloody campaign that was compelled upon us – to brotherhood, peace, and cooperation. We are the nation of peace we have come to build peace. We will found and build together our state as equal citizens with equal rights and equal duties, out of belief and mutual respect and out of true understanding of the needs of our fellow man. With belief and faith, the day is near where the Arabs of the state and our neighbors around us will be persuaded, like us, by the knowledge that our freedom is sibling to their freedom, and that our sincere partnership will affix a blessing to all the land and its all inhabitants and neighbors.

The foundations of our state have been laid before us, and its walls are rising before our eyes. Generations of pioneers have labored to set them, paying with the sacrifices of their lives: In the fields and vineyards, in the workshops and factories, in trade and industry, in valleys and mountains, on beaches and in the air, in the army, police, and public services, in literature and the arts and in the laboratories of science and all spaces of creative endeavor; the workers at their machines and the guardians at their posts and the faithful at their watch. The rafters will now be lifted and the building of state will be visible in its full scope.

And to the peoples of the world that courageously stood by us at the time of the Aliyah to correct together the injustice of the ages and to recognize our right to a life of independence: stand with us now in these most severe days of action and extend us a helping hand.

And to the global diaspora of Israel, refugees of disaster and prisoners of hope, whose battle is now the battle unfolding in the land, and for whose future it is happening, discover now the wellsprings of loyalty and love, bearing within them the longing for redemption, unite with us into one nation fighting for its liberation and for the future of an established independence.

We, our lives are dedicated to the protection of our people's freedom. And if greater trials and battles await us, with all our souls and all our might will we defend the project that is our hope.

Justice is on our side. With us are the longings of all the generations of our nation. With us is the conscience of the world. With us are the testaments of our martyrs and the steadfast desire for life of millions of survivors. We have the blessed heroism of our warriors and protectors, and the God of Israel is our pillar.

Bibliography

DECLARATION TEXTS AND PROTOCOLS

Copies of the drafts and edits of early versions of Israel's Declaration, as well as other related proclamations, memos, and texts, appear in several different cartons of the Israel State Archives, in 5664/20/ג, 111/3/ג, 366/2/ חצ, 2/8227-א. Much of this material has also now been digitized and is available directly through the website of the Israel State Archives or by request. We have also drawn extensively on the protocols (transcriptions of meetings) in the months leading up to independence, particularly the following: Protocols of *Mapai* Party: March 6, May 11–12, 1948 (available through the Labor Party Archives), the protocols of the National Administration (*Minhelet ha'Am*): April 18, May 12–13, 1948 (available through the Israel State Archives), protocols of the National Council (*Moetzet ha'Am*), May 14, 1948 (available through the Israel State Archives), and the protocols of the Zionist Actions Committee, April 6–12, 1948 (Available through the Central Zionist Archives).

Other Primary Materials and Basic Texts

Academic records in Inns of Court Archives, MT/13/BER/2/1, University of Cambridge. Archives, UA Graduati 12/20, Exam. L.47.

American Declaration of Independence (1776).

Adams, John, "Letter to Timothy Pickering," August 6, 1822.

Basic Law (Israel): Human Dignity and Liberty (1992).

Basic Law (Israel): Freedom of Occupation (1994).

Begin, Menachem, "Broadcast to the Nation," May 15, 1948. *Menachem Begin Heritage Center* publication.

Ben-Gurion, David, "Letter to A. Bein," November 13, 1972.

Bill of Rights (1689).

Blackstone, William, *Commentaries*, Avalon Project, https://avalon.law.yale.edu/18th_century/blackstone_bk4ch33.asp

Deuteronomy, King James translation and Jewish Publication Society (1917).
    The Declaration of the Establishment of the State (Hebrew and English) (1948).
Jefferson's original rough draft of the Declaration of Independence, From: *The Papers of Thomas Jefferson.* Vol. 1, 1760–1776. ed. Julian P. Boyd. (Princeton, NJ: Princeton University Press, 1950).
Leviticus, Jewish Publication Society, 1917.
L'heyot ezrachim b'yisrael (To Be Citizens in Israel), Textbook (2016).
Lincoln, Abraham, "Letter to Henry L. Pierce and Others," April 6, 1859.
"Palestine Report on Immigration, Land Settlement, and Development," London: 1930.
Pirkei Avot (Ethics of the Fathers).
Foreign Relations of the United States, 1948, vol. 5 (Available through history. state.gov).
Truman, Harry, "Address in San Francisco at the Closing Session of the United Nations Conference in San Francisco," June 26, 1945.
United Nations Charter (1945).
United Nations Palestine Commission Report (1948).
United Nations Resolution 181 (1947).
Virginia Declaration of Rights (1776).
Whartman, Eliezer, "Interviews with Signers of the Israeli Declaration of Independence,"
c. 1961, Israel National Library, 2= 2007 A 8945.

Israeli Supreme Court Cases
al-Karbutli v. *Minister of Defense (1948)*, *Ziv* v. *Tel Aviv Administrator (Gubernik)* (1948), *Kol Ha'am* v. *Minister of the Interior* (1953), *Lubin* v. *The Municipality of Tel Aviv* (1956), *Streit* v. *The Chief Rabbi* (1963), *Yeredor* v. *Chairman of the Central Election Committee* (1964), *Ressler* v. *Minister of Defense* (1988), *Shakdiel* v. *Minister of Religious Affairs* (1988), *Schnitzer* v. *Military Censor* (1989), *Klal Insurance Enterprises* v. *The Minister of the Treasury* (1994), *Mizrahi* v. *Migdal Cooperative* (1995), *Miller* v. *Minister of Defense* (1995), *Adalah* v. *Tel Aviv* (2002), *Central Elections Committee* v. *Ahmed Tibi* (2003), *Regional Council, Coast of Gaza* v. *Knesset* (2005), *Gal-On* v. *Attorney General* (2012), *Academic Center for Law and Business* v. *Knesset* (2017), *Beham* v. *State of Israel* [District and Supreme Court rulings] (2017–2018).

Books, Journals, Essays, Articles, and Pamphlets

Acacia, John, *Clark Clifford: The Wise Man of Washington* (Lexington: University Press of Kentucky, 2009).
Acemoglu, Daron and James A. Robinson, "Persistence of Power, Elites, and Institutions," *The American Economic Review*, 98, 1, 2008.

Adams Schmidt, Dana, "Ben-Gurion Urges Zionist Set-Up Now," *The New York Times*, April 6, 1948.

Adler, Jacob, "The Zionists and Spinoza," *Israel Studies Forum*, 24, 1, 2009.

Aksin, Bejamin, "Ha'khraza al ka'mat ha'medina," ("Declaration of the Founding of the State") In *Sefer ha'yovel l'Pinchas Rosen*, ed. Haim Cohen, 1962.

Torat ha'mishtarim (The Idea of Regimes) (Jerusalem: Hebrew University Student Union Press, 1964).

Alboim, Israel Dov, ed., *Megilat atzmaut em talmud yisrael (The Declaration of Independence with an Israeli Talmudic Commentary)* (Rishon LeZion: Yedioth Aharanoth, 2019).

Alexander, James, "Three Rival Views of Tradition, (Arendt, Oakeshott and MacIntyre)," *Journal of the Philosophy of History*, 6, 1, 2012.

Allen, Danielle, *Our Declaration* (New York: Norton, 2014).

Almog, Shmuel, Anita Shapira, and Jehuda Reinharz, eds., *Zionism and Religion* (Hanover, NH: University Press of New England, 1998).

Alroey, Gur, "'Zionism without Zion'? Territorialist Ideology and the Zionist Movement, 1882–1956," *Jewish Social Studies*, 18, 1, 2011.

Anastaplo, George, *Reflections on Freedom of Speech and the First Amendment* (Lexington: University Press of Kentucky, 2007).

Antieau, Chester James, "Natural Rights and the American Founders: The Virginians," *Washington and Lee Law Review*, 3, 1, 1960.

Aristotle, *The Politics*, trans. Benjamin Jowett (London: Dover, 2007).

Arkush, Allan, "Biblical Criticism and Cultural Zionism Prior to the First World War," *Jewish History*, 21, 2, 2007.

"Cultural Zionism Today," *Israel Studies*, 19, 2, 2014.

Armitage, David, *The Declaration of Independence: A Global History* (Cambridge, MA: Harvard University Press, 2007).

Aron, Leon, *Roads to the Temple: Truth, Memory, Ideas, and Ideals in the Making of the Russian Revolution, 1987–1991* (New Haven, CT: Yale University Press, 2012).

Atlas, Pierre M., "Defining the Fringe: Two Examples of the Marginalization of Revisionist Zionism in the 1930s," *Israel Studies Bulletin*, 9, 2, 1994.

Avihai, Avraham, "Israelocentrism: A Guiding Doctrine of David Ben-Gurion," *Proceedings of the World Congress of Jewish Studies* (1973).

Avineri, Shlomo, *Herzl's Vision* (Katonah, NY: Bluebridge, 2014).

Avner, Yehuda, *The Prime Ministers* (Jerusalem: Toby Press, 2012).

Avneri, Arieh, *Hetyashvut ha'yehudi ve'ta'anat ha'nishol (The Claim of Dispossession)* (Efal, Israel: Yad Tabenkin, 1982).

Bao, Limin and Lin Zhang, "'Justice Is Happiness'? – An Analysis of Plato's Strategies in Response to Challenges from the Sophists," *Frontiers of Philosophy in China*, 6, 2, 2011.

Bar-Adon, Aaron, "S. Y. Agnon and the Revival of Modern Hebrew," *Texas Studies in Literature and Language*, 14, 1, 1972.

Barak Aharon, "Al tafkidi ke'shofet" ("My Work as a Judge"), *Law and Government*, 7, 2003.

"Ha'Nasi Agranat: Kol Ha'am – Kolo shel ha'am," ("President Agranat: *Kol Ha'am*, the Voice of the Nation"), *Writings*, 1, 2000.

"Human Rights in Israel," *Israel Law Review*, 39, 2, 2006.

The Judge in a Democracy (Princeton, NJ: Princeton University Press, 2006).

"Megilat atzmaut ve'haKnesset k'reshut mechunenet," ("The Declaration of Independence and the Knesset as a Constituent Authority"), *Hukim*, 11, 2018.

"The Role of the Supreme Court in a Democracy," *Israel Studies*, 3, 2, 1998.

Barak, Aharon and Tana Spanitz, eds., *Sefer Uri Yadin* (*Uri Yadin Festschrift*) (Jerusalem: Bursi, 1990).

Bartlett, Robert C., "Aristotle's Introduction to the Problem of Happiness: On Book I of the 'Nicomachean Ethics,'" *American Journal of Political Science*, 52, 3, 2008.

Barzel, Neima, "The Attitude of Jews of German Origin in Israel to Germany and Germans after the Holocaust, 1945–1952," *The Leo Baeck Institute Year Book*, 39, 1, 1994.

Basri, Carole, "The Jewish Refugees from Arab Countries: An Examination of Legal Rights – A Case Study of the Human Rights Violations of Iraqi Jews," *Fordham International Law Journal*, 26, 3, 2002.

Begin, Menachem, *The Revolt* (Jerusalem: Steimatzsky, 1977).

Beloff, Max, "Is There an Anglo-American Political Tradition?," *History*, 36, 126/127, 1951.

Ben-Gurion, David, *Medinat yisrael ha'mehudeshet* (*The Renewed State of Israel*), vol. 1 (Tel Aviv: Am Oved, 1969).

"Speech to the Knesset's Committee on Constitution, Law, and Justice," July 13, 1949, trans. Neil Rogachevsky, *Mosaic*, March 10, 2021.

Ben-Israel, Hedva, "Zionism and European Nationalisms: Comparative Aspects," *Israel Studies*, 8, 1, 2003.

Benvenisti, Meron, *City of Stone*, trans. Maxine Nunn (Berkeley: University of California Press, 1996).

Sacred Landscape, trans. Maxine Kaufman-Lacusta (Berkeley: University of California Press, 2002).

Berenson, Tzvi, *Megilat ha'atzmaut (The Declaration of Independence)* (State of Israel Publications, 1988).

Sefer Berenson (Festschrift for Tzvi Berenson, with original writings), ed. Chaim Berenson and Aharon Barak, Navo, 1997.

Bergman, Ronen, "The KGB's Middle East Files," *Ynet*, October 28, 2016.

Berkowitz, Michael, "Toward an Understanding of Fundraising, Philanthropy and Charity in Western Zionism, 1897–1933," *Voluntas: International Journal of Voluntary and Nonprofit Organizations*, 7, 3, 1996.

Berlin, Isaiah, Annan Noel, and Lee Hermione, *Personal Impressions*, ed. *Henry Hardy* (Princeton, NJ: Princeton University Press, 2014).

Berlin, Isaiah, Annan Noel, and Lee Hermione, *Personal Impressions*, "Two Concepts of Liberty," *Four Essays on Liberty* (Oxford: Oxford University Press, 1969).

Bickerton, Ian J., "President Truman's Recognition of Israel," *American Jewish Historical Quarterly*, 58, 2, 1968.

Borochov, Ber, *Nationalism and the Class Struggle* (New York: Poale Zion Alliance of America, 1937).

Bovis, Eugene H., *The Jerusalem Question, 1917–1968* (Palo Alto, CA: Hoover Press, 1971).

Bowes, Alison M., "The Experiment That Did Not Fail: Image and Reality in the Israeli Kibbutz," *International Journal of Middle East Studies*, 22, 1, 1990.

Brown, Gordon, ed., "The Long and Influential Life of the Universal Declaration of Human Rights," in *The Universal Declaration of Human Rights in the 21st Century: A Living Document in a Changing World* (Cambridge: Open Book Publishers, 2016).

Burke, Edmund, *Reflections on the Revolution in France* (London: Everyman's Library, 2015).

Calderon, Ruth and Simon Rabinovitch, "On the Declaration of Independence as a Basic Law and the Meaning of a Jewish Nation State," in *Defining Israel*, ed. Simon Rabinovitch (New York: Hebrew Union College Press, 2018).

Ceaser, James, "*The First American Founder*," *National Affairs*, Summer: 2018.

Chapman, Anne, "Genetic Engineering: The Unnatural Argument," *Techné: Research in Philosophy and Technology*, 9, 2, 2005.

Chazan, Meir, "Israel Goes to the Polls: The Road to Elections for the Constituent Assembly, 1948–1949," *Israel Studies Review*, 31, 2, 2016.

Chesteron, G. K., *What I Saw in America* (London: Hodder & Stoughton, 1922).

Clifford, Clark, *Counsel to the President* (New York: Random House, 1991).

Cohen, Eliot A., *Conquered into Liberty* (New York: Free Press, 2012).

Supreme Command (New York: Free Press, 2002).

Cohen, Michael J., *Palestine and the Great Powers* (Princeton, NJ: Princeton University Press, 1982).

"Truman and the State Department: The Palestine Trusteeship Proposal, March 1948," *Jewish Social Studies*, 43, 2, 1981.

Cohen, Mitchell, "Labor Zionism, the State, and Beyond: An Interpretation of Changing Realities and Changing Histories," *Israel Studies Review*, 30, 2, 2015.

Cohen-Levinovsky, Nurit, *Plitim yehudim be'milhemet ha'atzmaut (Jewish Refugees in the War of Independence)* (Tel Aviv: Am Oved, 2014).

Cohen, Samy, "Politiques et Généraux en Israël Aux 20 E et 21 E Siècles," *Vingtième Siècle, Revue d'Histoire*, 124, 2014.

Cosgrove, Charles, "The Declaration of Independence in Constitutional Interpretation: A Selective History and Analysis," *University of Richmond Law Review*, 32, 1, 1998.

Cottrell, Patrick M., "Lost in Transition?: The League of Nations and the United Nations," in *Charter of the United Nations: Together with Scholarly Commentaries and Essential Historical Documents*, Ian Shapiro and Joseph Lampert, eds, (New Haven, CT: Yale University Press, 2014).

Diamond, James, *Maimonides and the Hermeneutics of Concealment* (Binghamton: State University of New York Press, 2012).

"Maimonides and *Medinat Yisrael*," *Jewish Review of Books*, April 28, 2020.

Maimonides and the Shaping of the Jewish Canon (Cambridge: Cambridge University Press, 2017).

Dallaire, Roméo, *Shake Hands with the Devil* (Cambridge: Da Capo Press, 2004).

Davidowitz, Harry S., "Recent Books on Palestine and Zionism," *The Jewish Quarterly Review, New Series*, 13, 2, 1922.

Donnelly, Jack, *Universal Human Rights in Theory and Practice* (Ithaca, NY: Cornell University Press, 2013).

Doumani, Beshara B., "The Political Economy of Population Counts in Ottoman Palestine: Nablus, circa 1850," *International Journal of Middle East Studies*, 26, 1, 1994.

Dowty, Alan, *The Jewish State: A Century Later* (Berkeley: University of California Press, 1998).

"Dropsie College Theses," *The Jewish Quarterly Review, New Series*, 24, 1, 1933.

Dvir, Boaz, *Saving Israel* (New York: Rowman & Littlefield, 2020).

Eban, Abba, *The Tide of Nationalism* (New York: Horizon Press, 1959).

Edelstein, Dan, *The Terror of Natural Right* (Chicago: University of Chicago Press, 2009).

Elboim, Dov, ed., *Megilat ha'atzmaut em talmud yisraeli (The Declaration of Independence with an Israeli Talmudic Commentary)* (Rishon Lezion: Yedioth Aharanoth, 2019).

Elqayam, Avi, "The Metaphysical, Epistemological, and Mystical Aspects of Happiness in the Treatise on Ultimate Happiness Attributed to Moses Maimonides," *Journal of Jewish Thought & Philosophy*, 26, 2018.

Al-Farabi, *The Philosophy of Plato and Aristotle*, trans. Muhsin Mahdi (Ithaca, NY: Cornell University Press, 2001).

Feldstein, Ariel, "One Meeting – Many Descriptions: The Resolution on the Establishment of the State of Israel," *Israel Studies Forum*, 23, 2, 2008.

Ferguson, Niall, *The Great Degeneration* (New York: Penguin, 2014).

Fine, Arlene, "Cantor's Jewish Journey Set to Music," *Cleveland Jewish News*, October 9, 2011.

Fine, Jonathan, "Establishing a New Governmental System: The Israeli Emergency Committee, October 1947–April 1948," *Middle Eastern Studies*, 44, 6, 2008.

A State Is Born (Albany: State University of New York Press, 2018).

Finkelman, Yoel, "The Ambivalent Haredi Jew," *Israel Studies*, 19, 2, 2014.

Foster, Zachary, "The Invention of Palestine," (Unpublished PhD thesis), Princeton University, 2017, https://dataspace.princeton .edu/handle/88435/dsp01g732dc66g

Franzén, Johan, "Communism versus Zionism: The Comintern, Yishuvism, and the Palestine Communist Party," *Journal of Palestine Studies*, 36, 2, 2007.

Furet, François, *Penser le Vingtième Siècle (Contemplating the Twentieth Century)* (Paris: Robert Lafont, 1997).

Fukuyama, Francis, *State-Building* (Ithaca, NY: Cornell University Press, 2004).

Galnoor, Itzhak, "The Zionist Debates on Partition (1919–1947)," *Israel Studies*, 14, 2, 2009.

Ganter, Herbert Lawrence, "Jefferson's 'Pursuit of Happiness' and Some Forgotten Men," *The William and Mary Quarterly*, 16, 4, 1936.

Garfinkle, Adam, "On the Origin, Meaning, Use and Abuse of a Phrase," *Middle Eastern Studies*, 27, 4, 1991.

Gartman, Eric, *The History of Modern Israel* (Omaha: University of Nebraska Press, 2015).

Gavison, Ruth, "Jewish and Democratic? A Rejoinder to the 'Ethnic Democracy' Debate," *Israel Studies*, 4, 1, 1999.

Gilbert, Martin, *Israel* (New York: William Morrow, 1998).

Golan, John, *Lavi* (Lincoln: University of Nebraska Press, 2016).

Golani, Motti, ed., *The End of the British Mandate for Palestine, 1948: The Diary of Sir Henry Gurney* (New York: Palgrave MacMillan, 2009).

Goldberg, Harvey E., "The Ethnographic Challenge of *Masorti* Religiosity Among Israeli Jews," *Ethnologie Française*, 43, 4, 2013.

Gordis, Daniel, *Israel* (New York: Harper Collins, 2016).

Menachem Begin (New York: Schocken, 2014).

Gordon, A. D., "The Dream of the Aliyah," in *Selected Essays* (New York: Arno Press, 1973).

Green, Abigail, "Rethinking Sir Moses Montefiore: Religion, Nationhood, and International Philanthropy in the Nineteenth Century," *The American Historical Review*, 110, 3, 2005.

Gruweis-Kovalsky, Ofra, "Between Ideology and Reality: The Right Wing Organizations, the Jerusalem Question, and the Role of Menachem Begin 1948–1949," *Israel Studies*, 21, 3, 2016.

Gurari, Moshe, "Galguliya shel megilat ha'atzmaut" ("The Scrolling of the Independence Scroll,") *Davar*, April 24, 1958.

"Havlei leidata shel megilat ha'atzmaut" ("The Birth Pangs of the Declaration of Independence,") *Davar*, May 11, 1973.

Ha'am, Ahad, *The Spiritual Revival*, trans. Leon Simon (London: The Zionist, 1917).

Halkin, Hillel, *Jabotinsky* (New Haven, CT: Yale University Press, 2014).

"The Self-Actualizing Zionism of A. D. Gordon," *Mosaic*, February 15, 2018.

Halpern, Ben, and Jehuda Reinharz, "The Cultural and Social Background of the Second Aliyah," *Middle Eastern Studies*, 27, 3, 1991.

Hansen-Glucklich, Jennifer, "Father, Goethe, Kant, and Rilke: The Ideal of *Bildung*, the Fifth Aliyah, and German-Jewish Integration into the Yishuv," *Shofar*, 35, 2, 2017.

Hazony, Yoram, "Did Herzl Want a Jewish State?" *Azure*, 9, 2000.

"The Jewish State at 100," *Azure*, 2, 1997.

Helfand, Jonathan, "Baron James de Rothschild and the Old Yishuv," *Proceedings of the World Congress of Jewish Studies*, 1985.

Herodotus, *The History*, trans. David Grene (Chicago: University of Chicago Press, 1988).

Herzl, Theodor, *The Jewish State* (London: Dover, 1988).

Himmelfarb, Gertrude, *People of the Book: Philosemitism in Britain from Cromwell to Churchill* (New York: Encounter, 2011).

Holland, Matthew S., *Bonds of Affection: Civic Charity and the Making of America – Winthrop, Jefferson, and Lincoln* (Washington, DC: Georgetown University Press, 2007).

Horowitz, Dan, and Moshe Lissak, "Authority without Sovereignty: The Case of the National Centre of the Jewish Community in Palestine," *Government and Opposition*, 8, 1, 1973.

Huntington, Samuel, "Democracy's Third Wave," *Journal of Democracy*, 2, 2, 1991.

Ibn Ezra, "Commentary on the Pentateuch," www.sefaria.org/Ibn_Ezra_on_Deuteronomy.4.5?lang=bi

Jabloner, Clemens, "Hans Kelsen," in *Weimar: A Jurisprudence of Crisis*, ed. Arthur J. Jacobson and Bernhard Schlink (Berkeley: University of California Press, 2000).

Jaffa, Harry V., *A New Birth of Freedom* (Lanham: Rowman & Littlefield, 2000).

"What Were the 'Original Intentions' of the Framers of the
Constitution of the United States?," *Seattle University Law
Review*, 351, 1987.

Jayne, Allen, *Jefferson's Declaration of Independence* (Lexington:
University of Kentucky Press, 2000).

Johnson, Alvin, "The Jewish Problem in America," *Social Research*,
14, 4, 1947.

Johnson, Glen M., "The Contributions of Eleanor and Franklin
Roosevelt to the Development of International Protection for
Human Rights," *Human Rights Quarterly*, 9, 1, 1987.

Kabalo, Paula, "Challenging Disempowerment in 1948: The Role of
the Jewish Third Sector during the Israeli War of
Independence," *Israel Studies Forum*, 24, 2, 2009.

Kaplan, Jonathan Zvi, "Rabbi Joel Teitelbaum, Zionism, and
Hungarian Ultra-Orthodoxy," *Modern Judaism*, 24, 2, 2004.

Kant, Immanuel, "Perpetual Peace: A Philosophical Sketch," trans.
Mary Cambell Smith (London: George Allen & Unwin, 1917).

Karsh, Efraim, "How Many Palestinian Arab Refugees Were There?"
Israel Affairs, 17, 2, 2011, pp. 224–246.

Palestine Betrayed (New Haven, CT: Yale University Press, 2011).

Kedar, Nir, *Ben-Gurion ve'hahuka (Ben-Gurion and the
Constitution)* (Ramat Gan: Bar Ilan Press, 2015).

"Democracy and Judicial Autonomy in Israel's Early Years," *Israel
Studies*, 15, 1, 2010.

Kennedy, David, *Freedom from Fear* (Oxford: Oxford University
Press, 2001).

Klagbrun, Francine, *Lioness: Golda Meir and the Nation of Israel*
(New York: Shocken, 2017).

Koestler, Arthur, *Promise and Fulfillment* (New York: Macmillan,
1983).

Kolodny, Daniella, "Why Israel's Independence Led to an Argument
over the Name of God," *The Jewish Chronicle*, April 16, 2018.

Koskenniemi, Martti, *The Gentle Civilizer of Nations: The Rise and
Fall of International Law 1870–1960* (Cambridge: Cambridge
University Press, 2004).

"Lauterpacht: The Victorian Tradition in International Law,"
European Journal of International Law, 8, 2, 1997.

Kotzin, Daniel P. "An Attempt to Americanize the Yishuv: Judah
L. Magnes in Mandatory Palestine," *Israel Studies*, 5, 1, 2000.

Kramer, Martin, "The May 1948 Vote that Made the State of Israel,"
Mosaic, April 2, 2018.

"1948, Why The Name Israel," https://martinkramer.org/2020/04/
27/1948-why-the-name- 17israel/, April 27, 2020.

Laqueur, Walter, *A History of Zionism* (New York: Schocken,
2003).

Lauterpacht, Elihu, *A History of Zionism* (New York: Schocken,
2003).

The Life of Hersch Lauterpacht (Cambridge: Cambridge University Press, 2010).

"Zionism and Its Liberal Critics, 1896–1948," *Journal of Contemporary History*, 6, 4, 1971.

Lenzner, Steven J., "Strauss's Three Burkes: The Problem of Edmund Burke in *Natural Right and History*," *Political Theory*, 19, 3, 1991.

Lerner, Ralph, "Jefferson's Summary View Reviewed, Yet Again," in *Principle and Prudence in Western Political Thought*, eds., Christopher Lynch and Jonathan Marks (Binghamton: State University of New York Press, 2016).

"Lincoln's Declaration – And Ours," *National Affairs*, 2011.

Naïve Readings (Chicago: University of Chicago Press, 2016).

Levenberg, H., "Bevin's Disillusionment: The London Conference, Autumn 1946," *Middle Eastern Studies* 27, 4, 1991.

Levenson, Allan T., "In Search of Ahad Ha'am's Bible," *The Journal of Israeli History*, 32, 2, 2013.

Levush, Ruth, "Israel Supreme Court Decision Invalidating the Law on Haredi Military Draft Postponement," Law Library of Congress Report, March, 2012.

Lind, Uriel, *Hukei Ha'yesod shel medinat yisrael (The Basic Laws of Israel)* Yosef Sapir Research Center, 2011.

Locke, John, Hebrew trans. Yosef Or (Jerusalem: Magnus Press, 1948).

Letter Concerning Toleration, ed. James Tully (New York: Hackett, 1983).

Two Treatises on Government, ed. Peter Laslett (Cambridge: Cambridge University Press, 1988).

Loeffler, James, "Zionism, International Law, and the Paradoxes of Hersch Zvi Lauterpacht," in *The Law of Strangers: Critical Perspectives on Jewish Lawyering and International Legal Thought* (Cambridge: Cambridge University Press, Forthcoming), https://papers.ssrn.com/sol3/papers.cfm?abstract_id=3313561

Lottholz, Philipp and Nicolas Lemay-Hébert, "Re-Reading Weber, Re-Conceptualizing State-Building: From Neo-Weberian to Post-Weberian Approaches to State, Legitimacy and State-Building," *Cambridge Review of International Affairs*, 29, 4, 2016.

Loughlin, Martin, "The Concept of Constituent Power," *European Journal of Political Theory*, 13, 2, 2014.

Lovejoy, David S., "Two American Revolutions, 1689 and 1776," in *Three British Revolutions*, ed. John Pocock (Princeton, NJ: Princeton University Press, 1980).

Lozowick, Yaacov, "Who Owns Israel's History?" *Tablet*, August 05, 2019.

Lucas, Stephen E., "The Rhetorical Ancestry of the Declaration of Independence," *Rhetoric and Public Affairs*, 1, 2, 1998.

Lynch, Allen, "Woodrow Wilson and the Principle of 'National Self-Determination': A Reconsideration," *Review of International Studies*, 28, 2, 2002.

Machiavelli, Niccolò, *The Prince*, trans. Harvey Mansfield (Chicago: University of Chicago Press, 1998).

MacPherson, C. B., *The Political Theory of Possessive Individualism* (Oxford: Clarendon Press, 1962).

Magnette, Paul, *Citizenship: The History of an Idea* (Essex: ECPR Press, 2005).

Maimonides, *Mishneh Torah*, www.Sefaria.org

Malcolm, Joyce Lee, "The Creation of a 'True Antient and Indubitable' Right: The English Bill of Rights and the Right to Be Armed," *Journal of British Studies*, 32, 3, 1993.

Marshall, George Catlett, *Papers*, vol. 6, eds., Larry Bland, Mark Stoler, Sharon Stevens, and Daniel Holt (Baltimore: Johns Hopkins University Press, 2013).

Marx, Karl and Friedrich Engels, *Collected Works*, vol. 6 (New York: International Publishers, 1976).

A Reader, ed. John Elster (Cambridge: Cambridge University Press, 1986).

Metzer, Jacob, "Jewish Immigration to Palestine in the Long 1920s: An Exploratory Examination," *Journal of Israeli History*, 27, 2, pp. 221–251, 2008.

Milstein, Uri, *History of Israel's War of Independence*, vol. 1, trans. Alan Sacks (Washington, DC: University Press of America, 1998).

Morris, Benny, *1948* (New Haven, CT: Yale University Press, 2008).

The Birth of the Palestinian Refugee Problem Revisited (Cambridge: Cambridge University Press, 2004).

"The Harvest of 1948 and the Creation of the Palestinian Refugee Problem," *Middle East Journal*, 40, 4, 1986.

Muñoz, Vincent P., "George Washington on Religious Liberty," *The Review of Politics*, 65, 1, 2003.

Muravchik, Joshua, "The UN and Israel," *World Affairs*, November/December 2013.

Nadler, Allan L., "Religious Movements in Nineteenth- and Twentieth-Century Eastern Europe," in *The Modern Jewish Experience*, ed. Jack Wertheimer (New York: New York University Press, 1993).

Naor, Mordechai, *Yom ha'shishi ha'gadol (The Great Friday)* (Tel Aviv: Dekel, 2014).

Naor, Moshe, "Israel's 1948 War of Independence as a Total War," *Journal of Contemporary History*, 43, 2, 2008.

ha'Netsiv, "Commentary on Deuteronomy," www.sefaria.org/Haamek_Davar_on_Deuteronomy.1.8?lang=bi

Netanyahu, Benzion, *The Founding Fathers of Zionism* (Geffen: Jerusalem, 2012).

Newton, Adam Zachary, *The Fence and the Neighbor* (Albany: State University of New York Press, 2001).

Novak, David, "Haunted by the Ghost of Weimar: Leo Strauss' Critique of Hans Kelsen," in *The Weimar Moment*, ed. L. V. Kaplan and R. Koshar (Lanham, MD: Lexington Books, 2012).

Ohana, David, "Kfar Etzion: The Community of Memory and the Myth of Return," *Israel Studies*, 7, 2, 2002.

Olyan, Saul, "Zadok's Origins and the Tribal Politics of David," *Journal of Biblical Literature*, 101, 2, 1982.

Ottolenghi, Michael, "Harry Truman's Recognition of Israel," *The Historical Journal*, 47, 4, 2004.

Van Ooyen, Robert, "Totalitarismustheorie Gegen Kelsen Und Schmitt: Eric Voegelins 'Politische Religionen' Als Kritik an Rechtspositivismus Und Politischer Theologie," *Zeitschrift Für Politik, Neue Folge*, 49, 1, 2002.

Orren, Elhannan, *Hetyashvut be'shnot ma'avak (Settlement Amid Struggles)* (Jerusalem: Yad Yitzhak Ben Tzvi, 1978).

Oz, Amos, *A Tale of Love and Darkness*, trans. Nicholas de Lange (New York: Harcourt, 2004).

Oz-Salzberger, Fania and Eli Salzberger, "Die Geheimen Deutschen Quellen Am Israelischen Obersten Gerichtshof," *Kritische Justiz*, 31, 3, 1998.

Penslar, Derek, "Rebels without a Patron State: How Israel Financed the 1948 War," in *Purchasing Power: The Economics of Modern Jewish History*, Rebecca Kobrin and Adam Teller, eds., (Philadelphia: University of Pennsylvania Press, 2015).

Della Pergola, Sergio, "World Jewish Population, 2006," in *The American Jewish Year Book*, vol. 106, 2006.

Perlmutter, Amos, "Berl Katznelson and the Theory and Practice of Revolutionary Constructivism," *Middle Eastern Studies*, 13, 1, 1977.

"A. D. Gordon: A Transcendental Zionist," *Middle Eastern Studies*, 7, 1, 1971.

Pestritto, R. J., ed. *American Progressivism: A Reader* (Lexington: Lexington Books, 2008).

Pinsker, Leon, "Auto-Emancipation," (London: Association of Youth Zionist Societies, 1932).

Plato, *Republic*, trans. Allan Bloom (New York: Basic Books, 1991).

Pogue, Forrest C., *George Marshall: Statesman* (New York: Viking, 1986).

Polish, David, "Rabbinic Views on Kingship – A Study in Jewish Sovereignty," *Jewish Political Studies Review*, 3, 1–2, 1991.

Publius, *The Federalist*, ed. Charles Kesler (New York: Signet, 2003).

Quinault, Roland, "Churchill and Democracy," *Transactions of the Royal Historical Society*, 11, 2001.

Rabkin, Jeremy, *Law without Nations* (Princeton, NJ: Princeton University Press, 2005).

Raphaël, Freddy, "Le Sionisme de Martin Buber," *Esprit*, 38, 2, 1980.

Ravndal, Ellen Jenny, "Exit Britain: British Withdrawal from the Palestine Mandate in the Early Cold War, 1947–1948," *Diplomacy & Statecraft*, 2010.

Reimer, Michael J., *The First Zionist Congress* (Albany: State University of New York Press, 2019).

Reuben, Julie A., "Beyond Politics: Community Civics and the Redefinition of Citizenship in the Progressive Era," *History of Education Quarterly*, 37, 4, 1997.

Rogachevsky, Neil, "The Man Who Willed a State," *Mosaic*, July 1, 2020.

"Nathan the Wise: An Ambiguous Plea for Religious Toleration," *Mosaic*, June 29, 2016.

"The Not-So-Strange Death of Labor Zionism," *American Affairs*, 4, 3, 2020.

"Who Was Abba Eban?" *Mosaic*, February 17, 2016.

Rosen, Stanley, "Reviewed Work: Against the Current: Essays in the History of Ideas by Isaiah Berlin," *The Journal of Modern History*, 53, 2, 1981.

Rosenne, Shabtai, "Revisiting Some Legal Aspects of the Transition from Mandate to Independence: December 1947–15 May 1948," in *Israel Among the Nations*, ed. Alfred Kellerman, Kurt Siehr, Talia Einhorn (The Hague: Kluwer Law International, 1998).

Rubin, Aviad, "Political-Elite Formation and Transition to Democracy in Pre-State Conditions: Comparing Israel and the Palestinian Authority," *Government and Opposition*, 44, 3, 2009.

Rubinstein, Elyakim, "The Declaration of Independence as a Basic Document of the State of Israel," *Israel Studies*, 3, 1, 1998.

Sager, Samuel, "Israel's Dilatory Constitution," *The American Journal of Comparative Law*, 24, 1, 1976.

"Israel's Provisional State Council and Government," *Middle Eastern Studies*, 14, 1, 1978.

Salkin, Jeffrey, ed., *A Dream of Zion: American Jews Reflect on Why Israel Matters to Them* (Nashville, TN: Jewish Lights, 2009).

Sampson, Geoffrey, "Liberalism and Nozick's 'Minimal State,'" *Mind*, 87, 345, 1978.

Sapir, Gideon, *The Israeli Constitution* (Oxford: Oxford University Press, 2008).

Seelig, Michael and Julie Seelig. "Architecture and Politics in Israel: 1920 to the Present," *Journal of Architectural and Planning Research*, 5, 1, 1988.

Segev, Tom, *A State at Any Cost: The Life of David Ben-Gurion*, trans. Haim Watzman (New York: Farrar, Straus, & Giroux, 2019).

One Palestine, Complete (New York: Henry Holt Press, 2000).

Sela, Avraham and Alon Kadish, eds., *The War of 1948: Representations of Israeli and Palestinian Memories and Narratives* (Bloomington: Indiana University Press, 2016).

Sen, Amartya, *Development as Freedom* (New York: Anchor, 2000).
    "Human Rights and Capabilities," *Journal of Human Development*, 6, 2, 2005.

Sever, Shmuel, "Some Social Aspects of Public Library Development in Israel," *The Library Quarterly*, 38, 4, 1968.

Shachar, Yoram, "Ha'teyotot ha'mukdamot shel hakhrazat ha'atzmaut" (The Early Drafts of the Declaration of Independence"), *Iyunei Mishpat* (2002).
    "Israel as a Two-Parent State," *Zmanim*, 2007.
    "Jefferson Goes East: The American Origins of the Israeli Declaration of Independence," *Theoretical Inquires in Law*, 10, 2, 2009.
    "Yomano shel Uri Yadin" ("Uri Yadin's Diary"), *Iyunei Mishpat*, 3, 1991.

Shachar, Yoram, and Eliav Lieblich, "Cosmopolitanism at a Crossroads: Hersch Lauterpacht and the Israeli Declaration of Independence," *British Yearbook of International Law*, 84, 1, 2014.

Shapira, Anita, *Ben Gurion: Father of Modern Israel* (New Haven, CT: Yale University Press, 2014).
    Berl: A Socialist Zionist, trans. Haya Galai (Cambridge: Cambridge University Press, 1984).
    "Herzl, Ahad Ha-'Am, and Berdichevsky: Comments on Their Nationalist Concepts," *Jewish History*, 4, 2, 1990.
    K'hol am ve'am (Like Every Other Nation) (Jerusalem: Zalman Shazar Center, 2014).

Shapira, Avraham, *Hope for Our Time: Key Trends in the Thought of Martin Buber*, trans. Jeffrey Green (Albany: State University of New York Press, 1999).

Shapiro, Marc B., "Maimonides' Thirteen Principles: The Last Word in Jewish Theology?" *The Torah U-Madda Journal*, 993, 4, 1993.

Sheffer, Gabriel, *Moshe Sharett: Biography of a Political Moderate* (Oxford: Oxford University Press, 1996).

Sharef, Ze'ev, *Three Days*, trans. Julian Meltzer (W. H. Allen, London: 1962).

Shetreet, Shimon, "Reflections on the Protection of the Rights of the Individual: Form and Substance," *Israel Law Review*, 12, 1, 1977.

Shilon, Avi, "Ben-Gurion's Pragmatic Approach to Borders," *Mosaic*, April 23, 2018.
    Menachem Begin, trans. Danielle Zilberberg and Yoram Sharett (New Haven, CT: Yale University Press, 2012).

Shimony, Tali Tadmor, "Teaching the Bible as a Common Culture," *Jewish History*, 21, 2, 2007.

Shindler, Colin, *A History of Modern Israel* (Cambridge: Cambridge University Press, 2008).

Shlaim, Avi, "Britain and the Arab-Israeli War of 1948," *Journal of Palestine Studies*, 16, 4, 1987.

Shumsky, Dmitry, *Beyond the Nation-State: The Zionist Political Imagination from Pinsker to Ben-Gurion* (New Haven, CT: Yale University Press, 2018).

Siniver, Asaf, *Abba Eban: A Biography* (New York: Harry Abrams, 2015).

Slonim, Shlomo, "The 1948 American Embargo on Arms to Palestine," *Political Science Quarterly*, 94, 3, 1979.

Snetsinger, John, *Truman, the Jewish Vote, and the Creation of Israel* (Stanford: Hoover Institution Press, 1974).

Spotton, John and Donald Britain, *Memorandum* (1965, National Film Board of Canada), film.

Steinberg, Gerald M., "The Politics of NGOs, Human Rights and the Arab-Israel Conflict," *Israel Studies*, 16, 2, 2011.

Sternhell, Ze'ev, *The Founding Myths of Israel*, trans. David Maisel (Princeton, NJ: Princeton University Press, 2000).

Stone, Dan, *The Liberation of the Camps: The End of the Holocaust and Its Aftermath* (New Haven, CT: Yale University Press, 2015).

Strauss, Leo, *Natural Right and History* (Chicago: University of Chicago Press, 1999).

"Why We Remain Jews," in *Jewish Philosophy and the Crisis of Modernity*, ed. Kenneth Hart Green (Albany: State University of New York Press, 1997).

Tananbaum, Duane, *Herbert Lehman: A Political Biography* (Albany: State University of New York Press, 2016).

Tessler, Mark, *A History of the Israeli-Palestinian Conflict* (Bloomington; Indianapolis: Indiana University Press, 2009).

Teveth, Shabtai, *Ben-Gurion: Burning Ground* (New York: Random House, 1989).

Tidhar, D., "Moshe Zilberg," *Entsiklopedyah le-halutse ha-yishuv u-vonav (Encyclopedia of the Pioneers of the Yishuv)*, 2, 1947.

Tooze, Adam, *The Wages of Destruction* (London: Penguin, 2006).

Troen, Ilan S., "The Discovery of America in the Israeli University: Historical, Cultural, and Methodological Perspectives," *The Journal of American History*, 81, 1, 1994.

"Israeli Views of the Land of Israel/Palestine," *Israel Studies*, 18, 2, 2013.

Troen, Ilan S., Tuvia Friling, "Proclaiming Independence: Five Days in May from Ben-Gurion's Diary," *Israel Studies*, 3, 1, 1998.

Vidmar, Jure, "Conceptualizing Declarations of Independence in International Law," *Oxford Journal of Legal Studies*, 32, 1, 2012.

Volovici, Marc, "Leon Pinsker's Autoemancipation! and the Emergence of German as a Language of Jewish Nationalism," *Central European History*, 50, 1, 2017.

Walzer, Michael, *Exodus and Revolution* (New York: Basic Books, 1986).

Walzer, Michael, Menachem Lorberbaum and Noam J. Zohar, ed. *The Jewish Political Tradition*, vol. 1 (New Haven, CT: Yale University Press, 2000).

Waxman, Dov, "What Are the Implications of Israel's 'Nation-State Law' for Jewish-Arab Relations?" *Pacific Standard*, July 24, 2018.

Weber, Max, "Politics as a Vocation," (1919) trans. H. H. Gerth and C. Wright Mills (New York: Oxford University Press, 1946).

Weiss, Amy, "1948's Forgotten Soldiers?: The Shifting Reception of American Volunteers in Israel's War of Independence," *Israel Studies*, 25, 1, 2020.

Weissbrod, Lilly, "Economic Factors and Political Strategies: The Defeat of the Revisionists in Mandatory Palestine," *Middle Eastern Studies*, 19, 3, 1983.

"From Labour Zionism to New Zionism: Ideological Change in Israel," *Theory and Society*, 10, 6, 1981.

Whelan, Daniel J., *Indivisible Human Rights: A History* (Philadelphia: University of Pennsylvania Press, 2010).

Wyschograd, Michael, "A King in Israel," *First Things*, May: 2010.

Xenophon, *Hellenika*, trans. John Maricola (New York: Anchor, 2010).

Yanai, Nathan, "Ben-Gurion's Concept of *Mamlahtiut* and the Forming Reality of the State of Israel," *Jewish Political Studies Review*, 1, 1/2, 1989.

Zamir, Meir, "Intelligence Documents Reveal What Ben-Gurion Learned on the Eve of Declaring Israel's Independence," *Ha'aretz*, May 18, 2020.

"The Role of MI6 in Egypt's Decision to Go to War against Israel in May 1948," *Intelligence and National Security*, 34, 6, 2019.

Zamir, Yitzhak, ed. *Sefer Klinghoffer (Klinghoffer Festschrift)* (Jerusalem: Hebrew University Law Faculty, 1993).

Ziegler, Reuven, *Majesty and Humility: The Thought of Rabbi Joseph B. Soloveitchik* (Jerusalem: OU Press, 2012).

Zilbershied, Uri, "The Legal and Political Development of the Israeli Declaration of Independence: A Victory of the Bourgeois Democratic Conception," *Democratic Culture*, 12, pp. 7–58.

Ziv, Guy, "Shimon Peres and the French-Israeli Alliance, 1954–9," *Journal of Contemporary History*, 45, 2, 2010.

Zuckert, Michael P., *Natural Rights and the New Republicanism* (Princeton, NJ: Princeton University Press, 1994).

"Self-Evident Truth and the Declaration of Independence," *The Review of Politics*, 49, 3, 1987.

Index

Abdullah, king of Jordan, 178
Abraham (patriarch), 11, 63–64, 74, 100, 186
Acre, 88
Adams, John, 278, 280–81
Agranat, Shimon, 9, 240, 242
Aharonovich, Zalman (Aranne), 31
Ahdut Ha'Avodah, 211
Aksin, Benjamin, 246
  dissent from conventional interpretation of Israel's Declaration of Independence of, 243–44
al-Farabi, 67
al-Husayni, Haj Amin, 22
aliyah, 38, 53, 89, 127
Altalena, 29, 181–82
Altman, Aryeh, 31–32
America's Declaration of Independence, 12, 44, 69, 71, 73–75, 77, 97, 99, 121, 149, 187, 192, 202, 206, 227, 243, 282
  as source text in first draft of Israel's Declaration, 58–59
  differences with United Declaration of Human Rights of, 91–92
  divergences from Virginia Declaration of Rights of, 67
  doctrine of consent of the governed in, 99
  doctrine of freedom, equality, and sovereignty in, 59–61
  edits to Thomas Jefferson's first draft of, 280–81
  relation to first draft of Israel's Declaration of, 49

removal of ideas from Israel's Declaration of, 76
  role in American jurisprudence of, 236
  role in American public life of, 193
Amidah (Jewish prayer), 188, 204
Anglo-Saxon imperialism, 28
anti-Semitism, 160
Arab Legion, 184
Arab Liberation Army, 22
Arabic, 6, 262
Aristotle, 11, 50, 67, 132
Arlosoroff, Chaim, 181
arms embargo, 141
  US enforcement on *Yishuv* of, 158
Assembly of Representatives (parliament of *Yishuv*), 226
Athens, 139, 193
Austin, Warren, 158, 162, 267, 271
  advocacy for Trusteeship and against partition at United Nations of, 154

Balad, 250
Balfour Declaration, 7, 48, 66, 97, 127, 149, 185
Balfour, Arthur, 56, 121
Bar Kohba, 212
Barak, Aharon, 9, 243–44
  interpetation of Israel's Declaration of, 252–53
  jurisprudence on Court's constitutional authority of, 245–47
Basic Laws, 9, 232, 245, 250–51
  Freedom of Occupation, 8, 248, 251
  Human Dignity and Liberty, 8, 248

Basic Laws (cont.)
  judicial interpretation of constitutional
    force of, 246–48
  Knesset, 245, 250
  The Jewish State, 8, 252
Beeley, Harold, 158
Begin, Menachem
  demand for statehood by, 47
  rejection of partition of the land of, 97
  rejection of retaliation after Altalena
    incident of, 182
  speech on Israeli independence of, 273–78
Beham, Mordechai, 12, 79–82, 96–102,
    107–8, 163, 168, 176, 188, 196, 202,
    206–8, 227, 244, 272–73, 277, 282–85
  aspirations in writing declaration of
    independence of, 49
  assignment of drafting declaration to, 45
  biography of, 51–52
  collaborative work with Legal
    Department of, 99–100
  Declaration of the Jewish state by,
    65–66
  dispute over provenance of draft of
    Israel's Declaration of, 56
  doctrine of liberty of, 69–71
  later life recollections about writing draft
    of Israel's Declaration of, 74–76
  relationship to Harry Davidowitz of, 55
  work on first draft of Israel's Declaration
    of, 43–78
Beham, Yehuda, 51–52
Beinisch, Dorit, 249
Ben-Gurion, David, 4–5, 11, 14, 19, 29–30,
    38, 46, 50, 78, 97, 109, 139, 153, 160,
    166, 168–69, 171, 173, 191, 235, 255,
    285
  actions on day of independence of, 1–3
  agenda at Zionist Actions Committee of,
    25–26
  attitude toward United Nations
    Resolution 181 of, 175–76
  biography of, 210–13
  consultation with Moshe Shertok during
    Declaration drafting process of, 143
  debate with Aharon Zisling over the name
    of God of, 203–4
  insistence on statehood without
    qualifications of, 177–78
  intention in writing Israel's Declaration,
    196

later reflections on Israel's Declaration of,
    228–30
  machinations to ensure control of
    government by, 36–37
  mythologization of debate over the name
    of God in Declaration of, 202
  prioritization of natural and historical
    rights over UN process in Declaration
    text of, 207–8
  referral to America's Declaration of
    Independence of, 183–84
  reflection on importance of Zionist
    Actions Committee of, 20
  rejection of declaring statehood in April
    1948 of, 33
  rejection of Soviet alliance by, 28–29
  reliance on Cultural Zionism in writing
    Declaration of, 221–22
  support for naming the state Israel of, 188
  understanding of governmental
    sovereignty of, 179–80
  understanding of the long-term
    importance of a declaration of
    independence of, 194
  understanding of the nature of law of,
    186
  view of nature of state of, 209
  war doctrine of, 98
Ben-Gurion, Paula, 211
Bentov, Mordechai, 190, 193, 236, 279
  advocacy for more detailed treatment of
    human rights in Declaration of, 192
Berenson, Tzvi, 12, 56, 77, 80, 90, 96, 99,
    103, 112, 142, 168–69, 201, 206,
    217–18, 225, 227, 244, 256, 258, 272
  biography of, 103
  characterization of the state as democratic
    by, 93–95
  Declaration on the Founding of a Jewish
    State by, 82
  departure from ideas of Mordechai
    Beham by, 85
  doctrine of labor of, 86–88
  doctrine of sovereignty in Declaration
    draft of, 98–99
  treatment of borders of the state in
    Declaration draft of, 97
  understanding of history and tradition of,
    85–86
  use of Zalman Rubashov's text in
    Declaration draft of, 84–85

Bergen-Belsen, 122
Bevin Plan, 151
Bevin, Ernest, 151
Bialik, Haim Nachman, 100
Bible, 23, 49, 58, 77, 86, 206–7, 257, 277
  invocation by Mordechai Beham of,
    63–64
  location of authorship of, 220
  potential universalism of appeal to, 219
  role in cultural Zionist thought of, 220
Black Friday, 156
Blackstone, William, 224
Bodenheimer, Max, 213
Bograshov, Haim, 30
Book of Books. *See* Bible
Book of Psalms, 188
borders, 10, 142, 269
  changing nature of, 212–13
  debate over at the founding of the state
    about, 183–87
  ideological dispute in the *Yishuv* over,
    97–98
  Revisionist party hard line on, 275
Borochov, Ber, 50, 80
Brewer, David, 236
Brisk, 214, 284
British Foreign Office, 158
British Mandate, 4–5, 11, 19–20, 26, 33,
    35, 45, 48, 51, 110, 170, 185, 226, 266
  la saison during, 181
  retreat from Palestine of, 22
  warning not to declare independence
    while British remained in country by
    authorities of, 31–32
Brodetsky, Selig, 32
Buber, Martin, 127
  opposition to Jewish state of, 216
Bundism, 127
Burke, Edmund, 62

Calderon, Ruth, 259
Cambridge, University of, 107, 114–15,
    128
Canaan, 68, 218
capital, 87, 105, 185
capitalism, 89
Central Intelligence Agency, 152
Chesin, Mishael, 247
Chicago, University of, 107
Churchill, Winston, 26, 121
Citizenship and Entry to Israel Act, 249

Clifford, Clark, 154, 158, 164, 188, 265
  politics advancing the founding of Israel
    of, 265–70
  support for Jewish statehood of, 161–62
Comay, Michael, 151
Communists, 12, 28, 32, 272, 278
  exclusion from *Minhelet ha'Am* of, 37
Conservative Judaism, 52
Constituent Assembly, 123, 230, 246, 248,
    253
constitution, 83, 180, 228, 238
  failed efforts in the post-independence
    years in drafting of, 230
Continental Congress, 280–81
Corfu Channel case, 114
Council of 13. *See Minhelet ha'Am*
Council of 37. *See Moetzet ha'Am*
Cultural Zionism, 54
  influence on Israel's Declaration of
    Independence of, 220–21
Czechoslovakia, 161

Davar, 19, 34, 84
David (king of Israel), 63
Davidowitz, Harry, 12, 49, 63–65, 74, 100,
    102, 272, 282
  biography of, 52–55
  uncertainty surrounding role in helping
    Mordechai Beham write draft of
    Israel's Declaration of, 55
Declaration of the Rights of Man and of the
  Citizen, 56, 91, 229
Defense, Department of, 148
democracy, 83–84, 107, 239,
    253, 258
  absence of word from Israel's Declaration
    of, 204
  emphasis by Supreme Court of
    substantive notion of, 244–45
  procedural and substantive understanding
    of, 93–95
  role of idea in Israel's Declaration,
    225–27
democratic socialism, 106
Department of State
  advocacy for UN Trusteeship for
    Palestine of, 153
Deuteronomy (book of Bible), 55, 74, 219,
    273, 276–77
  conventional doctrine of covenant in,
    63–64

Deuteronomy (book of Bible) (cont.)
  philosophic interpretation of the idea of
    the covenant in, 68–69
Diaspora, 21, 48, 96, 102, 147, 284
  Zionist understanding of, 95
displaced persons camps, 6
divine providence, 73–74, 78, 202
Dobkin, Eliyahu, 26

Earl of Shaftesbury (Anthony Ashley-
  Cooper), 87–88, 121
Eban, Aubrey (Abba), 13, 151
  relationship to Herschel Lauterpacht of,
    114–15
economic union (proposed union between
  Arab and Jewish states in Palestine), 24,
    123–24, 166, 173, 178, 257
Egypt, 43, 88, 110, 125, 140, 148, 153,
    159, 186, 201, 211, 265, 275
Elections Committee, 254
Eliot, George, 121
English Bill of Rights, 55, 58, 101, 206, 282
  doctrine of rights and tradition of, 61–63
Epicureanism, 190
Epstein, Eliahu, 151, 164
  diplomacy in Washington leading up to
    Israeli independence of, 268–70
  diplomacy with Harry Truman and Clark
    Clifford of, 164
Epstein, Judith, 25
  reflections on arriving in Palestine at war,
    21–23
Ethics of the Fathers, 220
Etzel. See Irgun
Exodus (book of Bible), 186
Eytan, Walter, 151, 189

First Zionist Congress, 213
Fishman, Yehuda Leib (Maimon), 190, 204
  advocacy for name of God in Declaration
    of, 191
  debate with Aharon Zisling and David
    Ben-Gurion over name of God in
    Declaration of, 202–3
Fletcher-Cooke, John, 24
Forrestal, James, 152
Four Freedoms, 70, 91–92, 107
Franklin, Benjamin, 278, 280–81

Galilee, 87–88, 184, 284
Gaza, 110, 112, 125, 249, 251

Gelber, Lionel, 151
General Zionist Council. *See* Zionist
  Actions Committee
General Zionists, 33
  Support for majority at the Zionist
    Actions Committee of, 30
Genesis (book of Bible), 23, 186
Glorious Revolution, 61
Goldmann, Nahum, 151
Goldstein, Israel, 34
Gordon, A. D., 80, 147
  influence on Labor Zionism of,
    90
Grabovsky, Meir, 279
Gromyko, Andrei, 148
Grossman, Meir, 31, 37
Gurari, Moshe, 143
Gurney, Henry, 20, 25, 124

Ha'am, Ahad, 56
  influence of ideas about Jewish ideas on
    Israel's Declaration of Independence of,
    220–21
Ha'aretz, 19
ha'Netziv, 64
Ha'Poel Ha'tzair, 90
Ha'Poel Mizrahi, 168
Hadassah, 21
Hagadah, 43, 201
Haganah, 22, 48, 79, 86
Haifa, 22, 88, 140, 176, 185, 284
Hamilton, Alexander, 71
Haredi (religious movement), 215, 249
Hashomer Ha'tzair, 79
Hatikvah, 1
Hebrew University, 32, 127, 215
Heinsheimer, Uri (Yadin), 56, 76,
    176–77
  biography of, 100
  dissatisfaction with Israel's Declaration
    of, 208–10
Henderson, Loy, 152, 162
Herut, 273
Herzl, Theodor, 1, 38, 48, 147, 263
  importance of actions over writings of, 58
  inclusion of reference to in Israel's
    Declaration of, 56
Herzliya Hebrew high school, 30
Histadrut, 79–80, 103, 211
Holocaust, 7, 68–69, 97, 101, 121, 127,
    129, 176, 213

role in labor Zionist discourse of, 95–96
Horowitz, David, 151
Hovevei Zion, 95, 210

Idelson, Beba, 30
ingathering of the exiles, 7, 95–96
International Court of Justice, 114, 126,
    129–30
International Criminal Court, 126, 130
international law, 4, 10, 13, 43, 82, 99, 119,
    121, 126, 174, 179, 206, 269, 293
    comparison with Zionism of, 127–29
    development in post-World War II era of,
        113–15
    use against Israel of, 129–30
Iraq, 140, 153, 159, 185
Irgun, 273–74, 276
    debate over integration into *Haganah*, 29
Isaac (patriarch), 63, 74, 100
Israel State Archives, 56
Israel, State of
    changes following the founding of, 6–7
    debate over naming of, 188–89
Israel's Declaration of Independence
    as a source of the Basic Laws, 8
    basic summary of contents of, 7–8
    doctrine of historical right of, 217–22
    doctrine of natural rights of, 213–16
    doctrine of civil rights of, 222–25
    full official English translation of, 197–200
    importance of studying of, 8
    likeness to early drafts of final text of,
        195–96
    period of composition of, 5
    reason for absence of word democracy in,
        225–27
    role in Israeli jurisprudence of, 235–55
    role in national life of, 235
    substantive departure of final text from
        pre-drafts of, 196

Jabotinsky, Vladimir, 31, 181
Jacob (patriarch), 63, 74, 100
Jacobson, Eddie, 160
Jaffa, 22, 60, 88, 104, 140, 289
    Arab flight from, 111
Jaffa, Harry V., 44
James II, King of England, 62
Japanese Empire, 93
Jefferson, Thomas, 59, 66, 80, 99, 101, 278,
    280

attitude to Glorious Revolution of, 61
Jerusalem, 88, 105, 124, 140, 185, 284
    Arab militia warfare in, 184
    literary reputation of, 53
    military pressure on, 48–49
    special international regime planned for,
        24
    United Nations plan for
        internationalization of, 122
Jerusalem Legal Department, 46
Jerusalem Post, 54
Jesus, 127
Jesus College, Cambridge, 103
Jewish Agency, 13, 26, 38, 48, 128, 143,
    156, 181, 267–68
Jewish Legion, 211
Jewish National Council, 79
Jezreel Valley, 22
John, king of England, 187
Jordan, 110, 122, 125, 130, 140, 148, 159,
    178, 184
Jordan River, 97, 219
Joshua, 63, 74
Judea, 189, 273, 284
Judean Kingdom, 195
Justice Ministry, 45, 48, 52

Kahany, Menachem, 151
Kant, Immanuel, 134
    ironic understanding of perpetual peace
        of, 130–33
Kaplan, Eliezer, 173
Katznelson, Avraham, 26
Katznelson, Berl, 50, 211
Kelsen, Hans, 128, 244
    influence on Israeli jurisprudence of,
        240
Kenen, Cy, 151
Kennan, George, 152
kibbutz, 73, 79, 88–89, 106, 184
King James Bible, 55, 63
Knesset, 21, 226, 229–31, 243, 253
    question of constitutional authority of,
        246–48
Kramer, Martin, 188

Labor Party. *See Mapai*
Labor Zionism, 12, 46, 50, 58, 81, 98, 102,
    104, 129, 139
    aspiration for coexistence with Arabs of,
        84–85

Labor Zionism (cont.)
dominance in the *Yishuv* of, 79
ideological aspirations and reality of,
105–6
Lake Success (UN headquarters), 114, 126,
128, 134
Landau, Moshe, 244
Lauterpacht, Herschel, 13, 114, 122, 133,
142, 150, 169–70, 173, 206, 217, 228,
272
Act of Independence and Declaration of
the Assumption of Power of, 116–21
Activites at United Nations, 114–15
biography of, 126–29
influence of Declaration draft on
deliberations regarding Jewish
statehood, 174
neo-Kantianism of, 131
univeralistic understanding of Judaism of,
219
Law of Return, 96, 259
League of Nations, 133, 144
Lebanon, 110, 140, 185
legal conventionalism, 127–28
Legal Department, 44, 46, 52, 56, 76–77,
79–80, 103, 108, 142, 163, 176,
208–9, 225, 263
edits to declaration draft of Mordechai
Beham of, 99–102
legal internationalism, 126, 128
Lehman, Herbert, 160
Levin, Shlomo, 247–48
Levy, Edmond, 250
liberalism, 83, 91, 106
libertarianism, 71, 108
Likud, 273
Lincoln, Abraham, 237
Livingston, Robert, 280
Locke, John, 66, 80, 88–89, 106, 227, 282
absence from the *Yishuv* of, 106
idea on labor and property of, 86–87
Loeffler, James, 129
London School of Economics, 51, 128
Lovett, Robert, 155–56, 264–68, 270–71
advocacy against Jewish independence of,
159–62
Lubianker, Pinhas (Lavon), 37
Lvov, 114, 127

Maccabees, 275
Machiavelli, Niccòlo, 50, 214

MacMillan, Harold, 154
Magna Carta, 187
Maimonides, 54, 67, 277
interpretation of Abraham of, 63
political understanding of Messianism of,
216–17
mamlichtiyut (political doctrine), 193
Mapai, 21, 29, 34, 36, 48, 79, 84, 168, 171,
173, 211, 258
deferral of decision on statehood at
Zionist Actions Committee by, 31–32
deliberations regarding the founding of a
government, 25–26
resolution at Zionist Actions Committee
of, 33
Mapam, 34, 190, 202
agenda at Zionist Actions Committee of,
28–29
resolution at Zionist Actions Committee
of, 32
Margoshes, Samuel, 34
Maritain, Jacques, 91
Marshall Plan, 151, 161
Marshall, George, 151, 153, 155, 159–60,
162
effort to persuade Jewish leaders not to
declare independence of, 157–58
politics regarding recognition of Israel of,
264–67
view of Palestine question of, 152–53
Marx, Karl, 50, 80, 89–90, 106
Marxism, 50, 89, 106
Mason, George, 67
Masuot Yitzhak, 185
Meyerson, Golda (Meir), 14, 182, 205
insistence on complete state sovereignty
of, 178–79
intervention at Zionist Actions
Committee of, 29
Middle Temple, 51
Minhelet ha'Am, 37, 45, 47, 74, 79, 109,
116, 123, 140–43, 157, 176, 223, 226,
246, 261, 270, 272, 278–79
debate over content of Declaration of,
167–93
naming of, 38
Mishnah, 11, 186, 220
Mizrahi, 33
Moetzet ha'Am, 37, 44–46, 74, 79, 150,
176, 180, 246, 258, 278–80
debate over the role of God at, 203

Mohilewer, Samuel, 214
Moses, 63, 68, 186, 220, 273
moshav, 88, 184
Murphy, Charles, 154

Nablus, 88
National Administration. *See Minhelet ha'Am*
National Council. *See Moetzet ha'Am*
National Security Council, 152
natural rights, 12, 61, 66, 70, 78, 81, 91–92, 99, 101, 107, 126, 192, 207, 228, 279, 281
  debate regarding relation to state of, 192
  invocation at Zionist Actions Committee of, 32
  role in America's Declaration of, 59–61
  role in Israel's Declaration of, 213–16
negative liberty, 69–71, 258
Netanyahu, Benzion, 57
Neumann, Emanuel, 30, 34
New Deal, 92
The New York Times, 20, 159
Niles, David, 265

Oslo Accords, 181
Oz, Amos, 53

Pale of Settlement, 105
Palestine, 4, 33, 74, 85
  geography of, 87–89
  population of, 185
  situation in 1948 of, 21–25
Palestine Commission, 122
Palestinian Refugee Crisis, 108–12
Pan-Arabism, 130
Partition Plan, 29, 155–56, 164, 172, 178, 185, 212
Passover, 12, 43
Peel Commission, 185
Philadelphia, 278, 281
Pinsker, Leon, 56, 95, 214
pioneers, 86–87
  invocation in Israel's Declaration of Independence of, 201
  Marxism among the ideological vanguard of, 89
  role in Zionism of, 88–89
Plato, 50
  relationship between *Republic* and *Laws* of, 193

Po'alei Zion, 211
political philosophy
  importance of studying Israel's founding in light of, 10–11
  role in the *Yishuv*, 49
positive liberty, 70–71, 92, 258
Progressivism, 52
Provisional government
  creation of, 38

Rabin, Yitzhak, 181–82
Rehavia, 53, 105
religious Zionism, 102
Remez, David, 142, 168, 173, 179, 182, 189
Revisionists, 12, 29, 31, 46–47, 97, 102, 129, 181, 274, 276
  demand for a state at the Zionist Actions Committee of, 32
  exclusion from *Minhelet ha'Am* of, 37
  resolution at Zionist Actions Committee of, 32–33
Riftin, Yaakov, 28
Robinson, Jacob, 115
Rock of Israel. *See Tzur Yisrael*
Roosevelt, Franklin, 70, 91, 107, 163
Rosenblüth, Felix (Pinchas Rosen), 76–77, 80–81, 142, 168, 182, 208
  attitude toward United Nations process of, 172–73
  debate with Ben-Gurion over the nature of law of, 186
  delegation of drafting Declaration by, 45–48
  introduction to Mordechai Beham of, 52
  relationship to Tzvi Berenson of, 103
  view on sovereignty of, 175
Rothschild Boulevard, 1, 143, 236
Rousseau, Jean-Jacques, 91
Rubashov, Zalman (Shazar), 12, 39, 81, 104, 112, 201–2, 256, 258, 272, 280
  call to the Arabs of the state in ZAC declaration of, 109
  Declaration on the Founding of the Government, 34–36
  influence on Tzvi Berenson's Declaration draft of, 84–85
Rubenstein, Elyakim, 251
Ruffer, Gideon, 151
Runnymede, 187
Rusk, Dean, 157
Russia, 105, 134, 148, 161, 185, 191, 210

Sabbath, 3, 99, 188, 199, 222, 274
Saudi Arabia, 161
Scots College, 103
Second *Aliyah*, 102, 189
Second Intifada, 130
Second Temple, 74
Segev, Tom, 212
Sen, Amartya, 92
Sepharadim v'Edot ha'Mizrakh, 109
Sha'ar Zion (library), 54
Shachar, Yoram, 9
Shakespeare, William, 54
Shapira, Moshe, 142, 168
    advocacy for inclusion of more religion in
        Declaration of, 191
Sharef, Ze'ev, 74, 76–77, 189, 229
Shechtman, Joseph, 33
Sheetrit, Bechor, 109–10, 183, 222
    advocacy for inclusion of Bible in
        Declaration by, 190
Shehecheyanu (Jewish prayer of gratitude),
    2
Sherman, Roger, 280
Shertok, Moshe (Sharett), 13–14, 115, 125,
        142, 150, 169–70, 187, 189, 206, 209,
        217–18, 225, 256, 273
    decision to edit Declaration draft of, 194
    diplomacy with American officials
        regarding Trusteeship Plan of, 155–56
    diplomatic considerations in Declaration
        draft of, 165–66
    discussion of statehood at *Mapai* party
        meeting of, 171–72
    draft Declaration of, 143–47
    foreign policy understanding of, 163
    meeting with George Marshall of, 157
    rivalry with David Ben-Gurion of,
        139–40
Shertok, Yael (Sharett), 139
Shkolnik, Levi (Eshkol), 31
    intervention at Zionist Actions
        Committee of, 29
Shoah. See Holocaust
Silver, Abba Hillel, 151, 156–57
Smoira, Moshe, 8, 252
Sneh, Moshe, 28, 32
socialism, 50
Socrates, 11, 67
Solon, 193
Soloveitchik, Chaim, 214
Soloveitchik, Joseph, 215

Soviet Union, 29, 204, 283
Sprinzak, Yosef, 21, 29, 38
Stalin, Josef, 28–29, 106, 134, 163
State, Department of, 141, 148, 151–52,
        156–57, 162–63, 265–66
statehood
    debate at Zionist Actions Committee over
        declaration of, 30–32
statesmanship, 5
Strauss, Leo, 128
    critique of Hans Kelsen of, 240
suicide bombings, 130
Supreme Court, 8, 12, 80, 100, 103, 237,
        263
    interpretation and use of Israel's
        Declaration of Independence by,
        237–38
    understanding of democratic character of
        Israel of, 244–45
Supreme Court cases
    al-Karbutli v. *Minister of Defense*, 238
    Beham v. *State of Israel*, 56
    Central Elections Committee v. *Tibi*, 254
    Kol Ha'am v. *Minister of the Interior*, 9,
        239
    Mizrahi v. *Migdal Cooperative*, 245–46
    MK Gal-On v. *The Attorney General*,
        249
    Movement for Quality Government v. *the
        Knesset*, 249
    Peretz v. *Kfar Shmaryahu*, 241
    Ressler v. *The Ministry of Defense*, 254
    Schnitzer v. *Military Censor*, 244
    Streit v. *the Chief Rabbi*, 241
    *The Academic Center for Law and
        Business* v. *Knesset*, 251
    Yeredor v. *Chairman of the Central
        Election Committee*, 242
    Ziv v. *The Tel Aviv Administrator
        (Gubernik)*, 8, 238
Syria, 110, 140, 153, 185

Tal Law, 249
Talmud, 30, 50, 100, 186, 190, 214, 235
Tel Aviv, 1, 10, 12, 21, 48, 51, 114, 140,
        157, 164, 185, 208, 264, 284
    founding of, 104
    literary reputation of, 53
Tel Aviv Museum, 1, 188, 235
The Federalist, 50
    doctrine of state power in, 71–72

Third Reich, 93, 95, 133
Thirteen Colonies, 183
Tibi, Ahmed, 250
Toff, Moshe, 151
Tohu va'Vohu (political void), 23, 26
Trotsky, Leon, 80, 106, 180
Truman, Harry, 113, 147–48, 154–55, 158,
    164, 166, 264
  contest with Department of State over
    Palestine policy of, 153–54
  foreign policy judgment of, 163
  politics that led to diplomatic recognition
    of Israel by, 265–71
  rationale for supporting Jewish statehood
    of, 160–63
Truman, Margaret, 154
Trusteeship Plan, 24, 140, 153–54, 215,
    265
  failure of, 156–57
Tzur Yisrael, 44, 73–74, 78, 85, 187, 201,
    275
  debate over inclusion in Israel's
    Declaration of, 202–4

United Nations, 4, 13, 77, 107, 116, 161,
    166, 175, 177, 212, 228, 256
  founding of, 127
United Nations Charter, 24, 83, 91, 93,
    107, 134
  rights doctrine in, 91
United Nations Declaration of Human
  Rights, 70
United Nations International Law
  Commission, 114
United Nations Resolution 181 47, 55, 64,
    91, 97, 104, 111, 113, 140, 148, 150,
    164–65, 170–71, 175, 177, 200, 223,
    235, 246, 266, 275, 282
  ambiguity toward at Zionist Actions
    Committee, 33–34
  details of, 122–23
  failure of, 23–25
  substance of, 23–24
Universal Declaration of Human Rights, 81,
    92, 241
University College London, 127
Ur Kasdim, 11, 186

Va'ad Ha'Poel Ha'Tzioni. See Zionist
  Actions Committee
Vardi, Herzl, 278

Vilner, Meir, 272, 278
Virginia Declaration of Rights, 66–67

War of Independence, 4, 98, 230, 246
  fighting in April 1948 of, 22
  Jewish refugees of, 111
  role of American pilots in, 159
Washington, George, 193
Weber, Max, 182
  idea of sovereignty of, 180–81
Weimar, 283
Weizmann, Chaim, 160, 169, 178
West Bank, 110, 249
White Paper, 82, 96–97, 122
Wilson, Woodrow, 121
Wolfsberg, Yeshayahu (Aviad), 34
World Jewish Congress, 128
World War I, 147, 180
World War II, 92–94, 128, 131, 135, 148,
    151, 274, 283–84
World Zionist Organization, 11
  transfer of power away from, 38

Xenophon, 212
Xiadong, Mao, 134

Yadin, Yigal, 213
Yesh Atid, 259
Yishuv, 1, 11, 13–14, 21–22, 24, 28–29,
    32–33, 35, 45, 50–51, 53–54, 56, 64,
    73, 84, 86–87, 91, 96, 99, 102, 104,
    106–7, 114, 121–22, 129, 148, 150,
    155, 157, 160, 163, 167–68, 170–72,
    174–79, 181, 188, 196, 200, 203,
    210–13, 215, 246, 258, 263, 270, 272,
    278
  Arab population flight from, 109–12
  chaotic political situation of, 46–48
  creation of a new government of, 37–39
  decisions faced leading up to British
    withdrawl from, 4–5
  democratic character of, 226
  diplomatic dilemmas facing, 139–42
  disconnect from Anglo-American political
    tradition of, 283–85
  dominance of Labor Zionism in, 79–80
  geographic and military situation of,
    184–86
  ideology of creative work in, 89–90
  importance of records of debates of the
    leadership of, 5–6

Yishuv (cont.)
   need for unified government in, 19–20
Yishuv Elections of 1944, 47
Yosef, Dov, 46

Zilberg, Moshe, 100
   biography of, 100
Zion, 189
Zionism, 7, 38, 48, 54, 95, 126, 150, 215,
      271, 284
   centrality of state sovereignty in, 213
   relation to political philosophy of, 10
   role in overturning opposition to state
      sovereignty in Judaism of, 216

Zionist Actions Committee, 11, 19, 45, 84,
      112, 150, 180, 201, 246, 256
   composition of, 21
   importance of, 19–21
Zisling, Aharon, 142, 168, 173, 272
   advocacy for removing belief in God from
      Declaration of, 191
   debate over role of God in Declaration of,
      202–3
   opposition to belief in God in Declaration
      of, 203
   opposition to the name of the state of, 188
   support for Shertok's Declaration text of,
      190